MAPPING THE STARS

MAPPING THE STARS

CELEBRITY, METONYMY, AND THE NETWORKED POLITICS OF IDENTITY

Claire Sisco King

THE OHIO STATE UNIVERSITY PRESS
COLUMBUS

Copyright © 2023 by The Ohio State University.
All rights reserved.

Library of Congress Cataloging-in-Publication Data
Names: King, Claire Sisco, author.
Title: Mapping the stars : celebrity, metonymy, and the networked politics of identity / Claire Sisco King.
Description: Columbus : The Ohio State University Press, [2023] | Includes bibliographical references and index. | Summary: "Analyzes the public images of Norman Rockwell, Will Smith, and Kim Kardashian across movie posters, magazines, cinema, and social media and deploys a rhetorical study of celebrity to challenge normative ideas about how we form selfhood, including conceptions of gender, race, and sexuality"—Provided by publisher.
Identifiers: LCCN 2023007349 | ISBN 9780814215500 (cloth) | ISBN 0814215505 (cloth) | ISBN 9780814282991 (ebook) | ISBN 0814282997 (ebook)
Subjects: LCSH: Rockwell, Norman, 1894–1978—Criticism and interpretation. | Smith, Will, 1968– | Kardashian, Kim, 1980– | Celebrities—Social aspects. | Celebrities in popular culture. | Celebrities in mass media. | Fame—Social aspects. | Metonyms—Social aspects.
Classification: LCC HM621 .K563 2023 | DDC 305.5/2—dc23/eng/20230501
LC record available at https://lccn.loc.gov/2023007349
Other identifiers: ISBN 9780814258804 (paper) | ISBN 0814258808 (paper)

Cover design by adam bohannon
Text composition by Stuart Rodriguez
Type set in Minion Pro

*For MP, Lolo, and Alfie . . .
You are the lamp that always lights my way*

CONTENTS

Acknowledgments		ix
INTRODUCTION		1
CHAPTER 1	Six Degrees of Subjectification: Theorizing and Practicing Metonymy	21
CHAPTER 2	American Queerer: Norman Rockwell and the Art of Queer Feminist Critique	58
INTERSTITIAL 1	A Chapter on AIDS	97
CHAPTER 3	Terms and Conditions: Reflections on and of Black Fame in the Case of Will Smith	108
INTERSTITIAL 2	The Eyes Have Had It	148
CHAPTER 4	Emotional Icons: Digital Culture, Networks of Affect, and Kim Kardashian	159
EPILOGUE		201
Bibliography		213
Index		239

ACKNOWLEDGMENTS

First, I want to thank my employer, Vanderbilt University, for providing me a dynamic intellectual home. I am particularly grateful for the Research Scholar Grant that afforded me a research leave so I could work on this book.

I also want to thank the members of the Department of Communication Studies: Jeff Bennett, Neil Butt, Bonnie Dow, Bohyeong Kim, John Koch, ML Sandoz, John Sloop, Paul Stob, Courtney Travers, Isaac West, and Dustin Wood. You are wonderful colleagues, and I have been so touched by the times you have listened to me discuss my work, provided feedback, and offered support for me as a scholar and a teacher. I am also so happy to be in community with the folks in Cinema & Media Arts, and I am especially glad to have had Jen Fay's mentorship and encouragement for this book and for my work at Vanderbilt.

I am so grateful for the writing group who shared their work with me and gave thoughtful, generous, and rigorous attention to mine: Brooke Ackerly, Vanessa Beasley, Josh Bazuin, Anna Carella, Joy Calico, Stacy Clifford, Aimi Hamraie, Brielle Harbin, Jennifer Mokos, Andrea Pitts, Melissa Snarr, and Sarah Suiter. This work is better because of your guidance, and I am better because of your care and community.

I am so lucky to have friends and colleagues from the field of communication studies who have supported my work and offered me opportunities to share it with others. In particular, I want to thank Caitlin Bruce, Suzanne Enck,

Leslie Hahner, Robert Hariman, Joan Hawkins, Kristen Hoerl, Paul Johnson, Casey Kelly, Barbara Klinger, John Louis Lucaites, Joan Faber McAlister, Roopali Mukherjee, Chuck Morris, Kendall Phillips, Erin Rand, and Jamie Skerski. You have challenged, mentored, and cared for me in so many ways, and I could not do this work without your presence in my life and scholarship.

During the time that I worked on this book, I had the honor of serving as editor of *Women's Studies in Communication*, an intersectional feminist journal sponsored by the Organization for Research on Women and Communication. That work was challenging and rewarding. I am honored that the ORWAC leadership, including Leslie Harris, Diane Keeling, Alyssa Samek, and Jenna Hanchey, entrusted me with this role and am thankful for the ways they made that work easier and more enjoyable. I want to give extra thanks to Joan Faber McAlister and Kristen Hoerl, who preceded me as editors of the journal and who were impeccable models and mentors, and to Marina Levina and Sarah J. Jackson, who worked alongside me as editors and were the most marvelous collaborators.

This book owes so much to Taralee Cyphers, Rebecca Bostock, and the other folks who compose the editorial and marketing teams at The Ohio State University Press. Tara is a kind and brilliant editor, and I will always treasure her support.

An earlier version of portions of chapter 2 was published as "American Queerer: Norman Rockwell and the Art of Queer Feminist Criticism," *Women's Studies in Communication* 39, no. 2 (2016): 157–76. Permission to use this material is courtesy of Taylor & Francis Group and ORWAC. An earlier version of portions of chapter 3 was published as "Hitching Wagons to Stars: Celebrity, Metonymy, Hegemony, and the Case of Will Smith," *Communication and Critical/Cultural Studies* 14, no. 1 (2017): 83–102. Permission to use this material is courtesy of Taylor & Francis Group and the National Communication Association.

Jeff Bennett and Isaac West, you have brought great joy and care to our work in communication studies, but you are so much more than departmental colleagues. As the Golden Girls might say, you are pals and confidants. Having you in my world for the last two decades has made my life so much sweeter. I've never met funnier people, and I feel so known when I am with you. Thank you for being my friends and a chosen family to me.

Vanessa Beasley, you have been such a steadfast presence in my life: a department colleague, a writing community member, a co-author, a mentor, a fellow music lover and traveler, a friend, and an honorary sister. Thank you for always seeing me and giving me grace. Even though we are no longer living in the same state or working at the same institution, knowing you always feels like being together "on the rock."

It feels like an unbearably rich gift to have friends who have done life with me for decades and who love my family and me. To my "Seniors 95," Davidson, and "Lady Island" crews, you are my people. You are laughs and tears. You are adventure and mischief. You are dancing till the point of ecstatic exhaustion and regaling in the same stories again and again. You are the treasure of growing old together, even if only in spirit.

To my parents, Ralph and Evelyn Sisco: thank you for all you've taught me over the years—like how to love music and art, how to make the world's best cornbread dressing, and how to tell a good story. I'm sorry that learning to drive took as long and involved as many bumps as it did. Thank you as well for giving me my "baby" brother, even after I declared that I would prefer a puppy. Kirk Sisco, you are fiercely intelligent; but it is your tender heart and care toward our parents that truly set you apart. Thanks for making sure Jenny and the Howells stayed in our family's lives. I love all of you and can't wait to see what bad puns pop up in our group-text thread next.

Finally, Matt King, I am blessed beyond measure to have you as my best friend and partner. Thank you for our beautiful children and our life of adventure. From cycling trips to water slides, I've dared—because you were at my side—to try things that I might never have considered on my own. You consistently remind me that I am strong and brave, and, with you, I've learned not to take myself too seriously. Your selflessness and care as a physician have always moved me but never more than in the last two years when, day in and day out, you worked tirelessly and in nearly impossible circumstances on behalf of your patients while giving all your heart to the kids and me. I love you and living our life together because it works better that way.

INTRODUCTION

> Fame is fleeting. But the internet is forever.
> —Phineas and Ferb

This book is not about Donald Trump. It is virtually impossible, however, to write about US celebrity culture in the twentieth and twenty-first centuries without his name making some appearances. During his presidency, in addition to such revenue sources as hotels and golf resorts, Trump earned royalties from media appearances he had made in the 1990s. For example, financial disclosure statements submitted to the US Office of Government Ethics listed cameos in the NBC sitcom *The Fresh Prince of Bel-Air* (1990–96) and the Universal Pictures film *The Little Rascals* (Penelope Spheeris, 1994). Trump also appeared as himself in other television series and films, including *The Nanny* (CBS, 1993–99), *Suddenly Susan* (NBC, 1996–2000), *Spin City* (ABC, 1996–2002), *Sex and the City* (HBO, 1998–2004), *Home Alone 2: Lost in New York* (Chris Columbus, 1992), and *Zoolander* (Ben Stiller, 2001).

In these roles, Trump-as-Trump operates as a metonym for extreme wealth and New York City, as most of the appearances identify Trump as a real estate developer in New York and reference his legacy buildings, including Trump Tower and the Plaza Hotel. There were certainly other New York real estate developers who received more respect or acclaim, but Trump had become a national symbol for a particular brand of wealth (and a wealthy brand). *Six Degrees of Separation* playwright John Guare documented this association in a 1998 retrospective about New York City during the 1980s, titled "My Dinner with Donald, and Other Happenings."[1] In this timeline, Guare recounts personal milestones and major public events: John Lennon's assassination, the invention of the Walkman, the AIDS crisis, John Hinckley Jr.'s attempted assassination of President Ronald Reagan, and the Challenger disaster. He concludes by describing a fundraiser at which he was seated at a table purchased by Trump, who passed Guare a business card, saying, "Call me with your problem. I'll connect you with the right guy."

Trump's practice of appearing as himself in the 1990s signifies a paradigm of celebrity culture that was just beginning to emerge. His series of cameos built what Sarah Banet-Weiser calls a "self-brand," anticipating increased expectations of access to celebrities that would develop in relationship to the genre of reality television, the internet, and social media. Trump was not the first celebrity to appear as himself or to promote his own brand, but his self-branding heralded and perhaps inaugurated a mode of fame wherein "authenticity itself is a brand."[2] Trump's persona illustrates Karen Sternheimer's description of the 1990s as an era when people increasingly sought to become "famous just for being you" while also becoming "rich in the process."[3] Developing in tandem with this new paradigm were calls for the already rich and famous to open more and more windows into (the penthouses of) their everyday lives. By 2000 the notions that ordinary people might become famous overnight and that famous people should demonstrate their ordinariness had become largely normalized. Although Trump's desire to "play himself" on screen might be written off as self-serving and narcissistic, his choices signal these new norms in celebrity culture. As Neal Gabler puts it, "Trump is the Kardashian of politics."[4]

The increasing porosity of the lines between public/private, famous/not-famous, and professional/amateur demonstrates that, as Banet-Weiser proffers, "the separation between the authentic self and the commodity self not only is more blurred, but this blurring is more expected and tolerated."[5] This development suggests changes within celebrity and media cultures, but fame has always affected and been affected by understandings of what it means to have, or to be, a "self." Such intensified rhetorics of authenticity, which have been wrought by reality television and social media, manifest elements of celebrity and self-fashioning that have always existed in US culture.

1. Guare, "My Dinner with Donald," 26.
2. Banet-Weiser, *Authentic*™, 3, 11. See also Dubrofsky, "Authentic Trump."
3. Sternheimer, *Celebrity Culture*, 244.
4. Gabler, "We All Enabled Donald Trump."
5. Banet-Weiser, *Authentic*™, 13. See also Bell, *American Idolatry*.

Although tabloid-driven claims that celebrities are "just like us" ring rather hollow, *Mapping the Stars* posits celebrity culture as a resource for rhetorical scholars interested in considering what it means for any human (famous or not) to fashion a sense of self. Taking up Tim Edwards's contention that celebrity performs itself "*as subjectivity*," I contend that rhetorical analyses of fame make visible the interdigitation of signification and subjectivity and the political and ethical entailments therein.[6] This project deploys rhetorical theories of metonymy, a linguistic device linking signifiers by shared associations, to analyze iterations of celebrity culture as they take shape across constellations of media, including cinema, television, movie posters, magazines, and social media. Deploying metonymic criticism, this book illustrates how the networked form of celebrity offers a heuristic for understanding all subjectivity as defined by intersubjectivity and relationality to other subjects, texts, media, norms, places, and even events. Through the use of an associative form of interpretation, *Mapping the Stars* writes not only *about* networked form but also *in* it.

WON'T YOU BE MY NEIGHBOR?

In 2017 *Vanity Fair* profiled a California neighborhood that imagined itself in crisis. Framing the "very-much-gated and until-very-recently sleepy enclave of Hidden Hills" as a "three-dimensional Norman Rockwell painting," the article describes the neighborhood as aiming for an elite but pastoral ethos maintained by strict regulations that allow horseback riding on the streets but prohibit Google Street View vehicles. The supposed crisis, or "cultural rift," facing Hidden Hills was owed to the influx of "ultra-celebrities" whose presence invited increasing media attention, traffic, and noise, as well as architectural and vehicular extravagance in stark contrast to the neighborhood's sensibility of understated splendor. Of note in the article were homes purchased by Black celebrities in the "once almost exclusively white" neighborhood, including Will and Jada Pinkett Smith, who purchased a home for their son Jaden, and Kanye West, who purchased a home with then wife Kim Kardashian.[7]

The *Vanity Fair* article alludes to long-standing anxieties about celebrity's threat to traditional structures of generational wealth and inherited privileged—as in, for instance, moral panics about Hollywood in the 1920s and

---

6. Edwards, "Medusa's Stare," 163.
7. Lee, "Inside Hidden Hills."

'30s that arose out of fear that the industry was improving the socioeconomic status and power of immigrants.[8] As one Hidden Hills resident says, "This was a quiet neighborhood... but Jaden and his entourage are turning it into their own personal kingdom." It is precisely such a complaint that is dramatized by the roles that made Hidden Hills homeowner Will Smith famous: in the television series *Fresh Prince of Bel-Air*, he plays a street-smart but troubled young man who moves to the elite California neighborhood of Bel-Air and disrupts the lives of his wealthy relatives; and in *Six Degrees of Separation* (Fred Schepisi, 1993), he plays a street-smart but troubled young man who moves to the elite New York neighborhood of the Upper East Side and disrupts the lives of wealthy strangers.

The article also demonstrates fears about celebrity culture's metaphorical capacity to bring white spectators into contact with bodies of color through cultural forms, practices, and sensibilities with which they are associated. Such anxieties reverberate through frequent characterizations of celebrity as a "low" cultural form—as superficial, trivial, and even "trash." By painting the neighborhood as a Norman Rockwell picture, the article illustrates forms of gate-keeping that deem certain celebrities as more acceptable, respectable, or palatable than others. The article signals how various public figures become associated with different registers of taste and modes of fame that are often constructed in hierarchical, if not oppositional, terms. In Hidden Hills, for instance, one might imagine that Rockwell's brand of fame, which was built on the disavowal of his fame through an enactment of "small town" sensibilities in his work, would be preferred over the "famous for being famous" ethos of the Kardashians (or the extravagance of the Trumps). Such preferences cannot be extricated from normative discourses about identity in US culture. Fantasies about race and class structure these concerns, and intersecting assumptions about gender and sexuality are at work as well—as evidenced by one resident's remark that "in Hidden Hills, there's more of an effort to keep things on the D.L.," which references hidden same-sex sexual practices associated with Black men (including Will Smith) as a metonym for performances of class.[9]

Although very few people in the US find themselves in such direct contact with celebrities as the residents of Hidden Hills, celebrity culture has significant impacts on how people fashion themselves, imagine others, and map their positions within larger social worlds. *Mapping the Stars* argues that the melodramatic and metonymic modalities of celebrity culture matter for cul-

---

8. Rogin, *Blackface, White Noise*.

9. See Wright, "Great Down-Low Debate"; King, *On the Down Low*; McCune, *Sexual Discretion*; Snorton, *Nobody Is Supposed to Know*; and Taylor, "Will Smith Gay Sex Bombshell."

tural figurations of identity and subjectivity. Although stardom is often associated with hegemonic discourses and subject positions, *Mapping the Stars* deploys celebrity culture as a resource for challenging normative ideas about gender, race, and sexuality and for modeling ontologies of subjectivity that resist the individualized, masterful fantasies of selfhood that prevail in US media culture.

Three of the figures referenced in this *Vanity Fair* story—Norman Rockwell, Will Smith, and Kim Kardashian—occupy very different spaces in the landscape of celebrity, but each figure offers a unique vantage point for mapping the operations of fame and its implications for understandings of subjectivity in US culture. Although Rockwell, Smith, and Kardashian may seem to have little in common with one another, their bodies of work share an explicit interest in the concept of celebrity itself. Self-reflexivity about their own fame makes these public figures valuable for considering how networked forms of celebrity can promote productive ways of thinking about selfhood in US culture. As my analysis reveals, these celebrities have more in common with one another—and with a host of others to whom they are all directly linked, including Trump, O. J. Simpson, and Andy Warhol—than might have been obvious. What links Rockwell, Smith, and Kardashian is their conspicuous interest in image-making—by which I mean both the making of images, or pictures, and the crafting of public images, or personae.

Each of these figures has built a brand that conspicuously blurs the boundaries between their public image and their allegedly authentic selves. They are quintessential creators of what Banet-Weiser calls "self-branding," in which the "authentic and commodity are intertwined."[10] Rockwell focused his art on his own community, often using friends, family members, and neighbors as models. He was also his own subject in self-portraits, including ones of him in the act of making images. Smith often collaborates with family members, borrows autobiographical details for fictional works, and has claimed at times that he is not acting but just "playing himself"—as illustrated by the fact that his character in his first television role, *Fresh Prince of Bel-Air*, shares his name.[11] As a celebrity working primarily in the realms of reality television and social media—and whose fame first emerged from the leaking of a supposedly private sex tape—Kardashian has built her brand on promises of access to her "real" life and family. As Anita Brady argues, few other stars "so readily embody the deliberate curating of self for the lenses of the world's media" as Kardashian and her clan.[12]

---

10. Banet-Weiser, *Authentic™*, 14.
11. Chambers, "Willing," 77.
12. Brady, "Keeping Away from the Kardashians," 115.

At the same time, these celebrities' works depict the contingent, mimetic, and collaborative processes with which people—both famous and non-famous—construct and present their images, troubling the very notion that any "authentic" self even exists. In contrast to assertions that their public and private selves are the same, Rockwell's, Smith's, and Kardashian's bodies of work abound with fictionalized versions of themselves and self-reflexive considerations of the nature of fame itself, and many of these rather "meta" works attend to the Frankensteinian processes by which celebrity personae are assembled and animated. For example, in addition to Rockwell's famous self-portrait of his self-portrait, his oeuvre is replete with images of people looking in mirrors, getting dressed or applying makeup, preparing for auditions or performances, or considering their own images in relation to those of famous people. Many of Smith's works center on image makeovers, including *The Fresh Prince of Bel-Air* and the films *Six Degrees of Separation, Men in Black* (1997), *Hitch* (2005), and *Hancock* (2008)—all of which feature men who, under the guidance of a Pygmalion-like mentor, change their appearance and manners of speaking in order to adopt a new persona and gain entry into a new (largely white) social world.[13] Kardashian has pioneered the genre of the selfie and structured her career around behind-the-scenes access to her image-making processes, including consistent depictions of makeup sessions, wardrobe fittings, and cosmetic and medical procedures. She has also repeatedly imitated other celebrities, including Madonna, Cher, Jackie Kennedy Onassis, Aaliyah, and Toukie Smith.

These stars' bodies of work demonstrate conspicuous attention to not only *what* fame means but also *how*. Having become famous, at least in part, by addressing what it means to be famous, these celebrities have created space for considering the citational and performative aspects of all forms of self-making. They are not the only famous folks to address their celebrity self-reflexively, but Rockwell, Smith, and Kardashian make valuable case studies because they are highly conspicuous and controversial figures. All three have experienced immense popularity with audiences and corresponding, or even consequent, critical disdain—their bodies of work often dismissed as lacking artistic merit

---

13. The makeover is a frequent narrative device in Hollywood cinema, but Smith's case is unique. First, most makeover cinema, from *My Fair Lady* (George Kukor, 1964) to *Clueless* (Amy Heckerling, 1995) to *Mean Girls* (Mark Waters, 2004), centers on a woman whose appearance is modified to increase her attractiveness to potential heterosexual mates, but Smith's makeover sequences often focus on men's transformations and, most often, his own. Second, Smith's makeovers often enact his transformation as a way to access networks and spaces defined by whiteness, while mainstream makeover films center white protagonists who revamp their images not to approximate whiteness but to amplify its associations with economic privilege, traditional gender norms, and/or heterosexuality. See Ferriss, *Chick Flicks*.

or integrity. For example, art critic Clement Greenberg proclaimed, "You have to put Rockwell down, down below the rank of minor artist. He chose not to be serious."[14] Regarding a 2001 exhibition of Rockwell's work at the Guggenheim, art critic Jerry Saltz decried Rockwell's work in even harsher terms, accusing the museum of "trashing the reputation won for it by generations of artists" by featuring Rockwell's paintings.[15] Although Smith was called one of Hollywood's most bankable stars in the 2000s, critics have been rather cruel in admonishing the actor for his cinematic flops.[16] Consider, for example, this series of epithets used to describe his Netflix production *Bright*, which was dubbed one of 2017's worst films:[17] "batshit bonkers," "a truly terrible, mountainous pile of genre-blending garbage," and "lazy nonsense that's too silly to be good and too self-serious to be any fun."[18] These reviews of *Bright* demonstrate the "disreputable entertainment value" that some critics attribute to Smith's career more generally, as illustrated by a headline claiming that "The 5 Worst Movies of the Decade All Starred Will Smith."[19] Kardashian has been the subject of countless critiques of reality television and social media, as in Caitlin Flanagan's sardonic description of Kardashian as having made a career for herself by "selling the idea that any young woman scanning barcodes at Kmart can vault out of that condition not by night school and thrift but by texting enough naked selfies and staging enough tear-filled mini-dramas that she gets discovered and ends up with her own McMansion and a diamond as big as the Ritz."[20] Such critiques have been met with rebuttals or attempts at recuperation, but critics' dismissal of these celebrities as iterations of "throwaway" culture might be said to synecdochize a presumption about celebrity itself, which, for some, is defined by "epic triviality."[21]

The presumption that these stars produce banal or even disposable works does not, however, negate their potential rhetorical significance. As Greg

---

14. Williams, "Clement Greenberg."
15. Saltz, "Middle Americana."
16. In 2009 *Forbes* ranked Smith the Hollywood actor with the most currency, giving him (and no other actors) a perfect 10 on their score chart, which measured a star's capacity for affecting a film's success. See Burman, "Forbes' Star Currency."
17. David Ehrlich declares *Bright* the worst film of 2017, writing, "There's boring, there's bad, and then there's 'Bright,' a movie so profoundly awful that Republicans will probably try to pass it into law over Christmas break." See Ehrlich, "'Bright' Review."
18. Rife, "Will Smith's Netflix Blockbuster"; Roeper, "Put an Orc in It"; Coggan, *"Bright."*
19. Hassenger, "Gemini Man"; Baldwin, "5 Worst Movies." Consider also A. O. Scott's description of Smith's 2008 flop *Seven Pounds* as "among the most transcendently, eye-poppingly, call-your-friend-ranting-in-the-middle-of-the-night-just-to-go-over-it-one-more-time crazily awful motion pictures ever made." See Scott, "An I.R.S. Do-Gooder."
20. Flanagan, "Feeling Special."
21. Farred, "Achilles," 1107.

Dickinson posits, "Our collective and individual subjectivities are always at stake, and they are always at stake even in, and perhaps especially in, the mundane and banal practices of the everyday."[22] To Dickinson's list of such quotidian activities as drinking coffee, purchasing magazines, and talking about the weather, we might add the so-called guilty pleasures of celebrity culture as sites where rhetoric is at work despite their supposed mundanity or banality. The rhetorical stakes of these stars' potential influence on cultural discourses about selfhood and identity are high even if they are dismissed as low culture.

Like most stars, each of these figures has been associated with the circulation of hegemonic discourses in US culture, including individualism and the American Dream, but they have also been subject to rumors and/or scandals about their identities and particularly their sexualities. As I discuss later, these stars have been accused of "covering up" aspects of their supposedly authentic selves, and such tabloid gossip points to a central paradox within celebrity culture: the faith that celebrities have authentic identities that can be documented and the suspicion that they are always performing. Given this tension, these celebrities' image cultures offer resources for questioning and challenging normative expectations about identity and subjectivity.

While I make the case that Rockwell's, Smith's, and Kardashian's conspicuous attention to celebrity has unique probative value for considering the fashioning of selves more generally, this project also argues that metonymic criticism has applicability beyond them. This analysis thus addresses a range of other public figures with intertextual links to these three figures, including not only Trump, Simpson, and Warhol but also Marina Abramović, Ta-Nehisi Coates, Joan Crawford, Marilyn Monroe, Sidney Poitier, Jean-Jacques Rousseau, Jerry Saltz, and Mary Shelley. The contributions of this project are owed to its individual case studies and its larger theoretical interventions, deploying intertextual analyses of celebrity images to disrupt hegemonic discourses in US culture that emphasize individuation at the expense of ethical considerations of intersubjectivity and interdependence. This approach echoes Nicholas Christakis and James Fowler's assertion that networks can be marshaled as resources for making social worlds more capacious and inclusive.[23]

Scholars in cinema, media, and cultural studies, beginning with Alexander Walker and James Monaco, as well as others in psychology, journalism studies, sociology of communications, and anthropology, have long shown that celebrities mean a great deal not only because they matter so much to their audiences but also because they invite interpretation and communicate

---

22. Dickinson, "Joe's Rhetoric," 6.
23. Christakis and Fowler, *Connected*.

cultural discourses.[24] Joseph Boone and Nancy J. Vickers argue, "Now more than ever we live in a culture saturated in celebrity images and stories, and it shows no sign of retreat. Such images and stories inform our notions of self and community; our sense of the intermingling spheres of public and private life; our fears, aspirations, dreams." More than "mere" entertainers, celebrities operate as significant sites for the production of cultural and countercultural knowledges, functioning as intertextual heuristics through which audiences, including fans, critics, and scholars, can articulate, negotiate, and even rewrite public narratives. "Created by, and subject to, the vagaries of public opinion, celebrities are," Boone and Vickers contend, "the very substance of a public discourse through which communities negotiate mores, values, and politics."[25]

As sites of identification and affective investment, celebrities guide the attitudes and feelings of viewing publics. While it has become commonplace to critique celebrities for their tendency to reinforce hegemonic cultural norms—such as faith in the individualistic logic of the American Dream or fantasies about masterful subjectivity—this book moves beyond suspicious frameworks of critique and, instead, asks how metonymic criticism might reframe celebrity culture to manifest ethical ways of becoming (with others) in the world. I read these celebrities (and their networks of associates) as articulating theories of subjectivity that are attentive to intersectionality, internormativity, and interconnectivity. Much of the significance of celebrity culture lies in its facility for creating relationships—between various stars, between different texts, between stars and their audiences—and this book traces myriad forms of such interdependence to demonstrate ontologies of selfhood defined by intersubjective relations. Understanding vulnerability to be both a condition and a consequence of interdependence and intersubjectivity, I make ethical and political calls for attention to unevenly dispersed precarities as forms of injustice that demand response.

Mapping the Stars practices what Kenneth Burke calls "perspective by incongruity," which strategically violates conventional "assumptions about what properly ought to go with what" to manifest "unsuspected linkages and relationships."[26] This project also asks *what goes with what* and *what else might*. What networks of association between celebrities, texts, signifiers, and practices already exist within and give shape to US culture? What new or unexpected associations might we uncover or create to challenge, or even change, hegemonic ways of thinking about identity and being in the US? Analyz-

---

24. See Walker, *Stardom*; Monaco, *Celebrity*; Boorstin, *The Image*; Alberoni, "Powerless Elite"; Barker, "Introduction," 4–6; and Bennett, "Historicising Celebrity Studies."
25. Boone and Vickers, "Introduction," 902, 908.
26. Whedbee, "Perspective by Incongruity," 48.

ing images of some of the world's most privileged people and the logics that articulate them, I aim to make visible the intersections between interdependence, vulnerability, and precarity. Because celebrity culture offers important resources with which people imagine what it is to be human, critical attention to power and difference within that world offers valuable opportunities for critiquing injustices that privilege some subjects over others and for disrupting hegemonic discourses about identity and subjectivity in US culture.

FLEETING FAME

Addressing celebrity's capacity to create meaningful associations requires attention to the multiplicative and often evanescent sites through which fame moves because celebrity "is a phenomenon that flares in the moment, is experienced in its noisy immediacy, and thrives on the ephemerality that is the condition of its being," as Boone and Vickers contend.[27] "The ephemeral," writes Paul Grainge, "connotes the evanescent, transient and brief; in definitional terms, it describes anything short-lived." The concept of ephemerality also signals the "peripheral and throwaway" and suggests "questions of cultural value."[28] Celebrity is itself often ephemeral and depends on a range of media practices and objects that are themselves characterized by ephemerality, in both senses of this word: the temporary and the insignificant. This book attends to media sites that it defines as ephemeral both strictly and loosely. In the former sense of the word, the ephemeral objects being interpreted here include movie posters, magazine covers, social media posts, and memes, which are often designed to be temporary and replaceable.

As Phil Wickham argues, it is "because of its specificity and its address to consumers" that an ephemeral object can offer unique insights into popular media's "role in everyday life and its place within individual lives." Furthermore, Wickham notes, the seemingly "incidental" text or artifact can prove particularly "illuminating because it represents assumptions and ideas held at the time," which are often taken for granted as common sense or just the way things are.[29] In the latter sense of the word *ephemera*, this analysis also includes a range of objects that are not necessarily "short-lived" but that are perceived as lacking "cultural value," including images, television shows, movies, and even books that have been marked by critics as lacking artistic significance—in part because they are associated with public figures who have

---

27. Boone and Vickers, "Introduction," 904.
28. Grainge, "Introduction," 2.
29. Wickham, "Scrapbooks," 317, 318.

themselves been seen as lacking enduring importance. Despite the relative longevities of their fame, critics have often described Rockwell, Smith, and Kardashian as producing disposable bodies of works or even as "trashing" the cultures from which they emerged.

According to William Uricchio, *ephemera* derives from the term for an insect that has a life span of a single day, such as the mayfly. This notion of temporal transience resonates with contemporary figurations of fame as fleeting, as in the concept of "fifteen minutes of fame," often attributed to Warhol.[30] It seems fitting that short-lived celebrity has association with insects given that the gossip industry that feeds and feeds off of celebrity also has an entomological etymology. The term *paparazzo* was used by Italian director Federico Fellini as the surname of a character in *La Dolce Vita* (1960) who works as a freelance photographer and associates with tabloid writers, and the term now signifies those photographers who make a living snapping presumably unauthorized, candid shots of famous people going about their everyday lives. Although the actual linguistic origins of the term remain uncertain, *Time* magazine asserted in 1961 that Fellini chose the word because it reminded him of a "buzzing insect, hovering, darting, stinging."[31] That same year, Daniel Boorstin lamented the conditions of contemporary celebrity, in which a person could become a "household word overnight," being well known for their "well-knownness." Boorstin writes, "The celebrity is born in the daily newspapers and never loses the mark of his [sic] fleeting origin. The very agency which first makes the celebrity in the long run inevitably destroys him [sic]."[32] Such a perspective echoes through presumptions that "celebrity decays with age," offering ever-diminishing returns.[33]

Since the advent of digital mediation, the relationship between ephemerality, media, and fame has gained increasing import. As Grainge remarks, because tensions between "speed and storage, immediacy and archiving" characterize the discourses and practices of digital mediation, "the ephemeral has assumed a particular cultural and textual significance."[34] For example, the speed with which people can achieve fame through social media is often matched only by the speed with which such fame dissipates. Some scholars

---

30. The line "In the future, everyone will be world famous for 15 minutes" appeared in the program for Warhol's 1968 exhibition of his work at the Moderna Museet in Sweden, but there exists some debate about whether Warhol himself uttered those words or whether they were suggested to him by someone else. Regardless, this concept has been associated with Warhol. See Guinn and Perry, *Sixteenth Minute*.
31. "Paparazzi on the Prowl," 81.
32. Boorstin, *The Image*, 47, 217, 63.
33. Kurzman et al., "Celebrity Status," 354.
34. Grainge, "Introduction," 3.

have presumed, therefore, that the conditions of digital mediation have meant that celebrity's "rate of decay has accelerated."[35] And yet the fact that some fame is produced and/or circulated digitally means that its residue may be collected and stored indefinitely. The cultural significance of this paradox can be seen, for example, in that it even found its way to children's programming, in which the main characters of the animated series *Phineas and Ferb* declare that "fame is fleeting" and yet "the internet is forever."

Grainge's figuration of the study of ephemeral media as an exploration of the "relation between stability and impermanence, the substantial and the evanescent, the monumental and the momentary"[36] seems an equally apt characterization of the study of fame in the late twentieth and twenty-first centuries, which, Richard Dyer notes, oscillates between the extraordinary and the ordinary, the otherworldly and the everyday, the epic and the banal.[37] As Jennifer Wicke argues, "No one is, in fact, famous simply for being famous, even for as little as Andy Warhol's fifteen minutes." Rather, Wicke continues, "celebrification happens for a reason." Those reasons are often engineered, but they also signal the extent to which particular figures may "resonate" with public longings.[38] This book begins with the presumption that it is not only particular figures but also the *very idea and form of celebrity* that resonate with such cultural desires and anxieties. Indeed, *Mapping the Stars* argues that even the most banal iterations of celebrity culture may become sites where people reckon, both privately and publicly, with monumental questions of what it is to be human—not the least of which includes facing life's transience. Boone and Vickers's claim that celebrity "thrives on the ephemerality that is the condition of its being" might, therefore, be amended to make the claim that celebrity thrives on the ephemerality that is the condition of being itself.

The study of art, media, and culture, Wickham argues, should attend to both objects marked as culturally or historically significant and those deemed insignificant. Describing his own work in an archive of cinematic ephemera that ranges from the "sublime to the ridiculous" and includes objects such as early film posters, novelty items, and toys, Wickham contends that "this juxtaposition is valuable, and indeed essential, because the exceptional, the original and the beautiful, are inseparable in cinema history from the apparently trivial, derivative or plain ugly."[39] Such insights seem true of cinema and media history as well as of the related culture and industry of celebrity.

---

35. Kurzman et al., "Celebrity Status," 354.
36. Grainge, "Introduction," 13.
37. Dyer, *Heavenly Bodies*.
38. Wicke, "Epilogue," 1135.
39. Wickham, "Scrapbooks," 316.

Ephemeral media offer valuable resources for rethinking hegemonic discourses of selfhood. Even problematic or normative images of/by celebrities can be animated toward counterhegemonic ends, disrupting the norms they seem to reiterate. *Mapping the Stars* takes up its objects of study as illustrations of the fact that human experience is often characterized by tensions and oscillations between the mundane and the monumental, the banal and the sublime. The quotidian stuff of everyday life often functions as a tool with which people make sense of life's more spectacular experiences, questions, and challenges. Celebrity culture is itself structured by such tensions. While it often constructs stars—not unlike the celestial objects that this term references—as extraordinary and out of reach, celebrity culture also depends on narratives of celebrity ordinariness—their *just-like-us-ness*—that aim to foster audience identifications and illusions of relatedness.

Celebrities, P. David Marshall proffers, shape cultural discourses of the self, defining the terms with which selfhood is imagined and performed. In the digital era, the culture of celebrity has helped shape the parameters of self-presentation, in which the role of "persona" has become increasingly important, even for the nonfamous.[40] As Ernest Sternberg contends, the contemporary "image" economy encourages individuals (not to mention institutions) to "raise their value through calculated self-presentation, using techniques originally meant for the making of celebrities."[41] A suspicious reading of this culture of fame might understand it as encouraging individuals to exploit themselves and monetize their identities as brands. Such a reading is not wrong, but a more generous reading of celebrity culture and its rather ubiquitous presence in the age of networked media might also posit stardom as revealing the performativity and relationality that characterize signification and, consequently, subjectification. Celebrity culture and networked mediation are not the causes or origins of these practices of subjectivity but, rather, amplify and make more visible conditions of selfhood often obscured by Western culture's emphasis on individualism and authenticity.

The networked nature of celebrity culture is not new, but its capacity for hypertrophic expansion has been animated by digital mediation. As noted earlier, the digitization of celebrity has generated modes of "short-lived celebrity," often associated with the notion of virality.[42] At the same time, the digital archiving of celebrity narratives and images enhances what Sharrona Pearl and Dana Polan describe as "celebrity's long historical reach," giving audiences

---

40. Marshall, "New Media New Self," 634. See also Marshall et al., *Persona Studies*.
41. Sternberg, "Phantasmagoric Labor," 4. See also Hearn, "'Meat, Mask, Burden'"; Grindstaff and Murray, "Reality Celebrity"; and Ouellette and Hay, *Better Living*.
42. Mole, "Hypertrophic Celebrity."

access to historical celebrity figures and storing evidence of celebrity culture for future audiences.[43] Rockwell, Smith, and Kardashian offer unique perspectives on the "enduring ephemerality" of celebrity, particularly as it relates to digital mediation.

First, although Rockwell was experiencing, illustrating, and theorizing celebrity long before the advent of the internet, his example demonstrates the importance of digital mediation for the recirculation and reconstitution of a celebrity's image and body of work. Rockwell's art continues to reach audiences not only because of its exhibition in museums around the world but also because of its online presence. For instance, the popular US periodical *The Saturday Evening Post* has digitized all of its magazine covers, including the hundreds that featured cover art by Rockwell during his lifetime and some published long after his death. Similarly, the Norman Rockwell Museum (NRM) has digitized most of his body of work with an explicit aim of amplifying its cultural significance and accessibility. The NRM's digital preservation efforts have included the archiving of the works themselves and reference materials and personal belongings associated with the artist's catalogue raisonné. Promotional coverage of the years-long project of photographing and/or scanning Rockwell's belongings and works declared, "Norman Rockwell and his work are going viral."[44] The NRM website also features a number of interactive digital applications that encourage audiences to explore and even play with Rockwell's work. Such forms of digitization have also enabled further citation and parody of his work by contemporary artists, including professionals and amateurs, critics and fans.

It is also worth noting that much of the critical disdain for Rockwell's work seems to derive as much from its associations with mass mediation and dissemination as from the art itself. When Rockwell began working as a commercial artist in the early twentieth century, the magazines in which his images appeared were, alongside newspapers, the "sole media for the broad dissemination of news and information" and "the primary source of new images for most people."[45] The placement of his images in magazines led many critics to interpret Rockwell's work as having more value for circulation than for collection. As Saltz writes, "It's not surprising to learn that many of the companies that commissioned work from [Rockwell] tossed the originals once they were reproduced. His work was never meant to be seen in the flesh; it was meant for reproduction."[46] The dismissal of the mass mediation of Rockwell's work

---

43. Pearl and Polan, "Bodies of Digital Celebrity," 187.
44. Hollenbaugh, "Rockwell Goes Digital."
45. Montgomery, *Norman Rockwell*, 11.
46. Saltz, "Middle Americana."

in the twentieth century parallels many of the criticisms of work produced and circulated via digital mediation in the twenty-first century, illustrating the maxim in media historiography that the differences between old and new media are never as stark as they might seem. As Lisa Gitelman argues, "New media are less points of epistemic rupture than they are socially embedded sites for the ongoing negotiation of meaning as such."[47]

Second, Smith's television and film career began alongside the emergence of the internet in the US imaginary. It was only one week before the television premiere of *The Fresh Prince of Bel-Air* that the *New York Times* announced efforts by so-called father of the internet Robert Kahn to create a "national highway system for data." Three years later, Smith starred in *Six Degrees of Separation*, a film about networked forms of communication and their capacity for spreading misinformation and creating unwanted associations. Although *Fresh Prince* and *Six Degrees of Separation* may seem to be wholly distinct textual forms—one a lowbrow sitcom, the other a critically acclaimed film—they share small-world narratives about a precaritized character who finds his way into the social lives (and homes) of wealthy elites. These depictions of the characters' capacity to network with the rich and powerful resonate, respectively, with what Wendy Hui Kyong Chun calls the "now-embarrassing utopian and dystopian hype around the internet" in the late 1990s.[48] The former text tells a rather utopian tale about upward mobility and the exploration of new worlds, as if to anticipate Internet Explorer's tagline, "Where do you want to go today?" The latter offers a more dystopian, or even paranoid, figuration of Smith's character as infiltrative and infective, bringing with him threats of contamination and contagion.

As a celebrity whose career has spanned decades and genres, falling in and out of favor, and as one of the world's most famous Black celebrities, Smith has also been subject to a great deal of online parody and critique. After experiencing a significant downturn in his career in the 2010s, Smith turned to digital mediation as a way to reconnect with audiences and rebuild his currency. Such efforts have included the development of a multimedia company called Westbrook, partnerships with the streaming service Netflix, and adoption of an active social media presence on such platforms as Facebook, Instagram, YouTube, and TikTok. As is characteristic of Smith's brand, these ventures often include his immediate family members, with much of his social media content offering seemingly intimate access to his wife and children and operating as a nodal point for the promotion of his family members' various other projects.

---

47. Gitelman, *Always Already New*, 6.
48. Chun, "Enduring Ephemeral," 149.

Third, Kardashian has made much of her fame in the interdigitated spheres of reality television and social media. Kardashian's career has depended on virality and spreadability, helping to define the category of online "influencer," and she has used such platforms as Instagram and Snapchat to offer access to her and her family's everyday lives and to promote her business ventures in the fields of fashion, beauty, and cosmetics. Kardashian's celebrity is so articulated with the concept of virality that she became the inaugural face of *Paper* magazine's (now copyrighted) "Break the Internet" feature. Showcased on multiple versions of the cover for the November 2014 issue, nude photographs of Kardashian were predicted to overload the magazine's web server and crash its site. Only one month after the cover ran, *Paper* reported that traffic to the magazine's website was "staggering," constituting "nearly 1% of the entire web browsing activity in the US."[49] The flare of attention around this controversial set of magazine covers illustrates a practice central to Kardashian's career: the creation, or at least courting, of controversies whose singular impact fades rather quickly but whose cumulative effect helps perform and maintain her public persona. Often likened to Warhol, Kardashian seems to have mastered the logic of enduring ephemerality, building her fame around fleeting moments of infamy.

Given her associations with reality television and social media, Kardashian has also been linked to critiques of "post-truth" sensibilities and practices, including accusations that her media presence helped create the pathway for Trump's election. In line with this critique, Kardashian was one of several celebrities—including Facebook founder Mark Zuckerberg, performance artist Marina Abramović, Warhol, and Trump himself—who were subjected to "deepfakes" by artists Bill Posters and Daniel Howe. Such viral videos manipulate footage of the stars generated with artificial intelligence to raise questions about data privacy, surveillance, and the digital manipulation of information. In her video, Kardashian appears to brag about exploiting the data of her fans and "haters" and "manipulating people online for money." Along with other parodies and memes of Kardashian—not unlike those referencing Rockwell and Smith—these deepfakes raise questions about the stability and permanence of meaning; but more than just illustrate the kinds of manipulations made possible by digital technologies, these media artifacts signal the instability and contingency of all signification, which themselves signal the instability and contingency of all subjectification.

Like most famous folks, Rockwell, Smith, and Kardashian have been subjected to gossip and accusations of cover-ups, particularly in relation to their

---

49. Hershkovits, "Kim Kardashian."

sexualities.⁵⁰ In 2013 Deborah Solomon published an unauthorized biography of Rockwell claiming that the artist had experienced repressed homosexual and even pedophilic desires. The controversial book received condemnation from Rockwell's family and prompted high-profile responses from Rockwell's supporters, critics, and fans. Similarly, throughout his career, Smith has been described as homophobic, closeted, and on the DL with other Black celebrities. Such rumors have also suggested that Smith's association with the Church of Scientology is owed to a desire to cure his alleged homosexuality. Kardashian has been subject to multiple leaks of her (purportedly) private sexual videos and images, including the sex tape that made her famous and a series of images that were part of the 2014 "Fappening," but gossip has also suggested that those leaks were not violations of her privacy but strategically engineered efforts at fame.⁵¹

Gossip and allegations of cover-ups suggest a desire to know who a celebrity "really" is while revealing the impossibility of this knowledge. The gossip industry insists on fantasies of authentic and stable selfhood while acknowledging the performative aspects of celebrity. People (famous or not) are never who we think they are, and things are never what they seem, because the conditions under which we come to know ourselves and others are always themselves unstable and unreliable. These conditions make us vulnerable—to misinterpretations and misunderstandings, for example—but they also create opportunities to forge new interpretations and connections. *Mapping the Stars* argues that leaning into conditions of instability as they pertain to both signification and subjectivity can afford us resources for knowing each other (and ourselves) differently and imagining new ways of being (together). This perspective has both ethical and political entailments, given that, as Armond Towns argues, white cishet masculinity has historically maintained its supremacy and "self-conceptions" by misrepresenting and misinterpreting those constructed as Other while asserting that such constructions are essential.⁵²

Although attention to such instability can create paranoid sensibilities—as illustrated by the conspiratorial logics of gossip industries—it can also animate hopefulness and possibilities for reparation because when signifiers are understood to be unstable and arbitrary, their meanings and associations are

---

50. See Gamson, *Claims to Fame,* and Mercer, "Introduction."

51. The phrase *The Fappening* refers to an event that began in August 2014, following an iCloud hack that leaked private nude photographs of celebrities without their consent. The term itself is a portmanteau of the words *fap,* which is a slang term referencing masturbation, and *happening.* The term also alludes to the M. Night Shyamalan film *The Happening* (2008), which is about a mysterious virus that travels through the atmosphere, much as the photos went viral after having been stolen from their storage "clouds."

52. Towns, "Toward a Black Media Philosophy," 852.

subject to change. Understanding paranoia and hope not as mutually exclusive sensibilities but, rather, as coextensive dispositions, *Mapping the Stars* deploys the study of networked celebrity culture to challenge the hegemonic structures and norms that fame seems to affirm. This book turns to the figures of Rockwell, Smith, and Kardashian to chart some of the paradoxes and possibilities of being with and in relation to others.

Consideration of each of these artists' presence in and/or engagement with various forms of networked communication enables analysis of the changing contours of celebrity in the context of different modes of mediation and metaphorical figuration of subjectivity as a networked form. Throughout this book, theories of intertextuality, via Roland Barthes and Julia Kristeva, underwrite conceptions of interdependence and intersubjectivity, which are both necessary aspects of human existence and preconditions for vulnerability. *Mapping the Stars* deploys analyses of Rockwell's, Smith's, and Kardashian's imagetexts to highlight the performative registers of subjectivity. While, as Kendall Phillips argues, a "sense of subjectivity as fluid, dynamic, and multiple has become almost orthodox throughout the humanities," fantasies of unified, masterful subjectivity persist in popular media and political discourse in the US.[53] This book aims to intervene against such hegemonic figurations of the autonomous subject, which Judith Butler dubs the "legacy of individualism," calling attention to the contingent processes with which selves are formed through analysis of the conspicuous self-making that characterizes the personae of stars like Rockwell, Smith, and Kardashian.[54]

Chapter 1, "Six Degrees of Subjectification: Theorizing and Practicing Metonymy," deploys metonymic criticism to read celebrity as illustrative of the conditions of intersubjectivity. Metonymy works by forging associations between different signifiers, texts, and subjects, while also obscuring and naturalizing the logics and assumptions structuring those links. Mike Arntfield describes metonymy as a "hegemonic shorthand," whose communicative efficiency reinforces its presumed inherency.[55] Metonymic criticism calls attention to implied linkages between rhetorical nodes in order to challenge discriminatory or exploitative logics and create new, counterhegemonic networks of association. This chapter argues that semiotic theories of intersubjectivity, which proffer subjectivity as marked by the same instability and interdependence as signification, offer ethical and political resources for acknowledging vulnerability as a definitive human experience and emphasizing unevenly

---

53. Phillips, "Rhetorical Maneuvers," 310.
54. Butler, *Force of Nonviolence*.
55. Arntfield, "Hegemonic Shorthand," 77.

distributed forms of vulnerability—or precarity—as particularly affecting the lives of women and BIPOC, LGBTQ, and/or disabled people.

Chapter 2, "American Queerer: Norman Rockwell and the Art of Queer Feminist Critique," offers a history of Rockwell's engagement with celebrity culture, positioning his art as interested in both the norms of fame and celebrity's affordances for helping people fashion their senses of self. This analysis includes many of Rockwell's paintings and movie posters, as well as multiple parodies of and artistic allusions to his work, reading his art against the grain of conventional wisdom about him, which suggests that this work only celebrates white, middle-class, heteronormative identity formations. To the contrary, Rockwell's art abounds with images of individuals questioning their own genders and sexualities in relation to cultural norms, celebrity culture, and other people, disrupting the metonymic associations that typically attach to hegemonic identity formations. The chapter concludes that Rockwell's art engenders queer feminist criticism by calling attention to internormativity and intersubjectivity and the complex processes with which people (famous and nonfamous) create their own images.

Chapter 3, "Terms and Conditions: Reflections on and of Black Fame in the Case of Will Smith," closely reads texts featuring Smith, including films, movie posters, social media, and parodies. The chapter also addresses a range of other texts with intertextual links to Smith's work including Mary Shelley's *Frankenstein*, Ta-Nehisi Coates's *Between the World and Me*, and Victor LaValle's graphic novel *Destroyer*. Chapter 3 positions Smith's work as interested in the interdigitated phenomena of networks and fame and the racial politics that metonymically organize both. Reading many of Smith's media texts as "metacelebrity" objects, the chapter argues that the star's body of work makes visible the norms that authorize and constrain Black fame. This analysis reveals Smith's work as addressing the symbolic and material forms of violence that structure the lives of Black folks, including those who are famous and those who are not.

Chapter 4, "Emotional Icons: Digital Culture, Networks of Affect, and Kim Kardashian," deploys the case study of Kardashian to consider the historical and theoretical links between melodrama and celebrity culture. Connecting Kardashian's body of work to Jean-Jacques Rousseau's inaugural melodrama *Pygmalion*, the chapter argues that Kardashian's career illustrates not only a "metacelebrity" focus but also a metatropological one in which Kardashian's works and images address the practices of signification and their implications for processes of subjectification. The chapter considers a range of media objects including magazine covers, Kardashian's line of bespoke emoji, and her book of selfies, entitled *Selfish*. It also considers how Kardashian's image participates in centuries-old practices of exploitation and violence toward Black women and women of color, demonstrating whiteness's metonymic dependence on cultural signifiers of Blackness.

Bridging chapters 2 through 4 are two shorter chapters, "Interstitial I" and "Interstitial II." The interstitial chapters analyze an incongruous textual assemblage that includes a Rockwell AIDS activism poster, an Elton John song, an issue of *Premiere* magazine that features Smith, a trio of films about serial killers, a filmic adaptation of a Christopher Isherwood novel by a fashion designer, and a digital parody of a *Paper* magazine cover photo of Kardashian. Although this claim might be made about many of the intertextual associations mapped by this book, these interstitial chapters, in particular, illustrate the "strength of weak ties."[56] Tracing loose links, as opposed to strong or close ones, between nodes in a network can yield new, perhaps unexpected, insights and reveal connections that might have otherwise been unnoticed. The chapters tie together a series of textual and extratextual nodes that may seem to have little connection in order to reveal the shared logics or investments that bind them. These readings demonstrate how analysis of celebrity culture's networked form reveals fantasies and anxieties about subjecthood in US culture while also manifesting the ethical entailments and entanglements of intersubjective relations. Finally, an epilogue, following chapter 4, shifts focus to the rhetorical device of portmanteaus, which manifest aspects of metonymic functions that often remain obscured. While metonymy signifies the extent to which all subjectivities exist in contingent relation to others, must be forged, and are subject to change, the portmanteau, which has a considerable place amid celebrity culture, serves as a reminder that all subjectivity is incomplete and combinatory.

---

56. Granovetter, "Strength of Weak Ties."

CHAPTER 1

Six Degrees of Subjectification

Theorizing and Practicing Metonymy

> If we accept that part of what a body is (and this is for the moment an ontological claim) is its dependency on other bodies and networks of support, then we are suggesting that it is not altogether right to conceive of individual bodies as completely distinct from one another.
>
> —Judith Butler

In 1929 Frigyes Karinthy published a short story titled "Chain-Links," introducing the theory of six degrees of separation and claiming that each person on the planet is connected to every other person by only five people. In 1967 Stanley Milgram traced such interconnectivity by sending mail through the US postal system. Having already gained notoriety for his obedience experiments at Yale University, Milgram proved that the theory of six degrees of separation was shockingly accurate. A similar "small world" logic instructs playwright John Guare's 1990 play *Six Degrees of Separation*, which Fred Schepisi then adapted as a film, giving a breakthrough leading role to rapper-turned-sitcom star Will Smith. The lead character, Paul, penetrates the ultra-privileged social circles of Manhattan's Upper East Side by claiming to be the son of actor Sidney Poitier. Guare based his play on the actual story of David Hampton, as recounted to him by Osborn Elliott, then dean of the Columbia University School of Journalism; and, like the characters in his play, Guare describes Elliott and his wife Inger as proclaiming "Have we got a story for you!"

Illustrating Frank Rich's claim that the phrase *six degrees of separation* had "passed into the language," in 1994 students at Albright College created the "Six Degrees of Kevin Bacon" game.[1] Popularized on MTV's *The Jon Stewart Show*, the game requires players to connect any actor to Kevin Bacon in

---

1. Rich, "'Six Degrees' Reopens."

fewer than six steps—as in: Donald Trump was in *Celebrity* (Woody Allen, 1998) with Charlize Theron, who was in *Trapped* (Luis Mandoki, 2002) with Kevin Bacon. Public discourse about Six Degrees of Kevin Bacon claims that the game derives from Bacon's assertion in the January 1994 issue of *Premiere* magazine that he had worked with almost everyone in Hollywood. Only no such interview exists. Rather, it seems this specious attribution is owed to the associative logic of metonymy, as it was this issue of *Premiere* that introduced its readers to the film *Six Degrees of Separation* and to its breakout star Smith.[2]

In the decades since its creation, the Kevin Bacon game has generated a board game, books, websites, smartphone apps, and more. Incorporating the game into his own celebrity persona, Bacon referenced it in a 2002 Visa commercial and created a nonprofit organization called SixDegrees.org, which aims to connect celebrities with charities around the world and to enable nonfamous people to "become celebrities for their own causes." In 2012 Google introduced the (now defunct) "Bacon number" search tool, allowing users to search for connections between actors and Bacon, drawing on data from Google's Knowledge Graph. Jacopo Maria Cinti made a short film about the search tool, in which Bacon connects himself to a range of figures, including Buster Keaton, Marlon Brando, and Miss Piggy. The film's tagline highlights that Donald Trump and Kim Kardashian share a Bacon number of 2. In 2020 Bacon starred as a fictionalized version of himself in a podcast, *The Last Degree of Kevin Bacon*, which depicts an actor seeking revenge on Bacon for beating him out for a role in *Footloose* (Herbert Ross, 1984) and ruining his chance at fame.

The Kevin Bacon game has also inspired an art installation about the subject of celebrity. In 2012 the Donald W. Reynolds Center for American Art and Portraiture launched an exhibition called *Six Degrees of Peggy Bacon*, demonstrating how a little-known celebrity caricaturist and magazine illustrator named Peggy Bacon (no relation to Kevin) was connected to an array of public figures, including Andy Warhol, Buckminster Fuller, Eleanor Roosevelt, and Frida Kahlo. The installation was inspired by both the Kevin Bacon game and the ways that "radio technology, telecommunications and most recently, social media" have "increased the connectedness among the world's inhabitants."[3]

Associations between the six degrees phenomenon and celebrity have spawned other derivations and parodies, making it a "forever meme." Examples include popular press about Monica Lewinsky, baseball player Rogers Hornsby, and O. J. Simpson; and Malcolm Gladwell's *Tipping Point* uses the

---

2. See Teotonio, "Google Adds Six Degrees"; and Perman, "What's Your 'Bacon Number?'" Bacon appears in the January 1994 issue of *Premiere*, but only in advertisements for Paul Michael Glaser's 1994 film *The Air Up There*. The following year, Bacon gave an interview to *Premiere* about the game, but only after it had been given national attention on MTV.

3. McAlpine, "It's a Small World After All."

language of "six degrees" to describe Chicago's former cultural affairs commissioner Lois Weisberg as so well networked that she might secretly "run the world."[4] Norman Rockwell has also been a frequent subject of six degrees rhetoric, including discourse about his capacity to connect a wide range of viewers and his relationships with other artists. The American Masters site on PBS includes a six degrees function, through which users can connect an artist like Rockwell to myriad other public figures, including Truman Capote, Alfred Hitchcock, or Buster Keaton. The concept of six degrees also serves as the template for the 2016 and 2019 seasons of Karina Longworth's podcast *You Must Remember This*, which respectively detail Joan Crawford's network of professional and romantic relationships and the history of Disney's controversial film *Song of the South*.[5] Similar rhetoric abounds in descriptions of Kim Kardashian, linking her rise to fame with other celebrities with whom she has had relationships; for example, comedian Rob Maher has a bit called "Six Degrees of Kim Kardashian," which claims Kardashian can be connected to almost any politician, athlete, or celebrity through people with whom she has had sex. Kardashian also makes an appearance in the nonfiction book *Six Degrees of Paris Hilton*, which recounts the story of an aspiring star named Darnell Riley who, not unlike Hampton, infiltrated the elite world of Hollywood through charm, fraud, and blackmail.

These examples suggest the centrality of networks to the culture of celebrity; but more than simply reminding us that fame often works through circuits of relatedness, the network logic of celebrity culture offers opportunities for considering a range of rhetorical, social, and political relations. *Mapping the Stars* argues that the study of celebrity as a networked, intertextual form offers theoretical resources for interrupting prevailing discourses and practices of selfhood in US media culture. Understanding metonymy as a networked form, this chapter identifies this rhetorical technology as integral to both the workings of stardom and the formation of subjects and deploys metonymy to challenge hegemonic discourses about subjectivity and the ideologies of individualism and exceptionalism that reaffirm them. In contrast

---

4. Schuessler, "Six Degrees Forevermore." See also Roeper, "Six Degrees of Monica Lewinsky"; Remes, "Six Degrees of Rogers Hornsby"; Wells, "Six Degrees of Simpson"; Moylan, "6 Degrees of the O. J. Simpson Trial"; Obell, "Can You Guess"; Griggs, "Kevin Bacon on 'Six Degrees Game'"; and Gladwell, *Tipping Point*, 52.

5. The podcast *The Thread* relies on network theory to connect "history's interlocking lives and events," although it does not reference the concept of six degrees explicitly. The first season connects John Lennon to Vladimir Lenin through Lennon's killer Mark David Chapman, author J. D. Salinger, socialite Oona O'Neill, playwright Eugene O'Neill, and journalist Louise Bryant. The story of Lennon's murder also appears in *Six Degrees of Separation*. Paul discusses *Catcher in the Rye* with Ouisa, recalling the network of men inspired by the book to kill others, including a substitute teacher from Long Island, Chapman, and John Hinckley Jr.

to popular US media's figurations of subjects as autonomous and masterful individuals, metonymic criticism of celebrity culture makes intersubjectivity and interdependence visible as hallmarks of human existence.

POWER CHAINS

The six degrees trope maintains links to celebrity culture because of its dependence on network logics and practices, as illustrated by the conventional wisdom that fame depends on "who you know."[6] This connection is central to *Six Degrees of Separation*, which interweaves theories of networks with tales of celebrity. To demonstrate, Paul uses the allure of fame to infiltrate the privileged social network of Flan and Ouisa Kittredge, a high-society couple whose fortune stems from the art world. Paul's (false) promise that Poitier, his (fake) father, can offer the Kittredges parts in a film adaptation of the musical *Cats* enthralls them, even though they express disdain for the supposedly lowbrow Broadway show and declare that they are not "star fuckers."[7]

Inversely, the Kittredges take advantage of their powerful network of associates to create fleeting acclaim for themselves, recounting (again and again) their stories about Paul. In Schepisi's film, for instance, within hours of discovering they have been defrauded and amid panic that they could have had their "throats slashed," the Kittredges narrate their encounter with Paul at a society wedding—despite not being able to remember whether they have links to the bride or groom. Recalling the scene in Rockwell's painting *The Gossips* (1948), wedding guests lean in, and the crowd grows to hear Ouisa and Flan name-drop their powerful friends and share stories about Paul.[8] As a form of mise-en-abyme, the flashback sequences that depict their narrated accounts show Ouisa and Flan similarly gathering around Paul as he tells stories about his famous father. So successful are the Kittredges' retellings of their story, each of which becomes a node in a larger network of stories, that they find their

---

6. See Ravid and Currid-Halkett, "Social Structure of Celebrity"; Currid-Halkett, *Starstruck*; and Huliaras and Tzifakis, "Personal Connections."

7. Hampton actually promised his marks a role in the film version of the musical *Dreamgirls*. Guare altered this detail from the case presumably because of understandings of *Cats* as a metonym for the supposed tension between highbrow art and mass market entertainment. See Hummler, "Cats."

8. Rockwell's *The Gossips* is constructed in the style of a grid, featuring the images of fifteen different people as each of them shares a rumor with another. Illustrating "small-worldness," the painting shows a secret being passed from one person to another until it arrives back at its source. The Kittredges likely would have taken offense at comparisons between them and the Rockwell painting because they snubbed their noses at popular or lowbrow art, as demonstrated by their disdain for *Cats*.

way to the *New York Times*. This narrative web includes Rick and Elizabeth, a young white couple from Utah who moved to New York to pursue fame; Paul tells them he is Flan's son, claiming that Flan met his mother while in Mississippi in the 1960s registering Black voters. Referencing the infamous "Murder in Mississippi," which would become the subject of one of Rockwell's civil rights paintings, Paul declares that Flan returned to the north after his friends were killed and resumed his life among Manhattan's elite.

Desire for celebrity motivated the incidents that inspired Guare's play and Schepisi's film. Hampton first impersonated Poitier's son to get into Studio 54, with a friend posing as the son of Gregory Peck, because both men wanted to become famous. Hampton told the *New York Times* that he felt he had three Black celebrities from whom to choose: Harry Belafonte, Sammy Davis Jr, and Poitier. Although he thought he resembled Belafonte, who coincidentally had a son named David, he chose Poitier because he had "so much more class"—suggesting that association with Poitier would have the most currency with white New York sophisticates.[9] When this scheme worked at Studio 54, Hampton tried it more widely, implicating many famous white people including Melanie Griffith, Gary Sinise, Calvin Klein, and Warhol. According to *The Andy Warhol Diaries*—Warhol's best-selling diary, which *Six Degrees of Separation* mocks as gossipy and distasteful—the "fake Poitier kid" tried to access Warhol's office multiple times.[10]

The links between theories of networks and celebrity culture also stem from their mutual relation to technologies of communication and mediation, as illustrated by such media historians as Richard DeCordova, Charles Ponce de Leon, Susan Murray, and Mingyi Hou.[11] For example, Karinthy's small-world theories reflect his narrator's claim that the world had "never been as tiny" as it was at that moment, having been "shrunk" by the "quickening pulse of both physical and verbal communication" brought on by such technologies as automobiles, telephones, and radios—as well as the growth of the newspaper industry. Karinthy's narrator explains the six degrees game by suggesting that he could be connected to an "anonymous riveter at the Ford Motor Company" through the "director of Hearst publishing."[12]

---

9. Witchel, "Impersonator."
10. Hackett, *Andy Warhol Diaries*, 505.
11. DeCordova, *Picture Personalities*; Ponce de Leon, *Human-Interest Journalism*; Murray, *Hitch Your Antenna*; Hou, "Social Media Celebrity."
12. Karinthy, "Chain-Links," 21, 23. See also Grossman, *Charles Dickens's Networks*, 6; and Marcus, "Celebrity 2.0," 30. Twenty years after Karinthy's story, Vannevar Bush also imagined a world made smaller by technology in his description of an imagined technology called the "memex," which would make associational connections between ideas similarly to the human mind ("As We May Think"). This idea has been described as placing Bush "six degrees" from the creation of the internet. See Zachary, "The Godfather."

Karinthy's reference to the Hearst empire illustrates Fred Inglis's description of celebrity as the "product of culture and technology."[13] As Sharon Marcus reminds us, "Without portrait busts and coins, without broadsides and woodcuts, without newspapers and photographs, without film and television—no celebrity."[14] For example, the development of movie stars in the early twentieth century depended on films, advertisements, newspapers like those published by William Randolph Hearst, and fan magazines such as *Motion Picture Story Magazine* and *Photoplay*. Hearst also published such magazines as *Cosmopolitan* and *Good Housekeeping*, which also became sites for the circulation of star names and images, and made feature films in partnership with Metro-Goldwyn-Mayer, one of Hollywood's oldest studios and an originator of the star system.[15]

Since the early 2000s, attention to the relationship between networks and technology has proliferated, particularly in relation to digital mediation, as illustrated by Albert-László Barabási, Manuel Castells, Nicholas Christakis and James Fowler, Zizi Papacharissi, Steven Shaviro, Jan van Dijk, and Duncan Watts.[16] So ubiquitous has the word *network* become that John Law describes it as a "hegemonic" frame for studying "sociotechnical" phenomena.[17] Offering a history of network studies, Mark Newman, Albert-László Barabási, and

---

13. Inglis, *Short History*, 10. See also Turner and Larson, "Network Celebrity."
14. Marcus, "Celebrity 2.0," 21.
15. Founder of a publishing empire, Hearst became the stuff of Hollywood legend, having been rumored to be at least one of the inspirations for Orson Welles's *Citizen Kane* (1941). Hearst tried to suppress the film and discredit its director, declining to run ads for the film and refusing to mention the film's distributor, RKO Pictures, in his newspapers and magazines. Louella Parsons, the gossip columnist who worked for Hearst, also led a campaign against Welles and threatened the members of the RKO board of directors that she would release previously buried stories about their sex lives and those of their stars if the studio did not kill the film. The Hearst organization characterized Welles as a Communist and even attempted entrapment, sending an underaged girl and photographers to Welles's hotel room. After unsuccessfully persuading RKO not to release the film, Hearst animated his powerful network of associates to convince other studio heads not to screen the film in their theaters, which led to *Citizen Kane* having a much narrower release than originally intended, opening in only seven cities throughout the United States. MGM is the studio responsible for Schepisi's film adaptation of *Six Degrees of Separation*. When David Hampton learned about the production of a film based on his life story, he became incensed. Having failed to convince Guare to let him star in the theatrical version of his story, Hampton threatened to sue MGM and all those associated with both the play and the film. He also threatened to use tactics not unlike those deployed by Louella Parsons, blackmailing various media executives and "destroying careers" until they compensated him. See Lebo, *Citizen Kane*, and Kasindorf, "Six Degrees of Impersonation," 45.
16. Barabási, *Linked*; Castells, *Rise of the Network Society*; Christakis and Fowler, *Connected*; Papacharissi, *Networked Self*; van Dijk, *Network Society*; Watts, *Small Worlds* and *Six Degrees*.
17. Law, "Networks, Relations, Cyborgs."

Duncan Watts explain that a diverse range of scholars, including "mathematicians, physicists, computer scientists, sociologists, and biologists" initiated the study of the "science of networks," noting that digital technologies allowed for a "dramatic increase" in such study. They write, "Not only has the Internet focused popular and scientific attention alike on the topic of networks and networked systems, but it has led to data collection methods" for the study of "social and other networks."[18]

For example, in 2001 Watts replicated Milgram's experiments using email and has written multiple books about "small world" phenomena. Jure Leskovec and Eric Horvitz confirmed Milgram's results using Microsoft instant messaging, and in 2012 two employees from Facebook and scholars from the University of Milan found that social media have made the world even "tinier," shrinking the degrees of separation between people from six to four.[19] In 2019 the Netflix Media Center released data indicating that Netflix subscribers share, on average, six degrees of separation from each other in terms of common viewings, which they call "Six Degrees of Netflix." As part of a promotional campaign, Netflix released a short film with the tagline "We all have six shows in common," coding its algorithmic processes as an opportunity for people to feel connected.

Although digital mediation (arguably) made the world seem smaller, it also expanded the bounds of celebrity culture. Šárka Gmiterková writes, "The growth of mass media throughout the twentieth century facilitated the development of the Hollywood star system, but it was the 1990s trend toward technological and industrial convergence that gave celebrity culture an unprecedented boost."[20] The emergence of social media, like reality television, has also collapsed the perceived distance between famous and nonfamous people: stars and their fans communicate on the same platforms, sometimes with each other; "ordinary" people can use social networks to become famous; and even those who do not become famous can perform their online persona, or brand, in the style of celebrities.[21] Social media sites such as Facebook, Twitter, and Instagram, argues Martin Shingler, "have changed the way in which people relate to each other and also how they relate to celebrities."[22] Such platforms have even changed relationships between celebrities, generating what Peter Turner calls "interstellar communities," which include the "visible network-

---

18. Newman et al., *Structure and Dynamics*, 5.

19. Milstein, "Using E-Mail"; Sanderson, "Six Degrees of Messaging"; Backstrom et al., "Four Degrees of Separation."

20. Gmiterková, "Transmedia Celebrity," 117.

21. See Dovey, *Freakshow*; Ellis, "How to Be in Public"; Arcy, "Digital Money Shot"; Thomas, "Celebrity in the 'Twitterverse'"; Marshall, "Promotion and Presentation"; Banet-Weiser, *Authentic*™; Khamis et al., "Self-Branding"; and Duffy and Pooley, "Idols of Promotion."

22. Shingler, "Star Studies," 445.

ing" that celebrities do on social media to demonstrate their connections to each other.[23] For example, the Instagram account @commentsbycelebs posts comments that famous people make on other famous people's posts because, as the account's profile reads, "even famous people love famous people."

The role of communicative technology in creating both small-world sensibilities and celebrity is central to *Six Degrees of Separation*, which opens with Ouisa and Flan frantically traversing their apartment after they discover Paul's fraud, worrying that they had been burgled, and inventorying their belongings. The most fetishized object is a silver Victorian inkwell—a technology of communication that was, in its own time, facing competition from electronic and networked means of communication, including the telegraph and radio. Telephonic technologies also play a conspicuous role in *Six Degrees*, connecting characters to one another and enabling the transmission of (mis)information. It is a telephone that facilitates the call to the member of the Kittredges' social network who facilitates the writing of a *Times* piece about them, which itself facilitates their temporary stardom. *Six Degrees* also gives a significant, if unexpected, place to a particular technology of physical communication: the dogsled. Sitting in Central Park, a bronzed statue of a husky named Balto memorializes the dog's service on a sled team spurred by a telegraph to deliver medicine to Alaska during a 1925 diphtheria outbreak. A touchstone for Paul when homelessness leads him to live in the park near the Kittredges, this Balto sculpture becomes the site where Paul spreads stories of wealth and privilege and transmits strategies for achieving social mobility to others who have come to New York chasing fame.[24]

The link between network logics and celebrity culture should be understood as related to both the ways celebrity status is created and circulated and to the ways audiences encounter and interpret star images. As Stuart Hall establishes, the processes of "encoding and decoding," or the creation and reception of meanings, "may not be perfectly symmetrical." The meanings audiences make from texts—including star images—will be affected both by the texts themselves and by audiences' agency and subject positions, generat-

---

23. Turner, "Fast Marketing," 469.

24. Having become a celebrity himself, Balto traveled in a vaudeville show, appeared in some silent films, and became part of a novelty museum and "freak" show in Los Angeles before being placed in a zoo in Ohio. After his death, his taxidermic remains circulated through multiple museums. In 1995, two years after the release of *Six Degrees of Separation*, an animated film about Balto's rescue mission featured Kevin Bacon as the lead voice actor—which is to say, one could play the Kevin Bacon game by noting that Will Smith was in *Six Degrees of Separation* with Balto, who was in *Balto* with Kevin Bacon. Balto also has one degree of separation from Norman Rockwell, as both worked on Mack Sennett's 1928 silent comedy *The Chicken*—Rockwell in props and Balto on screen—which is to say, Rockwell has a Bacon number of 2. See Jennifer Gillan, "'No One Knows,'" 52.

ing a range of possible interpretations and responses in relation to hegemonic discourses.[25] Celebrity culture depends on audiences' capacity and willingness to connect people, texts, media, and sites of discourse. Known beyond their own networks and even those of their fans, celebrities "become public hubs," argues Marcus, "linking even people who do not seek out information about them."[26] While every audience member has different access to transtextual codes and discourses about celebrity, viewing publics are positioned to experience a celebrity not as a discrete star but as a *constellation* of meanings. Just as the shape of a constellation does not reside in any single star, interpretations of a celebrity cannot be attributed to any single text or medium. In fact, contends Michael DeAngelis, it is the networked construction of "star texts" that both encourages audiences to feel connected to celebrities and creates sufficient "ambiguities in the star's textual and discursive constructions" to engender differing—sometimes contradictory—interpretations of them.[27]

As Gmiterková argues, celebrity has "always relied on transmedia functioning." The dawn of the star system in the US, for example, required that stars appear in films and that their names and images circulate through fan magazines.[28] Rockwell was one artist who helped facilitate such transmedia fame, painting portraits of celebrities and creating movie advertisements. Media convergence in the late twentieth century increased transmediation, making celebrity culture a "useful way" for media conglomerates in the post-studio era to connect their "cross-media" platforms, including film, television, music, publishing, and the internet.[29] Geoff King names Will Smith as a "textbook" example of transmedia stardom, citing Smith's fame in music, television, and film.[30] Likewise, Gmiterková frames the Kardashian family as central in "redefining" celebrity culture as a transmediated modality through reality television and social media, transforming "ephemeral" modes of fame into an "instantly recognizable, immensely profitable, highly participatory, and long-running branded celebrity storyworld."[31]

According to Thomas Austin, understanding fame as an "intertextual and multi-media phenomenon has become a truism in star studies," as readings of any celebrity necessarily move across multiple texts, including ones in which they have starred and even ones in which they have not appeared, and often

---

25. Hall, "Encoding/Decoding," 166, 171–73. See also Rahman, "Is Straight the New Queer?"; and Oh, "K-Pop Fans React."
26. Marcus, "Celebrity 2.0," 23. See Butler, *Television*, 51.
27. DeAngelis, *Gay Fandom*, 4–5.
28. Gmiterková, "Transmedia Celebrity," 116; DeCordova, *Picture Personalities*, 72.
29. Gmiterková, "Transmedia Celebrity," 117. See also Turner, *Understanding Celebrity*, 34–41.
30. King, "Stardom," 63.
31. Gmiterková, "Transmedia Celebrity," 122.

implicate other public figures, through or against whom the celebrity might be read.[32] As Marvin Carlson notes, audiences "view any new creation by an actor with some experience not only 'ghosted' by previous roles, but by an interpretive persona created and maintained by the institutional structures of media and publicity."[33] Audiences also interpret any given celebrity in relation to the extratextual discourse that orbits their work, which includes strategically generated publicity, such as talk show appearances, magazine interviews, and photographs that appear on a celebrity figure's official Facebook page, or gossip in tabloids that may be (or, at least, appear to be) outside a celebrity's control. Barry King likens such configurations to hypertextuality, noting that the constitution of a star's image across a "multiplicity of texts and performances" results in an image that remains elastic and never achieves "closure." King also notes that while a star's persona might be understood as metaphorical—that is, as a representation of the star's essence—stars, in fact, act as metonyms for the industry and corporate interests that they serve and with whom they are associated.[34]

The popularity of the Kevin Bacon game demonstrates that making such connections is pleasurable, but it is also political and ideological, and the continued popularity of this game raises the question of why Kevin Bacon is still so ubiquitous. This question could be answered with respect to hiring practices within Hollywood; Bacon's omnipresence might also be explained by referencing his network of associates, his likability, his professionalism, and any number of other attributes that could make him attractive to hire. These answers, however, tell only part of the story. Bacon's ubiquity should also be understood as indicative of ideological norms; Bacon moves so freely through Hollywood—across genres and decades—because of his "apparent unremarkability," which is itself owed to the "apparent unremarkability" of white masculinity.[35] Imagine, for instance, what connective pathways might be enabled or foreclosed if the six degrees game centered on a woman actor and/or an actor of color.[36]

Not only do stars exist in relation to such power structures; audiences do as well, and their views of celebrity derive from their positions within various fields of social relations, which may be characterized by inequities or imbalances of power. Audiences create connections by drawing on their subject

---

32. Austin, "Star Systems," 25.
33. Carlson, "Invisible Presences," 113. See also Ellis, *Visible Fictions*.
34. King, "Embodying an Elastic Self," 51, 60, 48.
35. Dyer, *White*, 1.
36. Such connective possibilities need not be left to the imagination. Patrick Reynolds, creator of the Oracle of Bacon, has addressed the gendered and racialized politics of the Kevin Bacon game. See Stuart, "Sorry Kevin Bacon."

positions, epistemic cultures, and interpretive communities. As Hall argues, a person's "conceptual maps"—a "set of correspondences or a chain of equivalence between things"—take shape in relation to the contexts that person inhabits.[37] This claim has been demonstrated by audience reception scholarship within and/or adjacent to cultural studies, including David Morley's empirical study of viewers of the BBC television program *Nationwide* and Janice Radway's feminist analysis of women readers of romance novels.[38] These connective possibilities reflect both audience members' agency and their emplacement within larger social and cultural contexts. Although it might appear to be just a simple diversion, the Kevin Bacon game reveals the usefulness of celebrity as a lens and associative logic as a means for examining ontologies of selfhood and their relationship to intersecting ideologies, including ones affecting cultural assumptions about race, gender, and sexuality. From a rhetorical perspective, these examples also reveal the centrality of metonymy to the circulation and interpretation of media texts and celebrity culture.

THE MATCH GAME

Derived from the Greek word *metōnumia*, which means "change of name," metonymy is, strictly speaking, a figure of speech that substitutes one word or phrase for another with which it is associated (as in *Hollywood* for the US film industry). While metaphor works by "indicating similarity" or correspondence, metonymy operates by "revealing contiguity" and contingency.[39] But metonymic logic does not only apply to language. Roman Jakobson describes film as a metonymic art form that relies on associations between shots, and Roland Barthes argues that metonymy structures the interpretation of images, in which signifiers create chains of connotative associations.[40] Analyzing an advertisement for Panzani pasta, Barthes notes how certain foods (spaghetti and tomatoes) and colors (red and green) connote "Italianicity," which may itself connote ideas such as authenticity, passion, or indulgence. Barthes also considers how close-ups of Greta Garbo and Audrey Hepburn become metonyms for different conceptions of femininity and how Marlon Brando's hairstyle in *Julius Caesar* (Joseph Mankiewicz, 1953) connotes "Roman-ness."[41]

---

37. Hall, "Work of Representation," 19.
38. Morley, *Nationwide Audience*; Radway, *Reading Romance*.
39. Lanham, *Rhetorical Terms*, 101. See also Dirvin and Pörings, *Metaphor and Metonymy*.
40. Jakobson, "Metaphoric and Metonymic Poles." For more on the associational properties among cinematic images, often described as the Kuleshov effect," see Perez, *Eloquent Screen*.
41. Barthes, *Image, Music, Text*, 33–34, and *Mythologies*, 56–57, 24.

Likewise, Charles Denroche argues that "metonymic processing," which he defines as logic predicated on conditions of "relatedness," has a "far wider 'reach' than just the creation of lexical formulations." Denroche identifies an "unexpectedly wide range of cultural and recreational phenomena" that illustrates metonymy, including "quiz shows, puzzles, games, [and] humour." Although he does not name the Kevin Bacon game, Denroche identifies celebrity culture as illustrative of metonymic processing, citing public fascination with celebrity nicknames, or changes of name, as evidence that "metonymy is not only prevalent but often salient in everyday communication."[42] Charlie Chaplin as "The Champ," Frank Sinatra as "Chairman of the Board," and Will Smith as "The Fresh Prince" illustrate metonymic nicknames based not on characteristics of the stars but on roles with which they are associated.

The ubiquity of metonymy in culture reflects the fact that all language is by definition metonymic. Christian Lundberg argues, "All signs and representations are tropologically inflected" because they depend on metonymic articulations between and among signifiers and signifieds. Lundberg contends, via rhetorical and semiotic theory, that metonymy is not a discrete figurative device but is the condition of all signification. If all signification is arbitrary and contingent, then no meaning inheres in any sign, and the relationship between every signifier and signified depends on forged associations, or imagined contiguities, between them. "Words and representations," Lundberg posits, "only function when subjects invest in them by acting or speaking as if speech stands in for the thing."[43] The forging of metonymic associations replays the feigning of unicity that undergirds fantasies of unified subjectivity, as if to guarantee that subjects have essences and self-sameness is possible.

Julia Kristeva makes similar arguments about the nature of signification, but, rather, than using the language of metonymy, she offers an ontological figuration of textuality that she calls *intertextuality*. Articulating Saussurian and Bakhtinian theories of signification, Kristeva argues that the lack of unicity between signifiers and signifieds means that all signification is necessarily intertextual: any signifier can only be connected to other signifiers in an unending chain of inextricable interdependence. Kristeva proffers, "Any text is constructed as a mosaic of quotations; any text is the absorption and transformation of another."[44] Law, therefore, describes semiotics as a study of networks, noting, "Nothing that enters into relations has fixed significance or attributes in and of itself" but, rather, is "defined in relation to other ele-

---

42. Denroche, *Metonymy and Language*, 5, 1.
43. Lundberg, *Lacan in Public*, 79, 78.
44. Irwin, "Against Intertextuality," 228.

ments in the system, to other nodes in the network."⁴⁵ Because signifiers only become meaningful in reference to (or association with) other signifiers, the relationship between signified and signifier must be feigned or imagined—meaning that Kristeva's theory of intertextuality demonstrates the operations of metonymy.

Subjects make affective investments in the feigned connectivity between symbols and their referents because investing in this understanding of signification also authorizes particular figurations of what it means to be a subject.⁴⁶ Fantasies that imagine subjects as whole, unified, and autonomous abound in US media culture, manifesting, for example, in hegemonic rhetorics of individualism (despite having long been challenged by scholars in such fields as philosophy, rhetoric, cultural studies, gender studies, queer theory, and critical race studies). Cultural commitment to this fantasy of subjectivity and the logic of unicity on which it depends helps to account for metonymy's "central role in a whole range of social and recreational activities, such that [metonymy] becomes what the activity is about."⁴⁷

Over time, cultural associations become naturalized, turning "history into nature," giving metonymy political and ideological implications.⁴⁸ Ernesto Laclau and Chantal Mouffe maintain, "Synonymy, metonymy, and metaphor are not forms of thought that add a second sense to a primary, constitutive literality of social relations; instead they are part of the primary terrain itself in which the social is constituted."⁴⁹ Laclau's theory of hegemony, which he characterizes as "always metonymic," hinges on the "ineradicable tension between metonymy (or synecdoche) and metaphor," aligning metonymy with contingency and contiguity, metaphor with necessity and analogy.⁵⁰

The hegemony of any particular group—of ideas or people—depends on contingent relations of contiguity. To demonstrate, the hegemony of whiteness in the US is contingent on contextually specific assumptions, practices, relations, and institutions, but to maintain hegemony, whiteness asserts its naturalness and universality, or "unremarkability." Fantasies of unified and stable subjecthood have historically been associated, Armond Towns argues, with "one 'genre' of humanness: White, male, heterosexual, middle-classed, and able-bodied."⁵¹ Cultural associations between whiteness and innocence,

---

45. Law, "Network, Relations, Cyborgs."
46. Lundberg, *Lacan in Public*, 116.
47. Denroche, *Metonymy and Language*, 180.
48. Barthes, *Mythologies*, 128.
49. Laclau and Mouffe, *Hegemony*, 110.
50. Laclau, *Rhetorical Foundations*, 88, 92.
51. Towns, "'What Do We Wanna Be?'" 79.

for example, are metonymic, but over time these links may become fixed or naturalized, illustrating "the movement from metonymy to metaphor, from contingent articulation to essential belonging."[52] Cultural associations with whiteness also exist in relation to, among other things, ideas about Blackness. Consider the use of the words *urban* or *street* as metonyms for Blackness, as in James Bond novelist Anthony Horowitz's claim that Black actor Idris Elba was "too 'street'" to play the British spy on film. Horowitz's remark illustrates the way that such a metonym articulates ideas about Black masculinity, violence, and criminality. It is also such logic that leads Flan and Ouisa to fear that Paul might have left them with their "throats slashed."

Simultaneously creating and obfuscating cultural assumptions about race, metonyms such as *street* illustrate the coextensive work of articulation and displacement, which, argues Begoña Aretxaga, makes metonymy both the "base of figuration" and a central aspect of "political culture." Creating connections through deflection, metonyms "articulate a knowledge that remains hidden," making ideological sutures all the more effective because of their apparent seamlessness.[53] Displacement creates conditions of possibility for making a racialized remark while claiming not to speak about race, as in Horowitz's claim that his assessment of Elba was not a "color issue." Inattention to the politics of metonymy allows associations to become metaphorized and imagined as necessary.

Mapping the Stars defines metonymic politics of association as the ground for figuring social relations, positing all identifications (of/with self and others) as necessarily contingent and contextual. Such a perspective situates calls for equity not via metaphor, which would argue for justice because of sameness or essential likeness, but via the networked logics of metonymy, which makes an ethical demand for equity for all humans based on their contiguity, or coexistence. As John Lucaites and Celeste Condit argue, a call for equality on the grounds of sameness risks reproducing oppressive norms grounded on impossible fantasies of sameness (and self-sameness).[54] This book, therefore, understands subjectivity as dependent on metonymy, in which figurations of the self are always forged via association with signifiers and other subjects (and texts, places, objects, events, etc.).

---

52. Laclau, *Rhetorical Foundations*, 63.
53. Aretxaga, "Madness and the Politically Real," 54.
54. Lucaites and Condit, "Reconstructing <Equality>," 20.

GETTING HITCHED

Celebrity features in Barthes's and Denroche's accounts of metonymy because of its networked form. It is such form that renders celebrity culture valuable for thinking about the ideological implications of metonymic processes. Beyond the fact that images of celebrities—like all images—may be decoded through metonymy, celebrity culture can be understood as structured through multiple associational relations, including ones between stars and audiences, ones across stars' intertextual bodies of work, and ones between stars and ideologies.

First, as demonstrated by John Fiske and Henry Jenkins, celebrity is predicated on fantasies of relatedness between stars and their viewing publics.[55] The concept of identification, which Kenneth Burke defines as central to all communication, applies to fans' imagined relationships with celebrities.[56] Celebrity culture constructs stars as both otherworldly and "just like us," as objects of admiration or aspiration and figures of identification. As Inglis argues, the "powerful contradiction at the heart of" celebrity is its capacity to conjoin "knowability with distance."[57] For instance, Sean Redmond argues that fans of so-called toxic women celebrities, such as Lindsay Lohan or Amy Winehouse, are often guided by a sense of "shared difference."[58] Consider, as other examples, Pamela Keogh's self-help books *What Would Audrey Do?* and *Are You a Jackie or a Marilyn?*, which use celebrity personae as shorthands for women's self-fashioning, or the dozens of articles, blog posts, and videos that instruct people how to "live like Kim Kardashian," asking "WWKD?"

While audiences might imagine themselves as essentially the same as celebrities with whom they identify, which is a fantasy suggestive of metaphor, these relations must be forged and feigned, which is a metonymic operation. The affective registers of such identifications, argues Richard Dyer, have ideological functions. When audiences feel that they are "identifying with a unique person," they are less likely to notice that they are "identifying with a normative figure," and when audiences make affective investments in celebrities, identifications may engender acceptance of ideologies with which the celebrities are associated. For instance, Dyer argues, identification with a celebrity

---

55. Fiske, "Cultural Economy of Fandom"; Jenkins, *Textual Poachers*.
56. Burke, *Rhetoric of Motives*.
57. Inglis, *Short History*, 11.
58. Redmond, "Sensing Celebrity," 394, 395. See also Basil, "Identification as a Mediator"; and Kosenko et al., "Celebrity Influence and Identification."

paradoxically reinforces and is reinforced by fantasies about coherent subjectivity and cultural narratives about individualism.[59]

Second, as sites of articulation, stars are necessarily intertextual and signify through metonymy. Beyond Kristeva's ontological account, the concept of intertextuality has been used to describe a variety of practices related to the composition of texts, interpretations of them, and their relationships to other texts, including both intended and accidental linkages between them.[60] In his study of television culture, for example, Fiske frames images as existing "in an infinite chain of intertextuality," where any given image is understood through the lens of another and another and so on.[61] Mary Orr notes that although much of the work on intertextuality has origins in French semiotic and poststructuralist theories, including the works of Barthes, Gérard Genette, and Michael Riffaterre, the term has also been complicated by "electronic media and text-messaging developments" in the late twentieth and twenty-first centuries with the advent of such concepts as "hypertextuality" and "transmediation" that increase the potential connectedness between texts.[62]

Semiotics and cultural studies show us that star images are intertextual both in ontological terms and in relation to the media practices with which they are constructed, circulated, and consumed. Linking various texts, mediums, and audiences, stars develop the appearance of what Lawrence Grossberg describes as "identities on top of differences, of unities out of fragments."[63] As many cultural and media studies scholars have demonstrated, a star's image is the cumulative effect of assumptions and associations that accrete around it, and metonymy acts as a primary rhetorical mechanism for establishing such intertextual relationships. While some texts have direct relationships to others—via overt allusions or as parodies, spin-offs, or sequels—audiences indirectly experience a great deal of intertextuality (intended or not) via metonymy because of associations between mediated texts. These associations stem from such factors as shared stylistic or thematic sensibilities, related modes or contexts of production, or temporal propinquity. Associations may also be triggered by the roles of particular people with whom the works are linked, including authors, directors, photographers, illustrators, and actors—particularly when those individuals are well known.

---

59. Dyer, *Stars*, 96–97.
60. See Hitchon and Jura, "Allegorically Speaking"; Meinhof and Smith, *Intertextuality and the Media*; Ott and Walter, "Intertextuality"; Bertetti, "Toward a Typology"; Alzamora, "Semiotic Approach"; Annesley, "Being Spike Jonze"; and Tollefson, "You're Not You."
61. Fiske, *Television Culture*, 94.
62. Orr, *Intertextuality*, 3. See also Riffaterre, "Intertextuality vs. Hypertextuality."
63. Grossberg, *We Gotta*, 54.

The presence of any given star, or another, affects a text's location(s) within metonymic topographies and its consequent ability to (or inability not to) animate recognition of other cultural references, figures, or texts. For example, the many descriptions of Smith that use the word *fresh* rely on metonymy to communicate their joke, referencing his role on the television sitcom *Fresh Prince of Bel-Air*.[64] Likewise, the presence of any given star or another may also affect how audiences interpret and engage with particular texts; for example, metonymic logic guides many critics' extratextual assumption that Smith's film *After Earth* (M. Night Shyamalan, 2013) is an allegory about Scientology, the religion with which Smith is often associated.

Third, star images also help to articulate cultural discourses.[65] As Graeme Turner argues, as much as celebrities are imagined as individuals, they gain traction by "actively reconciling competing principles."[66] Similarly, Dyer writes, "Star images function crucially in relation to contradictions within and between ideologies, which they seek variously to 'manage' or resolve." For instance, Dyer notes that celebrity culture often links bootstrap rhetoric, which characterizes celebrities as ordinary, hardworking individuals, with aspirational narratives about stars as extraordinary people whose good fortune catapults them to fame.[67] This rhetorical linkage allows audiences to identify with celebrities and aspire to their success while also offering a conciliatory explanation for why fans have not achieved similar eminence.

At the same time that stars often cover over ruptures within and between various ideologies, celebrity culture may also expose such tensions. Dyer notes, "Far from managing contradictions," star images may also "expose them or embody an alternative or oppositional ideological position."[68] Such seemingly divergent functions are often evident within a single star's image, which may be capable of resolving and revealing ideological contradictions—even simultaneously. As Tim Edwards argues, a "single celebrity may often exist across" multiple mediated platforms at once in "ways that contradict each

---

64. The television series *Fresh Prince of Bel-Air* makes two references to *Six Degrees of Separation*. In the episode "Six Degrees of Graduation," Will is one class away from getting his high school degree and engages in complex schemes to earn a passing grade. In the episode "I Know Why the Caged Bird Screams," which alludes to Maya Angelou's autobiography, Will explains that he claimed to be Sidney Poitier's son in order to evade arrest. This title also references, perhaps unwittingly, the fact that Diahann Carroll, Poitier's former fiancé who David Hampton claimed was his mother, starred in the 1979 made-for-television movie based on *I Know Why the Caged Bird Sings*.
65. See Rojek, "Sports Celebrity"; and Marshall and Rahman, "Celebrity."
66. Turner, *Understanding Celebrity*, 25.
67. Dyer, *Stars*, 34, 42.
68. Dyer, *Stars*, 34.

other" and manifest ideological ruptures.[69] The polysemic term *hitch* offers an apt metaphor for illustrating this tension. A hitch joins one thing to something else, forming a connection or an attachment—as in the hitching of a trailer, lorry, or wagon. Yet a hitch is also an obstacle, interruption, or delay—as in colloquial references to a "hitch in one's plans."

Members of the Frankfurt School understood the entertainment industry and its attendant star system as inclined toward the former process, deploying stars to hitch together conflicting ideologies and reinforce the interests of the powerful. Theodor Adorno contends that the culture industry "makes use of" the "supposedly great personalities" and "heart-throbs" of the "star system" to encourage conformity and normativity, such that paradoxically "individuality itself serves to reinforce ideology."[70] Leo Lowenthal critiques "mass idols" including "headlines of the movies, the ball parks, and the night clubs" as distractions that discourage critical attention to "large confusing issues" and structures of power.[71] Such skepticism echoes through Maureen Orth's depiction of the "celebrity-industrial-complex" as a land of illusions, which creates the "reality we think we see" through the "familiar faces" of celebrities that "provoke sympathy, trust, and identification."[72]

Star images articulate cultural discourses by enabling their audiences to engage ideology indirectly—or, "safely"—via fantasmic displacements. Celebrity culture works less by "reiterating dominant values [than] by concealing prevalent contradictions or problems."[73] Karen Sternheimer argues that in the wake of social traumas, such as the Great Depression, World War II, or 9/11, celebrity culture operates as a fantasmic "mechanism for keeping the American Dream alive," redirecting audiences' attention from cultural exigencies toward stars' narratives of recovery or moving on.[74] For example, shortly after 9/11, the *New York Times* reproduced images created by Rockwell, drawing on his persona to offer uplifting narratives about the nation's capacity to recover from trauma. In this regard, celebrities act as metonyms themselves, articulating and displacing the cultural discourses with which they are associated. Celebrities may exacerbate metonymy's transformation "into a metaphor" by personifying and, hence, reifying the cultural norms and ideals they are imagined to signify.[75] Hall refers to this process as a form of articulation, whereby

---

69. Edwards, "Medusa's Stare," 156.
70. Adorno and Rabinbach, "Culture Industry Reconsidered," 14.
71. Lowenthal, "Biographies," 517, 548.
72. Orth, *Importance of Being Famous*, 21.
73. Dyer, *Stars*, 27.
74. Sternheimer, *Celebrity Culture*, 73.
75. Laclau, *Rhetorical Foundations*, 75.

the relationship between a "sign" and a "referent" becomes so normalized that it appears to be "'naturally' given" and may achieve "'near-universality.'"[76]

Although the star system tends toward the concealment of ideological contradictions, it does not always succeed. It is a mistake, Adrian Wesolowski contends, to assume that the "cultural industry arisen around celebrity . . . is inseparably conjoined with the meanings ascribed to it, the judgements made about it, and the shape of discourse revolving around it."[77] Celebrities sometimes perform interruptive functions, and criticism can amplify these interruptions, calling attention to and disarticulating the metonymic accretions on which ideologies depend. If hegemony requires concealment of its contingency, the "dissolution of a hegemonic formation involves the reactivation of that contingency," transforming a "'sublime' metaphoric fixation to a humble metonymic association."[78] *Mapping the Stars* deploys metonymic criticism of celebrity texts to reveal the cultural associations that bind them and to manifest the metonymic nature of all signification and subjectivity. Such criticism attends to the "field of possibilities" from which, as Karen Barad puts it, "statements and subjects emerge" in a relationship that is both "dynamic and contingent."[79] The value of metonymy as a critical apparatus derives from its associational properties, which encourage us to look at the implied, and therefore invisible, logics that link one cultural node to another.

Ed Folsom traces threads throughout Walt Whitman's poems in relation to the cultural phenomena that shaped them, briefly framing this approach as a "kind of metonymic criticism."[80] Folsom contends that Whitman drew from moments of transformation, such as the creation of American English dictionaries and the emergence of photography, "not just as *subjects* for his poetry, but as generators of a new kind of language" encompassing "diction and pacing and rhythm and form." Folsom demonstrates that such associations develop throughout Whitman's body of work. Similarly, *Mapping the Stars* reads texts intertextually and in relation to cultural context, but the approach deployed in this book also differs from Folsom's reading strategy. While Folsom traces lines of connection between texts and contexts, his form of metonymic criticism does not forward a theory of subjectivity linked to such practices of signification. By contrast, *Mapping the Stars* contends that a central contribution of metonymy as a theoretical construct and critical appa-

---

76. Hall, "Encoding/Decoding," 167.
77. Wesolowski, "Beyond Celebrity History," 198.
78. Laclau, *Rhetorical Foundations*, 63.
79. Barad, "Posthumanist Performativity," 819.
80. Folsom, *Walt Whitman's Native Representations*, x.

ratus is the illustration of interdependence as conditions of both signification and subjectification.

The intertextual approach deployed in this project also has affinities with David Lubin's *Shooting Kennedy*, which identifies "artistic lineages" between photographs of the Kennedys and other image cultures. Proffering a small-world theory of images, Lubin traces "elastic chains of images from art, literature, and the media that constantly inform us, often in contradictory ways, of who we are, who we ought to be, and where we belong." As Lubin charts the "impact of images on images," he figures the connections between images as inherent in the texts themselves, offering little critical reflection on the politics involved in linking one image to another.[81] Instead, this book emphasizes the political implications of making such connections, acknowledging the agency and accountability of the critic who articulates these metonymies.

This project also takes seriously Megan Volpert's argument that tracing connections across texts, including celebrity personae, has intellectual and affective importance. Volpert's *Sonics in Warholia* unfolds through letters to Warhol's ghost, "playing six degrees of Andy Warhol," with each letter moving through a chain of associations and tropes that accrete to Warhol's image. Volpert contends that celebrities become part of the fabric of their audiences' lives, noting, "Everybody becomes Andy." She continues, "When you witness another person's life, and chart it, and connect it to your own until some moments of it appear starkly as belonging to both of you . . . that's a spiritual practice, that is the process of living."[82] Volpert's reading of intertextual fandom as a "spiritual practice" resonates with this book's understanding of celebrity culture as illustrative of and participant in the intersubjectivity that defines human life.

Articulating rhetorical, semiotic, and psychoanalytic theories of metonymy, *Mapping the Stars* understands subjectivity as a networked form characterized by instability, interdependence, and vulnerability. As Helen Foster argues, subjects are constituted by "discourse, others, and the world" with which they are "imbricated."[83] Metonymic criticism of celebrity culture offers opportunities to consider this conception of subjectivity because of the conspicuousness of fame's networked form. The concept of networked subjectivity mirrors an understanding of celebrity personae as constituted in and by networks of associations, both literal and figural. Tom Mole argues, "Although it appears to be centred on an individual, celebrity culture is in fact radically rhizomatic. It operates as an intertextual network in which texts from sev-

---

81. Lubin, *Shooting Kennedy*, xii.
82. Jensen, "Megan Volpert."
83. Foster, *Networked Process*.

eral media (film, TV, photography, print) collectively create a public profile that is not, finally, under anyone's control."[84] Likewise, Sharrona Pearl and Dana Polan position each celebrity as "part of broader social networks, a node that links disparate communities, including fans who become celebrities themselves."[85] As I argue in chapter 1, these networks of associations include the texts, mediums, fictional roles, and people that celebrities link and the cultural associations they help to construct (or critique) and discourses they help to circulate (or interrupt). Understanding celebrity in this way creates space for considering the extent to which all people exist in and through various rhizomatic webs that are both material and symbolic. Understanding of celebrities as metonyms that create and circulate meaning also makes visible the fact that all subjectivity depends on signification that is always already metonymic—which is to say forged, or feigned, through contingent associations.

As an analytic perspective, metonymy can signal (and, perhaps, interrupt) cultural associations that link various texts together and manifest ontological dependence within both signification and subjectification. Metonymic criticism has destabilizing implications, undoing various associations, or discursive relations, that have become reified over time. This critical practice attends to the importance of the network as a political form, tracing connections between various "bodies, objects, and discourses" and mapping the cultural associations that traverse them.[86] The chapters that follow offer counterhegemonic readings of Rockwell's, Smith's, and Kardashian's image cultures aimed at disrupting normative discourses about race, gender, and sexuality; they also demonstrate the instability and contingency of signifying relations, which themselves signify the instability and contingency of subjective relations. Given that celebrity culture typically reinforces the rhetorics of individualism and authenticity that maintain hegemony in US public discourse, *Mapping the Stars* deploys metonymic criticism to amplify theories, like those forwarded by Stuart Hall and Judith Butler, of subjectivity as always contingent and tropological.[87]

Beyond its disruptive aims, this critical practice also has performative implications. Because cultural metonymies are constitutive of social realities and relations and, as such, have "real" and material consequences, metonymic criticism can forge new articulations and associations. By not only destabilizing cultural associations but also generating new ones, this approach could be deployed in ways that contradict the politics this project espouses, allow-

---

84. Mole, "Hypertrophic Celebrity."
85. Pearl and Polan, "Bodies of Digital Celebrity," 186.
86. Levine, *Forms*, 113. See also Latour, *Reassembling the Social*.
87. Hall, "On Postmodernism and Articulation."

ing, for example, a textual assemblage that reinforces, rather than challenges, discriminatory logics. And yet, while the content of such of an assemblage might reinforce oppressive cultural associations and norms, its form belies the totalizing and naturalizing logics on which discrimination hinges. The formal properties of metonymy evince the contingency of all signification, insisting that meaning is relational and contextual, which is to say political and ideological. This position illustrates Gabriel Renggli's contention that metonymy has "emancipatory potential that opposes itself to the classic humanist topos of stability."[88] The value in metonymic criticism as a form of semiotic and rhetorical analysis, therefore, derives from its attention to the relationship between intertextuality and intersubjectivity and, even more specifically, to the networked form of subjectivity itself.

To attend to questions of form and to the intertextual networks that constitute and contextualize texts is itself a way of attending to their political implications. As Erin Rand argues, "Rhetorical forms . . . operate much like subject positions: they are sites within institutional matrices of power through which discourse becomes intelligible."[89] Similarly, Caroline Levine argues, "forms are the stuff of politics," and, as such, analysis of textual forms "turns out to be as valuable to understanding sociopolitical institutions as it is to reading literature." Levine proffers different types of forms that merit attention: wholes, rhythms, hierarchies, and—most significantly for this project—networks. Although she notes that networks are neither "consistently emancipatory . . . nor always threatening," Levine understands them as necessarily political; accordingly, the study of networks is always the study of power.[90] For example, Black Feminist media scholarship, including work by Safiya Umoja Noble and Sarah J. Jackson, Moya Bailey, and Brooke Foucault Welles, has shown that algorithms and search engines that frame themselves as neutral or objective technologies always take shape in relation to the politics of identity.[91]

Patrick Jagoda echoes this claim, contending, "Artworks that experiment with network aesthetics are political, fundamentally, not because of their representational tactics or strategic values" but because of their recognition of the structures and social relations that position "certain ways of being or particular lives" with different access to power and privilege.[92] Attention to networked, metonymic form has significant implications for ontological understandings of subjectivity and the ideologies that spring from them. Just as prevailing

---

88. Renggli, "Building Metonymic Meaning," 125.
89. Rand, "An Inflammatory Fag," 300.
90. Levine, *Forms*, 7, 115.
91. Noble, *Algorithms of Oppression*; Jackson et al., *#Hashtag Activism*.
92. Jagoda, *Network Aesthetics*, 18.

fantasies of the subject as coherent, autonomous, and masterful depend on the feigning of unicity between signifiers and signifieds, recognition of the failure of symbolic unicity and the metonymic form of all signification creates possibilities for interrupting hegemonic figurations of the subject as unified and, instead, manifesting subjectivity as radically contingent and always in flux.

Consider the role that Dyer identifies celebrity as playing in the maintenance of rhetorics of individualism in US culture. Dyer contends that both extratextual narratives about celebrities and the works they create often affirm rhetorics of the American Dream, offering stories of individuals whose drive, desire, and determination lead them toward success despite whatever obstacles they may have encountered along the way. For instance, Rockwell, Smith, and Kardashian articulate different versions of the American Dream. Invocations of Rockwell's name often signal a nostalgic figuration of the American Dream in relation to simplicity, small towns, and family-values rhetoric that might be construed as a rejection of fame and its trappings. Stories about Smith often emphasize his pursuit of fame as an ordinary teenager whose hard work led to success, a narrative of upward mobility that echoes through a number of his fictional roles, including *The Fresh Prince of Bel-Air* and *The Pursuit of Happyness* (Gabriele Muccino, 2006). Constructions of Kardashian typically stand in sharp contrast to both of these models, figuring her as "famous for being famous" and illustrative of a conspicuously consumptive version of the American Dream.

Despite this assertion of coherence within a star's persona and within much of the diegetic content of their work, however, consideration of the formal figuration of celebrity reveals not stability and fixity but dispersal and diffusion. Star images become meaningful in the interstices between and articulations of various texts—dependent on the very kind of contiguity and contingency that characterizes all signification in the first place. There is no *Rockwell* qua *Rockwell*, *Smith* qua *Smith*, or *Kardashian* qua *Kardashian*. These celebrity personae, like any others, become meaningful as part of intertextual and always shifting networks of texts, mediums, and other cultural objects. Such a figuration of celebrity also illustrates the performative dimensions of subjectivity, inviting attention to, as Butler might suggest, the importance of mimesis and citationality to the rendering of subjecthood as the effect of iterative enactments that accrete over time.[93]

Acknowledging the networked (and therefore unfixed) form of celebrity makes visible a figuration of subjects less as bounded individuals than as points of articulation that cannot exist outside of their relationality to and

---

93. Butler, *Gender Trouble* and *Bodies That Matter*.

coextensivity with other subjects. The intertextuality that shapes stardom has affordances for making visible the intersubjectivity that defines selfhood given that every subject exists always in relation to others, in ways both symbolic and material. Such a claim resonates with Kristeva's contention that the "notion of intertextuality replaces that of intersubjectivity," wherein the connection between texts becomes a substitution, or stand-in, for the connection between subjects.[94] While intersubjectivity is not unique to star images—just as intertextuality is not—celebrities offer a useful illustration of this concept because of their pronounced visibility, audiences' intense affective attachments to them, and the rhetorical role stars play in articulating cultural discourses about what it means to be a person.

ALONE TOGETHER

Butler situates intersubjective figurations of selfhood as central to efforts against oppression, arguing that the "very bodies for which we struggle are not quite ever only our own." It is wrong to see, Butler argues, "individual bodies as completely distinct from one another," because they are defined by interdependence and "networks of support."[95] Yet the hegemony of discourses of individualism in US culture disavows the fact that no human is ever unbound from others. Such disavowal often entails the projection of fantasies of dependency on the oppressed in an effort to affirm the imagined wholeness and mastery of the privileged, all while denying that humans "are never fully individuated."[96] As Kathy Dow Magnus explains, subjects should be understood as only and always existing in relation to one another and as, therefore, neither coherent nor autonomous. Magnus writes, "Because I am always already entangled in a web of relations, I can never reach the ground of my origin: I can never fully explain who I am or how I came to act as I do. I cannot account for myself in any ultimate way."[97] Magnus invites an understanding of subjectivity as a networked form: a system of connections and associations that never achieve stasis or self-sameness.

This theorization of subjectivity does not reproduce the model of "networked individualism" forwarded by Barry Wellman, which claims that advances in mediated communication have wrested people from "little boxes" of homogeneity and "traditional group solidarities" and plugged them into

---

94. Kristeva, *Desire in Language*, 66.
95. Butler, *Precarious Life*, 26, and "Rethinking," 16.
96. Butler, *Force of Nonviolence*.
97. Magnus, "Unaccountable Subject," 92.

larger, more diffuse social networks. Despite its emphasis on linkages, this framework imagines individuals as distinct nodes connected to others socially and/or technologically, and Wellman's figuration posits humans as discrete entities with "holistic individual identities" that may exist apart from their connections to others.[98] By contrast, the theorization of subjectivity forwarded here contends that no individual exists apart from or outside of connections to others. The increased presence of technological networks may have amplified and made more visible social networks, but there is no subject—no self—outside of associations with others. Subjects do not merely exist within networks; they exist *as* networks.

To suggest that the subject can never fully account for itself is not to minimize or discount the agency of subjects but to highlight the value of subjects' self-reflexivity about such incapacity and their understanding that the "lack of self-coherence" and abundance of "internal contradiction[s]" necessarily connect them to others. Magnus argues, "The awareness that the subject can never justify itself completely also makes it necessary to conceive of responsibility in social terms."[99] Donna Haraway figures this kind of intersubjective relationality as a "becoming with," writing, "To be one is to *become with* many," human and nonhuman alike.[100] As Rosi Braidotti argues, interconnection is not limited to the "symbiotic relationship between mother and child."[101] Nor, Cecilia Åsberg clarifies, is it simply that humans are "separate entities to start with" who then become connected throughout their lives." Rather, such "*relational and formative processes*" are always ongoing and unfinished.[102] Renggli, therefore, defines "becoming" as a "metonymic function" because subjects do not exist distinctly or separately from other subjects or objects but with reference and in relation to them. Renggli writes, "Like metonymy, becoming does not approach something else; it finds alterity in the subject."[103]

While advising readers to relinquish the "fantasy of climbing into heads, one's own or others', to get the full story from the inside," Haraway makes an ethical call for us to be "responsible" for our "mortal entanglements." Worldmaking, Haraway argues, requires a "praxis of care and response," or "response-ability," for one another.[104] Butler similarly frames "relationality" as not only a "descriptive or historical fact of our formation but also as an ongo-

---

98. Wellman, "Little Boxes," 13, 18.
99. Magnus, "Unaccountable Subject," 93.
100. Haraway, *When Species Meet*, 4.
101. Braidotti, *Metamorphoses*, 24.
102. Åsberg, "Feminist Posthumanities," 186.
103. Renggli, "Building Metonymic Meaning," 128, 131.
104. Haraway, *When Species Meet*, 226–27, and "Awash in Urine," 302.

ing normative dimension of our social and political lives." We should "take stock of our interdependence," Butler argues, because "we are not separate identities in the struggle for recognition but are already involved in a reciprocal exchange that dislocates us from our positions, our subject-positions, and allows us to see that community itself requires the recognition that we are all, in different ways, striving for recognition."[105] Barad also frames "recognition," along with "acknowledgment" and "loving attention," as critical components of a just world, which is "not a state that can be achieved once and for all" but requires an "ongoing practice of being open and alive to each meeting, each intra-action" with others and with things.[106]

It is this desire for recognition that renders celebrity useful for considering the politics of subjectification and identification. Insofar as fame hinges on recognizability, stardom presents a (hyperbolic) synecdoche for the politics of recognition. This is not to say that subjects should imagine themselves as/like stars or replicate the norms of celebrity—although, to be clear, a number of scholars have demonstrated the extent to which many subjects already do.[107] This is also not to advocate for the rhetorics of authenticity that permeate celebrity culture or to suggest that there are better or worse ways in which a subject might perform selfhood for an audience. Rather, attention to celebrity reminds us that subjects are always co-constituted by and subjected to the interpretation of others. Even for those subjects who do not desire to be, as Daniel Boorstin put it, "known for [their] well-knownness," the concept of fame signals the importance of being *known well*.[108]

As Magnus's and Haraway's work suggests, being known well does not entail being known fully or completely by either the self or an other, for such total accountability is impossible. Rather, knowing well and being known well depend on the premise that all subjects warrant recognition as lives that matter; but the impossibility of knowing or being known fully does not justify the refusal of recognition. It is precisely the impossibility of accounting fully for ourselves or others that calls for ethical commitment to the (always inadequate) approximation of such recognition. Knowledge of and connection to the other should be understood, therefore, as always metonymic. There is no essential self to be known and no essential likeness, or metaphor, to be experienced—only approximations of the self or other, which remain situated within networks of symbolic and material associations. Ethical recognition requires the expectation that the subject will receive "recognition from the

---

105. Butler, *Precarious Life*, 27, 44.
106. Barad, *Meeting the Universe Halfway*, x.
107. See Marshall, "Persona Studies."
108. Boorstin, *The Image*, 57.

other" and the assurance that the subject will seek to recognize the other and their relationality.[109]

Challenging the "dominant ontological understanding of the embodied subject," which is steeped in logics of mastery and sovereignty and attendant ideologies of individualism, Butler argues that subjects and bodies are not "discrete, singular, and self-sufficient" but, rather, constituted by relationships with social and material forces, which they affect and are affected by. Vulnerability entails being "exposed and agentic at the same time." The embodied subject is not simply acted on by social and material forces but acts within, through, and on this dynamic network. In turn, Butler contends, "dependency and vulnerability" should be "part of the performative account of agency" wherein the subject's capacity to act cannot be extricated from the subject's capacity to affect and to be affected by others. And in addition to "social and material forces," subjects also experience "linguistic vulnerability," having been subjected to (and by) names, categories, and norms that precede and exceed them.[110] When we presume the fixity and unicity of these signifiers, the conditions for precaritization increase, rendering some lives legible and sensible but others not. By contrast, when we acknowledge the instability and contingency of signification, we make room for figurations of subjectivity that account for intersubjective relations and interdependencies and that allow for more expansive views of what/who subjects can be. If we accept vulnerability as central to signification—replacing investments in metaphoric stability, which undergird hegemonic discourses of individualism and authenticity, with recognition of metonymic conditionality—we disrupt fantasies of masterful, individualized selfhood.

Recognition of our connectedness to others issues an ethical call not only to offer support but also to hold one another accountable, and such accountability is particularly important for those who maintain positions of privilege. Attention to conditions of interdependence and intersubjectivity acknowledges vulnerability as a constitutive and shared element of human experience, as we are "not only constituted by our relations but also dispossessed by them." Butler thus encourages her readers to see the political importance of an "apprehension of common human vulnerability," arguing that reckoning with our own vulnerability may yield "consideration of the vulnerability of others," which might, in turn, encourage critical opposition to "the conditions under which certain human lives are more vulnerable than others."[111] But attention to vulnerability as a shared human experience must acknowledge distinctions

---

109. Magnus, "Unaccountable Subject," 96.
110. Butler, "Rethinking," 21, 24, 19, 16.
111. Butler, *Precarious Life*, 24, 30.

between vulnerability and precarity because, Malini Johar Schueller argues, "some vulnerabilities are more vulnerable than others."[112]

This unequal sharing of vulnerability is what Butler calls *precarity*, which she defines as illustrating "that politically induced condition in which certain populations suffer from failing social and economic networks of support and become differentially exposed to injury, violence, and death."[113] In addition to what might be considered spectacular and eventual forms of violence, precarity, argues Lauren Berlant, entails "slow death," or "the physical wearing out of a population in a way that points to its deterioration as a defining condition of its experience and historical existence."[114] Precarity is felt at both monumental and mundane registers, in life-changing moments and everyday forms of living.

While all humans experience vulnerability, precarity entails uneven distribution of vulnerability caused by structural forces and systemic inequalities. Precarity is, thus, the structural engineering of "maximized vulnerability and exposure." As an example, Butler proffers that precarity should be understood as "directly linked with gender norms," given that "those who do not live their genders in intelligible ways are at heightened risk for harassment and violence." Such increased risks are likewise experienced in relation to the intersecting politics of race, sexuality, class, disability, nationality, and so forth. Vulnerability is both an "existential condition" and one that is "socially induced," and those who are precaritized experience "disproportionate exposure to suffering."[115]

Critical attention to distinctions between vulnerability and precarity is paramount given how often claims of vulnerability are co-opted by those in positions of privilege. Feminist scholarship, for instance, has long documented how white masculinity claims states of victimization as strategies for disavowing critiques of sexism and racism.[116] Likewise, Brittney Cooper contends that the "mythic nature of white female vulnerability" enables the oppression of both Black women and Black men by foreclosing considerations of white women's complicity in racialized sexism and sexualized racism and making it difficult to "conceptualize Black female vulnerability."[117]

---

112. Schueller, "Decolonizing Global Theories," 249.
113. Butler, *Frames of War*, ii.
114. Berlant, "Slow Death," 754.
115. Butler, *Frames of War*, ii; "Performativity, Precarity, and Sexual Politics," ii; and "Rethinking Vulnerability," 25.
116. See Modleski, *Feminism without Women*; Robinson, *Marked Men*; King, *Washed in Blood*; and Johnson, "Art of Masculine Victimhood."
117. Cooper, *Eloquent Rage*, 175, 187.

There is a decided counterintuitiveness to my choice to frame the culture of celebrity as a resource for animating such attention to vulnerability and precarity. Fame, after all, typically entails extreme conditions of privilege that most people can only imagine. Yet the language of vulnerability suffuses celebrity culture, with such rhetoric often framing celebrity as traumatic for those that attain it. Consider, for instance, how often fame (and child stardom, in particular) is blamed for the mental health crises of well-known individuals, including Marilyn Monroe, Michael Jackson, and Britney Spears.[118] Or, consider those cases in which famous people experience violence or trauma because they are famous, as in the murder of Charles Lindbergh's child, the assassination of John Lennon, the death of Princess Diana, or the robbery of Kardashian. The purported risks of fame can be felt in the multiple meanings of the word *exposure*, which is both a condition on which fame depends (and around which the entire publicity industry pivots) and a synonym for proximity to risk, harm, or danger.

I draw a link between celebrity and vulnerability not to make a case for greater empathy toward celebrities (although I do not disagree with such an impulse) nor to facilitate further co-optation of the concept of vulnerability by those in positions of power and privilege. I am describing not the vulnerability of actual celebrities but, rather, the unfixity signified by the structure of stardom itself because celebrity culture offers an important map for navigating human existence. As Dyer argues, "Stars articulate what it is to be a human being in contemporary society," expressing the "particular notion we hold of the person."[119] And while celebrity has, since its inception, always been a key site for the enactment of fantasies of personhood, the rise of what Banet-Weiser calls "brand culture" makes celebrity culture even more relevant to considerations of the fraught processes of becoming (with) humans.[120] As Inglis argues, the stories we tell about celebrities are "the stories we tell ourselves about ourselves."[121] For example, the prevalence of the rhetoric of trauma in celebrity culture illustrates a melodramatic performance of and reckoning with the affects and anxieties associated with human vulnerability and impermanence. Attention to evidence of vulnerability within celebrity culture has unique affordances for manifesting this condition as definitive of human life more generally and for challenging structures of inequity and systems of injustice that make some lives more vulnerable than others.

---

118. See Williamson, "Female Celebrities"; and Negra and Holmes, *In the Limelight*.
119. Dyer, *Heavenly Bodies*, 7.
120. Banet-Weiser, *Authentic™*, 5.
121. Inglis, *Short History*, 247.

Celebrity culture, argues Dyer, shapes not only ideological figurations of identity, such as individualism, but also ontological figurations of personhood, including the notion that at the center of every person exists an "irreducible core of being."[122] Stars have been, Dyer contends, essential to the maintenance of cultural fantasies about the coherence, unicity, and autonomy of the subject, but celebrity's role in affirming such ontologies is neither inherent nor necessary. Metonymic criticism of celebrity can disrupt this process, engendering new ways of imagining what/how subjects are. While the content of celebrity narratives typically affirms logics of mastery and individualism, the form of stardom belies these claims, revealing their impossibility. The popularity of network games and small-world theories within the culture of celebrity seems precisely, if unwittingly, to acknowledge such interconnectedness and interdependence. *Mapping the Stars* contends that the affective intensities and investments circulating in and around fame reflect cultural reckonings with ontologies and ideologies of selfhood, becoming fecund sites for redrawing the contours of what it means to be a subject.

INTERPRETIVE CARE

My analyses in *Mapping the Stars* reveal political and discursive investments, but they also demonstrate the pleasures I experience as an audience member and fan of media culture. Taking inspiration from nonacademic modes of spectatorship, including the Kevin Bacon game, this book aims to articulate scholarly modes of criticism with practices of fandom or audience engagement. The analysis in this book constructs and traverses an assemblage of images and texts, drawing attention to individual artifacts, pathways between them, and the meanings that accrete through their appositive accumulation. Such attention to the paths that connect various texts allows us to consider what becomes visible *precisely because of* the routes we have chosen to take. I do not claim that audiences have, do, or necessarily should read these texts in the ways I do. Rather than offering "the" definitive reading of a set of texts, I hope to inspire other readings—or even spur counter-readings—that are attentive to the politics and pleasures of conjuncture.

This approach responds to the call from scholars, including Rita Felski and Eve Kosofsky Sedgwick, to generate new modes of textual analysis that take pleasure seriously and more closely resemble fan practices. This call reflects an impulse "to reject the premise of a radical asymmetry between academic

---

122. Dyer, *Heavenly Bodies*, 7.

and everyday thought." "This is not," argues Felski, a call "to lapse into the populist mind-set that sometimes afflicts cultural studies: the contention that 'ordinary people' are inherently savvier, sharper, more intuitive, more authentic, or more radical than the academics who write about them."[123] Rather, this call asks critics to recognize the relations of interdependence between nonacademic and academic ways of thinking in order to trouble this binary. Or, as Sedgwick puts it, resisting the urge to draw too fine an "ontological distinction between academic theory and everyday theory" suggests recognition of and interest in "the quality of other people's and one's own practices of knowing and experiencing."[124] This approach signals the recognition that the form of academic writing has implications for its content and its political entailments, requiring self-reflexive consideration of modes of scholarly thinking and writing.

Janet Staiger also attends to the importance of pleasure, encouraging scholars to embrace their perversions. Staiger's figuration of "perverse spectatorship" enacts a turning away or deviation from normative modes of scholarly writing and models a mode of criticism that narrows the distance between scholar and spectator. In "Hitchcock in Texas," Staiger describes her own spectatorial experiences as a person who is concurrently a critic and fan, noting the arguably idiosyncratic intertextual links she finds between two different texts: *Psycho* (Alfred Hitchcock, 1960) and *Texas Chainsaw Massacre* (Tobe Hooper, 1974). Tracing such intertextual links, Staiger questions why she "or any other reader" might make one interpretive move or another and underscores that, amid the considerable scholarship on intertextuality, "little work has been accomplished on the functions of intertextuality for the reader or why the reader might be primed or cued to take up a particular function."[125] Concluding that "intertextuality obviously serves affective functions," which are connected to its "political effects," Staiger encourages scholars to pursue such questions. *Mapping the Stars* aims to answer this call by framing intertextual metonymy as central to celebrity culture and the networks through which subjects are effected.

The pleasures of intertextuality derive from desires for connectivity between subjects. As Kristeva and Georges Bataille remind us, humans have ambivalent relationships with the discourses of sovereignty and autonomy that have come to define the parameters of Western subjectivity. While humans long for connections to and articulation with others, such interconnectedness may threaten the integrity of the self and, as such, entail fear. In

---

123. Felski, *Limits of Critique*, 139.
124. Sedgwick, *Touching Feeling*, 145.
125. Staiger, *Perverse Spectators*, 32, 185.

response, humans seek "safe" ways to experience such connection, which is itself a way to approximate dispossession; intertextual reading practices and metonymic networked games exemplify these impulses at work—or play, as it were.[126] Such play may, thus, commingle pleasure and pain, evoking fantasies of wholeness and mastery at the same time that it reveals such relations to be always approximate and never complete, signaling the impossibility of self-sameness and stability.

Staiger's playful, associative writing style resonates with Robert Ray's contention that film and media scholars should experiment with forms of writing and analysis to produce new ways of thinking about and with film. Encouraging film critics to be bold, if not irreverent, in their approaches, Ray contends that "knowledge depends on a willingness to investigate the implications of strategies that initially seem bizarre."[127] He therefore figures the "experimental researcher" as a "gambler" who "refuses to be bound by a heuristic vocabulary's original meaning" and a "collagist who does not coin his [sic] own terms but who grafts (and thereby remotivates) ones already available." Ray challenges what he considers the hegemony within film studies of David Bordwell's commitment to a "Baconian empirical model" that focuses on production norms and industry history as the primary sites for discovering knowledge about cinema. Staiger is explicit in her deviation from Bordwell's approach, describing herself as having "gone another way" by turning her attention from the schematics of industry history to the unpredictability of spectatorial experience.[128] The approach adopted by this book can still be considered "Baconian" to a degree—only, it aligns more with Kevin than with Francis.

The associative and appropriative approaches forwarded by Staiger and Ray resemble Barbara Klinger's description of fan engagement in puzzle films and Jenkins's figuration of fan investment in transmedia formations. In Klinger's analysis of such films as *The Usual Suspects* (Bryan Singer, 1995) or *Pulp Fiction* (Quentin Tarantino, 1994), which have elaborate and complex plots that require the "labor of decoding to put together the pieces of the [narrative] puzzle," she finds that spectators' "intricate decoding strategies" illustrate deep investment in paradigms of mastery, allowing the fans and avid viewers of puzzle films to seek "prestige" and imagine themselves as distinguished from ordinary viewers by their own "powers of discernment."[129] Similarly, Jenkins notes that fans of transmedia webs, such as those surrounding *The Matrix* trilogy, pursue epistemophilic impulses by articulating links between the various

---

126. Bataille, *Literature and Evil*.
127. Ray, *How Film Theory Got Lost*, 35, 34.
128. Staiger, *Perverse Spectators*, 30.
129. Klinger, *Beyond the Multiplex*, 157, 162.

platforms of this transmedia assemblage, including a web series, an online game, and the films themselves and, in so doing, demonstrating their authority within this intertextual network.[130]

Although this project does not—nay, cannot—claim total divestment from the logic of mastery, it seeks to trouble the concept of the masterful critic who exists at a distance from the text. This refusal of mastery is an effect of attention to network form itself. As Levine suggests, a particular affordance of networks and our study of them is the constant reminder of the impossibility of ever apprehending the "the totality of the networks that organize us." It is, Levine contends, "a formal fact of networks" that they are "sprawling, overlapping, and indefinitely expanding processes of interconnectedness."[131] For example, while the six degrees theory of interconnectivity alleges the "smallness" of the world, this concept also calls attention to the myriad unpredictable connective pathways that subjects might construct. The notion of six degrees of separation may suggest that there is an inevitable link between one person and another, but it allows for the possibility of multiple routes of interconnectivity and suggests that most of the connections between any two people may be unexpected, unforeseen, or even undiscovered.

This attempt to divest from regimes of mastery also reflects a critical disposition—or, repositioning of the critic in relation to the text—drawn from Sedgwick's insistence on counterbalancing suspicious engagements with texts with an impulse toward hopefulness. Sedgwick's discussion of paranoid reading strategies, or hermeneutics of suspicion, has inspired what Robyn Wiegman and Heather Love, among others, call a "reparative turn" in queer feminist criticism. This turn shifts from critical dispositions of skepticism to ones of hopefulness, trading a determination to reveal hidden, pernicious meanings in a text for a desire to read generously. This change replaces critiques "forged by correction, rejection, and anger" with readings "crafted by affection, gratitude, solidarity, and love." Wiegman writes, "In dialogue with Sedgwick, much of the queer feminist archive . . . aims to rethink, if not resist, its paranoid inheritances, which means challenging the methodological strategies and critical priorities that have accrued to interpretative practices founded on the symptom," displacing paranoid readings with reparative ones.[132]

Sedgwick builds her theory of reparation from Melanie Klein's psychoanalytic work, which names the "reparative process" a form of "love." While a paranoid position tears its object apart, seeking evidence of danger or threat, the impetus of reparation is rebuilding or assembling. Sedgwick describes rep-

---

130. Jenkins, *Convergence Culture*, 94.
131. Levine, *Forms*, 129.
132. Wiegman, "The Times," 7, 6.

aration as "additive and accretive," desiring "to assemble and confer plentitude on an object" in order to provide resources for the self. She frames reparative practices—like camp, for example—as survival tactics of "selves and communities" aimed at "extracting sustenance from the objects of a culture—even of a culture whose avowed desire has often been not to sustain them." Like Klein, Sedgwick identifies "wholeness" as a desire of the reparative process, wherein a supposedly broken cultural object can be repaired to "something like a whole."[133] Klein frames reparative practices as tactics with which people negotiate the traumatic discovery of their separation from others, as in the child who discovers that they are separate or independent from their parents, which Klein figures as a loss. The trauma engendered by this loss owes paradoxically to fantasies of whole and masterful subjectivity and attendant discourses of individualism that insist on the embodied subject's discreteness from others at the expense of attention to intersubjective relations and interdependencies. Without fantasies of autonomous and sovereign selfhood, subjects might avoid the kind of trauma that can lead to paranoia or require reparation. In contradistinction to Klein and Sedgwick, this project aligns a reparative disposition not with wholeness but with a different form: the network. Rather than being constituted by wholeness, subjects remain necessarily linked to others—never fully joined but never wholly separated. Subjectivity is defined neither by unicity nor by discreteness but by shifting, contingent, and unstable nodes of articulation and relationality.

Furthermore, paranoid and reparative reading practices are not mutually exclusive. As Wiegman and Love argue, the theoretical opposition of reparation over and against paranoia can be reductive, obscuring how these approaches overlap and depend on one another. Love contends that Sedgwick's call for reparative reading should not be interpreted as "*only* a call for reparative reading." Rather, interpretive dispositions often "vacillate between these two positions without ever coming to rest," and Love encourages scholars to acknowledge the "impossibility of choosing between them," answering the call for coextensive reparation and paranoia, affection and anger.[134] Metonymic criticism acknowledges the inextricability of reparation and paranoia through its attention to form: even while offering a suspicious reading of a text, attention to the metonymic register of all signification heralds the potential for new meanings and relations between signifiers and signifieds—constituted as they are by arbitrary and feigned connections—and for the consequent possibility of resignification. Moreover, metonymic criticism operates through "additive

---

133. Sedgwick, *Touching Feeling*, 128, 150–51.
134. Love, "Truth and Consequences," 238, 239.

and accretive" operations aimed at assembling connections rather than only breaking down extant associations.

Networks offer useful objects of study for this interdigitated mode of criticism, as they invite both paranoid and reparative responses. On the one hand, Tung-Hui Hu argues, when networks manifest as a "desire to connect every piece of information to another piece," they may operate as a "sign of paranoia" and a feverish sense of incompleteness.[135] On the other hand, José Esteban Muñoz posits, networks can also build reparative spaces for inclusion, becoming systems of "associative belonging."[136] Consider, for instance, how often conspiracy theories, the apex of paranoid networks, help generate communities of belonging. That networks are "resistant to knowing" means that they never settle in either paranoid or reparative (dis)positions, and neither should critical treatments of them.[137]

Sedgwick's call for critical practices that seek "ways around the topos of depth or hiddenness" and the attendant "drama of exposure" seems especially apt for a study of celebrity.[138] The publicity, tabloid, and gossip industries have primed audiences to seek the "truth" of who a star "really is" by uncovering their secrets. This search for the supposed truth of who a celebrity "is" reinforces the fantasies of the irreducible selfhood that it presupposes. Critical practices aimed at disrupting fantasies of mastery must find new ways of figuring the relationship between critic and subject. In place of the positionality of the critic as over or above the text, Sedgwick forwards the idea of existing "beside" it, conceiving the text as an agent working alongside and with the critic. This approach renders texts not as passive objects that must be interrogated or examined so that their hidden truths can be exposed but as sites that theorize the social, the political, and the cultural.

Drawing from Sedgwick, as well as the insights of actor-network theory and object-oriented ontology, Felski argues for the need to complicate our approaches beyond the disposition of suspicious criticism, urging scholars to think self-reflexively about their affective relations with and orientations toward texts. Rather than taking up a "stance of heroic mastery" over a text, with its presuppositions of "possession" or ownership of the object, Felski urges critics to think about how we might also experience "dispossession" in relation to our objects of study, "exposing ourselves to a text as well as imposing ourselves on a text."[139] Similarly, writing from the perspective of feminist

---

135. Hu, *Prehistory of the Cloud*, 11.
136. Muñoz, *Cruising Utopia*, 117.
137. Hu, *Prehistory of the Cloud*, 15.
138. Sedgwick, *Touching Feeling*, 8.
139. Felski, *Limits of Critique*, 34.

science, technology, and society studies, Maria Puig de la Bellacasa encourages scholars to see their work as a form of caring and to remain open to the possibility of being affected by and passionate about our "relationship with the 'objects' of research" with which we engage and by which we are "affected."[140] Such positions call for scholars to acknowledge and accept their connection with and consequent vulnerability to other subjects, objects, and texts, highlighting the interdependence that structures the relationship between texts and their readers and identifying critique not as a mode of detachment but as a form of attachment. This perspective also understands texts, like critics (and subjects), as concurrently agentic and vulnerable.

Citing the networked form that shapes all texts, Felski notes that "works of art, by default, are linked to other texts, objects, people, and institutions, in relations of dependency, involvement, and interaction." These networks of interdigitation also include those of us who read (with) texts, and Felski encourages us to think of a text as a "coactor," or as "something that makes a difference, that helps make things happen." She reminds us that texts have the capacity to affect us (and to be affected by us). The interpretation of a text is thus less an "unmaking" of the thing itself than a "making," or a "coproduction between actors." We should, contends Felski, acknowledge the "distinctive agency of art works," which includes texts' capacity to act us on through content and form in relation to a range of other "texts, objects, people, and institutions."[141]

Christopher Carter similarly understands texts as nonhuman actors. Engaging with a text, he argues, "does not mean merely interpreting" it but understanding that it constitutes a "mode of theorizing in its own right" through its own "rhetorical vitality." Texts are "works of theory in themselves, performing their arguments in multiple, interlocking modes."[142] This is not to say that readers and critics do not act on texts but, instead, to understand this relationship as a dynamic interchange. Neither critics nor creators nor consumers of texts can ever have mastery over them, because texts have a "liveliness" to them; rather than disavowing such vibrancy, critics should strive to work with, or beside, texts and to recognize them as actors within multiple networks of affects and meanings. Like subjects, texts can never be fully accounted for or known in totality, but this fact does not preclude the critic's capacity to recognize the text and should not dampen the impulse to know it well.

---

140. De la Bellacasa, "Matters of Care," 98–99.
141. Felski, *Limits of Critique*, 11, 12–13.
142. Carter, *Metafilm*, 6, 12–13.

Perhaps paradoxically, Felski attributes the hegemony of suspicious reading practices to the "spread of poststructuralist theories" that assert the "unreliability of signs." She sees such theories of the instability of signification as having helped secure the "permanence of suspicion" and the intransigence of the "impulse to decipher and decode."[143] Yet these perspectives exist at odds with one another: if signification always refuses stability and fixity, there can be no *one* way to read a text, no way to secure or guarantee its meaning. *Mapping the Stars* finds useful resources in/of celebrity texts not because there is one way they might be interpreted but because reading illustrates hopefulness that texts and the interrelations between them have something lively to offer us.

---

143. Felski, *Limits of Critique*, 33.

CHAPTER 2

American Queerer

Norman Rockwell and the Art of Queer Feminist Critique

> I showed the America I knew and observed to others who might not have noticed.
> —Norman Rockwell

> Norman Rockwell was in Stagecoach with Bing Crosby, who was in Say One for Me with Robert Wagner, who was in Wild Things with Kevin Bacon.

Deborah Solomon incited considerable controversy with her 2013 biography *American Mirror: The Life and Art of Norman Rockwell*. Making claims that contradict conventional associations between Rockwell's work and traditional or even conservative values, Solomon alleges that Rockwell struggled with depression and anxiety, suffered immense personal loss and familial strife, sought to fit in but often felt like an outsider, and experienced desires for (but never had sex with) men and boys. Evidence of such feelings, according to Solomon, can be traced throughout Rockwell's paintings. Although not the central premise of *American Mirror*, Solomon's characterization of Rockwell's sexuality has become a primary focus of debate about the book. Rockwell's family and a number of public figures have denounced Solomon's claims. For example, a positive review published by art scholar John Wilmerding in the *New York Times* prompted author and radio personality Garrison Keillor to respond in that same publication, chiding Solomon for seeming "awfully eager to find homoeroticism" in Rockwell's images.[1]

Solomon's book and its attendant controversy participate in long-standing contestations over public memory about Rockwell, his public persona, and his work.[2] Since well before the appearance of Solomon's biography, for exam-

---

1. Keillor, "Norman Rockwell."
2. Another debate addresses the racial politics of Rockwell's art. See Toh, "White Fireman."

ple, critics and art historians have debated whether Rockwell's work should be valued as art or categorized as "mere" illustration, and Rockwell himself addresses these debates in his work and public discussions of it.[3] This controversy regarding Rockwell's sexuality also illustrates a cultural norm with respect to well-known people: audience expectations of authenticity and intimacy, based on the presumptions that audiences can and should know who celebrities "really are" and that correspondences should exist between a famous person's private life, public persona, and body of work. This chapter does not make claims about Rockwell's sexuality or aim to uncover a hidden "truth" within the artist's life or paintings, nor does it engage in disputations about the aesthetic value of Rockwell's art. Rather, it reads Rockwell's celebrity persona and work to complicate much of the prevailing discourse about it, disrupting public memory about the cultural politics his paintings engender.

First, this chapter considers Rockwell's engagements with celebrity, via public discourse about Rockwell as a star and depictions of stardom in his work, arguing that his images take celebrity seriously as a heuristic with which people make sense of themselves and others. Rockwell's art deploys representations of celebrity's limitations and affordances in order to emphasize interconnection and interdependence as constitutive elements of human identity and experience. Rockwell's art considers the vulnerability inherent in the processes through which humans develop their subjectivities in relation to others, including others they know in their everyday lives but also those they know through mediated representations of them. Rockwell's depictions of stars, would-be stars, and their fans act as reminders of the risk that all human actors face—though some more than others—as they perform their lives before audiences who may judge or place expectations on those performances.

Next, this chapter unsettles public memory about Rockwell's art by arguing for its potential as a resource for queer feminist criticism. My analysis aims to complicate both the conventional assumption that Rockwell only painted idealized versions of normative subjects and the less prevalent assertion that his paintings are haunted by repressed or prohibited desires—between men or for boys.[4] As Rockwell himself said, his paintings often show affects and experiences that others "might not have noticed."[5] Instead, Rockwell's paint-

---

3. For example, Jerry Saltz argues, "You can't prove Rembrandt is better than Norman Rockwell—although if you actually do prefer Rockwell, I'd say you were shunning complexity, were secretly conservative, and hadn't really looked at either painter's work." See Saltz, "Has Money Ruined Art?" and "Middle Americana."
4. Wallach, "Norman Rockwell and the Representation of Social Conflict."
5. "Norman Rockwell Biography."

ings negotiate the constraints of normative gender and sexual identifications *and* the possibility of transgressing them. At the same time that his art celebrates the prospect of challenging traditional gender and sexual norms, it concedes the potential difficulty of such radical acts. Acknowledging that people often exist between various intersecting—and sometimes conflicting—social classifications, much of Rockwell's work resists binary oppositions between categories such as assimilation/transgression, hegemony/subversion, and normativity/antinormativity.

The claim that traditional or conservative images can be recuperated for feminist and/or queer intervention is not groundbreaking, but Rockwell's art offers a significant example of this kind of cultural work; for this reason, this analysis of Rockwell's art makes multiple political and theoretical contributions. First, Rockwell's continued presence in the US imaginary and his persona as a traditionalist create unique conditions of possibility for articulating feminist and queer politics to American audiences. Second, Rockwell's work, which has been identified as operating as visual epideictic rhetoric, may complicate figurations of this genre's functions. Akin to their capacity to trouble the divide between "serious art" and "popular entertainment," Rockwell's images generate space for considering the complexity of gender and sexual identifications without reducing identities to being *either* praiseworthy *or* blameworthy. Such a nonbinary perspective is useful for a consideration of celebrity, which often elicits strong and even polarizing reactions—as in the love/hate dynamics that often characterize rhetoric about famous people. Third, Rockwell's epideictic art contributes to contemporary debates within queer feminist criticism on the subjects of reparative readings and antinormativity.

Finally, Rockwell's work merits consideration because of its significant influence on other art forms. For example, Andrew Mendelson argues, Rockwell's images have helped constitute the themes, tropes, and stylistics of photojournalism in the United States;[6] and, as Virginia Mecklenburg suggests, Rockwell's paintings have influenced other popular American media including cinema, television, and advertising.[7] Given the centrality of the concept of celebrity, as it relates to both Rockwell's own stardom and to depictions of fame and fandom within many of his visual considerations of the politics of gender, analysis of Rockwell's work first necessitates consideration of his public image and celebrity.

---

6. Mendelson, "Slice-of-Life Moments," 166.
7. Mecklenburg, *Telling Stories.*

ROCKWELL ON TOUR

The value of Rockwell's work both as a meditation on celebrity and as a resource for queer feminist criticism should be understood in the context of his place(s) in US culture. Although his career originated with and was associated with magazines, Rockwell's art continues to travel through shifting contexts, amplifying its rhetorical and political potential. Rockwell began his career in his teens as the art director of *Boys' Life*, the official magazine of the Boy Scouts of America.[8] Rockwell went on to produce artwork for multiple magazines, including *Life* and *Country Gentleman*, but was most known for the 323 covers he produced for *The Saturday Evening Post*, many of which depicted white children and scenes of white, heterosexual, middle-class family life.

Founded in 1969 in Stockbridge, Massachusetts, the Norman Rockwell Museum (NRM) represents the largest public collection of Rockwell's work and personal artifacts and aims to counteract long-standing dismissals of his work as "mere" illustration or "just" entertainment. Alan Wallach characterizes NRM as the beginning of a "concerted, thirty-year campaign to elevate Rockwell's paintings to the level of high art."[9] These efforts to mark Rockwell as a significant artist worthy of admiration, which themselves illustrate a form of epideictic rhetoric, have coexisted alongside attempts to make Rockwell's work both literally and figuratively accessible. Literally, multiple exhibitions of his work, including three major and highly successful installations—*Norman Rockwell: Pictures for the American People* (1999–2001), *American Chronicles: The Art of Norman Rockwell* (2007–16), and *Norman Rockwell: Behind the Camera* (2009–14)—have brought Rockwell's work to museums throughout the United States and around the world. The museum's official website, NRM.org, has also digitized almost all of Rockwell's images (and scores of accompanying artifacts), making them searchable and viewable online.[10]

---

8. In 2021 Boy Scouts of America announced that they would sell nearly sixty pieces created by Rockwell to help raise money for a settlement in response to more than 82,000 claims of sexual abuse that the organization faced. See Vigdor, "Boy Scouts."

9. Wallach, "Norman Rockwell at the Guggenheim," 110. Demonstrating, perhaps, the success of such efforts, Rockwell's work has gained increased importance in the world of art collection. Just one month after the publication of Solomon's biography in 2013, three of Rockwell's paintings sold at Sotheby's "for a total of nearly $57.8 million, about twice their high estimate." See Vogel, "Three Rockwell Classics."

10. Collectively, the major recent touring exhibitions of Rockwell's work have traveled to twenty-six museums in the United States, one in Canada, and one in Italy, and many of the museums have reported record-breaking attendance for these exhibitions. Since 2003 NRM's "ProjectNORMAN" initiative has digitized Rockwell's known drawings artworks and related artifacts, reaching over 57,000 archived items by 2018.

Figuratively, NRM accompanies collections of Rockwell's work with educational tools that guide viewers' interpretations of the paintings, elaborating on their artistry and historical contexts. According to NRM.org, the exhibitions and digitization projects aim to preserve the artist's catalog, increase the availability of his work, and maintain his "cultural importance."[11] The archival ventures of NRM negotiate the arguably contradictory interpretations of Rockwell as either a serious artist or a popular source of entertainment through encomia that characterize his work as instructive for US citizens. This rhetoric encourages viewers to value and learn from Rockwell's depictions of the "social issues of his day," casting his paintings as cultural heuristics that empower their viewers to make sense of the world around them.[12]

Rockwell's entry into the upper echelons of the art world also signals what Wallach identifies as the "historical triumph of a corporatized museum culture," as exemplified, since the 1960s, by the phenomenon of the "blockbuster exhibition." As corporations began to take on patronage roles for major museums around the United States, museum culture became more commercialized, relying increasingly on marketing and public relations strategies to boost membership, draw in large numbers of visitors, and reach populations that had not been considered museum-goers.[13] NRM is, Wallach notes, no exception; the museum's current home in Massachusetts, for example, boasts a building named after major donors Steven Spielberg and Time Warner Communications, and the George Lucas Family Foundation has also become a patron of the museum.

In this increasingly commercialized context, NRM's constructions of Rockwell as an artist with a notable "catalogue raisonné" and significant "legacy" coexist with the museum's reliance on the rhetoric of stardom, referencing the "rave reviews" and "high attendance" garnered by new exhibitions and framing Rockwell himself as a celebrity. Rockwell's association with celebrity culture is not solely a product of the museum's marketing efforts, however. He is one of the most famous popular artists in US history and has been described as a "major star" of the first half of the twentieth century.[14] To demonstrate, by the 1920s and 1930s, newspaper and magazine articles already described him as a household name "known and loved by all Americans," and Rockwell participated in various practices associated with celebrity culture, serving, for example, as a celebrity judge in the 1922 Miss America pageant. In 1930 the *Los Angeles Times* covered the story of Rockwell's latest arrival in Hollywood,

---

11. "Museum Shares."
12. Plunkett, "Gallery Guide," 3.
13. Wallach, "Norman Rockwell at the Guggenheim," 106–7.
14. Berridge, "Escape from Celebrity."

his divorce, and his marriage to his second wife, Mary Rhoads Barstow, with whom Rockwell would sometimes appear in society pages detailing their visits with other prominent people.[15] By the 1940s, Rockwell had made multiple appearances in the "Looking at Hollywood" feature penned by famed gossip columnist Hedda Hopper.

Rockwell also had a direct relationship with Hollywood and its star system. In 1920, for instance, Rockwell illustrated an advertisement for Paramount Pictures, which appeared in *The Saturday Evening Post,* featuring a family of four buying tickets to see a new film. Throughout his career, Rockwell made many visits to Hollywood to collaborate with studios and draw on the industry's resources to further his work, often incorporating Hollywood imagery and characters into his art. These visits helped establish a working relationship between Rockwell and the studios. For example, in 1936 Rockwell played a role in the preproduction of a film distributed by United Artists, *The Adventures of Tom Sawyer* (Norman Taurog, 1938).[16] Because Rockwell was creating illustrations for new printed editions of Mark Twain's *The Adventures of Huckleberry Finn* and *Tom Sawyer,* producer David Selznick invited Rockwell to New York to consult on his forthcoming film adaptation of Twain's work. Rockwell brought drawings "to acquaint local United Artists people" with the books' midwestern setting and introduced the studio to some of his models, who then did screen tests for the film.[17] Rockwell's relationship with Hollywood studios continued for decades. In 1949 Paramount Pictures commissioned Rockwell to create an illustration to coincide with the release of Cecil B. DeMille's *Samson and Delilah,* and throughout his career Rockwell hired aspiring actors from casting agents and studio lots to serve as models for his paintings, which—in the parlance of movie directors—he called "pictures."[18]

Between the 1940s and 1960s, three Hollywood studios (RKO Pictures, Twentieth-Century Fox, and Paramount Pictures) commissioned Rockwell to

---

15. "Rockwell May Decide to Remain." Rockwell had made one of his first trips to a Hollywood studio at the behest of author Harry Leon Wilson, who was working on his book *Merton of the Movies,* which tells the story of a small-town man who moves to Hollywood with dreams of becoming a star. *Merton of the Movies* first appeared in *The Saturday Evening Post* in 1919 before becoming a book three years later. Wilson commissioned Rockwell to illustrate the work, but after a visit to a studio, Rockwell struggled to finish the project. *Merton of the Movies* was later adapted as a Broadway play, multiple films, and a radio play. See "Draws Boys and Not Girls."

16. The NRM archives include several reference photos labeled for an "unused movie idea," suggesting that Rockwell had been, at least potentially, involved in the development of other films or was, perhaps, pursuing film production of his own.

17. Crisler, "Footnotes."

18. Moffatt, "Norman Rockwell Museum," 12.

illustrate posters and other advertising materials for their films: *The Magnificent Ambersons* (Orson Welles, 1942), *The Song of Bernadette* (Henry King, 1943), *Along Came Jones* (Stuart Heisler, 1945), *The Razor's Edge* (Edmund Goulding, 1946), *Cinderfella* (Frank Tashlin, 1960), and *Stagecoach* (Gordon Douglas, 1966), in which Rockwell also played an onscreen part as "Townsperson." Rockwell's movie posters deploy his characteristic style and his literal signature, illustrating "the movie studio's marketing plan to use a 'star' illustrator to sell a movie." In 1943 Twentieth-Century Fox used Rockwell's illustration for *The Song of Bernadette* for a 150-foot-high billboard over a Broadway theater marquee, leading the studio's advertising director, Charles Schlaifer, to declare that Rockwell's art "absolutely sold the picture." So convinced was Fox by Rockwell's marketing potential that they returned to his work to advertise *The Razor's Edge* in what was, at the time, the company's most "extensive billboard campaign."[19]

NRM has repeatedly showcased Rockwell's relationship with the film industry and celebrity culture. For instance, the museum declared the summer of 1999 the "Summer of Cinema," hosting an exhibition titled *Hooray for Rockwell's Hollywood*, which included movie posters, lobby cards, and original portraits of movie stars that he created. This exhibition also included movie poster art by Drew Struzan for such Spielberg films as *E.T. The Extraterrestrial* (1982) and *Hook* (1991), as well as a fundraising event that auctioned movie memorabilia from Lucas and Spielberg, who had both commissioned Struzan to create posters for many of the film franchises they directed and/or produced. Shortly thereafter, according to reports from *Variety*, Rockwell's son and estate executor, Thomas Rockwell, made (unsuccessful) plans to form the Norman Rockwell Picture Co., as a "brand for films, telepics, and movie theater chains" akin to Disney and Hallmark.[20]

In 2010 the Lucas Foundation organized an exhibition at the Smithsonian American Art Museum showcasing Lucas's and Spielberg's personal Rockwell collections, titled *Telling Stories: Norman Rockwell from the Collections of George Lucas and Steven Spielberg* (2010–11), and NRM opened a corresponding installation, *Rockwell and the Movies*, which showcased much of the work featured in the earlier *Hooray for Rockwell's Hollywood* exhibition. This exhibition addresses the "connections between Norman Rockwell's iconic images of American life and the movies," with both Spielberg and Lucas citing Rockwell's influence on their cinematic oeuvres. The directors note their childhood admiration for Rockwell and their direct citations of his work in their

---

19. Moffatt, "Norman Rockwell Museum," 6, 7.
20. Fleming, "Kirkwood."

various films. Lucas and Spielberg, like many commentators, frame Rockwell's approach to painting as akin to that of a filmmaker, often likening him to Frank Capra; this comparison is one that Rockwell drew himself, encouraging his models to think of themselves as actors responding to his direction. The Smithsonian event also included a number of film screenings, including works by Lucas, Spielberg, and Capra, and the exhibition catalog emphasizes the connections between Capra's and Rockwell's shared interests in ordinary people and American Dream narratives, contributions to the US war effort during World War II, and overlapping social circles within Hollywood.[21] These similarities, the exhibition suggests, helped establish a lineage from Rockwell and Capra to Lucas and Spielberg.

NRM has also produced exhibitions linking Rockwell to other famous artists, including Walt Disney and Andy Warhol. Both of these exhibits borrow from the "small world" logic of networks to frame Rockwell's links to these cultural icons. To demonstrate, in association with a larger exhibition focused on Disney's cinematic masterpiece *Snow White and the Seven Dwarfs*, NRM mounted a smaller show emphasizing Rockwell's personal and professional ties to Disney. *It's a Small World: Norman Rockwell Meets Walt Disney* includes correspondence between the two men, who traded art and memorabilia throughout their years-long friendship. The 2013 exhibition indicates that Rockwell gifted *Girl Reading the Post* (1941) to Disney, who hung the signed painting in his office for years before passing it along to his daughter, Daisy Disney Miller, who had modeled for Rockwell.[22]

In 2017 NRM launched *Inventing America: Rockwell and Warhol*, linking the artists as "iconic visual communicators" and "celebrated image makers" who "embraced populism." The exhibition emphasizes Rockwell's influence on Warhol's work, framing both artists as struggling with the "high/low" art binary and characterizing Warhol as a fan and collector of Rockwell's work.[23] *Inventing America* features multiple comparisons of the artists' works, highlighting their shared interest in celebrity culture and emphasizing linkages

---

21. Mecklenburg, *Telling Stories*, 102–3.
22. Rockwell gifted *Girl Reading Post* to Disney with a note reading "To Walt Disney, one of the really great artists—from an admirer, Norman Rockwell." Links between Rockwell and Disney had been made well before this exhibition. Robert Hughes notes, in his 1978 obituary for Rockwell, "Norman Rockwell shared with Walt Disney the extraordinary distinction of being one of the two artists familiar to nearly everyone in the U.S., rich or poor, black or white, museumgoer or not, illiterate or Ph.D." See Hughes, "Rembrandt of Punkin Creek." Likewise, several of Rockwell's paintings inspired and were imitated by works created for Disney's promotional materials.
23. See Stewart, "Norman Rockwell's Art," B1, B5.

between their images, including their unique "recognizability."[24] For instance, the exhibition compares Warhol's 1962 drawing of Joan Crawford to Rockwell's image of Jane Russell in his painting *Girl at Mirror* (1954). The exhibition further notes that Russell starred in *Gentlemen Prefer Blondes* (Howard Hawks, 1953) alongside Marilyn Monroe, who was a famous subject of Warhol's work. *Inventing America* also includes a comparison of Warhol's portraits of Monroe to Rockwell's depiction of Ann-Margret from *Stagecoach*, which was part of the film's advertising campaign. Other comparisons include Rockwell's and Warhol's depictions of President John F. Kennedy and their renderings of Jacqueline Kennedy Onassis, noting that Warhol owned Rockwell's 1963 portrait of the first lady, which would influence his depictions of her the following year. This portrait of Kennedy Onassis was one of two that Warhol purchased in 1968. The other painting was *Extra Good Boys and Girls* (1939), which depicts Santa Claus checking his list while mapping his complex network of delivery stops around the globe.

Portraits of celebrities were an important part of Rockwell's oeuvre, and he painted myriad entertainers such as Frank Sinatra, Johnny Carson, John Wayne, and Judy Garland and presidents such as Kennedy, Richard Nixon, and Ronald Reagan. Rockwell also took up the concept of celebrity in many paintings. For example, *Gary Cooper as the Texan*, or *Movie Star Being Made Up*, pokes fun at the Hollywood mythos of the cowboy, depicting a makeup artist applying lipstick to Cooper's mouth as a he prepares to go on camera for his lead role in *The Texan* (John Cromwell, 1930). Two of Rockwell's paintings also depict fictional women characters in show business: *Hollywood Dreams* (1930) features a white woman actor, who recalls Hollywood's first female star, Mary Pickford, waiting anxiously outside a closed Hollywood casting office, alongside two older character actors seeking work, and *Movie Starlet and Reporters* (1936) shows a young, white woman actor, reminiscent of Jean Harlow, who appears exasperated by a group of journalists, all of whom are white men, surrounding her invasively. Just as Rockwell's portrait of Cooper addresses the circulation of hegemonic discourses of masculinity within Hollywood westerns, Rockwell's paintings of women actors seem aware of the stringent and rather homogenous gendered, raced, and classed beauty norms to which starlets (and aspiring starlets) would be subject. Each of these paintings depicts its figures in moments of relative vulnerability: the Hollywood star making light of his own persona and the masculinist western mythology that had made him famous, the out-of-work actors seeking opportunities

---

24. Danto, "Age of Innocence."

and facing (literally and figuratively) closed doors, and the young woman star whose fame comes at the cost of her privacy and hinges on her objectification.

Rockwell also painted multiple images of ordinary people consuming artifacts related to Hollywood celebrity culture and the fan magazines that helped create and circulate star images: *Charlie Chaplin Fans* (1916), in which a family of white theatergoers lean over a balcony railing, holding images of Chaplin and looking entranced and delighted by the silent movie they presumably watch; *Maid with Movie Magazine* (1922), in which a white woman sits in a chair distractedly holding a broom in one hand and a magazine, opened to a close-up photograph of a white male star, in the other, as she looks plaintively into the distance; *Boy Gazing at Pictures of Glamorous Stars* (1934), in which a young white boy sits with his baseball glove and dog beside him while staring bemusedly at three head shots of white women stars; *Two Girls Looking at a Movie Star's Photo* (1938), in which two white, college-aged women stare longingly at a photo of a white male movie star reminiscent of Robert Taylor as they sit on a dormitory bed with other photos strewn around them; *Girl Reading the Post*, in which a white, school-aged girl reads an issue of *The Saturday Evening Post* with a glamorous model on its cover; and *Girl at Mirror*, in which a white adolescent girl contemplates her image in the mirror with a magazine opened to a photograph of Hollywood star Jane Russell sitting in her lap and a pile of cosmetic supplies resting at her feet.

Each painting gestures toward the role of star culture in engendering communal practices with which individuals define themselves and develop relationships. Chaplin, for instance, unites three generations of fans, both male and female, who take pleasure in the shared object of his onscreen image and performance. Each of these images, which depict fans gazing at headshots or magazines, also illustrates individuals defining their senses of self and their desires in relation to others, including others they meet in person and those they meet virtually through mass mediation. Many of these paintings also point to the particular role that stardom plays in the construction and circulation of discourses regarding gender and sexuality, a point I return to below.

In 1973 Rockwell also painted an image filled with celebrities as an illustration to accompany a short story published in *McCall's* magazine about a young girl whose fantasy life features whimsical characters and often revolves around famous people. Rockwell's *The Saturday People*, published as a large two-page spread, depicts a young girl standing in front of a throng of people, her attention caught by two Indian princes and an elephant. The crowded Manhattan street teems with celebrities, including actor David McCallum, artist Grandma Moses, New York City mayor John Lindsay, opera singer Maria Callas, actor Sean Connery, drummer Ringo Starr, Prince Philip of England, New York governor Nelson Rockefeller, comedian Jonathan Winters, composer Leonard Bernstein, and actor Tallulah Bankhead. The illustration also features images of Rockwell and his third wife, Mary "Molly" Punderson Rockwell, amid the assemblage of stars.

The Rita Madocs story that inspired the image describes its thirteen-year-old protagonist, Leslie, as inventing stories about celebrities she encounters both in reality on the streets of Manhattan and virtually through their art and public appearances. She turns her attention to these figures as a distraction from her personal traumas: her father has died and her mother has begun a new romantic relationship with a man Leslie identifies metonymically as "The Hat," in association with the green velvet fedora he leaves on their parlor table during his visits. Leslie, who dreams of becoming a "famous conductor," keeps a scrapbook "where, among clippings from magazines and quotes from books, she recorded happenings."[25] Leslie imagines that such figures as Bernstein, Starr, Lindsay, and McCallum (whom she briefly confuses for his character from *The Man from U.N.C.L.E.*) are better men than her mother's lover—a distinction made visible, to her, by the fact that they do not wear hats. One evening, Leslie believes that she hears the couple quarreling, only to discover that they have recorded themselves performing a scene from Chekhov's *The Bear*, and it is this glimpse into the adults' playful, imaginative life that enables Leslie to warm toward The Hat and to accept her mother's relationship.[26]

While *The Saturday People* frames celebrity as a resource with which fans might cope with their vulnerabilities and traumas, other works by Rockwell consider the challenges of fame, especially for those who achieve it, including the artist himself. In *Triple Self-Portrait*, Rockwell paints an image of himself painting an image of himself based on his reflection in a mirror. Viewers see three versions of Rockwell: the artist's back side as he sits in front of his easel with glasses on his face, paintbrush in hand, and pipe dangling from his lips; his reflection in the mirror, with opaque lenses, a drooping pipe, and a down-turned mouth; and his painted portrait with his glasses removed, his pipe lev-

---

25. Madocs, "Saturday People," 166, 119.

26. *The Bear* is a one-act farce based on a French play, *Les Jirons de Cadillac*. Both plays tell the story of a boorish man, "the bear," tamed by a widow whom he loves; a central theme of Chekhov's play is the character's lack of self-awareness. A decade after Madocs's story appeared in *McCall's*, Chekhov's play was adapted as the second half of a two-part musical comedy, *A Day in Hollywood / A Night in the Ukraine*, directed and choreographed by Tommy Tune. In the first half of the Broadway play, ushers from Grauman's Chinese Theatre perform a revue of classic and highly self-referential Hollywood songs of the 1930s, including "Just Go to the Movies," "Famous Feet," "I Love a Film Cliché," and "Doin' the Production Code." Revivals of the show also feature the 1937 hit "Hooray for Hollywood." The second act of the musical comedy features a version of Chekhov's play in the style of a Marx Brothers film.

eled, and his visage improved. The image also depicts a fictionalized version of Rockwell's studio, strewn with painting materials and pipe ashes smoldering in a trashcan, and his easel, adorned with self-portraits created by other artists, sketches of his own image, and a brass helmet.[27]

The differences between the three versions of Rockwell in *Triple Self-Portrait* signal the artist's anxious efforts at what, in the parlance of public relations, might be called image management, as the painting-within-the-painting offers an idealized version of Rockwell's appearance. The joke suggested by the manipulations of his image depends on the familiarity of his well-known face. And while the self-portraits of other artists suggest Rockwell's efforts to seek guidance and inspiration from them, these images also point toward his vulnerability and awareness of his uncertain status in the world of high art.[28] It matters that the artists depicted in *Triple Self-Portrait* are European masters—Albrecht Dürer, Rembrandt van Rijn, Pablo Picasso, and Vincent Van Gogh—whose credibility as great artists has been widely accepted and institutionally sanctioned.

That these visual allusions to culturally lauded artists should be read as referencing questions about Rockwell's artistic merit and attendant feelings of self-doubt seems confirmed by the highly circulated, extratextual anecdote about the brass helmet atop the easel. Rockwell bought the helmet from an

---

27. *Triple Self-Portrait* is one of Rockwell's most imitated and parodied works, examples of which include Charles Boyer's *Walt's Self Portrait*, which depicts Walt Disney using a mirror to paint himself as Mickey Mouse, and *Mickey's Self Portrait*, which depicts the inverse process. In 2010 *Billboard* published an homage to the painting on its cover as a memorial to Michael Jackson. In the image, a contemporary Jackson paints his portrait, recalling a more youthful version of himself from his highly successful *Thriller* era. The easel features other youthful images of Jackson, and in place of Rockwell's helmet sits the black fedora with which Jackson had become associated. The title of the cover story, "It's a Wonderful Afterlife," metonymically references Rockwellian filmmaker Frank Capra's *It's a Wonderful Life* to frame public memory about Jackson. The choice to paint Jackson in this style signals the iconic status he shared with Rockwell as a definitive American artist, while at the same time suggesting a resemblance between Jackson and Rockwell as figures who struggled with their public image. Given the long-standing accusations that Jackson experienced pedophilic desires for young boys, the cover also offers an uncanny anticipation of the claims Solomon would make about Rockwell just three years later in *American Mirror*. See Harding, "It's a Wonderful Afterlife."

28. Jean-Paul Goude alluded to *Triple Self-Portrait* for the May 1974 cover of *Esquire* to accompany a story by Norman Mailer about graffiti's status within the art world. The image features a gangly and bespectacled young Black man, who recalls the awkward earnestness of the teenage boys common within Rockwell's oeuvre, painting at an easel with a spray can. This cover image was not *Esquire*'s only reference to Rockwell. After *Newsweek* reprinted an image of Santa by Rockwell on its December 28, 1970, cover, the April 1971 issue of *Esquire* featured its own "homage to Rockwell," highlighting the work of Ron Borowski, who had created photographs that aimed to look as much like Rockwell paintings as possible. See "Homage to Rockwell."

antique dealer in France in the 1920s, believing it to be a historic military artifact and later learning that it was a contemporary firefighter's helmet. The inclusion of the misrepresented helmet gestures toward Rockwell's falsification of his own image within the painting and his recognition that many within the art world might consider him a fake or a joke.[29] Rockwell's self-portrait meditates on his credibility as an artist and his status as a well-known figure and recognizable face, which may appear, at least to some, to degrade the integrity of his work.

This consideration of fame and its arguable tension with artistry offers context for another text circulating around Rockwell's persona—but not one created by Rockwell himself. Rather, this work is one of many inspired by a Rockwell painting. In 2013 the Hallmark Movie Channel aired a made-for-television movie in which one of Rockwell's most acclaimed paintings, *Shuffleton's Barbershop*, becomes the basis for a narrative about the pitfalls of fame.[30] In the film, *Norman Rockwell's Shuffleton's Barbershop* (Mark Jean, 2013), a famous country music singer in the midst of a personal and professional crisis returns to his small hometown to seek guidance from the barber who acted as a surrogate father for him during his youth. Casting fame as having alienated the young musician from his origins and corrupted his love for his art form, the film nostalgically deploys tropes associated with family-values rhetoric to remind the lead character of what "really matters." Rockwell's famous painting, which depicts men playing instruments in the back room of a barbershop, becomes the literal and figurative backdrop for the protagonist's redemption, as the film opens with a close-up on *Shuffleton's Barbershop* and concludes with the star's declaration that he will give up his fame to rejoin his family and the local musicians in his small community.

In addition to the fact that *Shuffleton's Barbershop* has been considered one of Rockwell's greatest works, two aspects of it help account for its adaptation as a film with this particular narrative: its cinematic stylistics and its attention to the subjects of fame and art. Rockwell's image positions view-

---

29. In the excerpt of *My Adventures as an Illustrator* that appears in the same issue of the *Post* as this cover image, Rockwell addresses his reputation directly, noting that critics had described his work in terms "derogatory" of "popular art." He also notes that he will "never be a fine-arts painter or a modern artist" and instead identifies here as an illustrator. See Rockwell, *Adventures*, 110.

30. Illustrating the ongoing trend of museum commercialization, the Berkshire Museum in Pittsfield, Massachusetts, announced plans in 2018 to sell this painting (along with others) in attempts to save itself from massive debt and to fund "reinvention" efforts that would make the museum more multimedia and interactive. Famed Rockwell collector George Lucas purchased *Shuffleton's Barbershop* and agreed to lend it to the Norman Rockwell Museum until it would be relocated to the Lucas Museum of Narrative Art upon the facility's completion.

ers on the outside of a barbershop, peering through a window. The shop sits empty and dark, but the well-illuminated background of the image reveals a group of older white men playing instruments in a backroom. The image, which Rockwell produced using over fifty reference photographs, illustrates a number of qualities that have been called "cinematic." For example, film critic Todd McCarthy describes the image as deploying "what in cinematography is known as is 'deep focus,'" which translates in this painting as visual "clarity" in all three planes of the image: foreground, midground, and background.[31]

The intricately staged mise-en-scène enables this deep-focus rendering of the image's subtle attention to fame and art. The foreground includes a rack lined with magazines and comic books, including the November 1949 issue of *Cosmopolitan*, featuring an illustration of a white woman model by well-known illustrator Coby Whitmore, and a December 1949 issue of *Walt Disney's Comic Book and Stories*, featuring a Walt Kelly illustration of Donald Duck and his nephews. The midground of the image shows an empty barber's chair draped with a towel, a wood-burning fireplace with glowing embers, and a poster on a wall that depicts a tattered US flag at half-staff and the partially obscured phrase "REMEMBER DEC. 7th!" The background clearly depicts three musicians playing, respectively, a violin, a clarinet, and a cello. That the viewer can see all these details clearly from outside the shop through the panes of a window adds to the sense of depth in the image.

The magazines, with images associated with famous artists and characters, function as metonyms for commercial success and fame, while the amateur musicians evoke the pleasures of creating art for art's sake. The position of the magazine rack in the foreground of the image close to the window and the location of the musicians in the background of the image in a partially obscured room suggest a potential tension between the pursuit of fame and the creation of art, as if the two endeavors necessarily exist at odds with one another. This image might be read to suggest that whereas fame is superficial and based on spectacle and display, real art is personal, intimate, and authentic—the perspective that *Norman Rockwell's Shuffleton's Barbershop* adopts. Yet the use of deep-space composition and deep-focus stylistics suggests that the image does not situate celebrity and art in opposition or stark contrast to each other but locates them along a continuum in which the pursuit of fame and the creation of art can be mutually enabling and constraining.

The very idea of authentic art for art's sake derives its meaning, at least in part, in relation to ideas about fame and commerce. Such a reading of *Shuffleton's Barbershop* accords with Rockwell's depiction of his three "selves" in *Tri-*

---

31. Mecklenburg, *Telling Stories*, 207.

ple Self-Portrait, in which his fame enables him and his art to be seen by others but also constrains how others might expect to see him and the work he creates. This reading aligns with Rockwell's own persona as an artist. Although public discourse about him frequently characterized Rockwell as fleeing his celebrity and preferring the purported authenticity of small towns over Hollywood spectacle, it was precisely his investment in the aesthetics of small-town authenticity that gave Rockwell his fame; he quite literally traveled to Hollywood to make use of movie industry resources—from props to cameras to actors—to create his supposedly authentic renditions of small-town life.

Rather than reading this painting as critical of celebrity, I argue that Rockwell's body of work offers an ambivalent characterization of fame that understands both its limitations and its affordances, without framing fame as either praiseworthy or blameworthy. As the work of a famous person who was aware of the industry mechanisms with which star images are created and circulated, Rockwell's images value the role that celebrity culture can play in the lives of those who encounter it, giving recurrent attention to the ways that it enables audiences to fashion their senses of self. His work also considers how celebrity constructs and circulates cultural ideas about gender and sexuality. This emphasis exists in relation to a more general concern in Rockwell's work with the politics of identification and his treatment of both gender and sexuality not in binary terms but, instead, as defined along continua and in interstices.

READING (WITH) ROCKWELL

In addition to framing Rockwell as both a serious artist and a beloved celebrity, NRM's rhetoric encourages viewers to engage actively with his paintings. For example, the *American Chronicles* "Gallery Guide" invites "visitors to compare their American experience with that portrayed by Rockwell, and to consider how the artist's vision may have inspired their own."[32] Similarly, the "Family Guide" for *Norman Rockwell Pictures* invites visitors to offer their own interpretations of his works, explaining that "Rockwell gives us lots of clues to help us understand the story he's telling. Sometimes he leaves things hidden so we can imagine stories of our own."[33] NRM.org enhances active reading practices through "Digital Experiences." With its "Explore Norman Rockwell" app, for instance, the museum's website allows users to visit an interactive virtual

---

32. Plunkett, "Gallery Guide," 4.
33. *Norman Rockwell Pictures*, 14.

gallery of Rockwell's paintings.[34] As Gallagher and Zagacki note, the fact that Rockwell's paintings have been "digitized, enlarged, layered, reproduced, and recontextualized" amplifies their capacity to "make new meanings in shifting contexts."[35]

This chapter takes up the invitation to engage actively with Rockwell's work as a cultural heuristic, finding resources in his paintings for challenging restrictive gender and sexual norms. This analysis does not, and cannot, account for all of Rockwell's art or posit a totalizing interpretation of the artist's body of work. To be sure, many of Rockwell's paintings have been deployed to reaffirm the hegemony of white, middle-class, Christian, and heterosexual values and subject positions. Images such as the iconic *Freedom from Want* (1943), which depicts a white, middle-class family eating Thanksgiving dinner, or *Freedom from Fear* (1943), which depicts white, heterosexual parents putting their children to bed, are those for which Rockwell is perhaps best known, and they have often functioned to reinforce dominant cultural narratives. To emphasize only these images and suspicious interpretations of them, however, misses an opportunity to consider how Rockwell's work might add to queer feminist archives of US history and to rethink the epideictic genre in relation to the politics of privilege. Just as Rockwell's position of privilege as a white, presumably heterosexual, and famous man affects the reception and implications of his work, his art encourages viewers not to judge his characters without consideration of their positions within larger social worlds.

NRM's encomia for Rockwell as an artist (and a celebrity) parallel what Lester Olson and Gallagher and Zagacki have identified as the primary rhetorical functions of Rockwell's paintings themselves: defining what is praiseworthy and valuable to a culture and, by contrast, what is not. Locating Rockwell's work within the epideictic genre, Olson's and Gallagher and Zagacki's analyses suggest that Rockwell's paintings demonstrate the interaction of aesthetic display, encomium, and civic education that characterizes the genre. Describing Rockwell's *Four Freedoms* posters, Olson writes, "Visualization of the praise-

---

34. Clicking on a thumbnail of a painting, visitors can access a range of materials, including historical information about each work of art, artifacts Rockwell referenced when creating his paintings, recorded segments of the NRM's audio tours, and videotaped interviews discussing the works. For some of the virtual paintings, users can click on different parts of the image to access even more specific information and activities. The NRM's Annual Report for 2019 indicates that over 550,000 participants engaged with the site's digital experiences, a dramatic increase over the two years prior, which, respectively, saw approximately 40,000 and 62,000 users. See https://annualreport.nrm.org/numbers/.

35. Gallagher and Zagacki, "Visibility and Rhetoric," 194.

worthy or the blameworthy allows for the union of aesthetics and society, since a people's aesthetic artifacts can both reflect and reform social action."[36]

Likewise, Gallagher and Zagacki argue that in his civil rights paintings, which include *The Problem We All Live With* (1964), *Murder in Mississippi* (1965), and *New Kids in the Neighborhood* (1967), "Rockwell functioned much like an epideictic orator, visualizing human virtue and vice and thus proving his subjects worthy of praise or blame." Gallagher and Zagacki contend that Rockwell's nonthreatening persona, popularity with white middle-class audiences, and reliance on traditional visual aesthetics increased the efficacy of his critiques of long-standing racist iconographies and ideologies.[37] This argument resonates with Cindy Koenig Richards's claim that, contrary to understandings of the genre as upholding traditional values, "epideictic can in fact be both conservative and revolutionary." Often deploying rather conventional signifiers, epideictic rhetoric can marshal culturally shared associations in order to render subversive ideas more acceptable and "promote alternative public norms, identities, and practices."[38]

Visual texts have a unique capacity for such articulatory work because they operate differently from verbal arguments.[39] Similar to interpretations of epideictic rhetoric as depending less on the "well-reasoned arguments" expected of other genres and more on aesthetic or "poetic appeal,"[40] rhetorical scholars have argued that visual texts may offer "stronger inducement" than propositional claims because of their capacity to reduce "complex situations into simpler visual abstractions."[41] This suasory force depends, in large part, on what remains unsaid in iconic texts, which, Barthes argues, communicate through metonymic, or associative, logic. Collapsing the distance between perception and interpretation—denotation and connotation—images forge associations that become naturalized, transforming "history into nature" and making the contingent seem essential.[42]

For example, the covers of popular US magazines have played a significant role in naturalizing normative expectations regarding what is praiseworthy about women. These images have maintained metonymic links between femaleness, femininity, and physical beauty, declaring that women must be feminine and equating femininity with beauty. When Rockwell began pub-

---

36. Olson, "Portraits," 24.
37. Gallagher and Zagacki, "Visibility and Rhetoric," 178, 180.
38. Richards, "Inventing Sacagawea," 2.
39. See O'Gorman, "Aristotle's Phantasia."
40. LaWare, "Encountering Visions," 144.
41. Cloud, "'To Veil the Threat,'" 289.
42. Barthes, *Image Music Text*, 39, and *Mythologies*, 129.

lishing covers for *The Saturday Evening Post* in 1916, that periodical and other popular magazines (such as *Life, Collier's,* and the *Ladies Home Journal*) circulated ideas about American women that derived and deviated from the nineteenth-century Cult of True Womanhood with its emphasis on "piety, purity, submissiveness, and domesticity." While some covers in the early twentieth century began to depart from these expectations by depicting women as active, adventurous, and ambitious (in contrast to earlier depictions of women as passive and confined to the private sphere), these magazine images continued to link physical beauty to femininity and to define beauty in terms of white, Eurocentric, and upper-class standards.[43] Such epideictic images create metonymic chains that identify certain female bodies and subjectivities as praiseworthy, excluding women marked as *not* white, Euro-American, and/or upper-class from the interarticulated categories of "feminine" and "beautiful."

Much of Rockwell's art, including some covers for *The Saturday Evening Post*, can be understood as disrupting these metonymic associations, which continue to circulate through magazines and popular culture to this day. For instance, many of Rockwell's paintings challenge links between femininity and beauty, while others dispute the assumption that women must be conventionally feminine. These visual texts do not merely operate according to the logic of inversion, however; paintings such as *Girl at Mirror* and *Girl with Black Eye* (1953), which I discuss below, depict characters who exist between various gender classifications, creating space for denaturalized understandings of all gender identifications as fluid, unstable, and radically contingent. At the same time that Rockwell's work draws from metonymy in order to communicate its ideas, it also attends to its own metonymic registers, marking gender and sex as socially produced and regulated through such channels as mass mediation and celebrity culture.

Many of Rockwell's paintings highlight the arbitrariness of gender categories and norms by visualizing characters that exist between and struggle with them. These images also invite understanding of praise as existing coextensively with discipline and blame, wherein adulation of some may entail disregard for or denigration of others. Not only might the celebration of normative identity formations engender castigation of those *not* identified as adherent to such cultural norms; the celebration of antinormative identifications may also create exclusions and hierarchies. As Robyn Wiegman demonstrates, the "queer critical desire to champion gender transitivity reveals normativities of its own," and the queer critical choice to call "normativity pathological [is]

---

43. Kitch, *Girl on the Magazine Cover*, 20.

to participate in the logic of normalization itself."[44] Rockwell's art attends to such paradoxes, troubling figurations of both normativity and antinormativity by emphasizing its characters' interstitiality and indeterminacy. Rockwell's work also maintains a productive tension between hermeneutics of suspicion and reparation, squaring critical attention to the politics of gender and sex with what José Esteban Muñoz might call the queer politics of hope.[45] This balancing act resonates with the claim made by Wiegman and Heather Love that paranoid and reparative reading practices—dispositions of suspicion and love—should be understood as coextensive and inextricable. In other words, this body of work seems to recognize Isaac West's claim that "texts and lived practices rarely, if ever, fit neatly into theoretical binaries," and, as a result, Rockwell's work helps generate "more capacious theories of norms, the normative, and normativities capable of capturing the multiplicities of texts and practices."[46]

Rockwell's art encourages his audiences to look at his characters with compassion and empathy without losing sight of their shortcomings or struggles. Inviting an attitude of love toward his characters that does not imagine them as above reproach, his images construct their subjects not as worthy of praise or blame but as deserving consideration and recognition. His well-known works ask their viewers to know their characters well, whether they are well known or not. This chapter assumes an analogous stance toward Rockwell's art, reading his images as filled with potential—but far from perfect—in their capacity to promote attitudes of acceptance and inclusion. Three rhetorical strategies within Rockwell's work illustrate its queer feminist potential: these images critique essentialized understandings of gender, depict characters whose gender transitivity confounds various categorizations, and envision bonds between people that unsettle prevailing relational norms. Central to many of these images are Rockwell's conceptions of celebrity.

MIRROR, MIRROR

As a motif in Rockwell's paintings, images of young girls in front of mirrors critique both essentialist understandings of gender identity and oppressive gender norms. Such portraits as *Little Girl with Lipstick* (1922), *Going Out* (1933), *Prom Dress* (1949), and *Girl at Mirror* frame gender as a social and cultural construct while acknowledging women's particular subjugation to

---

44. Wiegman, "Interchanges," 97.
45. Muñoz, *Cruising Utopia*, 4.
46. West, "Queer Generosities," 539.

cultural expectations regarding feminine beauty. Focusing on white women's negotiation with white, middle-class feminine beauty norms, this series of paintings resembles Rockwell's civil rights images by reminding viewers that abstract cultural norms have material consequences "relative to the individuals or groups whose lives were most directly influenced by their presence or absence."[47] And while Rockwell's work often emphasizes the ways that US culture subjects girls to unrealistic beauty norms and expectations, his paintings also understand masculine gender identifications as citational and mimetic. For example, *Boy Lifting Weights* (1922) depicts a spindly, bespectacled young boy attempting to lift weights while staring at a poster of a brawny body builder, captioned "Be a Man."

In *Going Out,* an affluent white woman sits at her vanity table in a floor-length gown, her makeup and hair expertly styled as she dresses for a formal event. The gown she wears mimics one of the most famous dresses from film history, created by MGM designer Adrian for Joan Crawford in *Letty Lynton* (Clarence Brown, 1932).[48] Two mirrors frame her face: the large mirror attached to the vanity table and the mirror held in her hand, toward which she directs her gaze. Behind the woman stands a young girl, holding a brush and watching the beauty ritual that unfolds before her. The young girl, who is also white, wears a white T-shirt and white overalls; she has her hair tied in two braids, each adorned with a red ribbon that recalls the red in her shoes and hairbrush. We cannot see the child's face, but the plainness of her wardrobe suggests that she wears no cosmetics. The brush in her hand implies a certain level of interest in the ritualized practices of beauty, such that viewers might imagine her face to express awe, her eyes wide with wonderment. Yet Rockwell's choice to depict the young girl in all-white, gender-neutral overalls connotes not only her young age and innocence but also a lack of investment in traditional signifiers of femininity.

This image illustrates what Olson calls the "productive ambiguity" that characterizes much of Rockwell's art.[49] The white clothing recalls the typical uniform of a painter, suggesting that the girl might be expected, at some point, to "paint her face" as her elder does; however, she remains, at this moment, a partially blank canvas—not fully invested in the norms on display in front of

---

47. Gallagher and Zagacki, "Visibility and Rhetoric," 180.
48. Mecklenburg, *Telling Stories,* 75. The film *Letty Lynton* (Clarence Brown, 1932) stars Joan Crawford as a woman who gets away with murdering her abusive lover. The film has remained largely unavailable to audiences because of a legal determination that the script produced by the film's studio, MGM, relied too heavily on the 1930 play *Dishonored Lady* without securing the rights to that work.
49. Olson, "Portraits," 16.

her. The simple clothing also suggests that the girl might be a tomboy; perhaps, then, the expression on her face connotes puzzlement or skepticism, her eyes rolled in disbelief. Rockwell's choice *not* to depict her face encourages this ambiguity or indeterminacy; but regardless of how one might imagine the young girl's attitude, the painting illustrates Judith Butler's arguments that gendered identification is learned through mimetic and citational practices and enacted through stylized performance.[50] The painting's acknowledgment of this fact denaturalizes gender identifications as learned choices rather than innate characteristics.

The choice of dress for the woman in the image merits detailed discussion. Adrian's gown, on which this dress is based, influenced women's fashion throughout the 1930s, offering "dramatic evidence of motion picture 'influence' on fashion behavior."[51] *Vogue* magazine described (and helped engender) the dress's mimetic appeal: "Every little girl, all over the country, within two weeks of Joan Crawford's picture, felt she would die if couldn't have a dress like that. With the results that the country was flooded with little Joan Crawfords." The *Vogue* article frames Hollywood stars as capable of influencing not only style but also the "prejudices," "etiquette," and "morals" of their audiences.[52] Adrian designed his dress with incredibly complex lines and structure to prevent imitations of it, but "references to it abounded" in women's fashion and media culture. The dress also played a significant role in the construction of Crawford's celebrity persona as not only a fashion sophisticate but also a woman, born with very little, who used style to elevate her class status.[53] Rockwell's choice to depict this particular, very famous dress matters for multiple reasons.

First, this choice highlights not only the citational structure of gender performances but also the mimetic role that celebrity plays in shaping cultural desires and practices, as if the painting asks whether the little girl in the overalls will become another "little Joan Crawford." Second, this choice points toward the ways that celebrity can be both enabling and constraining. As Robert Corber argues, a key task for Adrian as a designer at MGM was the creation of clothing that could establish a distinct stylistic for Crawford, which he did so effectively that at least one industry insider identified her metonymically with "her goddamn shoulder pads." Such close association, however, risked limiting Crawford's image and range such that some critics commented on "her vivid screen presence and glamorous wardrobe rather

---

50. Butler, "Imitation," 26–28.
51. Herzog and Gaines, "'Puffed Sleeves,'" 25.
52. "Does Hollywood Create?" 61, 76.
53. Herzog and Gaines, "'Puffed Sleeves,'" 75, 84. See also Corber, "Padded Shoulders," 1.

than the quality of her acting when reviewing her movies," a problem that is both specific to Crawford's persona and illustrative of the sexism that has long typified the industry.[54]

Third, this dress illustrates not only the instability of star images but also the undergirding instability of gender categories. As Corber argues, the gown's chiffon fabric, puffed sleeves, and fitted bodice signify traditional feminine norms that frequently govern the figuration of Hollywood's women stars as "glamorous, decorative, and alluring." At the same time, however, the exaggerated sleeves on the gown accentuate "Crawford's masculine mode of embodiment by making her shoulders appear broader." This aspect of Crawford's embodiment, Corber notes, acts as a signifier of those aspects of her star persona often associated with masculinity, including her career ambition.[55] Thus, the tension between traditionally feminine and masculine stylistics that characterizes Rockwell's renderings of the characters in *Going Out* finds extratextual resonance with Crawford's "female masculinity" and her star image as both a feminine clotheshorse and a masculine workhorse.

Rockwell also addresses the subjects of fame, fashion, and femininity in *Girl at Mirror*.[56] Dressed in a white slip, her brown hair braided and pinned to the top of her head, this girl, who is also white, seems like an older version of the child in *Going Out*. She sits on a red stool before a framed mirror, contemplating her reflection in comparison to the glamorous image of Jane Russell, whose picture appears in a magazine opened on her lap. Her expression appears thoughtful and fraught with uncertainty. Immediately to her left rests a pile of cosmetic tools, including red lipstick, red rouge, and a red brush, and tossed to the side sits an upturned doll. The prominence of the color red, which has metonymic associations with desire, passion, and romance, signals her emergent sexuality and the cultural processes that may sexualize and objectify her in ways that she is only beginning to apprehend. The private, self-surveillance of the child in *Girl at Mirror* anticipates the judgment to which she will soon be subjected, and the expression on her face suggests

---

54. Corber, "Padded Shoulders," 2.
55. Corber, "Padded Shoulders," 4, 2.
56. *Girl at Mirror* inspired a 1987 parody by Disney artist Charles Boyer, created to commemorate the fiftieth anniversary of Disney's *Snow White and the Seven Dwarfs*. Boyer created at least one other Rockwell parody for Disney, which imitates Rockwell's 1936 *Barbershop Quartet*, with Donald Duck, Br'er Bear, Goofy, and Mickey Mouse standing in front of a masthead that reads "The Disney Evening Post." This Charles Boyer, the master illustrator at Disney, is not to be confused with Charles Boyer the Hollywood actor. It was the latter Charles Boyer, and not the former, who announced that Crawford defeated Bergman, among others, for the Academy Award for Best Actress for her role in *Mildred Pierce* (Michael Curtiz, 1945), the film that effectively ended Crawford's "clotheshorse" period as an actor.

her anxiety about how her appearance will be evaluated in relation to others (including Russell) whose performances of femininity she may imitate.

The presence of the girl's doll also identifies gender mimesis as an ongoing process. Noting its antiquated appearance, Richard Halpern suggests that the doll was inherited from the girl's mother or grandmother.[57] In this way, *Girl at Mirror* anticipates what Butler describes as the unremitting process of mimetic gender identifications.[58] Just as this girl must imitate others, so too did—or, more to the point, *do*—the women who came before (and will come after) her. Intertextual connections between *Girl at Mirror* and other Rockwell paintings further reinforce this figuration of gender imitations. For example, visual similarities between the girl in this painting and the young girl depicted in *Going Out*—both have braided brown hair and wear all white with touches of red on or near them—proffer a theme of gender citationality and performativity as incessant. The very resemblances between these paintings, like many repetitions across Rockwell's work, seem to embody Butler's description of gender as a copy of a copy with no original.[59]

I take issue, therefore, with Halpern's claim that the realization that the girl's "mother and grandmother probably grew up in exactly the same way" should convince viewers that the "rituals of maturity are reassuringly familiar."[60] Not only does this assertion risk reproducing heteronormative timelines that equate growing up, or maturing, with adopting normative gender and sexual stylizations; it also misses some of the angst and uncertainty on display in the image.[61] The look on the girl's face reveals discomfort and apprehension. Her eyebrows are raised in what might be imagined as puzzlement about how she looks and how she is supposed to look; but her downturned chin, resting on clinched fists, also evokes the potential for disappointment, the fear that she will not live up to expectations or resemble the icon whose image she studies. This process of self-surveillance and stylization is, no doubt, recognizable, but its familiarity does not necessarily connote reassurance. Rather, its familiarity signals what Butler identifies as the compulsoriness of normative gender and sexual expectations.[62] The image's emphasis on the girl's affective experience thus invites empathetic responses from imagined viewers, asking them to consider the serious implications of this act of playing dress up.

Similar disquietude characterizes *Little Girl Observing Lovers on a Train* (1944), which depicts an act of voyeurism that is both specular and specula-

---

57. Halpern, *Norman Rockwell*, 122.
58. Butler, *Gender Trouble*, 179–80.
59. Butler, "Imitation," 21.
60. Halpern, *Norman Rockwell*, 123–24.
61. Halberstam, *Queer Time and Place*, 4–5.
62. Butler, "Imitation," 24.

tive. In this image, a girl sits on her knees, facing backward in her train seat, leaning over the edge, and staring intently at a heterosexual couple in the row behind her. Her mesmerized gaze mirrors that of other Rockwell characters looking longingly at images of celebrities on the pages of magazines. The couple shares an intimate moment—heads nestled together, legs entangled. The woman, with red hair almost identical to that of the little girl who watches her, wears a dress and high-heeled shoes, and the man wears a military uniform. The girl's countenance appears melancholy, suggesting an interest in the lovers that is neither eager nor erotic.

Perhaps her expression reveals discomfort with public displays of adult sexuality and/or sadness at recognizing the separation this couple may face during World War II. We might also read the image as depicting the girl's ambivalent recognition as she looks in a phantasmatic mirror that reveals a normative version of her future reflected back at her. The little girl is observing how to perform traditional femininity as it is defined with respect to heterosexuality, linking *Little Girl Observing Lovers on a Train* to Rockwell's paintings that construct gender identification as a mimetic process. This image further denaturalizes heterosexual identification as a learned and performative act rather than a natural expression of innate desires, and it suggests an understanding of gender and sexuality as interarticulated. Seen in relation to the paintings of girls observing their own reflections in the mirror, *Little Girl Observing Lovers on a Train* also points toward heterosexuality as a compulsory cultural institution.

While these images depict girls being shaped by the world around them, it matters that they suspend their female characters in liminal states of self-reflection. Revealing the performativity of gender, these moments visualize the thorny process of gender identification while recognizing that these young women have agency and make choices about whether (and how) they accept or reject normative gender expectations. Neither praising nor blaming their girlish subjects, these paintings invite empathetic, self-reflexive responses from their imagined viewers by framing gender as both a discursive construct and an embodied, felt experience. Commingling fear with hope, Rockwell's portraits allow these subjects a moment of indeterminacy, considering but never prescribing what futures might await them.

LAUDED OUTLAWS

A second series of Rockwell's works portrays characters that challenge easy oppositions between normative and antinormative performances of gender. For example, Rockwell created a famous iteration of Rosie the Riveter, as well as the less well-known Liberty Girl, both of which suggested the possibility of female masculinity as a productive response to wartime traumas and social upheavals. Rockwell's Rosie the Riveter was part of a government-commissioned campaign to encourage women to assume temporary ownership of wartime jobs (and certain traits of masculinity) that had typically been understood as belonging to men. *Liberty Girl* similarly depicts a masculine women whose wardrobe recalls that of Uncle Sam and who, quite literally, shoulders heaps of responsibilities—including ones that would have been coded as feminine and as masculine—during the war.

Girl with Black Eye depicts a preadolescent girl sitting on a bench outside a school principal's office. Her braids are disheveled, one red ribbon hanging loosely over her shoulder. Her white school shirt is ruffled, one sleeve rolled up, and her shirttail partially untucked. Her legs are muscular and bruised, one knee bandaged from this (or perhaps another) skirmish. The girl's arms grip the edge of the bench, her elbows bent, in a pose that is active, if not exuberant. She looks at her imagined viewers, smiling eagerly despite her bruised eye and the unhappy encounter that awaits her in the principal's office. Her expression suggests that, her injury notwithstanding, she is no victim. There is but one word to describe the look on her face: *pride*.[63]

Like Rosie and Liberty Girl, this girl is strong and active—concerned more with what she does than with how she appears. Unlike Rockwell's wartime heroines, however, she does not seem bound and determined to work in the service of social order. Instead, this girl appears unabashed in her deviant behavior, which includes (at the very least) breaking school rules by getting into a fight as well as violating normative expectations about femininity. Her robust confidence stands in stark contrast to the young character featured in *Girl at Mirror,* who worriedly contemplates her reflection. This bruised and battered girl throws conventionally feminine beauty norms to the side as fiercely as she may be imagined to throw a punch.

One might read these two girls as utterly distinct from one another; yet Rockwell used the same model, Mary Whalen, for both characters. With Whalen as their absent referent, these paintings point toward the instability of gender identifications: they are malleable over time, and individuals tend to move in and out of—across and between—various social categories throughout their lives. The extratextual link between these images also invites intertextual narrativization of them. A suspicious reading might imagine, for instance, that

---

63. An imitation of this image appears in *Forrest Gump* (Robert Zemeckis, 1994), with young Forrest sitting on a bench outside the principal's office—awaiting not punishment but, rather, acceptance—as his mother advocates for his inclusion in school despite his intellectual disability.

the young girl who once sat gleefully outside the principal's office, proud of her indiscretions, would, one year later, become the girl who sat at her mirror worried about her reflection, invested in celebrity culture, and perplexed by her place in the social world—while a reparative reading might reverse this chronology to queer its implications.[64] Rockwell's body of work encourages a third reading that imagines this girl as moving indefinitely and interstitially between such identificatory registers, never firmly in nor fully free of either.

Although such paintings celebrate those girls who choose *not* to make themselves over in accordance with hegemonic beauty norms—or, at the very least, celebrate the possibility that such girls *might* choose not to do so—they neither condemn nor blame those who do conform to normative cultural expectations. Rather, the paintings ask their imagined viewers to attend to the often-vexing processes of identification. The girl boasting the black eye seems pleased with her indiscretions, but Rockwell's painting calls attention to the disciplinary regime that awaits her—she is sitting, after all, outside the principal's office and is subject to both her principal's and her teacher's troubled gazes. This painting avoids overly romanticizing transgression and, instead, reminds viewers that cultural disobedience can be pleasurable, powerful, and politically important at the same time that it may be painful, risky, or dangerous.

Yet another Rockwell painting considers the rewards and costs of transgression while also challenging metonymic links between femininity and passivity. In 1963's *The Marriage Counselor,* a heterosexual couple sits on a couch in the lobby of a therapist's office, depicted from the therapist's point of view. The man sits with his arms crossed, sporting a dark business suit, an unhappy look on his face, and a conspicuous black eye. The woman sits next to him, wearing a paisley dress and high heels, holding the man's hat in her lap, and cutting a mischievous, sideways glance in the man's direction. The look on her face, coupled with their location in a marriage counselor's office, implies that she is responsible for her husband's shiner.

This image exists in relation to a series of others that depict scenes of marital discord, troubling the "happily ever after" mythology that typifies many popular media representations of heterosexual romance or marriage. These images—including *Election Debate* (1920), *Breakfast Table, or Behind the Newspaper* (1930), *The Gaiety Dance Team* (1947), and *Breakfast Table Politi-*

---

64. A similar narrative characterizes the first work in which Whalen appeared, *A Day in the Life of a Little Girl* (1952). In this painting, twenty-five small images in gridlike form depict moments from a young girl's day, gradually demonstrating her transformation from being unconcerned with to acutely aware of normative gender expectations and compulsory heterosexuality.

cal Argument (1948)—reveal ideological fault lines and power imbalances that may characterize heterosexual relationships, calling attention to gendered hierarchies that have historically functioned to restrict women's access to the public sphere and portraying heterosexual marriage as an institution complicit in reproducing structural inequalities between men and women. From this perspective, the young woman's violence against her husband might be understood as a form of protest against the institutions of marriage and heterosexuality themselves.

A number of striking resemblances and reversals link *Marriage Counselor* and *Girl with Black Eye*. First, both narratives center on violence signified by a black eye and feature the primary characters sitting outside an open but marked door. The color and texture of the wooden doors are virtually identical, as is the lettering that reads "Principal" on one and "Marriage Counselor" on the other. The paintings are also mirror images of one another. In *Girl with Black Eye*, the girl sits to the left and in front of the open door. In *Marriage Counselor*, the couple sits to the right of and behind the open door. Second, the woman in *Marriage Counselor*, although decidedly more traditional in her performance of femininity, recalls the teenaged subject from *Girl with Black Eye*. Her hair is redder and her frame thinner, but they share the same mischievous grin and rebellious attitude. Both women, through their presumed violence, violate cultural expectations about feminine tractability and weakness. And yet, in each case, this female character finds herself subject to a disciplinary gaze that presumably aims to correct, or at least address, her transgressive behavior.

Perhaps the girl with the black eye did become, first, the girl at the mirror, and then the woman at the marriage counselor. Though she may feel compelled to don traditional signifiers of feminine beauty and to imitate screen sirens like Jane Russell, such choices may not have evacuated her penchant for disobedience. The violence that is referenced in these paintings challenges metonymic associations between femininity and docility or passivity. At the same time, the traces of violence recall the struggles that these characters, like all people, may face in wrestling with normative gender categories and expectations, which may themselves be understood, as Butler argues, as forms of symbolic violence.[65]

These images offer depictions of normative and antinormative gender performances whose coexistence has political value for queer feminist criticism. Women (like all people) must confront, on a daily basis, conflicting and constricting expectations for who and what they should be; women (like all

---

65. Butler, *Gender Trouble*, 148.

people) might enact these many, conflicting forms of identification simultaneously or variously at any given moment or in any given context, finding themselves, more often than not, betwixt and between—rather than squarely within—a range of categories and classifications. I read these images, therefore, as highlighting the unfixity and multiplicity of all identifications and as marking gender as enacted through ongoing, unstable, and often interstitial performances.

Consider the subject of another painting, *Girl Reading the Post* (1941), which depicts a white, middle-class, adolescent girl trying on a version of femininity that, at first glance, fits her like a glove; as in *Girl at Mirror*, a magazine plays a powerful role in shaping her performance. She sits on a bench, wearing a sweater set and plaid school skirt, resting a pile of books in her lap, and holding a fictitious issue of *The Saturday Evening Post* in front of her face. On the cover of the magazine appear the head and shoulders of a beautiful and glamorous woman, who is presumably a celebrity. The image of the woman on the magazine cover is positioned and scaled to match precisely with that of the girl holding the magazine, so that the woman's face appears in the place of the teenaged girl's. The image might signify the naturalness of female beauty and the inevitability or "reassuring familiarity" of "growing up." Yet closer inspection reveals something more insidious; the image offers less a match or continuity between the teenaged girl and the icon on the magazine than an act of displacement or erasure.

We might imagine that what captures the girl's attention is an article about the glamorous model on the *Post* cover—one that may offer her hope of better imitating or becoming more like this icon of traditional feminine beauty. The structure of this image calls attention to the ideological work of metonymy as a form of displacement, visualizing their subjects' interpellation as they come to imagine themselves as a self in relation to something or someone else; for instance, the values and cultural codes with which the cover model is associated have affected who the young girl understands herself to be. This painting therefore offers critical commentary about mass mediation, celebrity, and the circulation of normative gender expectations, in ways similar to *Girl at Mirror*, and it generates self-reflexive attention to Rockwell's role in shaping those norms. The girl is reading *The Saturday Evening Post*, which was the publication that established Rockwell's fame and which has become metonymically associated with the artist and the white, upper-middle-class, heteronormative values he is often imagined to represent.

This painting also envisions a character who is (at least) two people at once: she is, in part, an adolescent schoolgirl whose muscular legs and scuffed saddle oxfords recall the tomboyish girl with the black eye as much as they recall many of Rockwell's male characters, but she is also the glamorous woman on the magazine cover. This image thus offers a consideration of intersubjectivity, which is mirrored in its self-referential intertextuality. Poised somewhere between adolescent tomboy and elegant model, she can be fixed in neither category nor said to fit perfectly in either role, despite Rockwell's rather seamlessly executed graphic match between the figures behind and on the magazine. Rockwell's celebratory visions of outsiders who do not lament their failure, or refusal, to "fit in" operate alongside his empathetic visions of those who struggle with or find themselves at the mercy of normative cultural narratives, reminding us that many people find themselves not solely in one of those camps or the other but somewhere between them.

Even those individuals—like the characters in *Girl with Black Eye* or *Marriage Counselor*—who violate normative expectations of gender must rely on acts of citation and mimesis for their gender performances; no bodies, no matter how unruly, can exist fully outside of or apart from gender norms.[66] These paintings call attention to the ways that their characters negotiate various norms (sometimes challenging them, sometimes adhering to them, sometimes doing both) and carve out spaces for themselves between and within the categories that seem available to them. Troubling the reductive binary between transgression and assimilation, these images also disrupt the opposition between praise and blame, asking spectators to attend to the complexity of gender and sexual identifications before casting judgment on their subjects. Rather than declaring what is praiseworthy or blameworthy about the characters themselves, Rockwell's epideictic images affirm the act of looking compassionately as being worthy of praise.

TESTING THE WATERS

In addition to those paintings that complicate normative understandings of gender, Rockwell's body of work features many images that confound conventional relational categories, such as hetero/homo or social/erotic/sexual. Such paintings as *Sailor Dreaming of Girlfriend* (1919), *No Swimming* (1921), *No Swimming* (1929), *A Guiding Hand* (1946), *Two Old Men and Dog: No Swimming* (1953), and *Two Old Men and Dog: No Swimming* (1956) invite recognition of the pleasures and tenderness that may be shared between characters presented as white men. They also playfully call attention to the cultural norms that aim—but often fail—to regulate such relational practices.

---

66. Butler, "Imitation," 24.

Consider Rockwell's "No Swimming" paintings, a series of four images featuring a sign that prohibits swimming at an outdoor body of water. In the 1921 *No Swimming*, three white boys and a dog run away from a swimming hole, dripping wet and in various stages of undress. Two boys face forward, but one boy looks nervously over his shoulder, presumably at the authority figures chasing them away from their spot. Behind them appears a sign that reads "No Swimming." The later of the *Two Old Men and Dog* paintings, from 1956, imitates the first *No Swimming* painting so closely that their nearly identical compositions seem to suggest that two of the young boys have grown up to be the old men.

The 1921 *No Swimming* emulates *The Swimming Hole* (1884–85), a famous painting by Thomas Eakins, whose style and use of reference photographs to create realistic paintings influenced Rockwell. In fact, the NRM archive of Rockwell's personal belongings includes prints of images by Eakins, books about the artist, and a 1971 article from *Life* magazine about Eakins's use of photography as part of his process. Eakins's painting depicts six nude men and a dog at a swimming hole. Three men stand or recline on the bank of Dove Lake, another dives off the shore, and another stands in the water, while a sixth man, whose image derives from Eakins himself, swims toward them. *Swimming Hole* has been considered one of the earliest examples of homoeroticism in American art, and homoerotic male desire abounds throughout Eakins's body of work such that debates about Eakins's sexuality have also been a staple in conversations about him as a public figure and artist.[67]

The "No Swimming" paintings by Rockwell, not unlike Eakins's *Swimming Hole*, illustrate the pleasures of deviance: part of the fun for the characters, both young and old, was the swimming, but the violation of rules was, no doubt, also part of the swimming hole's allure. That the young characters in the first *No Swimming* painting were apparently skinny-dipping—one boy wears no clothes, his naked torso and legs exposed, his genitals covered by the clothes he carries—adds to the illicit pleasure of the act and of the image itself. Not only were the boys swimming in a prohibited body of water; they also violated cultural taboos and laws against public nakedness. It matters, then, that the image depicts only boys. The intimacy evoked by this scene declares that affection, desire, and pleasure are not solely the province of hetero/sexual relationships.

Whether or not these young boys grew up to be the old men at the swimming hole, the latter painting further demonstrates that the pleasures of transgression and of same-sex intimacy are not just child's play—refusing the

---

67. Adams, *Eakins Revealed*.

heteronormative equation of "growing up" with "settling down." These paintings also reveal the illusoriness of normativity itself. With this claim, I mean not to underestimate how compulsory or powerful normative expectations may feel but to highlight the impossibility of the natural conditions that such norms presuppose. For instance, even the most ardent heterosexuals likely fail to meet the expectations of heteronormativity in various ways, wittingly or not. The "No Swimming" sign, then, becomes a metonym for the instability of social and cultural dictates, which individuals may variously obey, resist, ignore, mistake, or otherwise fail to follow.

The fact that the "No Swimming" paintings take particular interest in the limits of gender and sexual norms is further demonstrated by the other two images in this series. In the 1953 *Two Old Men* painting, two older men and a dog approach a swimming hole to discover that they've been beaten to the punch. Draped over the "No Swimming" sign are a woman's hat, undergarments, and clothing, while a pair of red high heels sits on the ground. The men look shocked and unsettled, eyes bulging and mouths gaping, as they stare at the clothing hanging on the sign. Significantly, the painting does not depict the presumably female swimmer's body, refusing to participate in her objectification. Rather, it puts the gaze itself on display at the same time that it signals the possibility of the woman's agency and transgressive pleasure as she swims alone in a prohibited body of water.

Consider the contrast between this image, in which the two men stop and stare at an ostensibly naked female swimmer, and the 1929 *No Swimming*, in which a young white girl refuses to look at presumably naked male swimmers. In the latter painting, the girl walks past a "No Swimming" sign draped with what appears to be boys' clothing. Turning her head, closing both eyes, and covering one eye with her hand, she has internalized the cultural prohibition against the female gaze—as is reiterated by the subtitle of the painting, "No Peeking." Unlike the two men, she does not imagine herself as having the prerogative to look, let alone join in or interrupt. Taking these paintings together encourages viewers to consider the politics of looking / being seen and to imagine the affective responses of those involved in the encounter. For example, might the female swimmer enjoy the thrill of getting "caught"? Might she feel vulnerable and in peril? How will she respond now that she has been discovered? These paintings may also remind viewers that while opposition to social regulations and norms can be pleasurable, not all transgressions—or transgressors—are treated equally. It is not simply that some transgressions are considered more consequential than others. Rather, the "No Swimming" paintings also demonstrate that not all bodies have equal access to oppositional pleasures and that not all bodies are subject to the same disciplinary norms.

The men's shock in *Two Old Men and Dog* (1953) may signify the privileged position of white men who have enjoyed greater license to ignore or violate certain kinds of social regulations, as exemplified by the sexist logic that "boys will be boys." It might never have occurred to them that a woman might swim (alone) in "their" forbidden spot. Furthermore, as much as they may be startled by what they *see*, this scene reveals that they may also be reacting to the very idea of *being seen* (by the swimmer) themselves. This disbelief thus also reveals a privilege afforded to white men as typical bearers—but not objects—of the gaze, which, as many of Rockwell's paintings acknowledge, is a privilege reaffirmed by popular media (including magazines) and celebrity culture. Yet the gaze on display in this image is not a masterful one. The men approach the swimming hole not to see a naked woman—but to enjoy time alone, together. The juxtaposition of the men's co-presence with the female swimmer's absent presence calls attention to a range of pleasures and intimacies that can be experienced outside of heterosexual economies.

Another aspect of queer potentiality in *Two Old Men and Dog* becomes visible when we consider this painting alongside other Rockwell paintings that feature characters looking simultaneously at shared objects of desire. Consider *Two Girls Looking at a Movie Star's Photo*, in which two women stare desirously at a headshot that resembles Hollywood star Robert Taylor. As they sit nuzzled together on the same dormitory bed, one character holds a photograph of the star while the other places her hands gently on her companion's shoulders. Although the women's attention fixes on the movie star's image, their physical proximity on the bed and comfort with one another suggests a connection and intimacy between them that is not fully reducible to their affection for the star. Likewise, in *Sailor Dreaming of Girlfriend*, two white Navy men sit close together as one holds a photograph of a white woman signed "Love to my Sailorboy, from Irene xxxxx." While the woman in the photo presumably holds the affection of her "Sailorboy," he rests his hand with familiarity on his companion's leg, once again pointing toward an affective charge that may surpass the norms of heterosexuality and/or monogamy and may signify what Sedgwick has dubbed the "triangulation of desire." The theme of triangulated desire appears in at least two other Rockwell paintings, including *Willie Gillis: Girls with Letters* (1942), in which two young white women hold letters and copies of the same autographed image of Gillis, implying a rivalry between them over the deployed soldier. *Man Courting Two Girls* (1929) shows two white women, almost identical to each other, sitting nestled together on a settee, across from a white man attempting to woo one or both of them.

These paintings neither praise nor blame their subjects for their practices or their desires but, instead, invite audiences to consider the choices the characters are able (or unable) to make. Like the other images discussed in this chapter, these paintings illustrate the politics of privilege, demonstrating Muñoz's contention that not all bodies are equally positioned to thwart normative gender and sexual expectations.[68] Intimating that transgression may be easier for some than for others, the paintings point most clearly toward the importance of gender in this equation, but it also matters that they depict gender trouble only in bodies (un)marked as white and middle-class.

A suspicious reading might argue that these images do not disrupt the hegemony of whiteness or middle-classness, whereas a reparative reading might suggest that the homogeneity of Rockwell's characters makes such race and class privilege visible. This latter interpretation finds support in Gallagher and Zagacki's reading of Rockwell's civil rights paintings. Acutely aware of the interarticulation of race, class, and gender, these images advocate for people of color by relying on evidence—if not exaggerations—of the Black characters' adherence to normative class and gender expectations.[69] From a queer feminist perspective, Rockwell's images of subjects questioning gender norms may inspire both hope and critique, love and anger. They contribute to ongoing conversations about the variability of lived experience and its interpretations, but they do not, and cannot, tell the whole story. Neither the beginning nor the end of such conversations, Rockwell's images occupy a position of *in-betweenness* that has value for queer feminist critique.

Rockwell's images may offer theoretical resources to queer feminist critics at a time when many scholars have suggested that queer theory should reconsider its relationship to antinormativity. The canonization, or "axiomatic centrality," of antinormativity within queer theory, Robyn Wiegman and Elizabeth Wilson argue, risks becoming occlusive and normative in its own right; in turn, they call for approaches that bring "into focus" positionalities other than "anti," "contra," or "non."[70] What Rockwell's work offers, then, is an opportunity to attend to "inter" as a framework for thinking about normativity, drawing attention to the extent to which subjects (not unlike works of art) are rarely (if ever) fully opposed to or outside of norms but, more likely, positioned between and among them. If normativity reveals itself as an illusion, then antinormativity also proves to be impossible, as the opposition to one set of norms entails adherence to others—including oppositionality as one such norm.

The limits of antinormativity become even clearer when considered intersectionally, given that opposition to one set of norms may impede resistance

---

68. Muñoz, *Cruising Utopia*, 94.
69. Gallagher and Zagacki, "Visibility and Rhetoric," 186.
70. Wiegman and Wilson, "Introduction," 10, 12.

to others; for example, transgressing gender norms may depend on upholding raced or classed ones (or vice versa). Furthermore, identifications are not only interstitial and intersectional but also relational and social; cultural norms operate on bodies, but they also operate in the affectively charged spaces between them. Active engagement with Rockwell's art, therefore, creates conditions of possibility for acknowledging and exploring this range of interstitial and intervening spaces and relations.

PARTING REFLECTIONS

In 2001 the *New York Times* ran a series of self-promotional advertisements featuring Rockwell's work in relation to 9/11, framing both Rockwell's art and the newspaper as resources for coming to grips with the nation's trauma. In November 2001, the *Times* ran a colorized version of Rockwell's *Freedom from Fear* (1943) with the caption "Make Sense of Our Times." In the original *Freedom from Fear*, the father holds a newspaper whose above-the-fold headline references "Bombings" and "Horror." The altered version of the image transforms the newspaper into an exact replica of the front cover of the *New York Times* on September 12, 2001, with the headline "U.S. ATTACKED: HIJACKED JETS DESTROY TWIN TOWERS AND HIT PENTAGON IN DAY OF TERROR." Over the next month, four other modified Rockwell images appeared with the same directive to "Make sense of our times": *The Stay at Homes (Outward Bound)* (1927), *Teacher's Birthday* (1956), *First Love* (1926), and *Brooks Robinson* (1971). Minor alterations to each image directly reference 9/11 and the nation's response. The epideictic images produced by the *Times*, argues Francis Frascina, construct a "particular type of American home and family" characterized by "racial, heterosexual, and ethnic uniformity" as worthy of praise *and* in need of protection."[71]

These advertisements indicate the significant role that Rockwell's paintings play as cultural heuristics, while also making clear that appropriations of his images may function to reinforce oppressive cultural narratives. Such use of Rockwell hardly seems surprising with respect to prevailing public memory about his work. After all, the term *Rockwellian* often operates as a metonym for, at best, sentimental, idealized, and hopeful depictions of life in the United States or, at worst, simplistic and exclusionary figurations of the nation—case in point, one review of Solomon's biography characterizes the "right-wing activists" associated with the Tea Party as desiring a "'Rockwellian' myth of

---

71. Frascina, "Advertisements for Itself," 75, 82.

America."[72] Yet we may also find evidence of other uses of Rockwell's work that challenge hegemonic cultural narratives about identity in the US and that echo the political project of this chapter.

In 1994 cartoonist Alison Bechdel parodied Rockwell's *Freedom from Want* in the catalog for her series *Dykes to Watch Out For* (*DTWOF*) depicting a group of lesbians gathered around a table for a birthday celebration, and the cover of the 2008 anthologized collection of Bechdel's *DTWOF* comics features a parodic version of Rockwell's *The Gossips,* in which recurrent characters from *DTWOF* circulate a rumor that begins and ends with Bechdel's animated version of herself. More recently, the artist Maurice "Pops" Peterson turned to Rockwell's art as inspiration for mixed-media images that critique racial injustice and heteronormativity in US culture. Peterson's *Freedom from What* (2014), for example, modifies *Freedom from Fear,* depicting African American parents putting their son and daughter to bed at a moment when they must fear their children's vulnerability to anti-Black racism. The father, who anxiously looks through his children's bedroom window to a threatening world outside, holds a newspaper with the headline "I Can't Breathe," referencing Eric Garner's death at the hands of white police officers. Peterson's *It Hasn't Ended* borrows Rockwell's image of Ruby Bridges entering her newly integrated school amid racist threats, from *The Problem We All Live With,* and transports Ruby's image to contemporary Ferguson, Missouri—her walk to school disrupted by evidence of violence and social injustice. Peterson also created a photographic version of Rockwell's *Freedom from Want,* portraying himself, a man who is Black and gay, along with his white partner and their family.[73]

The subjects of anti-Black racism and police brutality have inspired other Rockwell parodies as well. In 2015 *Mad* magazine published an illustration by Richard Williams that imitates Rockwell's *The Runaway*.[74] In the original, a

---

72. Davis, "Mi Gosh and By-heck."

73. Photographer Maggie Meiners also created a series of photographs that reimagines Rockwell paintings, in light of contemporary contexts, called *Revisiting Rockwell*. For example, *Captain Carrie* refigures Rosie the Riveter as a woman in the US Army, *Dream Act* recasts Ruby Bridges as a Latinx child being detained by border patrol agents, and *It Went Viral* replays the scene of gossip spreading from cell phone user to cell phone user via text messages.

74. Williams was one of *Mad* magazine's most prolific cover artists, and many of his images featured parodies of Hollywood films, stars, and celebrity culture, as well as other parodies of Rockwell's work, including a 2004 reimagining of Rockwell's *Marriage License* (1955), which features two gay white men preparing to wed, and a 2007 spoof of Rockwell's *Freedom from Want,* which features celebrity women Lindsay Lohan, Nicole Ritchie, Britney Spears, and Paris Hilton in various states of intoxication at the Thanksgiving table—much to the horror of the older white couple that hosts them. This *Mad* cover adopts a cynical attitude toward celebrity akin to that in the film *Norman Rockwell's Shuffleton's Barbershop,* framing fame as antithetical to and destructive of family values.

young white boy who has run away from home sits next to a white male police officer at a soda shop, as the officer comforts the child and persuades him to return home. In Williams's version, a young Black boy sits fearfully next to a heavily armed white police officer with military-grade gear. The magazine retweeted the image in 2017 after President Donald Trump lifted the ban on military gear for local police. Similarly, in anticipation of the 2016 presidential election, political cartoonist Mr. Fish recirculated his 2013 parody of Rockwell's *Triple Self-Portrait,* which is titled *Through a Looking Glass Darkly* and features a hooded member of the Ku Klux Klan painting an image of himself, based on his mirrored reflection, as comic book superhero Captain America.[75] These parodies, which aim to illustrate the cruelty of white supremacy and the Trump administration, draw their rhetorical force from their contrast with the empathy and compassion that typify Rockwell's work.

Beginning in 2016, a large-scale multimedia project, *For Freedoms,* turned to Rockwell's work for inspiration, featuring the work of over eight hundred artists. Created by Hank Willis Thomas and Eric Gottesman, this campaign involves exhibitions and public programming around the United States that address such issues as homophobia, racism, campaign reform, gun control, and reproductive rights. Some of the works are original pieces; others are parodies of Rockwell's works, including different versions of the *Four Freedoms* images that represent diversity and inclusivity in terms of ethnicity, race, gender, and sexuality. Many of the images also include celebrities of color such as Rosario Dawson, Public Enemy's Chuck D, Jesse Williams, Van Jones, Michael Ealy, and Saul Williams. Like Peterson's works, many of these parodic repetitions feature Black and Brown parents fearfully putting their children to bed in an iteration of *Freedom from Fear,* as well as same-sex and/or interracial couples setting the Thanksgiving scene in *Freedom from Want.*

Such images exemplify the freedom of expression that much of Rockwell's work might be said to encourage. The parodic images manipulate Rockwell's art to make new meanings and offer cultural critique, but this chapter argues that such critical resources already circulate in Rockwell's work itself. Perhaps

---

75. Just one day prior, Mr. Fish also posted *Go Back to Sleep, America—Nothing to See Here,* in which Donald Trump wears a Captain America costume with sticks of dynamite strapped around his chest and his hand on the detonator. This allusion to the figure of Captain America matters because it was the *Captain America* comic book series that introduced one of the first Black comic book characters, The Falcon, whose story invokes histories and practices of anti-Black racism. Rockwell has other connections to superheroic imagery as well. In 1928 Rockwell published *Uncle Sam Flying* for the *Post,* depicting Uncle Sam as a superheroic figure flying alongside military planes. Comic book illustrator Alex Ross imitated this image in 2011 to create *Andy Warhol,* which depicts the artist flying through the sky. Digital artist Marco D'Alfonso also illustrates images of superheroes in Rockwell's style, posing them on mocked-up covers of the *Post.*

another indication of this potential already within Rockwell's work can be seen in a November 2016 photograph taken at the White House. During the first meeting of President-elect Trump and President Barack Obama in the Oval Office, Kevin Lamarque photographed the two men in a commonly staged setting: both in armchairs in front of the white marble fireplace. Framing them on the walls behind them are three pieces of art: Rembrandt Peale's portrait of George Washington (c. 1823) above the mantle between them, Thomas Moran's *Three Tetons* (1895) on the wall behind Obama, and Rockwell's *Statue of Liberty* behind Trump. Rockwell's painting, which first appeared on the cover of *The Saturday Evening Post* in 1946 and which was donated to the permanent collection of the White House in 1994 by Spielberg, features five men, one of them Black, repairing Lady Liberty's torch; the angle of the torch and the stations of the laboring men evoke Joe Rosenthal's iconic *Raising the Flag on Iwo Jima* (1945), and both images have circulated in public memory as characterizing the United States as a site where diverse people can come together to support freedom.

Shortly after Lamarque's photograph first appeared, Rockwell's granddaughter Abigail Rockwell published an essay on *Huffington Post* asking, "Who moved the Norman Rockwell in the Oval Office?"[76] Rockwell notes that her grandfather's painting is "clearly too small" for the space and originally hung on the other side of the room, to the right of the Resolute Desk. She concludes that the move was a strategic effort to encourage Trump to be more inclusive toward people of color and immigrants. Rockwell contends that the White House staff slipped the painting into a new location in the same way that her grandfather sneaked a man of color into his *Post* image, despite the fact that the magazine discouraged representations of people of color. Other news outlets reported on Abigail Rockwell's article and similarly concluded that the painting was meant as a message to Trump as a sort of hoax or performance art piece.[77]

As it turns out, Abigail Rockwell was right that *Statue of Liberty* originally hung by Obama's desk and was moved, but she was wrong about the timing. The painting was moved on February 7, 2014, and was not, therefore,

---

76. Rockwell, "Who Moved the Norman Rockwell?"

77. See Boucher, "Did Obama Troll Donald Trump?"; and Jones, "Norman Rockwell's Statue of Liberty." It is worth reiterating, then, that critics have framed Rockwell's art both as complicit in the rise of Trump-era politics and as a rejoinder to them. For examples of articles that cite Rockwell's complicity in or contributions to the increasing presence of right-wing ideology in US culture, see Smee, "Nostalgia, Norman Rockwell, and . . . Donald Trump?"; and Jones, *The End*.

intended as a message to Trump.[78] This error does not, however, change the fact that the placement of this image does significant rhetorical work both in Lamarque's image of Trump and Obama or in many of the other images in which it appears in its various locations in the Oval Office—including a 2010 image of Obama discussing the repeal of "Don't Ask, Don't Tell," a 2012 image of Obama bending over so a young Black boy can touch his hair, and a 2013 image of Obama meeting with seven DREAMers. The presence of *Statue of Liberty* in such images illustrates the capacity of Rockwell's work to argue for acceptance and inclusion—a fact further demonstrated by Obama's choice to hang *The Problem We All Live With* in the White House during part of his two terms as president.[79]

Although the articulation of conventional ideologies in Rockwell's *Four Freedoms* posters is in some ways quintessentially "Rockwellian," this chapter has threaded these images together to inspire new interpretations of Rockwell's original works, new understandings of what counts as "Rockwellian," and new visions of what "Freedom from Fear" and "Freedom from Want" might look like. Those characters who exist between various gender and sexual categories may allow viewers to imagine lives not governed entirely by compulsory and exclusionary norms and to envision pleasures that transcend extant categories and expectations. These works make it possible to imagine worlds free from the fear of violating compulsory gender norms and free from want for queer forms of worldmaking.

While Solomon's biography of Rockwell adopts a suspicious attitude toward the artist's work and life, this chapter has argued for the importance of balancing skepticism with generous reading strategies, which Rockwell's images themselves encourage. Both Solomon and I deploy interpretive strategies that depend on reading Rockwell's work closely with an eye toward its

---

78. The White House staff moved *Statue of Liberty* to accommodate two new Edward Hopper paintings, *Cobb's Barns, South Truro* (1930–33) and *Burly Cobb's House, South Truro* (1930–33), on loan from the Whitney Museum of American Art. The Rockwell piece assumed the location of a printed copy of the Emancipation Proclamation, which required removal for preservation purposes.

79. This painting was the first of Rockwell's works purchased by NRM for its permanent collection in 1975. The museum loaned the painting to the White House in 2011. A reproduction of this painting also played a significant role in the O. J. Simpson trial. During efforts to restage Simpson's home with more signifiers of cultural Blackness, attorney Johnny Cochrane replaced Simpson's print of a Rockwell painting of white boys playing football with *The Problem We All Live With*. It is worth noting that Rockwell's painting strategically darkened Ruby Bridge's skin tone to prevent white viewers from ignoring the image's argument about racism. That artistic choice has problematic ethical and political implications as exemplified, for instance, by *Time*'s choice to darken Simpson's mug shot for its "An American Tragedy" cover story.

depths of meaning—which is to say, we both seek to read between Rockwell's lines. Within the critical disposition adopted by this chapter, however, reading between the lines aims less at revealing hidden truths or desires and more at striving to see the various categories, norms, and social positions *between* which Rockwell's characters may find themselves. Rockwell's body of work becomes a resource for complicating theories of normativity and its interstices and for encouraging nuanced and empathetic attention to the lives that his art imagines and reflects. Furthermore, Rockwell's fame and his artistic interest in stardom illustrate the value of celebrity for thinking about the complex, changing, always vulnerable, and sometimes precarious positions that subjects inhabit over the course of their lives.

INTERSTITIAL 1

A Chapter on AIDS

Norman Rockwell's *Facts of Life,* originally published as a 1951 *Saturday Evening Post* cover, features a white father introducing the topic of sex to his red-faced son. With a sex education book opened across his knee, the father leans in as he speaks to his son, who hides behind tightly clenched fists. The image features mostly black, white, and gray hues, including on the father's and son's clothing, the book, their chair, a framed silhouette hanging behind them, and cats gathered around them. The exceptions to this color palette are a red wall in the background and the son's rosy cheeks. In 1987 the AIDS Action Committee (AAC) reappropriated the famous *Facts of Life* painting for an AIDS awareness poster with the caption "Don't Forget the Chapter on AIDS!" On the eve of the internet's emergence, posters were key sites for shaping public discourse about AIDS.[1] AAC chose the Rockwell image because of Rockwell's fame and "precisely because he is associated with family values."[2] The prominence of the red wall also makes this image a fitting choice, as that color was emerging as an important signifier within AIDS activism, metonymically signifying both blood and intense emotions, including desire, love, and anger.

The poster typifies what Daniel Harris describes as two patterns in AIDS activism of the late 1980s and early 1990s: use of folk-art sensibilities and reli-

---

1. Brier and Wizinsky, "Worlds of Signification," 9.
2. "Rockwell Cover."

ance on the cultural capital of celebrities. Harris cites two examples of AIDS awareness campaigns "modeled on the pictorial conventions of folk art": Cleve Jones's AIDS Memorial Quilt, which Harris describes as conjuring the "archaic innocence of folk traditions straight out of a pastoral world of buggies and butter churns," and a controversial 1992 advertisement for the clothing line Benetton.[3] The Benetton advertisement colorized a black-and-white photojournalistic image, originally published in *Life*, that shows David Kirby as he lay dying of AIDS in a hospice bed beneath a framed painting of Jesus while his sobbing father embraced him.[4] Like the Rockwell image, Benetton's ad emphasizes father–son relationships as important sites for AIDS awareness and acceptance.

To this assemblage of folksy AIDS Americana, we might add the Red Ribbon Project, which used red ribbons fastened in a simple loop to promote awareness of the epidemic. Initiated in 1991 by the Visual AIDS Artists' Collective, the red ribbons were modeled after the yellow ribbons used as symbols of dedication to loved ones in the US military, as in the 1917 song "Round Her Neck She Wears a Yeller Ribbon (For Her Lover Who Is Far, Far Away)" or the John Wayne film *She Wore a Yellow Ribbon* (John Ford, 1949). Visual AIDS organized thousands of "ribbon bees" to assemble ribbons, recalling the colonial practice of collective quilting.[5] These approximations of folk-art sensibilities metonymically signal associations with family, domesticity, and even the "iconography of the Christian church," framing the AIDS epidemic as something that white heterosexual people should care about.[6]

As much as the down-home and domestic sensibilities of folk were central to 1990s-era AIDS activism, so too were the high-fashion and highfalutin stylistics of Hollywood. Celebrities, argues Harris, became "unofficial statesmen" and "glamorous panhandlers" for AIDS research and development, with scores of famous faces appearing at events and in magazine spreads to raise funds. What resulted was an admixture of Hollywood opulence with "kitschy

---

3. Harris, *Rise and Fall*, 222–27, 220.

4. Therese Frare's original photograph, originally titled *Final Moments* before being retitled as *The Faces of AIDS*, became one of the most well-known images of the AIDS epidemic. See Span, "Colored with Controversy"; and Cosgrove, "Photo."

5. "Red Ribbon Project."

6. Harris, *Rise and Fall*, 227. Activists using the internet in the 1990s also deployed folk sensibilities to make the newly emergent World Wide Web seem more welcoming. Andrew Wood and Tyrone Adams argue that Kathy Daliberti's *Yellow Ribbon* website, which advocated for her husband's release from Iraqi custody following the Persian Gulf War, used not only the trope of the yellow ribbon but also the "quilt and quilting as metonyms" to cast the internet as "an environment of community, liberation, and safety." See Wood and Adams, "Embracing the Machine," 225.

public appeals designed to elicit pity" and family-values rhetoric from such stars as Elton John, Elizabeth Taylor, and Madonna.[7] For example, the Red Ribbon Project depended heavily on celebrity culture for its success, having first gained visibility on national television at the forty-fifth Annual Tony Awards, when numerous attendees and presenters wore ribbons. The distribution of the ribbons at the Tonys stemmed from the hope that the campaign could, Jesse Green argues, "persuade mass audiences of the existence of AIDS and . . . destigmatize it by associating it with stars."[8] Soon the red ribbons featured prominently at star-studded events, including the Grammys, Emmys, and Oscars, leading *Brandweek* to call the ribbon the "most powerful icon of the '90s."[9]

In 1993 HBO aired *And the Band Played On* (Roger Spottiswoode), which was based on the 1987 book of the same name by journalist Randy Shilts, who died of AIDS in February 1994.[10] Featuring well-known actors including Matthew Modine, Alan Alda, Richard Gere, and Anjelica Huston, *And the Band Played On* depicts epidemiologist Don Francis's quest to discover the truth about the so-called gay plague. It ends with Elton John's "The Last Song" playing under a montage of celebrities who contracted or even died of the disease, including Rock Hudson, Anthony Perkins, Arthur Ashe, Freddy Mercury, Magic Johnson, Halston, and Willi Smith. Like the AAC Rockwell poster and the Benetton ad, "The Last Song" focuses on father–son relationships, recounting the story of a father who comes to accept his son's sexuality and "things that were never spoken" just as the child loses his life to AIDS.

Perhaps the apotheosis of this intersection of folk sensibility with celebrity culture was Jonathan Demme's 1993 film *Philadelphia*. Starring Tom Hanks and Denzel Washington, *Philadelphia* tells the story of the uneasy friendship that develops between Andy, a white gay man with AIDS, and Joe, a straight Black man. When Andy is fired because of his AIDS diagnosis, he enlists Joe as his attorney in his fight against workplace discrimination. The film relies heavily of the star power of its two leads but also references the folksy sensibilities of other AIDS awareness efforts. It boasts a folk-rock-laden soundtrack featuring such Americana legends as Bruce Springsteen and Neil Young, and it casts Joe, not unlike the abashed preteen in the Rockwell poster, as a neophyte

---

7. Harris, *Rise and Fall,* 222, 223. See also Chouliaraki, "Theatricality of Humanitarianism"; and Kapoor, *Celebrity Humanitarianism.*

8. Green, "Year of the Ribbon."

9. Fleury, "Most Powerful Icon." The ribbon eventually earned a spot in the Museum of Modern Art's Design Collection in 2015.

10. One month after Shilts's passing, NBC aired an edited version of the movie, with a parental advisory. NBC had originally bought the rights to the book in 1989 but dropped the project before HBO and producer Aaron Spelling picked it up. See Weinstein, "NBC Takes."

who must be gently ushered into his understanding of AIDS. Famously, when he encounters unfamiliar ideas or experiences, Joe says, "Explain it to me like I'm a four-year-old."

Promoting the film, Hanks and Washington appeared on the cover of the January 1994 issue of *Premiere* magazine. It is this issue with which the Kevin Bacon game has been erroneously associated—likely because the issue features an article about a breakout performer from *Six Degrees of Separation* (Fred Schepisi, 1993), with a cover line that reads "Will Smith Gets Fresh in 'Six Degrees.'" The photograph of Hanks and Washington appears in black and white, as does much of the text on the cover. Like the Rockwell poster, the only other color that appears is red, which is used for both *Premiere*'s masthead and the AIDS awareness ribbons pinned to both stars' shirts. The cover for this issue deploys a complex network of metonymies. Literally, the choice to use black-and-white photography and to edit the image so that the ribbon appears in bright red emphasizes the fact that *Philadelphia* is a film about AIDS.[11] Figuratively, the use of black-and-white photography conveys an impression of *Philadelphia* as a historically significant and artistic film. The palette also concurrently encourages and discourages attention to race. On the one hand, it reductively defines racial difference along only black and white lines. On the other hand, it also invites a color-blind reading of the film, as if to literalize the euphemism that one does not "see color." In such a postracial fantasy, race might be imagined as not mattering to the film's story of homophobia and AIDS, even though *Philadelphia* relies heavily on racialized logics. For example, the film's characterization of Washington's character as homophobic recalls long-standing assumptions about homophobia within Black cultures.[12]

Beyond their similar release dates and proximity on this magazine cover, *Six Degrees of Separation* and *Philadelphia* have much in common: both address same-sex desire, register traumas of the AIDS epidemic, and tell stories of Black men navigating unfamiliar terrain alongside wealthy white urbanites. For instance, while AIDS occupies a central place in *Philadelphia*, its specter can be felt in *Six Degrees of Separation*, as illustrated when Ouisa

---

11. Within this issue of *Premiere*, ten advertisements deploy this exact visual affectation, including ads for Ford Ranger trucks, Diesel clothing, Folger's coffee, Oliver Stone's film *Heaven & Earth*, and Kate Bush's *The Red Shoes* album. Most notable is an advertisement for Spielberg's *Schindler's List* with a black-and-white photograph that includes a red coat worn by a young girl. The colorization of the coat also occurs within Spielberg's black-and-white film, operating as a metonym for the bloodshed and inhumanity that characterized the Holocaust. The similar aesthetics of the *Premiere* cover photograph and the iconography of *Schindler's List* suggest metonymic connections between the tragedies of the AIDS epidemic and the Holocaust as embodied, for instance, by Larry Kramer's famous description of the AIDS crisis as the "gay Holocaust."

12. See Johnson, "Specter"; and Connell, "Contesting Racialized Discourses."

asks Paul, who is both gay and a sex worker, "Do you have AIDS? Are you infected?" David Hampton, the actual person on whom Smith's character was based, did die of an AIDS-related complication ten years after the film was released. Additionally, while *Six Degrees of Separation* hinges on Paul's entrée into the seemingly exclusively white world of Manhattan's elites, *Philadelphia* charts Joe's anxious introduction to gay culture, which the film casts as mostly white.

Philadelphia and *Six Degrees of Separation* also have an extratextual link through the offscreen relationship between Washington and Smith, which this issue of *Premiere* emphasizes. Not only does the magazine position Washington as a father figure to Smith; it also suggests an analogy between Washington's fictional character in *Philadelphia* and Smith-the-actor in *Six Degrees of Separation,* framing both as homophobic. At issue in Veronica Chambers's *Premiere* article about Smith, entitled "Willing," is the actor's now famous confession that, based on advice from Washington, he refused to shoot a same-sex love scene for *Six Degrees of Separation*.[13] Chambers discusses Washington's influence on Smith at length, which is significant given Washington's position in the issue's cover story about AIDS and homophobia. Chambers's article also includes a pull quote, printed in bold type along the top of two pages, that reads "Smith says Denzel Washington told him, 'Don't be kissing no man.'"[14] While most of the pull quote is printed in black type, Washington's name appears in bright red; this choice not only calls attention to Washington's complicity in Smith's decision but also animates metonymic recognition of the *Philadelphia* cover story.[15] This emphasis on Washington's rhetoric and Smith's refusal to kiss a man onscreen notably obscures the fact that Hanks refused to kiss Antonio Banderas, the actor playing his partner in *Philadelphia*, which neither article addresses.[16]

---

13. Chambers, "Willing."

14. In a *Rolling Stone* interview, Demme apologizes for Washington, declaring that Hollywood actors cannot provoke audiences like Larry Kramer's polemical work does. See DeCurtis, "Jonathan Demme."

15. As his career progressed, Smith seems to have become aware of the political implications of pull quotes. In a 2013 interview with Claire Hoffman for *New York* magazine, he references a past pull quote that claimed he didn't discipline his children, lamenting how that remark was taken out of context and turned into a soundbite. He then directly asks Hoffman, "What's the blurb gonna be from this one?" See Hoffman, "Will Smith."

16. Despite the fact that *Philadelphia* casts Hanks's and Banderas's characters as loving and committed to each other, the film shows little to no amorous connection between the men, except for one slow dance at a party, an implied kiss in a hospital room, and a kiss on the hand as Hanks's character lays dying. Banderas reported to *Inside the Actor's Studio* host, James Lipton, that he had been willing to shoot a kissing scene but that Hanks had declined. In his Best Actor acceptance speech for his role in *Philadelphia,* Hanks aims, perhaps, to counter perceptions of him as homophobic by quipping that Banderas is the only person he would "trade" for his wife Rita Wilson.

The coincidence of Washington's place in the magazine and the emphasis within "Willing" on Washington's place in Smith's life may be just that—coincidence, but the conspicuous attention to Smith's choice to take Washington's arguably homophobic advice suggests a potentially castigatory attitude toward both Black actors. The *Philadelphia* cover story by Jesse Green, who earlier declared 1992 the "Year of the Ribbon," corroborates such a suspicious reading.[17] The article, "The Philadelphia Experiment," asserts that "art, profit, and AIDS awareness" can "coexist in the same movie."[18] The article devotes much, rather hagiographic, attention to white director Demme, white screenwriter Ron Nyswaner, and white actor Hanks but only one paragraph to Washington, whose quoted response seems to do as much, if not more, to undercut the film as it does to promote it. While Green quotes Hanks as predicting that *Philadelphia* "will last because it tells its truth for its time," he quotes Washington as remarking, "I hope *Philadelphia* makes a difference, but let's not go overboard either." Washington pessimistically concludes, "It's only a movie. It ain't gonna change the world."

Chambers's article also critiques Smith for his supposed homophobia, repeatedly reminding readers that Smith was not willing to kiss another man while shooting *Six Degrees of Separation*, as illustrated by the article's tagline: "To move beyond the *Fresh Prince* and into a movie career, Will Smith says he'll do anything. Well, almost anything." Framing Smith as something of a hustler himself, *Premiere* also includes a teaser quotation in the table of contents, in which Smith admits, "I waited till they gave me my check to tell them I wasn't going to do what the script called for." Chambers ends her article with Smith's declaration that he would "do anything" in order "to be considered for the dramatic, artistic pieces" associated with actors like Washington. This framing suggests a parallel between Smith, his fictional character in the film, and the person on whom the character is based—all of whom wanted to be taken seriously in the art world. Instead of giving Smith the last word, however, Chambers concludes that he would do anything "except, perhaps, kiss a man."[19] Thus, *Premiere*'s punitive attitude toward Washington also seems to structure its portrayal of Smith.

Taken together, the treatments of Washington and Smith might be understood as reaffirming metonymic associations between Black masculinity and

---

17. Green, "Year of the Ribbon." Green is a theater and cultural critic who wrote in the *New York Times* and *New York* magazine in the 1990s about gay culture and AIDS. See also Green, "Flirting with Suicide." He also wrote a memoir about his experiences becoming a father as a gay man. See Green, *Velveteen Father*.

18. Green, "Philadelphia Experiment."

19. Chambers, "Willing," 77.

homophobia. The articles also do not acknowledge the risks that men of color face in Hollywood, wherein, for instance, a Black actor might experience more fallout than a white actor for the choice to play an LGBTQ character. As a result, a suspicious reading of this issue of *Premiere* might find the magazine guilty of being more invested in a rather self-congratulatory story about (white) Hollywood than in a critical assessment of the double binds faced by Black actors in the industry. We might also understand these articles as illustrative of paranoia about the network as a form. *Premiere*'s disciplinary treatment of Washington and the attendant implication that Smith "caught" his homophobia from Washington imply that networks may become, at best, closed systems or, at worst, dangerous mechanisms of transmission. Such affects replay worries at the heart of *Six Degrees of Separation* itself, which— not unlike *Philadelphia*—is a text haunted by anxieties about transmission as a potential consequence of network form.

Note, for instance, the curious incident of the dog statue in the park in *Six Degrees of Separation*: much of the narrative takes place next to the Central Park sculpture commemorating Balto, a dog who earned his fame stopping the spread of a communicable disease. In addition to referencing the literal transmission of diseases, this narrative device echoes the film's depiction of stories spreading like contagions. For example, Flan worries that circulating rumors about Paul being his illegitimate son will damage his social and economic positions, and the Kittredges go to great lengths to uncover how their private information was leaked to Paul. The text also constructs Paul's entrance into the lives of Manhattan's elite as a kind of infection itself. Like a virus, Paul infiltrates the Kittredges' social circle and begins to replicate their way of life. He learns information about the lives and habits of the Kittredges' wealthy friends, as well as how to talk, dress, and think like them. Just as Smith purportedly aims to imitate Washington, Paul deploys an imagined association with Poitier to enable his replication of and connections to the Kittredges. Paul then shares this information and mimetic performance with other struggling artists so that they too may break into the world of Manhattan's elite.

These literal and figurative concerns about virality resonate with what Wendy Hui Kyong Chun describes as a (racialized and sexualized) paranoia in the 1990s about the "deviance" of networked media and their capacity to circulate "obscene material," such as pornography, and infect private spaces and personal computers with dangerous, or perverse, materials.[20] The twinning of these concerns about the spreadability of both information and disease also echoes Paula Treichler's description of AIDS as an "epidemic of signi-

---

20. Chun, *Control and Freedom*.

fication": a "transmissible lethal disease" that was also a web of "meanings or signification."[21] Concern about the transmission of information also had particular significance in the early 1990s, when public discourse about the internet was increasing, often expressing anxiety about privacy, data security, identity theft, and attacks related to the World Wide Web.[22]

Six Degrees of Separation and *Philadelphia* thus not only share temporal propinquity and Black actors who were famously linked to one another; they also similarly embody affects of paranoia that, as Janet Staiger notes, characterized US culture in the late 1980s and early 1990s in relation to both the spread of AIDS and the emergence of networked media. It was also this context, particularly as it related to AIDS, that informed Sedgwick's theorizations of paranoid reading styles.[23] My interpretation of these films and their treatments in *Premiere* has itself taken a paranoid turn, offering suspicious critiques of their intersecting gender, sexual, and racial politics. But paranoid and reparative readings always exist in relation to one another. Attention to the ideological problematics of these texts does not foreclose the possibility that they may also offer useful considerations of ontologies of subjectivity and the politics of identity. For example, as much as they seem to fetishize white victimization at the expense of attention to Black vulnerability, *Philadelphia*, *Six Degrees of Separation*, and this issue of *Premiere* also make space for considering conditions of precarity created by anti-Black racism in Hollywood.

Such space can be seen, for example, in *Premiere*'s attention to the "small worldness" of Smith's and Washington's connection. The emphasis on Washington's influence on Smith makes clear that Black actors in Hollywood have historically had few options for Black mentors because of the history of anti-Blackness in the industry. Such a perspective seems reinforced by Chambers, a Black woman journalist, who has stated that she was hired as the only Black person on staff at *Premiere* because "Spike Lee insisted on having black journalists on his set."[24] It also matters that Washington has himself described

---

21. Treichler, "AIDS, Homophobia, and Biomedical Discourse," 32.
22. Consider, for example, the following headlines from the *New York Times* in 1993 and 1994: "Computer Insecurity on the Rise: Intruders Set Snares on Data Highway," "Computer Jokes and Threats Ignite Debate on Anonymity," "Software That Pits Alarmists Against Devil's Advocates: A Test for Chinks in Network Armor Could Also Be a Hacker's Lance," "A Rise in Internet Break-Ins Sets Off a Security Alarm," "A Secret Computer Code Is Out: Key to Data Security Appears on Internet," and "Newcomers to Internet Need Combat Training."
23. Kerr and O'Rourke, "Sedgwick Sense and Sensibility."
24. Ledbetter, "Unbearable Whiteness." Further evidence for this reading can also be found in another article written by Chambers in this 1994 issue that directly addresses racism in Hollywood. See Chambers, "On-Color Remarks."

Poitier as a significant mentor to and influence on himself.[25] Thus, the assertion by the actual David Hampton that he had only three famous Black actors to claim as his father resonates quite literally with Smith's and Washington's positions within Hollywood. Even long after Smith was established as a bona fide star, he continued to frame Washington as a father figure. For example, in 2022, after he made the controversial choice to slap comedian Chris Rock on stage during the Oscars telecast in response to a joke Rock made about Jada Pinkett Smith, Smith apologized during his Best Actor acceptance speech, referencing spiritual counsel he received from Washington (who was also nominated for the award).

Washington's suspicious attitude toward Hollywood's capacity to effect social change might also be understood as illustrating disappointment that commercial films have limited capacity to activate change because of their inclination to appeal to hegemonic audiences and cultural norms, including representations of sexuality and treatments of racism and racial difference. In other words, we might read this pair of articles as both critiquing the homophobia implied by Washington's and Smith's choices *and* registering Smith's and Washington's (and Chambers's) relative positions of vulnerability within Hollywood's racialized hierarchy, which has a long history of constraining and exploiting people of color.[26] Washington was not alone in his expression of cynicism about Hollywood's capacity to change public discourse about AIDS, which was echoed by many people living with HIV/AIDS and/or working as activists. For example, the inaugural 1994 issue of *POZ* magazine, a periodical for folks living with HIV and AIDS, asked whether the critical and commercial success of *Philadelphia* would lead to a "Hollywood bandwagon." Questioning the likelihood of "Philly the sequel," the article indicates that the industry's commitment to the "bottom line" over "art or social conscience" made such a possibility doubtful.[27] The fact that the other AIDS projects the article mentions—*Angels in America* (Mike Nichols, 2003) and *The Normal*

---

25. For example, in 1998 Washington said that it was advice from Poitier that helped shape his career. See "Denzel Washington" and Rottenberg, "Denzel Washington Reflects." In 2002 Washington won a Best Actor Oscar for his role in *Training Day* at the same ceremony at which Poitier—the first Black actor to receive a Best Actor Academy Award—received a lifetime achievement honor, which Washington presented to him. In his acceptance speech, Washington acknowledges both this coincidence and his relationship with Poitier, stating, "I'll always be chasing you, Sidney. I'll always be following in your footsteps. There's nothing I'd rather do, sir." That same year, Halle Berry became the first Black woman to win the Best Actress Award, and Smith was also nominated for Best Actor for his portrayal of Muhammad Ali.
26. Washington, *Blasian Invasion*, 19–20.
27. Davidson, "Philly, the Sequel?"

Heart (Ryan Murphy, 2013)—would take, respectively, almost ten and twenty years to get made suggests that Washington's cynicism was not off the mark.

There was also, at the time of *Philadelphia*'s release, skepticism about the Red Ribbon Project. While some celebrated the iconicity of the red ribbon, others lamented its ubiquity and associations with celebrity. In 1993 some HIV/AIDS activists warned against the "tyranny of the red ribbon," wherein the ribbon itself and the celebrities who wore it were celebrated at the expense of actual activism or policy change on behalf of people with HIV and AIDS.[28] Such concerns echo what Harris describes as the late 1990s "kitschification" of AIDS, in which images of the disease/d were exploited as a "vehicle for advancing the economic interests" of major corporations. But, Harris reminds us, the reliance on celebrity culture was a tactic—imperfect though it was—that was owed to the homophobic refusals on the part of the Reagan and Bush administrations to respond to the public health crisis.[29]

This chain of texts and celebrity appearances reveals both the limitations and affordances of the celebrity-industrial complex for effecting social change. Celebrity-driven activism is likely to be, as Harris suggests, harnessed for economic gain or used to garner cultural capital; moreover, when celebrities benefit from not only the privilege of fame but also the privileges of whiteness and/or cisheterosexuality, these efforts usually involve little, if any, disruption to normative structures of power. Such limitations were on display more recently in 2020, when more than a dozen white Hollywood actors took part in a PSA titled "#ITakeResponsibility."[30] The video features a series of black-and-white clips of such celebrities as Kristen Bell, Julianne Moore, Aaron Paul, and Stanley Tucci wearing black shirts and apologizing for their complicity in anti-Black racism. The PSA prompted fierce and immediate backlash, including a parody that called it out for its lack of action in response to racism and its fetishization of white celebrities as saviors. The video illustrates what Francesca Sobande describes as white-dominated celebrity culture's affinity for "flexing" its "power and authority" rather than "relinquishing" it.[31]

The limitations of celebrity culture to counter hegemonic discourses and structures are compounded by the fact that the star system remains embedded

---

28. Peyser, "Tyranny."

29. Harris, *Rise and Fall*, 219–20, 223.

30. This video came just weeks after the celebrity-helmed cover of John Lennon's "Imagine," which was offered in response to the COVID-19 pandemic. In March 2020, while in quarantine, movie star Gal Gadot gathered members of her celebrity social network to sing parts of the song for a stitched-together viral Instagram video that elicited considerable online critique for being out of touch with most people's lived experiences of the pandemic, leading the *New York Times* to joke, "It is proof that even if no one meets up in person, horribleness can spread." See Caramanica, "'Imagine' Cover."

31. Sobande, "Celebrity Whitewashing," 134.

in white supremacist and cisheterosexist cultures, such that some famous folks experience more privilege and license than others. As Spring-Serenity Duvall and Nicole Heckemeyer demonstrate, "Celebrity culture is defined by both the constant visibility and invisibility of whiteness."[32] As a result, contends Sarah J. Jackson, "Black celebrities are subject to incredibly limited conditions for inclusion and acceptance," which often results in their being "vilified for their activism while being pressured to remain apolitical."[33] For instance, Duvall and Heckemeyer note that despite Poitier's stardom and acclaim, his position within the celebrity-industrial complex remained "precarious and inseparable from the ongoing criminalization of blackness through systemic racism."[34] Such constraints were more recently evinced in 2022, when Black filmmaker and director of *Black Panther* (2018) Ryan Coogler was mistaken for a bank robber while attempting to withdraw money from his account.

Critical attention to inequities within even the most privileged and elite networks demonstrates and may intervene against the normalization of such oppression. Moreover, even as celebrity culture's capacity to engage in ideological critique may be constrained, its networked and metonymic form offers opportunities to counter hegemonic constructions of subjecthood in US culture. Like metonymic criticism itself, the content of celebrity culture might be deployed to reaffirm oppressive discourses and practices, but its intertextual and associative form undercuts the essentializing logics that typically undergird oppressive ideologies. As Alexander Montgomery argues, network analysis reveals all structures and subjects to be defined by conditions of mutual dependence, "transmission and co-constitution," and "patterns of association . . . that can define, enable, and restrict."[35] Analysis of celebrity culture has unique affordances for promoting theories of subjectivity as performative and structured by mimesis and citationality, relationality and interdependence—as illustrated, for example, by the multiple dyads of father figures and symbolic sons within the textual formation under analysis here. Just as cultural discourses about the AIDS virus, as Treichler argues, activate and challenge such "semantic oppositions" as "self and other," metonymic criticism of celebrity culture troubles discourses of individualism and fantasies of self-sufficiency, suggesting that there is never a clear or certain answer to the question "What is self and what is not self?"[36]

---

32. Duvall and Heckemeyer, "#BlackLivesMatter," 395.
33. Jackson, *Black Celebrity*, 1.
34. Duvall and Heckemeyer, "#BlackLivesMatter," 396.
35. Montgomery, "Centrality," 20.
36. Treichler, "AIDS, Homophobia, and Biomedical Discourse," 64.

CHAPTER 3

Terms and Conditions

Reflections on and of Black Fame in the Case of Will Smith

> Will Smith is no more "real" than Paul—they're both characters that were invented, practiced, and performed, reinforced, and refined by friends, loved ones, and the external world. What you think of as your "self" is a fragile construct.
> —Will Smith

> *Will Smith was in* Hancock *with Charlize Theron, who was in* Trapped *with Kevin Bacon.*

In December 1993, a cinematic kiss became a source of controversy, not because it happened but because it did not. In *Six Degrees of Separation*, Will Smith's character Paul has an erotic encounter with a man. Because Smith refused to kiss a man in the film, Schepisi shot the scene to imply but never show a kiss. Criticized for the refusal, Smith publicly apologized and famously attributed the choice to guidance from Denzel Washington. That purported advice reflects cultural norms imposed on Black masculinity, acknowledging that actors of color face higher risks than their white counterparts. As Sarah J. Jackson argues, Black celebrities face extraordinary "public scrutiny" and heightened expectations of normativity, including heteronormativity.[1]

Vershawn A. Young contends, "The normative gender behavior and sexuality that black men respond to are not the same as the heteronormative sexuality held out for white men."[2] As Young explains, Black men must "navigate through zones of contradiction" that regulate their masculinity in inconsistent and often irreconcilable ways. If white audiences perceive a Black man as "too" masculine, he may be coded as a threat, but if they perceive a Black man as "insufficiently" masculine, he may be presumed gay and/or coded as "insufficiently black."[3] Such contradictory expectations circulate in a white supremacist culture that often constructs Black men as more homophobic and

---

1. Jackson, *Black Celebrity*, 5.
2. Young, "Compulsory Homosexuality."
3. Young, "Compulsory Homosexuality."

misogynistic than white men. For example, outrage about Smith's slapping of Chris Rock at the 2022 Oscars, in response to a joke the comedian made about Smith's wife, reflects constructions of Black men as violent and homophobic, but had Smith not defended his wife, he might have been coded as "unmanly."[4]

That Smith has found himself in these "zones of contradiction" throughout much of his career can also be seen in tabloid accusations that he is homophobic, in the closet, and on the "down low."[5] Consider another incident in which a refused kiss caused controversy for Smith. While greeting reporters at a 2012 premiere of *Men in Black 3*, Smith spoke with Ukrainian television personality Vitalii Sediuk, who attempted to kiss Smith twice while on the red carpet. Smith pushed Sediuk away, slapped his face, and asked, "What the hell is your problem, buddy?" Then, turning to cameras, Smith said, "He tried to kiss me on my mouth. This joker—he's lucky I ain't sucker punched him." Various tabloid outlets criticized Smith, leading him to issue an apology on late-night television—although the controversy over that red-carpet slap paled in comparison to the uproar elicited by the 2022 slap "heard 'round the world."[6]

Not unlike the case of Rockwell, these examples illustrate intersections of heteronormativity with cultural expectations about the transparency of celebrities, which suggest that audiences should know who celebrities "really are" while also implying that celebrities often have something to cover up. It is precisely this tension on which the entertainment journalism and tabloid industries depend. Furthermore, these examples illustrate constraints felt by Black celebrities, which Smith's image culture frequently addresses. This chapter frames Smith's persona as visualizing Young's account of such "zones of contradiction," showing how Smith's persona and career have been limited by white cultural norms and fantasies and how, as Towns argues, Smith is but one of many "Black bodies" used as "media for white self-concepts."[7] This chapter also argues that Smith's image culture takes up the subject of celebrity in relation to the politics of race, gender, and sexuality, inviting consideration of the precaritization of Black bodies that do not enjoy the privileges of fame.

POLITICAL CONNECTIONS

Born in Philadelphia, Smith began as a hip-hop performer under the moniker "The Fresh Prince" and became a household name through the popular NBC sitcom *The Fresh Prince of Bel-Air* (1990–96). This sitcom drew on extratextual

---

4. Boston, "Underlying Lesbophobia."
5. See "Will & Jada's Divorce Secret" and Deino, "Will Smith."
6. Stitch, "Will Smith & Chris Rock."
7. Towns, "Toward a Black Media Philosophy," 863.

information about Smith's actual life, casting him as a "street smart" young man from Philadelphia sent to live with his wealthy relatives in California after a brush with violence in his hometown. In 1990 Smith told *Interview* magazine, "I'm not having to do too much acting—I'm just being myself." He added, "[Fresh] Prince is not really a character. It's me."[8] Smith has maintained this porous understanding of character and self, noting in his 2021 memoir that he and his *Six Degrees of Separation* character Paul are equally "invented," "performed," and shaped by their relationships with "friends, loved ones, and the external world."[9]

Such autobiographical sensibilities have carried over into Smith's larger body of work, which often features his family, including films in which he and his children have costarred, such as *Pursuit of Happyness* (Gabriele Muccino, 2006) and *After Earth* (M. Night Shyamalan, 2013). For example, in 2018 Smith's wife Jada Pinkett Smith began *Red Table Talk,* a reality series for Facebook Watch in which she has intimate and frank discussions with family and friends about their lives. An infamous 2020 episode features the Smiths addressing rumors about their relationship, including speculations about their sexuality, accusations of infidelity, and assertions that their marriage is a business arrangement, and in 2022 Pinkett Smith turned to *Red Table Talk* to discuss her husband's choice to slap Rock.

Despite these collaborations, Smith has denied that "fame" is the "family business." In a *New York* magazine cover story, the famous father explicitly distinguishes his family from the famous-for-being-famous Kardashian family, despite their having been neighbors.[10] Such differentiation demonstrates what Pamela Ingleton and Lorraine York describe as a cultural aversion to "reality-show, Kardashian-esque over-self-promotion" that gets coded as "quintessentially shameful."[11] It also illustrates what Banet-Weiser describes as the "cultural value" of authenticity as a brand, as Smith frames his familial relations as genuine rather than staged. (Notably, in 2022, amid their divorce, Kanye West differentiated his relationship with Kardashian from the Smiths,

---

   8. Sturley, "Fresh Prince." As much as Smith framed the show as telling his stories, the concept from the sitcom also derived from the experiences of Black music executive Benny Medina, who as a teenager moved in with white composer Jack Elliott in order to pursue a career in music. Among Medina's many clients was Smith, and it was Medina who chose Smith for the part. Tabloid rumors about Smith's sexuality have often suggested that he had a relationship with Medina, who was openly gay. For example, see Greenwood, "'Absolutely Not True.'" In 2017 actor Jason Dottley accused Benny Medina of attempting to rape him in 2008; Medina was also accused of sexual assault in 2004. See Artavia, "*Sordid Lives.*"
   9. Smith, *Will.*
   10. Hoffman, "Will Smith."
   11. Banet-Weiser, *Authentic™,* 5; Ingleton and York, "From Clooney to Kardashian," 369.

claiming that they would not be "going for a 'Will and Jada'" approach to disclosing personal information.)[12]

While on *Fresh Prince,* Smith had his breakout film role in *Six Degrees of Separation* and launched his first film franchise, *Bad Boys* (Michael Bay, 1995), becoming known as one of the most "bankable" stars in Hollywood.[13] Since Roland Emmerich's *Independence Day,* his first major blockbuster in 1996, Smith's films in the late 1990s and early 2000s grossed an average of over $400 million in global box office receipts. Smith's career during that period featured primarily science fiction films and action-comedies, most of which were commercially successful and often critically panned, with Smith himself often receiving great critical vitriol.[14]

Despite Academy Award nominations for the dramas *Ali* (Michael Mann, 2001) and *The Pursuit of Happyness* and a win for *King Richard* (Reinaldo Marcus Green, 2021), Smith's forays into genres with darker themes have not fared as well commercially and, in many cases, critically—with *Collateral Beauty* (David Frankel, 2016), *Concussion* (Peter Landesman, 2015), *Focus* (Glenn Ficarra and John Requa, 2015), and *Seven Pounds* (Gabriele Muccino, 2008) averaging just over $100 million. Smith's later return to action, comedy, and/or special effects–driven films, such as *Suicide Squad* (David Ayer, 2016) and *Aladdin* (Guy Ritchie 2019), proved much more successful, respectively grossing approximately $750 million and $1 billion worldwide; *Bad Boys For Life* (Adil and Bilall, 2020), the third installment in one of Smith's action-comedy franchises, broke box office records and earned over $300 million globally in just its first three weeks.

As a Black actor who is successful in historically white genres and with diverse audiences, Smith is something of an anomaly. This position affords him, argues Jackson, "unique access to mainstream debates around race and nation," with some framing Smith as a trailblazer and others calling him a "sell-out" dependent on assimilation into white culture.[15] Smith may be exceptional in many ways; however, his role as a cultural heuristic hardly makes him an exception, as he exemplifies metonymic labor done to/with representations

---

12. Gulla, "Kanye West."
13. Burman, "Hollywood's Most Valuable Actors."
14. Oliver Burkeman offers a sardonic critique of an interview Smith gave to Hoffman at *New York* magazine, asserting, "Everyone knows you rarely learn much by reading interviews with movie stars. It's a less commonplace experience, though, to feel yourself becoming actively less well-informed as you read, as if the celebrity's words were eliminating your brain-cells, one by one, like bubble-wrap being popped." Burkeman, "Will and Jaden Smith."
15. Jackson, *Black Celebrity,* 5. See also Nama, *Black Space,* 39; and McLeod, "Authenticity within Hip-Hop," 144–45. For more on the impossible demands placed on Black stars to be "Black enough" but not "too Black," see Koojiman, "True Voice of Whitney Houston."

of myriad other celebrities. His case therefore offers productive opportunities for analysis because of its specific iterations of Black masculinity and celebrity and because of its self-reflexive attention to the terms and conditions by which white media industries and cultures have imagined Black fame to be possible.

Consider, for instance, a photo from Smith's official Facebook page. This black-and-white photograph from Ft. Hood in Texas depicts Smith and his son Jaden on stage in front of soldiers and their families, who look to be primarily white. Other photographs of this event reveal the crowd to be racially diverse, but the framing of this image whitewashes the audience. The Smiths appeared at the base for a USO-sponsored special premiere of their film *After Earth*. Everything in the image, including Smith's and Jaden's clothing, is in black and white—except for an American flag, which has been rendered in color. This stylistic choice, not unlike the technique used on the January 1994 cover of *Premiere*, implies that the only colors that matter in the United States are red, white, and blue, forwarding fantasies of the American Dream as color-blind. While attempting to displace race from the image, this use of color asserts the exceptionality of the US as a land of opportunity. The image also invites interpretations of Smith and his son, with connotations of black-and-white photography as timeless or classic, as "stars." Likewise, the white color of Smith's and Jaden's shirts connotes their wholesomeness or innocence, just as the military setting of the image may ascribe nobility or virtuousness to a promotional stunt. This image further casts Smith and his son as proof of both the color-blindness and the accessibility of the American Dream, which aligns with much of Smith's oeuvre.[16]

For example, in 2001 Smith published a children's book, *Just the Two of Us*, based on the lyrics of his song by the same name, which reimagines a romantic love song by Bill Withers and Grover Washington Jr. as one about fatherly love. The book and song celebrate the "dignity, integrity, and honor" of fatherhood, declaring, "Just the two of us, building castles in the sky." The book's illustrator is Kadir Nelson, a Black artist whose style recalls that of Norman Rockwell, whom Nelson cites as a major inspiration for his work. Many illustrations in Smith's book allude to Rockwell paintings, including *Coming and Going* (1947), *Freedom from Fear* (1943), and *Shuffleton's Barbershop* (1950), suggesting appeals to the so-called traditional values with which

---

16. Consider comments made by *Six Degrees of Separation* author John Guare, as quoted by Veronica Chambers, who notes that "even after months of knowing Smith," the playwright assumed that Smith turned to acting to find "another life" and a way to "[get] himself out." In response, Chambers retorts, "Out of what? Smith isn't from the ghetto, and he's never pretended to be." Chambers critiques Guare for reifying metonymic associations between Blackness, adversity, and suffering in service of American Dream rhetoric. See Chambers, "Willing," 76.

Rockwell is associated.[17] Seen in the context of the star's larger persona, then, this Facebook image positions Smith and his son as metonyms for articulating postracial fantasies, American Dream rhetoric, and narratives of American exceptionalism. These actors may be understood to confirm narratives about equal opportunity in US culture, their photographed bodies seeming to confirm such ideologies, while also obscuring structural or cultural injustices that privilege some and punish others.

Though celebrity culture's investment in American Dream rhetoric encourages this interpretation of the image, a reparative reading can resist the photograph's whitewashing by demonstrating how uncommon positions of privilege are for people of color in the US and how often such positions require the approval of white audiences. This positioning emphasizes the relative vulnerability of Black celebrities, which reflects the precarity faced by all Black people. Furthermore, this photograph destabilizes the presumed normativity of whiteness, making visible the process by which white culture defines itself in an imagined relationship with otherness, exposing a representative moment in which "white culture has assigned black culture a central role in its own self-definition."[18] This image does not fully displace race and reveals the extent to which Smith's persona "presents white anxieties over black manhood and assuages them through the fantastic resolution of America's racial contradictions."[19] The erasure of most color from the image, therefore, replays what Towns describes as the invisibilizing of racial exploitation and violence as a medium for "white self-creation."[20]

The photograph's ability to confirm postracial American Dream rhetoric derives in part from its position within much larger metonymic fields of discourse in which similar images and associations circulate. As much as this image may articulate and *stand in* for cultural discourses, it may be effective because its logics do not *stand out*. The photograph articulates with a network of texts that maintain both the invisibility and the presumed naturalness of its assumptions. In response, metonymic criticism of Smith's body of work—from movie posters to the films they promote—reveals displaced articulatory associations, reactivating their contingency and disrupting ideological slippage into metaphor.

---

17. Seth Abramovitch, "'New Yorker' Cover Artist"; Booker, "Award-Winning Illustrator." In 2022 the Norman Rockwell Museum featured Nelson's work in its exhibition titled *Imprinted: Illustrating Race*, which celebrates how images can affect public discourse about race and racism.
18. Gabbard, *Black Magic*, 6. See also Yancy, *Black Bodies, White Gazes*.
19. Magill, "Celebrity Culture," 127.
20. Towns, "Toward a Black Media Philosophy," 865.

STARS FOR SALE

One of Hollywood's oldest promotional strategies, movie posters occupy an important space in the political economy of the film industry. Spectators, Jonathan Gray argues, encounter more promotional material than the "thing itself."[21] As Thomas Stubblefield explains, in the age of ubiquitous advertising and promotional discourse, "'seeing' the film no longer necessitates the theater or even the film itself."[22] Advertisements operate by "hailing an audience for a text," and they help "create meanings for those who will not be in the audience."[23] Necessarily intertextual, posters exist in relation to the films they advertise and also articulate with other texts, including other film advertisements and the works of the celebrities whose names or images they feature.

Although designed as disposable goods to be discarded after a film's theatrical run, posters have experienced unintended longevity and mobility, becoming elements of home or office décor and sometimes amassing great value as collector's items. Since the advent of home entertainment systems, the packaging for VHS cassettes, laserdiscs, DVDs, and Blu-ray discs has replicated movie posters' designs. Posters also circulate digitally, appearing on sites where consumers purchase, stream, and/or research movies, including Amazon, Netflix, Hulu, IMDB, Fandango, and Google. For example, a Google search for the phrase "Will Smith movies" results in a visual archive of posters for his movies.

While movie posters may not be the primary sites at which audiences seek information about celebrities—social media, magazine interviews, or television appearances are more obvious resources—they are useful objects of study because of their metonymic logic. Movie posters do not promote the celebrities they feature but, rather, illustrate distributors' attempts to *use* stars as metonyms for promoting the movies in which they appear. Articulating genre norms and star images as communicative shortcuts, much as audiences do, posters aim to "police proper interpretations" of the films they advertise and the intertextual stars they feature, revealing the assumptive logics they help naturalize.[24] As Emily King argues, "The history of the film poster is the ongoing story of the link between cinema and society."[25]

A movie poster for the first public film screening features spectators gathered to see short actuality films by Auguste and Louis Jean Lumière at the

---

21. Gray, *Show Sold Separately*, 52.
22. Stubblefield, "Disassembling the Cinema," 88.
23. Gray, *Show Sold Separately*, 52.
24. Gray, *Show Sold Separately*, 79.
25. King, *Century of Movie Posters*, 6.

Grand Café in Paris in 1895. Another advertisement for this film screening shows audience members cheering with delight in response to the black-and-white image of a man being sprayed in the face with a water hose. These depictions of the audience's pleasure anticipate the convention of contemporary movie posters including a "short enthusiastic quote from an established critic."[26] The "audience image" also illustrates another function of early film advertisements: acculturating audiences to practices and norms of spectatorship.[27] The only text on the poster does not reference, or even name, the film being depicted but, rather, identifies the "Cinématographe Lumière," the Lumière Brothers' patented film camera, projector, and printer with which the film had been made. This emphasis on the cinématographe reflects what Richard DeCordova describes as the technological fascination that characterized early discourse about the cinema: more important than what audiences saw was the fact that they were seeing moving images at all.[28]

Posters during the early decades of the twentieth century often showcased significant scenes from the advertised film. As Kathryn H. Fuller notes, many film posters featured "boldly colored lithographs of artists' interpretations of a film's most exciting, sensual, or dramatic scenes."[29] For example, one *Birth of a Nation* (D. W. Griffith, 1915) poster depicts the scene of Abraham Lincoln's assassination, showing Lincoln's collapsing body and John Wilkes Booth's narrow escape. The poster describes the film as a "mighty spectacle" with a caption for the illustrated image that reads "Lincoln's Assassination. The Fatal Blow that Robbed the South of its Best Friend." King likens this format to the covers of contemporaneous magazines, which combined illustrated images with cover lines that explained their significance. The only names included on this poster, aside from Lincoln's, belong to director D. W. Griffith and author Thomas Dixon. The poster does not name actors, because at that early stage in film history, the discourse of acting was just emerging and actors were only beginning to develop name recognition.

As the discourse on acting arose, alongside the continued development of feature-length narrative films, promotional efforts began to reference actors as well. Emergent fan magazines helped make the names and faces of actors recognizable to audiences, and the film industry increased attention to actors' intertextual bodies of work, as well as to their offscreen personae.[30] The development of the star system had significant implications

---

26. King, *Century of Movie Posters*, 12.
27. Stubblefield, "Disassembling the Cinema," 86. See also Fuller, *At the Picture Show*.
28. DeCordova, *Picture Personalities*, 26.
29. Fuller, *At the Picture Show*, 58.
30. DeCordova, *Picture Personalities*, 12.

for the history of film posters and movie advertising generally. King notes, "The twinned emergence of feature films and recognizable stars promoted the development of the movie poster" because promoters learned that "nothing attracted an audience more surely than a familiar face."[31] It would not take long for picture personalities, and eventually stars, to find their way to prominence on movie posters. In the 1920s, for example, posters advertising movies starring Charlie Chaplin conspicuously displayed his name and image, along with other crucial information about the film, establishing conventions still largely in place today.[32]

While the visual depictions of actors on movie posters reference the film being advertised, posters also rely on audiences' extratextual recognition of the stars they depict, as illustrated by movie posters' characteristic use of actors' and not characters' names. By the 1940s, as audiences had increasing knowledge about the private lives of the stars, movie posters often attempted to "reflect stars' perceived off-screen personalities" in their visual characterizations of actors.[33] Consider Norman Rockwell's 1945 poster for the film *Along Came Jones,* a western-comedy in which Gary Cooper pokes fun at his own persona and rise to stardom through the western genre. Cooper stands before a barn with a saddle in his hand, wearing the western genre's version of a three-piece suit—thick trousers, a denim jacket, and a gun holster. Rockwell's depiction of Cooper in this poster, not unlike the film itself, relies on audience familiarity with Cooper's offscreen persona and oeuvre, including his childhood on a ranch in Montana, his past successes in the western genre, and the fact that Rockwell had already painted a picture of Cooper spoofing his cowboy persona in his film *The Texan* (John Cromwell, 1930).

By the second half of the twentieth century, movie posters began to circulate in contexts beyond movie theaters, including museums and auction houses. In the 1960s, the Museum of Modern Art and the Smithsonian launched some of the earliest public exhibitions of movie posters in museum settings. The Norman Rockwell Museum has also had multiple exhibitions of movie posters, including those by Rockwell as well as those of famed illustrator Drew Struzan; film posters now appear in many museum collections around the world and are archived by the Academy of Motion Picture Arts and Sciences.[34] The notion that movie posters should be classified and treated as art is further reflected in the choice by Texas-based theater chain Alamo Drafthouse, via its gallery and retail site Mondo, to commission artists to

---

31. King, *Century of Movie Posters*, 13.
32. Haralovich, "Advertising Heterosexuality," 52.
33. King, *Century of Movie Posters*, 78.
34. Murphy, "Hand-Drawn Homage."

create alternative posters for films. So notable are these commissioned posters that they have also been included in the Academy's archives—with the first entry into that collection being Struzan's alternate version of a poster for James Whale's *Frankenstein* (1931).

Film posters have also garnered much attention as high-priced auction items. In 1980 the *Chicago Tribune* proclaimed that movie posters had become "stars" themselves, often selling for considerable money. Popular subjects throughout the history of movie poster collection include *Casablanca*, *The Wizard of Oz*, and *Gone with the Wind*; such stars as Greta Garbo, Marlene Dietrich, and Jean Harlow; and such eras as the 1930s horror films of Universal Studios.[35] Posters for Whale's *Frankenstein*, for example, are the highest-priced posters in movie history, with some selling for hundreds of thousands of dollars.[36]

Circulating digitally, movie posters have become searchable and accessible but also more malleable, as audiences collect, connect, and manipulate them. Many websites, including Joy Reactor, Freaking News, Reddit, and Tumblr, feature the creation and circulation of fake movie posters. Smith is one star whose image has been subjected to multiple manipulations on faux posters. For example, in 2013 internet rumors claiming that Robert Zemeckis would direct Smith as the eponymous lead in an Obama biopic materialized as a counterfeit movie poster. The joke of this image, which mimics the poster for Smith's film *Seven Pounds*, derives from public speculation about the likelihood of Smith playing Obama in a film about his presidency, with both Smith and Obama endorsing this possibility. Suggestions that Smith should play Obama assert that physical similarities exist between the men, but they also rely on associations that accrete around both men's images with respect to postracial American Dream rhetoric.[37]

WHERE THERE'S A WILL

Although Smith may be a "poster boy" for science fiction / disaster films, his transtextual persona enacts a melodrama that negotiates postracial fantasies

---

35. Shepard, "Movie Posters Become Stars." See also Del Costello, "Movie Posters Being Coveted."
36. One poster sold for almost $200,000 at a Los Angeles auction in 1994. Heritage Auctions, one of the largest purveyors of collectibles in the US, sold one poster for almost $300,000 in 2013 and another for almost $400,000 at a 2015 auction. For more on movie poster sales, see Chang, "Artists Are Poster Boys."
37. See Hughes, "Will Smith Recycles Joke," and Raphael, "Barack Obama."

of the American Dream. The genres with which Smith is associated, contends Despina Kakoudaki, operate in a melodramatic mode to offer displaced consideration of racial politics in US culture, using near-apocalyptic scenarios to stage scenes of racial reconciliation between Black and white characters. These narratives aim to defuse cultural anxieties about racism, deflect attention from persistent inequalities, and "propose a fantasy/utopian alternative to complex political conditions."[38]

A survey of Smith's body of work makes clear that melodramatic narratives about racial reconciliation are not confined to his science fiction / disaster films. Many of Smith's films, across genres, position him as a helpmate and inspiration to white men. Recalling the "magical Negro" trope, Smith's charismatic characters often enable white male heroes to reaffirm their subjectivities, positions of authority, and virility. In *Independence Day*, Smith's character inspires a gawky white male scientist to discover his strength, save the world, and win back his lost love; in the Jim Crow–era *Legend of Bagger Vance* (Robert Redford, 2000), Smith's character helps restore a struggling white golfer to professional and romantic glory; and in *Hitch* (Andy Tennant, 2005), Smith plays a dating consultant who teaches an awkward white attorney how to be cool in order to win the affection of his beautiful celebrity client, making him a better lover and lawyer along the way. Such films invite Smith into historically white spaces without disrupting the "racist ideologies that continue to keep white people" in positions of privilege.[39]

Smith's literal position in many posters, which feature him in front of or between a pair of white bodies, visualizes this tension. Examples include posters for *Six Degrees of Separation, Independence Day, Wild Wild West* (Barry Sonnenfeld, 1999), *The Legend of Bagger Vance,* and *Men in Black 3* (Barry Sonnenfeld, 2012). This staging of a movie poster is not uncommon; but the compositional scheme takes on additional registers of meaning when considered in relationship to Smith's persona, illustrating how Smith hitches together sites that might not necessarily overlap, including the musical genre of hiphop and the cinematic genre of science fiction. Smith has gained access to spaces historically predominated by whiteness, and industry discourse frequently characterizes Smith as being unique as an actor of color who attracts white audiences.[40] His position on these posters mirrors his imagined role as a mediator and site of articulation, figuring Smith as a signifier of postraciality in ways that reinforce the invisible normativity of whiteness.

---

38. Kakoudaki, "Spectacles of History," 112–13.
39. Gabbard, *Black Magic*, 144.
40. Palmer, "Black Man/White Machine," 34.

Consider the poster for *Hitch*, in which Smith's character, Alex "Hitch" Hitchens, offers confidential dating services to a selective network of male clients seeking romance with women. Hitch only accepts clients who have been referred to him by existing ones, and his "small world" of clients (and their love interests) is entirely white.[41] Unlike the posters cited above, only Smith's body appears; yet the image nonetheless positions Smith as a link between white bodies, which operate as absent referents. Smith stands at the center of the mostly white poster behind the word *hitch*, written in bright red capital letters, leaning on the word, as if it is a physical object. His hands rest, respectively, on the letter *h* that begins and ends the word *hitch*, his arms connecting them like an arch. Larger than the other letters in the word, these letters frame Smith's body between and behind them, becoming metonymic stand-ins for the white bodies (*his and hers*) not pictured in the poster. Coupled with the use of hitch as a pun ("getting hitched"), this positioning signals the character's role in bringing (white) people together and stabilizing their social relations. Marking Smith as a source of salvation for white masculinity, the poster's tagline reads "The cure for the common man," with *common* operating as a metonym for *white*. Smith's smile and confident expression suggest that he is happy to perform this redemptive labor on behalf of common, or unremarkable, white, heterosexual masculinity.

As much as posters like this one link postracial fantasies and American Dream narratives, they also signal a hitch in this articulation, highlighting what Young calls the "zones of contradiction" that Black men must negotiate. Not simply concealing ideological contradictions, these posters manifest how often media texts understand Black lives to matter in ways that buttress the hegemony of whiteness. Smith's foregrounded, detached position in the posters highlights the anomalous, even tokenistic, state of his career: he is a rarity as a Black star whose films appeal to wide audiences across multiple genres. Smith may have gone "places few black actors have ever gone before," but his position in these images frames him as operating in spaces where whiteness maintains hegemony.[42] Smith's visual circumscription within these posters reveals that the landscape, though altered, has not been radically restructured.

Notice, then, the poster for *MIB 3*: Smith stands in front of white actors Josh Brolin and Tommy Lee Jones, whose positions create intersecting diagonal lines that frame Smith inside an invisible "X." While the *MIB 3* poster

---

41. Sony addressed the racial politics of casting with *Hitch*, indicating that they chose Latinx actress Eva Mendes because of worries that an interracial relationship with a white actress would offend audiences and that a Black actress would fail to attract white viewers. See Graham, "Casting Film Couples."

42. Nama, *Black Space*, 39.

casts Smith and his character as devoted to white structures of authority, it also acknowledges that people of color often struggle with and against limits opposed by normative white culture, complicating the claim that a figure like Smith could be *either* transgressive *or* assimilative, subversive *or* acquiescent, with respect to cultural expectations about race. Furthermore, the visual composition of this poster reminds viewers that there is no "outside" of race, and its positioning of Smith at the center of an invisible "X" points toward intersections among racialized and gendered ideologies. It is not just figurations of Smith as *Black* that matter but also figurations of him as a *Black man*.

This poster visualizes how much whiteness depends on figurations of otherness as its constitutive outside. Lee and Brolin do not simply wear black; their whiteness depends on contiguous relationality with Blackness, and, more to the point, their white masculinity depends on contiguous relationality with Black masculinity. Accordingly, Smith's image may foster counterhegemonic critiques of naturalized discourses about race (and gender). Just as the phrase *men in black* operates as a metonym for covert governmental organizations that secretly maintain the social order, this poster reveals how often Blackness, as Towns argues, becomes a construct with or against which whiteness defines itself.[43] Although the *Hitch* poster depicts Smith depending on the word *hitch* for support, it also reveals white masculinity's dependence on and appropriation of the metonymic links between Black masculinity, coolness, and sexual ability.

Consider also one of the posters advertising *Six Degrees of Separation*: Smith sits on a Rolls-Royce, dressed in casual clothes associated with performances of Black masculinity, including an athletic jersey and Nike high-tops; white actors Stockard Channing and Donald Sutherland stand behind Smith in formal attire, gazing at him intently. This arrangement highlights how out of place Smith's character is in the uberwhite world of the Upper East Side, where he would likely be perceived as "too street"; yet this image also illustrates the appropriative desire that structures the white characters' imagined relationship with him. The wealthy, white characters in *Six Degrees of Separation* do not believe Smith's character belongs in their world, and the film unfolds through flashbacks as white characters entertain friends and earn fame with stories about his disruptive presence in their lives. Smith was also quite out of place in the film itself: he was a popular rapper and sitcom actor who had never had a major film role, and he is one of only two African American men with a leading role in a film by Schepisi.[44]

---

43. Towns, "Toward a Black Media Philosophy," 863.

44. Schepisi's other US film to include a Black actor in a prominent role is *Mr. Baseball* (1992), which features Dennis Haysbert. Schepisi's *The Chant of Jimmie Blacksmith* (1978), which he made in his native Australia, features Indigenous actors.

The visual composition of the poster connotes a buoyant tone; although Channing and Sutherland seem aloof, Smith appears approachable and comfortable. Bright colors dominate the artwork and copy on the image, and the primary type on the poster appears cartoonish. Excerpts from thirteen reviews frame the poster, describing the film as a lighthearted comedy: "hilarious," "uproariously funny," "wickedly funny," "hot stuff." There are some comedic moments in this film, but the poster's tone feels incongruous with the film's dramatic treatment of racism, classism, homophobia, and suicide. As out of place as Smith's character is in Channing and Sutherland's fictional world, and as out of place as Smith may be in Schepisi's oeuvre, this poster appears similarly incompatible with its referent—so much so that on first seeing the advertisement, I assumed it was another fake.

One explanation for this advertising anomaly might be that the colorful *Six Degrees* poster aims to reach fans of Smith but not of Schepisi, but this poster reveals more than just an effort to market a dramatic film through the conventions of comedy. The poster's uncertainty about how to manage Smith's presence (and how to attract Black audiences to a white film) exposes the white privilege of which it is a symptom. Race (and class) differences may be metonymically displaced, but they cannot be fully denied or contained. The poster depends on Smith while also maintaining a degree of distance from him.

Note its contrast to another poster advertising the film, whose black-and-white palette—with occasional traces of red—evokes a more refined, artistic characterization of the film, connoting a somber tone more befitting the complex subject matter of the narrative. This "color-less" ad, which ran in *Premiere*, quotes five reviewers, including several of those cited on the more colorful image, revealing that many of those quotations were taken somewhat out of context. For example, *Glamour* magazine does call the film "uproariously funny," but only after describing it as "searing social commentary." *Rolling Stone* magazine does describe the film as "hilarious," but it describes it as "elegantly" so and frames the film as a "comedy of manners." The contrasts between these posters manifest the very hitch that Smith may signify in US culture: although he travels through and maintains a notable presence within sites that have historically privileged whiteness, he is mobile only to a degree and remains largely separated from the white worlds he inhabits.

Also consider what becomes evident when the colorful *Six Degrees* image is read in relation to promotional materials for *The Fresh Prince of Bel-Air*, which also cast Smith as a poor teenager struggling to navigate an unfamiliar world of extreme wealth and privilege—although, unlike in *Six Degrees*, Smith's *Fresh Prince* character enters a world populated by affluent Black Americans, making him almost-but-not-quite "too street" to belong. Ads for *Fresh Prince* similarly use bright colors and graffiti-inspired graphics as metonyms for Black culture. The links between these images illustrate how mainstream media construct representations of Black bodies as constitutive foils for white normativity. White characters in *Six Degrees of Separation* use Smith's character to enrich their life stories, and these posters uncover white media culture's use of signifiers of Blackness to give meaning and stability to whiteness.

FOLLOWING SUITS

In the similarly styled *Six Degrees* and *Fresh Prince* advertisements, Smith's clothes connote a version of masculinity associated with Black culture: athletic jerseys and tracksuits. In many of his other posters, however, Smith wears a different kind of suit: a business suit. Examples include *Six Degrees of Separation*; the *MIB* franchise; *Enemy of the State* (Tony Scott, 1998); *The Legend of Bagger Vance, The Pursuit of Happyness, Seven Pounds* (Gabriele Muccino, 2008); *Focus* (Glenn Ficarra and John Requa, 2015); and *Concussion* (Peter Landesman, 2015). Photographs of Smith wearing a dark suit also abound in his image culture more generally, including social media posts and magazine cover photos. This recurrent wardrobe choice matters because of its racialized and classed history.

The iterations of the suit seen in these images of Smith—dark, simple, and conservative—connote centuries-old bourgeois norms of respectability. In seventeenth-century England, the three-piece suit displaced the ornamentality of the doublet and hose as the norm in men's fashion, reversing the "long-held association between elaborate display and high social status" and linking "male gentility" to "modesty and plainness in dress."[45] While masculine norms inaugurated by the three-piece suit were conceived as presumptively white, they also constrain and enable presentations of Black masculinity, which have negotiated white masculine norms for centuries.[46] In contrast to minimalistic white fashion norms, performances of Black male dress often refashion white bourgeois norms through exaggeration and hyperstylization. The zoot suits of the 1940s or hip-hop styles of the 1990s, for instance, emphasize dramatic lines, oversized clothing, and bright colors, similar to the aesthetics of the *Six Degrees* and *Fresh Prince* advertisements cited earlier.

If Black men's fashion operates as a form of political engagement responsive to oppressive white norms, it matters that the version of the suit predominant in Smith's image culture is the understated suit associated with white

---

45. Kuchta, *Three-Piece Suit*, 2.
46. See Lynch, *Dress, Gender, and Cultural Change*; and Miller, *Slaves to Fashion*.

culture—not the zoot suit or the tracksuit. Such stylization influences perceptions of Smith as assimilationist, as in Amy Taubin's characterization of Smith as "probably the only African American actor in Hollywood guaranteed to be nonthreatening to a white middle-class audience"[47] or Adilifu Nama's description of Smith as illustrating the "racially nonthreatening posture of Sidney Poitier," who was the fictional father to Smith's character in *Six Degrees* and the actual mentor to Smith's mentor, Denzel Washington.[48]

The suit, however, signifies more than just assimilation or an uncomplicated hitching of Smith's persona to white norms. Its striking visibility within Smith's image culture marks the suit as a signifier of whiteness and its alleged unremarkability. The intersecting grammars of whiteness and masculinity frame white (heterosexual) masculinity as "nonimitative or nonperformative" in contrast to more (purportedly) theatrical iterations of race, gender, and/or sexuality; thus, Smith's adoption of this signifier puts the performative codes of white (heterosexual) masculinity on conspicuous display.[49] These images reveal whiteness and masculinity as metonymic sites of cultural performance that exist only insofar as they are instantiated through a network of signifiers.

This recurrent wardrobe choice also invites attention to expectations placed on Smith himself as a Black public figure and his agency to resist them. Consider a famous scene from *MIB*, in which Smith's character, James Darrel Edwards III, enters MIB headquarters to begin his career as a secret agent. Upon arrival, Edwards wears a colorful striped T-shirt and track pants, recalling his racialized *Fresh Prince* wardrobe. The MIB director, a white man, instructs him to put on "the last suit you'll ever wear." As the new recruit enters the program, the MIB director proclaims the erasure of Edwards's identity and his transformation into Agent J, explaining, "You will conform to the identity we give you.... Your entire image is crafted to leave no lasting image on anyone you encounter." Meanwhile, a montage sequence depicts Smith's character removing signifiers of his unique identity that operate as metonyms for cultural Blackness, including his earring and colorful wardrobe.

This scene dramatizes Edwards's interpellation into the (white) Men in Black system, as he becomes one of "them." This scene also evokes white Hollywood's terms and conditions for Smith's celebrity—so much so that one might imagine a white studio executive issuing a similar directive to Smith himself. However, as much as Smith's character consents to this assimilative transformation, he insists on his alterity to the system, rhetorically asking his white partner, "You know what the difference is between you and me?" Slipping on a pair of wayfarer sunglasses, Edwards continues, "I make this [suit] look

---

47. Taubin, "Playing It Straight," 8. See also Write, *Crossover Stardom*.
48. Nama, *Black Space*, 39.
49. Halberstam, "Mackdaddy, Superfly, Rapper."

good." Asserting his capacity to affect what the suit means, Edwards acknowledges the contingency of all signifiers. He exposes white culture's attachment to and dependence on the "cool" or "street" sensibilities that whiteness associates with cultural Blackness; at the same time, this scene reveals a double bind within US media culture's attitude toward Black masculinity, in which a Black public figure such as Smith is expected to be both the same as and different from normative whiteness—to fit in and to stand out, to belong and to remain separate.

A similar scenario unfolds in *Hancock,* in which Smith plays the title role as a troubled superhero receiving tutelage from a white man on how to gain public approval. This transformation, aimed at increasing Hancock's respectability to presumptively white authority figures and citizens, changes his wardrobe from disheveled street clothes to a sleek and understated black (superhero) suit. The prominence of the dark suit within Smith's image culture highlights the limited choices that white media culture deems suitable for Black men in the public eye in relation to interarticulated discourses of respectability politics and white normativity.

A HERO BY ANY OTHER NAME

Discussing Smith's dramatic movies, including *Collateral Beauty, Suicide Squad, Concussion,* and *Seven Pounds,* Steve Rose laments the displacement of Smith's "fun-loving but in no way threatening" persona by roles in which the actor plays a traumatized or depressed character. Rose appropriates political rhetoric associated with Donald Trump's presidential campaign to implore Hollywood to "Make Will Smith Great Again," declaring that "fixing Smith ought to be a national priority." He asserts that the US needs figures like Smith to "heal" the nation in a time of intense racial discord. Rose's desire for Hollywood to revive the "confident, cocky, charming, *funny* Will" as a therapeutic response to national trauma illustrates a nostalgic reading of Smith's early persona as a signifier of postracial American Dream rhetoric.[50] Furthermore, the impulse to ask a Black man to save white America from its own racism illustrates a long-standing practice wherein hegemonic whiteness relies on Blackness as its redemptive savior.

Rose contrasts his ideal version of Smith with what he calls "Sad Will," affirming performances of positivity that disavow ongoing cultural traumas and avoid making white audiences uncomfortable. The "bankable" and "non-

---

50. Rose, "Make Will Smith Great Again."

threatening" aspects of Smith's persona praised by Rose exist not only in contrast to public feelings of depression but also in opposition to stereotypes about Black men as angry, violent, and/or hypersexual.[51] The likeability that Rose attributes to Smith's early persona presupposes and only becomes meaningful in relation to cultural constructions of Black masculinity as dangerous and carnal, and it is such expectations about Smith that contributed to the shock that white audiences claimed at seeing Smith slap Rock in 2022. It is no accident that the kiss from *Six Degrees of Separation* is not the only love scene conspicuously absent from Smith's career. His films rarely picture him in any romantic relationships and almost never visualize him in erotic or sexual encounters, because such depictions might disrupt Hollywood's attempts to position the star as not threatening to the hegemony of white heterosexual masculinity.

White male audiences' investments in Black superstars, including athletes and hip-hop artists, reflect this tension, positioning Black masculinity as just dangerous enough to be exciting but not so dangerous as to threaten hegemonic whiteness. This popularity reflects an impulse to appropriate the "street" or "cool" sensibilities associated with Black men while buttressing the hegemony of white masculinity. These expectations are ones faced by Smith throughout his career, having become rather definitive of his persona, and *Hancock* directly addresses these contradictory norms. Central to this film's critique are mediated figurations of Black masculinity and of whiteness, including the figures of the benevolent white man and the forbidden white woman.

Although Smith is known by many for his "likable" parts in science fiction and action films, his first role as a superhero plays against type.[52] In *Hancock*, Smith stars as the eponymous hero, a disaffected supernatural being who often causes more damage than he prevents. Frequently drunk, foul-mouthed, and womanizing, Hancock is well known but not well liked by the public, facing scrutiny from the media and law enforcement agencies. *Hancock* depicts its titular hero as having a bad temper and a hostile disposition, recalling stereotypes of the "angry black man." The film's narrative centers on efforts by Hancock and his PR team to rehabilitate his image. Hancock learns to behave with more "civility," receiving a new wardrobe and elocution lessons offered

---

51. See Cvetkovich, *Depression*; Ehrenreich, *Bright-Sided*; and Gates, *Double Negative*.

52. Since *Hancock*, Smith has starred as another super antihero scarred by a violent past, in *Suicide Squad* (David Ayer, 2016). Smith did not return for the film's sequel, *The Suicide Squad* (James Gunn, 2021), so Idris Elba took over the role. Elba also had a leading role in the filmic adaptation of *Cats* (Tom Hooper, 2019), which was made over twenty-five years after Paul promised the Kittredges parts in it in *Six Degrees of Separation*.

by his Pygmalion-like white publicist. As Nama notes, the film's narrative satirizes the image management of Black public figures by white institutions, as exemplified by the often-concurrent attempts to exploit and contain the "black superstar persona" associated with the "gangster rapper and professional athlete."[53]

The antihero's makeover is not the only transformation at work in the film, which itself undergoes a generic transformation. Beginning as a comedic satire of the superhero subgenre, *Hancock* transforms rather (melo)dramatically, revealing its protagonist's life (and body) to be scarred by considerable trauma and loss caused by anti-Black racism. *Hancock* may be understood as a film not only about Hollywood's affection for superhero films but also about its ambivalence toward Black celebrities and Black lives. As a film about a talented and famous Black man who refuses to please his audiences or adhere to the politics of respectability, *Hancock* addresses the racist logics that structure the thorny relationship between Blackness and fame in US culture.

Initially, Hancock seems unconcerned with his public image problem until he meets white public relations expert Ray (played by Jason Bateman). After Hancock saves him from an accident with a train, Ray commits himself to stopping the train wreck that is Hancock's public image. Ray's PR campaign invokes the role of the "white savior," coaching Hancock on how to speak more politely, improving his wardrobe and physical appearance, and submitting Hancock to jail time to atone for his past mistakes.[54] Hancock confesses to Ray that he has no knowledge of who or what he is—having awoken, some fifty years prior, in a hospital emergency room with amnesia and no traces of his past life, except for two movie ticket stubs for the Universal horror classic *Frankenstein*.

During Hancock's first visit to Ray's house, Ray's wife, Mary (played by white actor Charlize Theron), has an intense but conflicted reaction to the superhero, toward whom she seems both attracted and hostile. The erotic tension between these characters culminates one afternoon when Hancock attempts to kiss Mary, catalyzing a physical altercation and revealing that Mary secretly shares Hancock's supernatural strength. Later, when Hancock is mortally wounded, Mary divulges to him that they are celestial beings, created as a pair; although they have been in love for centuries, their relationship always leads to conflict and disaster, as well as the loss of their supernatural abilities. It was their relationship, Mary explains, that led to the near-fatal injuries that destroyed Hancock's memory, so she has spent the last five

---

53. Nama, *Superblack*, 148.
54. See Hughey, *White Savior Film*; and Vera and Gordon, *Screen Saviors*.

decades hiding from him. Realizing the dangers of his connection to Mary, Hancock bids her to stay with Ray and commits to becoming a more likable, less destructive superhero.[55]

The film's construction of Hancock calls attention to three figures implicated in cultural constructions of Black masculinity: the comic book superhero, the professional athlete, and Frankenstein's monster. *Hancock*'s references to these figures critique the exploitative treatment of Black bodies and subjectivities by popular media, encouraging audiences to read the film through self-reflexive lenses attentive to celebrity culture. For instance, *Hancock*'s poster features a close-up shot of Smith's unshaven face contorted into a grimace that bears little resemblance to the toothy smile typical of his promotional materials. He wears a sock cap, embroidered with an eagle, and sunglasses with reflective lenses. Visible in the lenses are the Los Angeles skyline and a large bird in flight, with the city appearing in one lens and the bird in the other; these choices merit consideration for multiple reasons. First, the cityscape points toward the metonymic link between Blackness and urbanity, which itself operates as a dog whistle regarding presumptions of Black criminality. The film further signals such metonymic associations through its depictions of Hancock as publicly intoxicated, drinking alcohol from a paper bag, and sleeping on a park bench.

Second, the choice to show a reflected image of Los Angeles illustrates the extent to which a fictional character like Hancock or a public figure like Smith operates as a fantasy projection of those who construct, circulate, and consume his image, including the Hollywood industry and its white target audience. The reflected images in Hancock's glasses also encourage imagined audiences to consider Hancock's perspective, as what we see in the lenses is what he sees. This emphasis on perspective invites consideration of the famous antihero's own viewpoints regarding the terms of his fame; and, in asking audiences to consider how Hancock might see his lifeworld, the film encourages viewers to consider the stakes of their investments in particular images of Hancock's—and, by extension, Smith's—worlds.

Third, the choice to depict the bird at a remove from the city—contained literally by the other hemisphere of the glasses' frame—points toward both Hancock's and Smith's fraught relationship with Los Angeles and the enter-

---

55. Prior to *Hancock*, Theron appeared with Smith in *The Legend of Bagger Vance*, another film whose narrative depends on a triangulated relationship between a Black man, a white man (played by Matt Damon), and a white woman. In the earlier film, Smith played the role of a "magical Negro" who helped a struggling white man both regain professional success (as a golfer) and reclaim his lost childhood love (played by Theron). Not unlike *Hancock*, *The Legend of Bagger Vance* ends with Smith's character deciding to disappear from the lives of the white couple so that they may maintain their romantic partnership.

tainment industry with which the city is associated; this framing positions Black public figures as only partially of the Hollywood dreamworld—in, or near, but not of it. This gesture echoes framing of Smith in those posters discussed earlier, in which he exists close to but also at a remove from his white counterparts. In all, the poster invites audiences to think about the role that Hollywood and related entertainment industries have played in creating and constraining cultural constructions of Blackness, a subject to which *Hancock* returns through its depictions of its antihero's fame and infamy.

SUPERHEROES, SUPERSTARS, AND SUPERPREDATORS

Although Hancock is not sure of his origins, Smith's role as a Black superhero has a rich history, which *Hancock* self-reflexively acknowledges. As Ray revamps Hancock's image, he shows him comic books and encourages him to think metonymically, asking, "What springs to mind when you see this?" Looking at three cartoon drawings of superheroes on the comic book covers, Hancock responds, "Homo," "homo in Red," "Norwegian homo." His answers, which demonstrate Hancock's frequent recourse to homophobic rhetoric, suggest that he does not take comic book iconography seriously as a part of his own identity.[56] While this dismissive attitude might seem to align with the film's satirical take on superhero iconography, much of Hancock's story mirrors that of one of the most famous Black superheroes in the largely white history of comic books: The Falcon.

This history merits consideration because, Nama argues, constructions of Black superheroes address the "accepted wisdom regarding racial justice and the shifting politics of black racial formation in America." The introduction of such Black superheroes as Black Panther, The Falcon, and Luke Cage offered opportunities for comics to critique the "cultural politics of race and blackness in America."[57] As Ramzi Fawaz argues, The Falcon's "proximity to urban realities," including "the social and economic inequality experienced by people of color," invites reconsideration of cultural norms of both heroism and masculinity.[58] Likewise, Nama notes that The Falcon offers critical consideration of the discursive relationship between Blackness and whiteness, rhetorics of upward mobility and the "American Dream," and presumptions of Black crim-

---

56. On associations between Black masculinity and homophobia, see McCune, *Sexual Discretion*.

57. Nama, *Super Black*, 4, 3. See also Howard and Jackson, *Black Comics*; and Howard, *Encyclopedia of Black Comics*.

58. Fawaz, *New Mutants*, 170.

inality—all of which make the figure of The Falcon pertinent to a discussion of both Hancock and Smith's star persona.[59]

The Falcon first appeared in the *Captain America* comic series in 1969 and was the second Black superhero, following Black Panther, in the comic book universe.[60] Falcon's origin story begins on a Caribbean island and addresses the enslavement of Black men and women. Steve Rogers (aka Captain America) meets Sam Wilson, a social worker from Harlem, who is held captive on the island. Aiming to enlist Wilson in the fight to free the enslaved natives, Rogers teaches Wilson how to become a superhero. Becoming The Falcon, Wilson joins forces with Captain America, only later discovering that a villain named Red Skull had falsified his identity and memories as Sam Wilson. Prior to his time in captivity, Wilson was not Sam, a professionally successful and morally conscious social worker; he was actually Snap, a low-level criminal with ties to organized crime in Los Angeles. Red Skull had hoped that the idea of a friendship with an "upright and cheerful Negro" would appeal to Rogers's "sniveling liberalism," only to destroy him when Wilson's purportedly true criminal nature resurfaced.

This narrative parallels *Hancock*'s in multiple ways. First, both Wilson and Hancock experience amnesia caused by racist violence. In the former case, Red Skull targets Wilson and erases his memory because he believes that being defeated by a man who is Black would humiliate Captain America; in the latter case, Hancock learns from Mary that he suffered traumatic brain injury inflicted by a white mob.[61] Mary explains their history, "reading" Hancock's body as close-up shots highlight his scars. Mary implies that each scar is owed to an attack by racists that objected to a relationship between a Black man and white woman.

---

59. Nama, *Super Black*, 2.

60. Black Panther first appeared in an issue of the Marvel comic series *Fantastic Four* in 1966, as T'Challa, the leader of the fictional African nation of Wakanda. In anticipation of *Black Panther* (Ryan Coogler, 2018), the first major Hollywood superhero film to feature a Black actor in a leading role as well as a Black director, Ta-Nehisi Coates wrote new Black Panther graphic novels. Roxane Gay also collaborated with Coates on *Black Panther: World of Wakanda*, graphic novels about Wakandan women. In 2018 Coates also wrote a new iteration of the *Captain America* series, featuring art by the famed illustrator Alex Ross, who has been called the "Norman Rockwell of comics." In 2012 the Norman Rockwell Museum sponsored the exhibition *Heroes & Villains: The Comic Book Art of Alex Ross*, which was organized by the Andy Warhol Museum, and which includes Ross's paintings and sketches; works by artists who influenced his style, including Rockwell, Warhol, Andrew Loomis, and J. C. Leyendecker; and much of Warhol's personal comic book collection.

61. This film is not the only one in which Smith plays a character reckoning with traumatic brain injuries caused by violence. In *Concussion* (Peter Landesman, 2015), Smith plays Dr. Bennet Omalu, a forensic pathologist who discovers the link between head injuries and a degenerative condition called chronic traumatic encephalopathy, which disproportionately affects Black football players. See Shah, "Sporting Chance."

Second, each man must determine how to construct his identity in relation to long-standing assumptions about Black criminality and fantasies of upward mobility, which are literalized in each superhero's ability to fly.[62] Furthermore, each character finds himself under the tutelage of a white man during this process. In the comic, Captain America must convince Sam/Snap Wilson to adopt a superhero identity, explaining that in order to lead the slave rebellion, he needs to "serve as a symbol to the natives." When Captain America suggests that Wilson adopt a "mask and costume," as well as a "stirring name—like The Falcon," Wilson at first appears skeptical, asking, "Me, a costumed clown?" But two frames later, the comic depicts Wilson-as-Falcon, his tattered wardrobe traded for a sleek superhero suit. With Captain America's guidance, The Falcon has improved his own image so that he can guide other enslaved people out of their impoverishment as well, illustrating a hyperbolic version of labor that Wilson might have imagined himself as performing as a social worker.

Likewise, Hancock owes his identity to white characters: Ray fashions Hancock's revised image, and the antihero's amnesia means that he must depend on Mary for an understanding of who he is. All that Hancock knows about his history is owed to Mary's narrative account of his life. The name *Hancock* itself also signifies the extent to which whiteness has constrained his agency to define himself: he chose the name when his memory loss prevented him from being able to sign his actual name on hospital paperwork. This naming choice deploys *John Hancock* as a metonym for the term *signature*, but it also alludes to the history of slave naming practices, wherein enslaved people were forcibly assigned new names by those that enslaved them.[63] Using the surname *Hancock* as a first name critically references the history of slavery given that most enslaved people were denied surnames and often created new names after gaining their freedom.

The Falcon's and Hancock's stories invite explorations of a "black character" whose existence depends on the "ideas and boundaries created by [a] central white protagonist," but these constraints are not ones only faced by Black superheroes; they also affect Black superstars. *Hancock* registers this link, illustrating similarities between his superhero persona and mediated figurations of Black professional athletes as "immensely talented but troubled" men.[64] For example, the film opens with a high-speed car chase involving a white SUV that careens through the streets of Los Angeles, intercutting these scenes of carnage with images of Hancock unconscious and surrounded by

---

62. Nama, *Super Black*, 2.

63. John Hancock lived in a household that enslaved people. See Fowler, *Baron of Beacon Hill*.

64. Nama, *Super Black*, 70, 148.

empty bottles of alcohol on a bus bench. Close-ups of Smith's muscular physique juxtaposed with shots of multiple television screens showing news footage of the car chase recall public memory of O. J. Simpson's infamous car chase, signaling the film's interest in the complicated relationship between Black masculinity, athleticism, and celebrity.

When Hancock springs to action, the film accompanies images of his physical feats with such hip-hop songs as Ludacris's "Move Bitch" and Ice-T's "Colors," which feature profanities and references to violence. In contrast to the mild hip-hop music with which Smith himself has been associated, these songs act as metonyms for constructions of "urban black masculinity" as explosive and dangerous, reinforcing cultural associations between Black athleticism and violence or criminality.[65] Hancock's violent, erotically charged relationship with Mary also alludes to cultural constructions of Black men, and athletes in particular, as hypersexual, violent, and threatening to white women. The significance of this allusion seems confirmed by the fact that the final version of *Hancock* eliminated a scene in which a sexual encounter with a woman nearly causes Hancock to injure his lover through the sheer force of his orgasm.

Many of the film's expository scenes emphasize Hancock's bad public image and the mediated documentation of his misdeeds, framing him as not only a bad superhero but also a bad celebrity. News coverage of Hancock's "so-called heroics" chastises him for being "notoriously publicity shy," noting that "as usual" Hancock could not be reached for comment. The film depicts Hancock as the star of multiple YouTube videos that document his bad behavior and as the subject of a monologue by Nancy Grace, in which she chides Hancock for believing he is "above the law." When Hancock consents to Ray's plan for rehabilitating his image and agrees to serve jail time as an act of atonement, he delivers an apologia at a press conference. As Nama remarks, "His pretend public confession is clearly evocative of various real press conferences held by black superstar athletes such as Kobe Bryant, Tiger Woods, and Michael Vick, who confessed to misdeeds and asked for public forgiveness."[66] *Hancock*, thus, seems to recognize what Sarah J. Jackson and Spring-Serenity Duvall and Nicole Heckemeyer describe as the precarious positions of Black stars within the celebrity-industrial complex.[67]

Nama reads *Hancock* as being "less about imaginary black superheroes in comics, cartoons, television, and film and more about real black superstars in the music industry and sports entertainment field that are criticized for

---

65. Nama, *Super Black*, 148.
66. Nama, *Super Black*, 148.
67. Jackson, *Black Celebrity*, 1; Duvall and Heckemeyer, "#BlackLivesMatter," 396.

flaunting their above-the-law status."[68] A suspicious reading of *Hancock* might conclude that it reinforces metonymic links between Blackness and criminality; a more generous reading might find that the film, which is an origin story of sorts, encourages audiences to think about the source of such narratives. In particular, *Hancock* asks viewers to think about its hero's bad behavior in the context of his history and, more to the point, the history of anti-Black racism. As Hancock explains to Ray, his misdeeds owe to his loneliness and alienation.

This depiction of Hancock wandering aimlessly, namelessly, and alone calls attention to the third cultural figure that shapes the film's depiction of its antihero: Frankenstein's monster. *Hancock* makes this connection explicit through the reference to the movie ticket stubs for *Frankenstein* that Hancock carries, for reasons he does not understand, in his pocket. When Mary narrates Hancock's history to him, she explains that they saw *Frankenstein* on their last night together. Beyond this overt reference, *Hancock* also contains a number of repetitions and reversals of Frankenstein mythology, illustrating Elizabeth Young's contention that Frankenstein's monster reveals white anxieties about Blackness.

Young identifies a "network of affiliations clustering at particular historical moments and across literary, cinematic, and other cultural forms," including "scientific discourse," in which the metaphor of Frankenstein's monster appears. Mary Shelley's novel, which borrows from Greek mythology about Prometheus and Pygmalion, has inspired countless imitations and parodies—many of which address the subject of Blackness and how race is "intertwined with fantasies and anxieties about masculinity, relations between men, and the male iconography of the American nation."[69] Tracing this intertextual arc of depictions of and allusions to the figure of the "Black Frankenstein," Young reads this metaphor as critiquing anti-Black racism by appropriating and resignifying constructions of Black monstrosity. She argues, "In a racist culture that already considered Black men monstrous and contained them within paternalist rhetoric, the Frankenstein story, with its focus on the literal making of monsters and the unmaking of fathers, provided a stylized rhetoric with which to turn an existing discourse of black monstrosity against itself." Young argues that because analysis of "cultural constructions of race" is also, "necessarily, an investigation of gender and sexuality in U.S. culture," we should also understand Frankenstein stories as explorations of "relationships between men, from the homoerotic to the homophobic."[70]

---

68. Nama, *Super Black*, 149.
69. Young, *Black Frankenstein*, 3, 5.
70. Young, *Black Frankenstein*, 5, 9, 10.

Young reads Shelley's novel as offering "an oblique account of white anxiety in the face of slave rebellion," as illustrated, in part, by the fact that the novel itself was referenced in nineteenth-century debates about slavery. Young also reads James Whale's adaptations of Shelley's novel—*Frankenstein* and *Bride of Frankenstein* (1935)—as "commentaries on race relations in the United States."[71] For example, Universal released *Frankenstein* in 1931, which was also the year of the Scottsboro case, "in which an all-white jury sentenced nine young black men to death for allegedly raping two white women." Young contends, "Whale's films resonate with contemporary accounts of lynching," as *Frankenstein* ends with images of "the monster's flight from a crowd of angry townspeople, whose pursuit of him is represented with the visual markers— barking dogs, fiery torches, angry shouts—of a lynch mob."[72]

Young notes that as much as Whale's film seems to offer ethical and empathetic consideration of the experiences of people of color in a racist society, the film also forwards complex but problematic notions about Black male sexuality. The *Frankenstein* films point toward the potential of homosocial relationships, including the monster's intense ties to his creator, that may challenge "normative sexual bonds"; but they also "depict [the monster] as a black man who menaces white women," including the wife of his creator, whom he terrifies in her bedroom, and a young girl whom he accidentally drowns.[73] This construction of Frankenstein's monster as both aligned with and opposed to the man who created him illustrates the "zones of contradiction" that Black men must navigate.[74]

The now highly valuable advertising materials for Whale's *Frankenstein* invite readings of it in relation to such a view. Although multiple styles of *Frankenstein* posters exist, many include a close-up of the monster's head above the unconscious body of a blonde white woman draped over the side of a bed, using color and shadow to darken the monster's visage in contrast to the light pastel colors used to depict the woman. This imagery implies romantic elements within the film that are not in fact present in the narrative, which Mary Beth Haralovich describes as a common advertising tactic in classic Hollywood designed to attract women viewers.[75] But it also exploits cultural assumptions about the dangers of Black masculinity and the vulnerability of white femininity—as would be similarly reinforced two years later by *King Kong* (Merian Cooper and Ernest Schoedsack, 1933).

71. Young, *Black Frankenstein*, 20–21, 174.
72. Young, *Black Frankenstein*, 175, 177.
73. Young, *Black Frankenstein*, 183.
74. Young, "Compulsory Homosexuality."
75. Haralovich, "Advertising Heterosexuality," 52.

Young's genealogy of Black Frankenstein mythology also includes *Blackenstein* (William Levey, 1973), which Young describes as a problematic attempt by "white Hollywood" to appropriate and capitalize on the culture of Blaxploitation films, a subgenre of films that respond to Hollywood's "erasure of black protagonists" or inclusion of only Black actors/characters with "saintly" personae, like that of Poitier.[76] Young additionally discusses the prevalence of Frankenstein tropes in the work of the Black comic, actor, and activist Dick Gregory. Throughout his career Gregory referenced Frankenstein's monster "as a sustained critique of white America," including an account in his autobiography of seeing Whale's film in the theater as a child, identifying with the monster, and interpreting him as a signifier of resistance against oppression.[77]

Beyond direct allusions to Whale's film in *Hancock*, other traces of Frankenstein mythology exist. First, Ray serves as a metaphoric "creator" who turns Hancock into a creature of his own making. This effort signifies the extent to which Hancock's identity was already, literally and figuratively, the product of white imaginaries and violence. Ray's re-creation of Hancock as a "saintly" hero responds to the ways in which racism had already shaped him through trauma; but rather than celebrating Ray as a white savior, the film critiques the impulses of whiteness to regulate and discipline Blackness.

Second, Hancock's trauma and alienation mirror that of Frankenstein's monster. Like the monster's, Hancock's poor behavior derives from his experiences of "abandonment and abuse." Hancock and Frankenstein's monster also share the condition of namelessness; while Hancock chooses the name of another man, the monster has had such a name applied to him. Although neither Shelley nor Dr. Frankenstein named the creature, he has since been identified colloquially by the name of his creator. As Young notes, "Like the [enslaved person] who is forced to take his master's surname," Shelley's creature "has come mistakenly to be known only as 'Frankenstein,' which is the surname of his creator.[78] This metonymic slippage is owed, at least partly, to those posters advertising Whale's film that depict the monster, but not his creator, atop the word *Frankenstein*. The links between Hancock's name change and the historic practice of slave naming also resonate with this extratextual aspect of Frankenstein mythology.

Third, *Hancock* also references raced Frankenstein mythologies in its characterization of Hancock's prohibited relationship with Mary, whose name and role as narrator of Hancock's life allude to Shelley herself. While Young reads Whale's *Frankenstein* as contributing to characterizations of Black

---

76. Young, *Black Frankenstein*, 188.
77. Young, *Black Frankenstein*, 204, 208.
78. Young, *Black Frankenstein*, 22.

men as threatening to white women, *Hancock* reverses this association. Telling Hancock, "They come after you through me," Mary acknowledges how white supremacist patriarchy uses the bodies of white women as resources for oppressing Black men, weaponizing fantasies about the "sanctity of white women and whiteness itself" as justifications for violence against Black male bodies.[79] Such overvaluation of white women's vulnerability, as epitomized in "white-lady tears," argues Brittney Cooper, also enables violence against Black women who "grow up being denied the protections of femininity that are always afforded to white women."[80]

Mary's accounts of violence against Hancock emphasize moments of US history with significance in public memory about anti-Black racism. For instance, Mary describes an incident in 1850 when an anonymous "they" burned down the house that she and Hancock shared. This reference to the antebellum period in US history (during the year in which the Fugitive Slave Act became law) and the burning of their home by a mob frames Mary and Hancock's relationship in relation to the institution of slavery and anti-Black racism. Mary's account of the night she and Hancock saw *Frankenstein* also alludes to anti-Black racism and prejudice against interracial relationships. Mary explains that, while leaving the movie theater, Hancock took her hand. Then, once again, an unnamed "they" attacked them, beating Hancock almost to death in an alley. Rather than reinforcing perceptions of white feminine sanctity, *Hancock* positions the Black male body as a target for violence and a site of precarity.

Hancock's deployment of Black Frankenstein mythology acknowledges that white imaginaries define themselves in relation to (nightmarish) fantasies of their own creation about Black inhumanity. Just as Dr. Frankenstein's creature represents an anxious extension of him and a reflection of his own desire for wholeness and mastery, white culture's figurations of Blackness and Black masculinity illustrate attempts to give meaning and life to whiteness. Not unlike Shelley's Promethean tragedy, white culture's attempts to revivify itself depend on figurations of Black folks as monsters in order to justify killing them through violence that is at once literal, symbolic, and structural.

While the trope of the Black Frankenstein illustrates how whiteness depends on fantasy projections of Blackness, other aspects of Smith's oeuvre point toward white appropriations of Black culture. For example, Smith's film *Seven Pounds* suggests an inversion of Frankenstein tropology, dramatiz-

---

79. Leiter, *In the Shadow*, 15.
80. Cooper, *Eloquent Rage*, 172. It is precisely this historical pattern that might be understood as motivating Smith's choice to defend his wife Jada against Rock's jokes about her hair loss and femininity.

ing the picking apart—rather than piecing together—of the Black body. After causing a fatal car accident, Smith's character atones for his mistake by giving up his life and donating his organs to save others. Dramatizing the character's self-sacrificial offering, *Seven Pounds* meditates on the demands that whiteness places on people of color, seeming to ask a version of the question posed by Black actor and activist Amandla Sternberg, "What if we loved black people as much as black culture?" In a YouTube video titled *Don't Cash Crop on My Cornrows,* Sternberg and white high school classmate Quinn Masterson critique appropriations of cultural signifiers of Blackness by white people, using Black hair as one representative example, in the context of police brutality against Black bodies. *Seven Pounds* highlights how often not only signifiers of Black culture but also Black bodies themselves are deployed by others for their own ends.

AFTER *AFTER EARTH*

The depiction of the Black body as a site of vulnerability becomes even more pronounced in Smith's critical and commercial failure *After Earth*. Costarring Smith's son Jaden, the film centers on the father–son relationship. Given Smith's record of success in both the science fiction genre and in films that costar his children, the failure of *After Earth* was a surprise to many, prompting speculation about why the film did not find favor with critics or audiences. *Time* magazine, for instance, compiled a list of circulating explanations for why the film "bombed," including audience distaste for its perceived nepotism, its alleged references to the controversial religion of Scientology, and Shyamalan's embattled status as a filmmaker. Other critics have attributed negative reception of the film to racism and, in particular, to a refusal to support a famous Black actor promoting his son's acting career.[81]

The failure of *After Earth* may also owe to its critique of white supremacist culture, which visualizes what Toni Morrison, speaking of Ta-Nehisi Coates's *Between the World and Me,* has called the "hazards and hopes of black male life." Accordingly, this film has overlooked potential as a counterhegemonic resource against anti-Black racism. Revisiting the film in light of subsequent critiques of white supremacist violence, I interpret *After Earth* as allegorizing the tactics often deployed by Black folks as survival mechanisms in a racist world. Just as the film seems to dramatize Smith's experience as a Black father of a famous Black son, whose choices play out before him, quite literally, on a

---

81. Agyeman-Fisher, "Will and Jaden."

screen to be watched, its depictions of the struggles faced by Smith's character also evoke the experiences of the parents of Black sons more generally.

After Earth depicts diaspora following the destruction and abandonment of Earth. Seeking refuge on the planet Nova Prime, humans face attacks from blind aliens bred to track and kill them, called Ursa. Ursa hunt humans by smelling pheromones they release when experiencing fear. The only way to survive these monsters is to suppress all feelings of fear—a rare practice known as ghosting, which makes humans invisible to their predators. Smith plays Colonel Cypher Raige, a military leader famous for his ability to ghost. His illustrious career means that he is often physically absent and emotionally distant from his son Kitai, whom Cypher treats less as his child and more as his cadet. Played by Jaden, Kitai longs to earn his father's respect and to follow in his career path.

On the eve of retirement, Cypher brings Kitai on his last mission to improve the young cadet's military training, but catastrophe amplifies this training in ways neither Cypher nor Kitai could have imagined. When their plane crashes on the long-abandoned planet Earth, Cypher and Kitai are the only survivors. Severe injury immobilizes Cypher, so Kitai must venture alone into the wilderness to seek help. A surveillance camera attached to Kitai's body enables Cypher to follow his son's every move, and he offers him step-by-step guidance for how to survive. Cypher sees the myriad hazards that his son encounters—at times certain he will witness his son's death—while also hoping that his watchfulness will allow him to protect his son from a distance.

Numerous critics have read *After Earth* allegorically. Some read it as an allegory about celebrity and Smith's professional aims for his son, ushering Jaden into a film career and sending him out to become a star in his own right. Conceived by Smith himself, the film was designed as a star vehicle for Jaden, meant to capitalize on his prior success in the remake of *The Karate Kid* (Harald Zwart, 2010). Reviewing the film, Coates asks, "Who subjects their kid to such high-profile panning at such a young age?" Coates describes what he imagines as Jaden's experience of the excoriating reviews as a kind of violent trauma: "This is you stretched out in the street, and the full weight of the internet leaping on you with both feet. And it happens with the backdrop of your Dad being a mega-star." The article critiques Smith for not protecting his son, contrasting Smith's choice with what Coates presumes would be his own: "If I were famous, I think I'd hide my kids away somewhere—or break out the blanket like Michael Jackson."[82] Others have read the film as an allegory about Scientology, the religion with which Smith (and Michael Jackson)

---

82. Coates, "After Earth."

had been associated. Such readings suggest that the film's emphasis on the suppression of fear points toward a particular preoccupation of Scientology founder L. Ron Hubbard.[83]

In addition, we might also read this film as an allegory about Black families living—or, more to the point, trying to survive—in a racist world. Deploying both Afrofuturistic and Afropessimistic sensibilities, *After Earth* evokes the affective experiences of a Black father who must watch his son navigate a world filled with forces designed specifically to destroy him. Consider the two posters for *After Earth*, which position audiences to think about the film's allegorical potential and its attention to the affects of Black fatherhood and fame. One features Smith's and Jaden's faces bifurcated at the edges of the frame, revealing only half of their symmetrical and similar faces, as if they are mirror images of one another. The other depicts Jaden and Smith standing in almost identical poses, their matching space suits overlaid with a shot of the abandoned planet Earth. Within this landscape, located in the middle of Jaden Smith's chest, is a smaller image of his body, standing atop the fiery wreckage of their spaceship.

The stylization of these images recalls magazine covers that the Smiths share. Posing for *New York*, *Ebony*, and *Entertainment Weekly*, the duo wear coordinating or matching outfits and assume parallel or mirrored poses. For example, the *New York* cover story shows Smith and Jaden bent slightly forward, right hands raised to their chests, assuming the pugilistic stance that typifies many of Smith's magazine cover photos. Both wear white shirts and pants and share similar facial expressions: lips parted, eyes directed at the camera, eyebrows raised. A cover line that reads "Mr. and Mr. Smith" reinforces the symmetry between them.[84]

---

83. Abramovitch, "'After Earth.'"

84. The cover for this issue warrants attention itself. Smith and his son wear similar white T-shirts and assume the same pugilistic pose. The cover lines along the right edge are patterned in colors suggestive of a rainbow, except for two: those introducing Hoffman's article about the Smiths and Frank Rich's article about the legalization of same-sex marriage, "My Gay Surrogate Dad." The color scheme, the choice to title the Smith interview "Mr. and Mr." (language that typically signals marriage), and Rich's cover line emphasize the queer sensibilities of the issue. The visual link between these seemingly unrelated cover lines may, therefore, encourage readers to read the interview with the Smiths in connection with Rich's article about the intersecting histories of racism and homophobia in the United States. The use of the phrase "Mr. and Mr. Smith" itself reinforces attention to this link, animating a wide range of metonymic possibilities for thinking about the relationship between race, gender, and sexuality. Writing about the likelihood of the Supreme Court ruling in favor of same-sex marriage, Rich links the histories of the civil rights movement and the gay rights movement, likening bans on interracial marriage to bans on gay marriage. Soon after the Supreme Court's felicitously named *Loving v. Virginia* decision overturned laws prohibiting interracial marriage, another serendipitously named interracial couple, Mr. and Mrs. Smith, "came out" after having kept their three-year relationship hidden from the public eye. Guy Smith, an African American man, and Margaret

This staging illustrates the interconnectedness of the two figures, insofar as Jaden's celebrity persona and pursuit of fame remain inseparable from his father's public image, and Jaden's efforts to imitate his father or follow in his footsteps recall expectations that, as a Black celebrity, Smith act as a role model. This pattern in representations of Smith and his son, which emphasize his presence and involvement in his children's lives, also responds to extant cultural assumptions about the myth of the "absent black father." White supremacy expects Smith to do more than white men to prove to presumptively white audiences that he is a "good" father, and his performances of fatherhood also articulate with expectations about his performance of Black masculinity, including norms of respectability politics and stereotypes characterizing Black men as angry. As such, Smith's performances of masculinity and fatherhood not only signify the particularities of his relationship with his son but also illustrate how Smith may be expected to bear the "burden of representation," operating as a stand-in for all Black men.[85] Emphasizing the mirroring of the two Smith men, the posters for *After Earth* frame this burden as transgenerational, redoubling the "burden of synecdoche" as the son must navigate the legacy of his father's fame.[86]

After Earth attends to transgenerational histories of racism in several ways. First, multiple images recur throughout the film, which may be understood as evoking and, in some cases, anticipating iconic signifiers of anti-Black violence in the US. Repeated shots depict bodies hanging from trees, recalling the iconography and intentions of lynching rituals as spectacles. Ursa, Cypher explains to Kitai, stage these spectacles to trigger fear responses in the humans

---

"Peggy" Rusk, a white woman and daughter of then secretary of state Dean Rusk, were wed in 1967, earning a cover photograph and story in *Time* magazine, which discusses the high-profile wedding in light of the Supreme Court decision and Rusk's fame. The September 29, 1967, *Time* cover showcases a black-and-white photograph of the newly married couple walking out—literally, coming out—of the door of the Methodist church where they wed toward an uncertain future, with a cover line that reads "Mr. and Mrs. Guy Smith / An Interracial Marriage." *New York*'s reference to "Mr. and Mr. Smith" suggests the extent to which an institution like marriage is as raced as it is gendered and sexualized. Perhaps the choice to use the metonymically rich phrase "Mr. and Mr. Smith" to describe two Black actors in a magazine issue with a particular focus on gay marriage offers a winking nod to the rumors surrounding Smith's sexuality or an implicit acknowledgment of the fact that, one month earlier, Smith had publicly endorsed President Obama's stance in favor of same-sex marriage. The phrase also likely animates recognition of the films titled *Mr. and Mrs. Smith*—especially the version starring Brad Pitt in a role for which Will Smith was originally considered. It is that film about a married couple who are also spies working for opposing organizations that Lee Daniels, a Hollywood filmmaker who is Black and gay, references in his description to *Out* magazine of an idea he has for an action film about an interracial gay couple, which he pitched as "a gay *Mr. and Mrs. Smith*." See "Lee Daniels Wants to Make."

85. Mercer, "Black Art."
86. Taylor, "On Being an Exemplary Lesbian."

that see them, because if the human spectators become fearful, they become easier to hunt and kill. Additionally, *After Earth* includes multiple images of Black bodies lying bloodied, dying, or dead on the ground. Such shots resemble images that have become central to the visual rhetoric of the Black Lives Matter movement, including the photograph of Trayvon Martin's body lying on the grass after George Zimmerman killed him—one year before *After Earth* was released—as well as the photograph of Michael Brown's body after Darren Wilson killed him—one year after *After Earth*.

Second, multiple plot devices evoke the material conditions of structural and/or state-sanctioned violence against Black bodies in the US. Aside from dangerous predators, one of the greatest threats facing Kitai on planet Earth is his inability to breathe in an atmosphere made toxic by human actions. This attention to the human causes and costs of environmental destruction echoes Coates's argument that the "plunder" of the "bodies of humans" and the "body of the Earth itself" are often concomitant. The images of Kitai struggling in the toxic environment visualize what Reverend Benjamin Chavis named "environmental racism," wherein environmental harms disproportionately affect people of color.[87] At the time of *After Earth*'s release, for instance, a number of studies suggested that African American children were likelier to suffer from asthma and breathing disorders with higher morbidity rates than their white counterparts because of disparities that are socioeconomic, environmental, and policy related.[88]

Kitai's difficulty breathing takes on additional allegorical significance when reconsidered in relation to highly mediated acts of violence against Black men. As Cypher watches his son struggle for air on multiple occasions, contemporary viewers who are attentive to the histories and materialities of racism might find it difficult *not* to think of the footage of Eric Garner's killing and his last words: "I can't breathe." From this perspective, the conspicuous role of the body camera also takes on additional meaning. As a form of surveillance and protection for Kitai, this camera also invites a reading of *After Earth* in relation to the contemporary moment of racialized violence *and* its resistance; for Cypher, the camera becomes both a source of horror, exposing him to his son's vulnerability, and a resource for action, enabling him to identify and fend off potential threats.

Third, *After Earth*'s metaphors of ghosting and invisibility and its overt discussions of fear/lessness also evoke and anticipate key tropes within antiracist discourse. In addition to its allusions—intended or otherwise—to Elli-

---

87. See Holifield, "Defining Environmental Justice."
88. Edelstein, "Will and Jaden."

son's description of invisibility as both an injury and a survival mechanism, *After Earth* also recalls Coates's *Between the World and Me*, which is replete with metaphors of both ghosts and space travel. Written two years after his review of *After Earth* as a letter to his son, Coates's book recalls his own childhood and maturation as a Black man in the US. Not unlike Cypher's spoken words to his son, Coates's written words warn his child of dangers that await him at every turn. Coates locates himself and his son within a spectral economy populated by ghosts and haunted by ever-present danger. He frames this world as its own galaxy in which fear is both ubiquitous and always under cover as "extinction-level events" target Black bodies with a "singular and discriminating interest."[89]

As suggested by his name, Cypher Raige operates at one of two affective registers: anger or indifference. He is hot or cold but never warm. When Cypher's anger flares at his son, he recalls what Coates describes as the "rough manner" of elders quick to take a switch or a belt to their children—as in his own father's mantra, "Either I can beat him or the police." Such practices, Coates advises, must be seen in context and understood as driven by an impossible desire to drive out fear. Cypher's performances of hardness mirror what Coates describes as a familiar coping mechanism meant to "obscure the fear" of those who live in a "galaxy where [Black] bodies were enslaved by a tenacious gravity." Cypher's "rough manner" toward Kitai suggests his understanding that Black children "come to us endangered."[90] *After Earth* reveals this understanding to be not only learned but also lived, as multiple flashbacks reveal that Kitai witnessed the murder of his sister in the home they shared.

Despite moments in which Cypher shows rage, anger does not typify his disposition as much as disaffection does. For most of the film, Cypher appears not to have emotions at all. Aimed at suppressing fear, Cypher's inexpressivity acknowledges the interarticulation of emotions: expressions of joy or pleasure create spaces of vulnerability where there is also room for fear. Cypher's flat affect and emotional distance resemble Coates's descriptions of civil rights activists and parents of murdered Black children who appear "neither angry, nor sad, nor joyous" because betraying emotions is a luxury they cannot afford. Playing Cypher required Smith to deviate from the persona and style with which he had become associated. He does not play to his "charms" in *After Earth* and almost never flashes his "winning smile." These acting choices became the target of many of the negative reviews of the film, which rebuked Smith for not playing to type. For example, the *Wall Street Journal* diagnoses

---

89. Coates, *Between the World*, 90.
90. Coates, *Between the World*, 15, 20–21, 82.

Smith as having "undergone a radical charismaectomy," *Village Voice* chides Smith for not bringing "that charisma to the set," and, in his call to "Make Will Smith Great Again," Burkeman accuses *After Earth* as having broken Smith's film career.[91]

As noted earlier, words like *charisma* and *charm* abound in positive reviews of Smith's films, operating as metonyms for figurations of Smith as "racially nonthreatening." Geoff King explains, "That the Will Smith persona is 'nice,' charming and unthreatening has already been seen as a major factor in his ability to be seen as a performer appealing to white and/or middle-class audiences. This has ideological-political undertones: only by appearing 'safe,' or by appearing to mask the existence of racial divisions, can a black performer become a major Hollywood star."[92] Some negative responses to the film—many aimed at Smith and Jaden in personal, sometimes vitriolic, terms—can be understood as reacting to Smith's choice not to perform a version of Black masculinity that makes white audiences comfortable.

Cypher frames his fearlessness not as antithetical to his endangerment but as inextricable from it. Recounting a nearly fatal encounter with an Ursa, Cypher explains, "Fear is not real. The only place that fear can exist is in our thoughts of the future." He feels no fear in that moment because he does not believe in his own futurity. Cypher has recognized and internalized the condition of social death; living, for him, depends on already being, or at least feeling, dead. It is such logic that structures the rumored comment of one film executive who claimed, "Black people don't like science fiction . . . because they don't see themselves in the future," and it is precisely against such a sentiment of antifuturity that Black speculative fiction and Afrofuturism struggle.[93]

Coined in 1994 by Mark Dery, *Afrofuturism* describes an iteration of "speculative fiction that treats African-American themes and addresses African-American concerns in the context of twentieth-century techno-culture," as well as, "more generally, African-American signification that appropriates images of technology and a prosthetically enhanced future."[94] Science fiction, argues Ricardo Guthrie, typically either "expunges race" to foster postracial fantasies of futurity or reinscribes new versions of "racial hierarchy and white dominance." Afrofuturism offers an "antidote to these white imaginaries," positing visions of the future as a way to think through the problem of anti-Black

---

91. Morganstern, "Muddle-'Earth'"; Scherstuhl, "After Earth"; Burkeman, "Will and Jaden Smith."

92. King, *New Hollywood Cinema*, 168.

93. These words were reportedly spoken to Black authors Erika Alexander and Tim Puryear, discouraging them from pursuing a film adaptation of their graphic novel *Concrete Park*, which is set in a postapocalyptic future and centers on a Black woman hero. See Concrete Park Press Room, "TV and Film Star Erika Alexander."

94. Anderson and Jones, "Introduction," viii.

racism and, often, forwarding optimistic visions of emancipation.[95] Afrofuturism does not deny the existence of racial hierarchies or inequities, but neither does it assume that such obstacles are impassable.

As a science fiction film focused on a technocentric future, *After Earth* bears traces of Afrofuturistic sensibilities; yet its emphasis on the affects/effects of social death also articulates the perspectives of Afropessimism. As Jared Sexton argues, Afropessimism understands that "black life is *lived* in social *death*."[96] The film's depiction of Kitai's vulnerability and Cypher's disaffection echoes Frank Wilderson's description of Blackness as "always haunted by a shared sense that violence and captivity are the grammar and ghosts of [its] every gesture."[97] Afropessimism, Guthrie contends, marks what Wilderson names "natal alienation," or "death through enslavement," as central to the affective experiences of people of color. White society, argues Afropessimism, renders Black people "available for labor but constrained through gratuitous violence within civil society." Even Black celebrities, notes Guthrie, are subject to these terms, as Hollywood often asks them to perform traumas associated with natal alienation in service of narratives aimed at reassuring white audiences that "racial antagonisms are no longer present or significant"—a fact that is purportedly evidenced by the fame and privilege of the Black celebrities themselves.[98]

Cypher lives under the terms of Afropessimism, having lost hope in futurity, become alienated from his emotions, and forsaken emotional ties to others. Yet the development of *After Earth*'s narrative dramatizes the collapse of Cypher's ghosting under the weight of his connection to his son. Fearlessness, *After Earth* reveals, is feigned. As much as ghosting has become constitutive of Cypher's subjectivity, he begins to "unlearn" this skill when face-to-face with *both the precariousness and possibility* of his son's life and his future.[99] *After Earth* suggests that the vulnerability inherent in the interconnectedness of people is coeval with the possibilities of hope and love. To be connected to another person is to risk loss, particularly if precarity defines that person's

95. Guthrie, "Real Ghosts," 47.
96. Sexton, "Social Life."
97. Wilderson, "Grammar and Ghosts," 122–23.
98. Guthrie, "Real Ghosts," 50, 51.
99. This transformation of Smith's character from pessimism to optimism mirrors his evolution in another science fiction film, *I, Robot* (Alex Proyas, 2004). In this film, which offers another iteration of Frankenstein mythology, Smith plays Del Spooner, a cynical police detective investigating the murder of a scientist who may have been killed by a sentient-but-enslaved robot of his own creation. Over the course of the narrative, Spooner's disposition changes, making him more trusting and hopeful. As Ricardo Guthrie contends, "Spooner represents a type of Afro-Pessimist (Wilderson 2008) whose cynicism is gradually replaced by a soulful, Afro-futurist merger of black cultural ethos and commitment to struggle." See Guthrie, "Real Ghosts," 46.

life; but that connection also enables hope for the future. Paradoxically, it is Cypher's fear for his son's futurity that breathes new life into his own sense of self, demonstrating what Muñoz might call hope's queer potential. Or, as Coates explains to his son, "your very vulnerability brings you closer to the meaning of life."[100]

Kitai survives by learning to ghost but, having felt his own social death, ultimately refuses pessimism and insists on his own futurity. In a gesture contrary to the matching poses typical of the film's promotional materials, Kitai decides that he no longer wants to follow in his father's (famous) footsteps, choosing instead his mother's path of nonviolence and a life led outside the spotlight. *After Earth*, thus, maintains a productive tension between Afrofuturistic and Afropessimistic sensibilities, rejecting wholly optimistic visions of the future and resisting utterly pessimistic ones as well. Both *After Earth* and *Between the World and Me* illustrate Sexton's assertion that pessimism and optimism are not "negations" of one another but are mutually imbricated, mirroring the queer feminist recognition of paranoia and reparation as coextensive, rather than conflicting, interpretive perspectives.

The choice within *After Earth* to conclude with attention to Kitai's mother parallels Coates's choice in *Between the World and Me* to end with recollections of conversations with the mother of a college friend, Prince Jones, who was killed by police. Discussing the film *12 Years a Slave* (Steve McQueen, 2013), which was released five months following *After Earth*, Coates frames his friend's mother as using the film as a resource to help her process the loss of her son. The mother's story of her son, who has become a ghost to her, reflects the nightmare that Cypher imagines within the diegesis of *After Earth* and that Coates faces in his open letter to his son.[101]

A similar story animates another contemporary iteration of Black Frankenstein mythology: *Victor LaValle's Destroyer*. This futuristic graphic novel from 2017 tells the story of the mother of a murdered son and her attempts to bring her son back to life.[102] The last living descendant of Victor Frankenstein, Dr. Josephine "Jo" Baker is the nation's top scientist, a mother, and a Black woman. When police kill twelve-year-old Akai on his way home from

---

100. Coates, *Between the World*, 107.

101. *Raising Dion* (2019), a Netflix series based on a comic book of the same name, addresses similar themes, telling the story of a single mom trying to protect her Black son with superpowers in a racist world.

102. Victor LaValle is a Black writer known for work in the science fiction and horror genres. Weeks after his *Destroyer* series first appeared, LaValle also published an edited collection of short stories by science fiction writer Richard Matheson. LaValle's introduction to the collection begins with a brief discussion of Matheson's famous novel, *I Am Legend*, which inspired the Smith film of the same name. See LaValle, "Introduction," xviii.

a baseball game, mistaking his bat for a weapon, Baker reanimates her son's corpse, using state-of-the-art robotics technology and her ancestor's notes. *After Earth* implicitly references anti-Black racism, but *Destroyer* overtly juxtaposes images of violence against Black bodies with Shelley's novel.

In the first issue of *Destroyer*, Baker prepares her reanimation experiment, remembering her son's life and her choices as a parent.[103] She recalls telling Akai that he was too "tenderhearted" and needed to toughen up, which resembles those parental directives described by Coates and enacted by Cypher to choose toughness over kindness as a survival strategy. By issue 2, Baker has weaponized Akai's murdered and reanimated body with armor to protect his tender flesh, enlisting him in her fight against her former employer, an evil corporation that wants to hold Baker hostage as a valuable "asset." This narrative mirrors *After Earth* quite closely, as both texts hold in tension a parent's desire to keep a watchful eye over a child with the knowledge that the child can never be fully protected from peril.

The third issue of *Destroyer* opens with Baker's traumatic flashback to the day Akai died; she relives their last conversation as he left the house in his baseball uniform while she offered him banal advice about not eating too much junk food before dinner. Interrupting this flashback, two white agents from the corporation for which Baker worked infiltrate her lab. The agents marvel over Akai's technologized body, touching his arms and hands in ways reminiscent of the ways in which white people have historically fetishized the hair and bodies of people of color. Standing guard over Akai, Baker warns, "Stop touching my son," recognizing that these agents, like the company and society they represent, only value her son's body and life to the extent that they can exploit it.

Even after Akai has been armored with nanotechnology, Baker must goad her gentle son into using his powers against the agents who aim to take both of them hostage. Like Kitai, Akai had not become hard or fearless. Violence and cruelty are not in his nature, even as his body itself signifies power and aggression. As Baker talks to the agents, she describes being "let go" by the corporation when she became pregnant and then taking a university job so she could pursue her research honestly. With tenure and her son in a good school, Baker remembers thinking that they'd "made it" and "were safe," but

---

103. In his postscript to the first issue, LaValle emphasizes the importance of mother figures and the experience of loss to both his graphic novel and Shelley's source novel, noting that Shelley's mother lost her life during a pregnancy and that Shelley herself lost a child; he describes such fears being animated in him, a Black man and father, by mediated coverage of violence against Black bodies in 2014 and 2015. In a footnote of the third issue, LaValle defines a "just society" as one that recognizes the value of all its "Creations."

the memory of two white police officers at her door with the news of her son's death illustrates the destruction of that fantasy. This account of Baker's false belief that she and her son were safe mirrors what Coates recounts of his conversation with Prince Jones's mother, Mable Jones. Coates cites Dr. Jones, a scientist herself, as lamenting the fact that despite a life of "'developing a career, acquiring assets, engaging responsibilities,'" she could not protect her son's "body from the ritual violence that had claimed" him.[104]

Like *Frankenstein* and *Hancock,* the subject of naming also becomes significant in LaValle's *Destroyer.* The main character bears the name of Josephine Baker, one of the first Black people to star in a Hollywood film who was also known for her refusal to perform for segregated crowds; Akai's name also has metonymic resonance. Translating from Japanese to mean "red," *Akai* suggests an association between this boy's life and the spilling of blood, as is literalized by Akai's bloody handprint on Baker's lab apron. This color suggests the vulnerability and precarity that have defined Akai's life, but the color red also connotes love and anger—the mutually defining emotions that Baker feels as the "mother of a dead black boy."[105]

The histories of violence made explicit in *Destroyer,* through its return to Frankenstein mythology, also animate a resurrection of Smith's sitcom *The Fresh Prince of Bel-Air.* In 2018 cinematographer and self-described *Fresh Prince* fan Morgan Cooper directed *Bel-Air,* a short film presented as a trailer for a film that dramatically reimagines Smith's comedic series. In 2022 Smith and his multimedia production company Westbrook Studios actualized this speculative trailer, adapting it as a dramatic series for NBCUniversal's streaming service Peacock.

In *Bel-Air,* Philadelphia police find Will with a gun in his possession. In an effort to keep him alive, his mother sends him to live with his wealthy aunt and uncle in California. *Bel-Air* uses dialogue from the sitcom and lyrics from its title song verbatim but turns the comedic series upside down by focusing on the painful, if not traumatic, experiences of its lead character as he navigates classism and racism in the uberwealthy world of Bel-Air. One scene from Cooper's film, for instance, shows the palpable discomfort of white people as Will explains that he had trouble with a gun in Philly, which contrasts with another scene in which the white basketball coach of a private high school marvels over Will's athleticism. Later, Will's cousin explains that she will take him to Rodeo Drive so that he can remake his image to befit his new home. In this way, Cooper's film also alludes to the dramatic ethos of *Six Degrees of*

---

104. Coates, *Between the World,* 145, 144.
105. Coates, *Between the World,* xx.

Separation and the satire of *Hancock,* which share an interest in white people's desires to make over and recreate Black bodies and subjectivities.

The references to violence in Cooper's film summon the specter of Black death and the precarity of Black life. *Bel-Air* might be understood as a return of the anti-Black racism and violence that were largely repressed in Smith's sitcom; but not unlike the parodies of Rockwell's work that I discuss at the end of chapter 2, this film makes visible racial critiques that were already articulated throughout Smith's body of work. In fact, the tagline for *Bel-Air* interrogates the racialized conditions of Smith's celebrity. Asking "What would happen if Will Smith made *The Fresh Prince* today?," *Bel-Air* acknowledges the cultural and industrial constraints that would have made it difficult, if not impossible, for Smith to achieve stardom with work that made pointed critiques of anti-Black racism. Cooper might not have expected that Smith would, in fact, return to *Fresh Prince,* but Smith's choice (and capacity) to turn Cooper's film into a full series reboot suggests that the conditions of the star's fame may have changed (to a degree) since he first became famous.

Regardless of Smith's actual choice to reboot the series with which he was first associated, the conditional mood suggested by the hypotheticality of Cooper's original "what if" question bears noting. It invites consideration of other examples of Smith's early work: "What would happen if Will Smith made *Six Degrees of Separation* today?" Even more so, it calls attention to the conditions of possibility that have enabled (and constrained) Smith's performances of stardom, as well as the conditions of possibility enabled (and constrained) by Smith's performances of stardom. Such questions of Smith's past and future are the subject of *Gemini Man* (Ang Lee, 2019), in which Smith directly confronts the choices of his younger self. Playing an aging assassin pitted against Junior, a younger clone of himself, Smith must save his younger self from pursuing the life that he did. It is perhaps no accident that *Gemini Man* confronts Smith with a version of himself from twenty-five years prior— at almost the exact moment he gained fame through *The Fresh Prince* and *Six Degrees of Separation.* Collectively, the textual assemblage offered by this chapter understands Smith's career as a complex and increasingly self-aware meditation on the terms and conditions that shape Black fame in Hollywood. In turn, these considerations deploy fame as a lens through which to refract questions about the vulnerabilities and precarities that affect all Black lives.

INTERSTITIAL 2

The Eyes Have Had It

In his acceptance speech for his Best Actor Oscar for *Philadelphia,* Tom Hanks declared that his success in the film was only made possible by the thousands of lives lost to AIDS, leaving the "streets of heaven too crowded with angels." It was such an emphasis on suffering and loss that led many critics to read *Philadelphia,* not unlike like *Six Degrees of Separation,* as participant in a paradigm prevalent in popular US cinema of the twentieth century: the tragic gay narrative.[1] Although both films depict their leading gay characters as sympathetic figures, they ultimately deny them full lives or fulfillment: Andy dies at the end of *Philadelphia,* and Paul ends *Six Degrees of Separation* alone and impoverished. More recent films critiqued for reinforcing this tragic frame include *Brokeback Mountain* (Ang Lee, 2005), *Milk* (Gus Van Sant, 2008), *Pedro* (Nick Oceano, 2008), and *A Single Man* (Tom Ford, 2009), all of which involve gay men who lose a lover and/or die themselves.[2]

Critics typically understand this tragic frame as deviating from the cinematic paradigm that historically reinforced associations between queerness and criminality or monstrosity, as illustrated by such serial killer films as *Dressed to Kill* (Brian De Palma, 1980), *Cruising* (William Friedkin, 1980), and *Silence of the Lambs* (Jonathan Demme, 1991). Writing about *Silence of the*

---

1. Critics have also taken issue with this film's reliance on the trope of the straight savior. See Gittell, "*Dallas Buyers Club.*"
2. Pullen, "Heroic Gay Characters"; Mennel, *Queer Cinema.*

Lambs, for example, Janet Staiger notes that many critics felt "that in a time of paranoia over AIDS and increased violence toward gays in the United States, even suggesting connections between homosexuals and serial murderers was irresponsible."[3] *Philadelphia* might be understood as a particularly direct and notable response to such critiques, as it was the next of Demme's films to follow *Silence of the Lambs,* leading some to read it as an apologia. For instance, Larry Kramer describes *Silence* as "one of the most virulently and insidiously homophobic films ever made," asking, "Is 'Philadelphia' some sort of attempt on his part to offer an apology?"[4]

Demme denied that explanation for *Philadelphia,* offering a different backstory for the film. In 1994 Demme identified the film's inspiration as his friend Juan Suarez Botas, a filmmaker and magazine illustrator who had died of AIDS.[5] Others have suggested another, even more complex origin for *Philadelphia.* Shortly after its release, almost everyone involved in its production was sued by the survivors of Geoffrey Bowers, a New York–based attorney who died of AIDS in 1987 and who was one of the first plaintiffs in an HIV/AIDS discrimination suit. Alleging that the film misappropriated Bowers's story, the suit against the makers of *Philadelphia,* which asked for $10 million in damages and was presented in front of Judge Sonia Sotomayor, claimed that Bowers shared his story with the film's original producer, Scott Rudin. The film's distributor, TriStar Pictures, admitted that *Philadelphia* was inspired "in part" by Bowers, offering his family an undisclosed settlement in 1996.[6] *Six Degrees of Separation* also involved the threat of a lawsuit from the person on whom it was based. David Hampton demanded $1 million in compensation from John Guare for use of his life story, which led to charges of harassment from the playwright on top of the charges of petty larceny, criminal impersonation, and fraudulent accosting for which Hampton was convicted. To be clear, then, both films (released just one month apart) involved lawsuits from actual people in positions of precarity who died of AIDS in their thirties.

Demme's *Silence of the Lambs* did not generate lawsuits, but it did ignite firestorms because of its LGBTQ-phobic depictions of serial killer Buffalo Bill and because of the refusal of the film's lead actress, Jodie Foster, to address her sexuality. As Staiger recounts, many LGBTQ activists criticized Foster, rumored for years to be a lesbian, for not speaking out against homophobia.[7] One tactic of these activists was to "out" Foster without her consent, includ-

---

3. Staiger, *Perverse Spectators,* 161.
4. Kramer, "Why I Hated 'Philadelphia.'" See also Bliss and Banks, *What Goes Around,* 136.
5. DeCurtis, "Jonathan Demme."
6. Pristin, "'Philadelphia' Screenplay Suit," 47, 53.
7. Staiger, *Perverse Spectators,* 142–43.

ing via posters featuring a photograph of Foster with the caption "Oscar winner. Yale graduate. Ex-Disney Moppet. Dyke." Kramer's eulogy for Vito Russo decried the screening of *Silence of the Lambs* at an AIDS fundraiser while accusing Foster of being in the closet.[8] Foster did not publicly come out until decades after the film's release, and, as Clare Whatling notes, promotional campaigns for films Foster made shortly after *Silence of the Lambs* conspicuously framed her as traditionally feminine and heterosexual.[9]

Although Staiger discusses *Silence of the Lambs* in *Perverse Spectators*, she does not link it to her discussions of *Psycho* and *The Texas Chainsaw Massacre*, despite their shared source story. Based on the story of the murderer Ed Gein, all three films include some details from Gein's actual crimes, featuring killers who collect human remains and sometimes fabricate them into household items. The films also involve elements of gender transformation loosely borrowed from Gein's source story: in *Psycho*, Norman Bates assumes the identity of his mother; in *The Texas Chainsaw Massacre*, Leatherface wears a mask of a woman's face heavily adorned with makeup; and in *Silence of the Lambs*, Buffalo Bill wants to make himself a suit made from women's skin. The films also depict grotesque violence targeted at women, centering on an intrepid woman who survives the serial killers' attacks.

These films share other links as well. As noted in chapter 1, Staiger's "perverse" reading of *The Texas Chainsaw Massacre* cites this film as intertextually linked to Alfred Hitchcock's *Psycho* because they share fetishistic attachment to the human eye. Both films, Staiger notes, "use excessive close-ups of eyes matched to other round objects," fixating on the eyes of women as they experience extreme violence: Sally as she is tortured at the dining table and Marion Crane as Norman Bates stabs her to death in the shower. Staiger reads such shots as enacting a "symbolic chain of meaning" but never specifies what such meaning(s) might be.[10] This stylistic and symbolic choice also connects these films to *Silence of the Lambs*, which features multiple tight close-ups of both Hannibal Lecter's and Clarice Starling's eyes, demonstrating interest in the gaze and vision as concepts.

Perhaps unexpectedly, this aesthetic fixation also links these films to a much later one, *A Single Man*, which derives from Christopher Isherwood's 1964 novel of the same name and which has been called "*Philadelphia* for the art house crowd."[11] *A Single Man* stars Colin Firth as George Falconer, a

---

8. Crimp, "Right On, Girlfriend!," 16, 3.

9. For example, Whatling describes how the promotional materials for her romantic drama *Sommersby* (Jon Amiel, 1993) emphasized her chemistry and sexual tension with costar Richard Gere, who was also rumored to be gay and closeted. See Whatling, *Screen Dreams*.

10. Staiger, *Perverse Spectators*, 180.

11. Anderson, "Closet Case." See also DeAngelis, "Queer Memories."

white gay college professor on what will be the last day of his life as he ambles around his home, has a brief exchange with a hustler in a parking lot, and makes a brief but meaningful connection with a young man in one of his classes. Contemplating suicide, George plans to spend the evening with his best friend and former lover, a white heterosexual woman named Charley, played by Julianne Moore. Not part of Isherwood's source novel, George's suicidal ideations were added by Ford's adaptation, contributing to readings of the film as a "tragic gay narrative."

Reviews of *A Single Man* often frame its lead character as playing a role, including Mahnola Dargis's description of George as wearing a "beautiful and gently furrowed mask." He is a man hiding behind a carefully crafted image of restraint that aims both to protect him from the homophobic world he inhabits and to help him keep himself together as his life falls apart.[12] As George says in voice-over, "It takes time in the morning for me to become George. By the time I've dressed and put the final layer of polish on the now slightly stiff but quite perfect George, I know fully what part I'm supposed to play." As critics note, these efforts at image-making often leave George feeling like a contradiction, an impasse personified. For example, while he spends much of his day disdainfully scrutinizing the forced wholesomeness of "the Norman Rockwell-ish folks next door,"[13] he also comports himself "like a living, breathing cliché of a Norman Rockwell painting, an iconic American man of a certain age," so buttoned up that you can hardly seem him breathe.[14]

Given that Ford's film is a melodrama and not a horror film, it may seem to have very little, if anything, in common with *Psycho* or *The Texas Chainsaw Massacre*.[15] Nonetheless, *A Single Man* can be linked with these films on multiple registers, including its reliance on multiple close-ups of women's eyes. One example of this motif makes a direct allusion to Hitchcock's *Psycho*, featuring an oversized poster for the movie plastered on the exterior wall of a building.[16] The poster prominently depicts the terrified face of Janet Leigh as Mar-

---

12. Dargis, "A Love."
13. Romney, "A Single Man."
14. Atkinson, "Parting."
15. It is worth noting that both *Psycho* and *The Texas Chainsaw Massacre* have been read as operating in a melodramatic mode, given their emphasis on familial relations and affects. See Hemmeter, "Hitchcock's Melodramatic Silence"; and Donaldson, "Access and Excess." Similar takes have been offered about *Silence of the Lambs*, for example, Canby, "Methods of Madness."
16. In her review of the film for *Film Comment*, Amy Taubin notes that *A Single Man* also pays homage to Hitchcock's *Vertigo* through its "subjective use of color" to suggest the affects and psychological states of its white cis male protagonist. *A Single Man*'s soundtrack also includes a song called "A Variation on Scotty Tails Madeline," by Shigeru Umebayashi, which reimagines Bernard Herrmann's "Scotty Tails Madeline" from the *Vertigo* score. See Taubin, "Single Man."

ion Crane, and *A Single Man*'s cinematography and mise-en-scène emphasize Leigh's eyes on the poster.

Other close-up shots in *A Single Man* fixate on the eyes of Moore, who plays Charley as a narcissistic addict whose primary interests in life seem to be fashion, beauty, and George's fawning attention. One scene depicts Charley applying makeup at her vanity with extreme close-ups of her eye, seen in the distorted reflection of her handheld mirror, offering a Baroque rendition of Rockwell's *Going Out*—a painting discussed more fully in chapter 2. In both images, a white woman with curled red hair sits at a vanity table skirted with fabric as she applies her makeup in anticipation of a special event. While Rockwell's character sits at a forty-five-degree angle in her Joan Crawford–inspired gown on a stool draped with a white fur coat, Charley sits at a forty-five-degree angle in her lingerie on a white fur chair with her coat draped over the back. Both tables boast a large, framed mirror with smaller handheld mirrors and assorted cosmetics scattered on their tops. While Rockwell's image has a mostly black-and-white palette with occasional uses of reds and greens, Ford's image contrasts a variety of colors, patterns, and textures, in keeping with the opulence of Baroque style.

Perhaps Ford's choice to include allusions to *Psycho*, which were also deviations from Isherwood's source novel, references the fact that the film was set just two years after the release of Hitchcock's film; but given that *Psycho* would have been two years old within the diegesis of Ford's film, it seems unlikely that a billboard of this size would still be intact on the side of a building. *A Single Man*'s links to *Psycho*, as well as others to *Vertigo*, might also reference long-standing arguments that Hitchcock's oeuvre is filled with queer characters and/or repressed same-sex desires, including Norman Bates in *Psycho*—who, like George, relies on figurative masks to create an illusion of restraint.[17] But these allusions within *A Single Man* also point toward the fact that Moore herself has a direct connection to *Psycho*, having starred as Marion's sister, Lila Crane, in Gus Van Sant's 1998 shot-for-shot remake of the film.[18]

Moore's role as Lila in *Psycho*, a character originally played by Vera Miles, was not the first time Moore stepped into a part made famous by another

---

17. Taubin, "Single Man"; Doty, *Flaming Classics*; Greven, "Death-Mother."
18. Van Sant directed the music video for Elton John's "The Last Song," which played in the final sequence of *And the Band Played On* and was the first song to raise funds for John's eponymous AIDS foundation. Van Sant's *My Own Private Idaho* (1991) is a film that, like *Six Degrees of Separation*, tells the story of a young gay sex worker who was in search of a sense of belonging. While *My Own Private Idaho* has been considered a hallmark of the New Queer Cinema movement of the 1990s, Van Sant's film *Milk* has been called a "tragic gay narrative."

actor.[19] Just three years after Van Sant's film, she took over Foster's role as Clarice Starling in *Hannibal*, Ridley Scott's sequel to *Silence of the Lambs*. As both Crain and Starling, Moore plays a version of Carol Clover's Final Girl—the lone woman to survive a horror film because of her intelligence, strength, and willingness to engage the monster, all characteristics that signal her deviation from hegemonic feminine norms.[20] Crain's and Starling's nonconformity with gender norms has also led some scholars to read them as queer; in Starling's case, interpretations of her sexuality are impossible to separate from extratextual speculations about Foster, even when Moore plays her onscreen.[21]

Although *Hannibal* generated neither the acclaim nor the controversy that *Silence of the Lambs* did, it caused some uproar about an infamous scene that depicts Moore-as-Starling held captive at a dinner table by Lecter (played, as in *Silence of the Lambs*, by Anthony Hopkins).[22] Immobilized by a gunshot wound and powerful sedatives, Starling is forced to watch the cannibalistic serial killer feed her FBI colleague pieces of his own brain. This scene acts as an homage to the infamous dinner scene from *The Texas Chainsaw Massacre*, which is based on stories about Gein's crimes and, perhaps unexpectedly, on one of Rockwell's most famous paintings.

In Hooper's 1974 exploitation horror film, a family of cannibals kidnaps a young white woman named Sally. Binding and gagging her, the family traps her at the dining table for a meal at which she will be the entrée. The kidnappers cut Sally's finger so that the nearly dead patriarch of the family can drink her blood, causing Sally to lose consciousness. When she awakens, a point-of-view (POV) shot from Sally's perspective reveals an extreme close-up of the eye sockets of an animal skull resting on the table. Multiple shots of the eye sockets of this and other skulls, along with more POV shots from Sally's vantage, punctuate the scene. As the men prepare to kill and eat Sally, she screams in agony, and a series of increasingly tight extreme close-ups of her

---

19. Miles and Moore have at least one other intertextual relationship. Miles appeared in the pilot episode of the 1963 television series *The Fugitive*, which was adapted as a film thirty years later and featured Moore in an analogous supporting role. Moore has appeared in other remakes as well. In 2002 she starred in Todd Haynes's *Far from Heaven*, which remade Douglas Sirk's 1955 melodrama *All That Heaven Allows*. Sirk's film starred Rock Hudson as its straight male lead, but extratextual knowledge of his sexuality has helped foster a queer following for the film. Haynes's film folds those extratextual connotations into the narrative of his film, depicting a leading male character who comes out of the closet and leaves his wife, played by Moore, for a man. More recently, Moore starred in two other remakes, *Gloria Bell* (Sebastián Lelio, 2018) and *After the Wedding* (Bart Freundlich, 2019).
20. Greven, "Death-Mother," 168; Clover, *Men, Women, and Chain Saws*, 35.
21. Doty, *Flaming Classics*, 177.
22. Clinton, "Bloody 'Hannibal'"; Wilson, "Lecter's Bloody Second Course."

eyes emphasize her horror and fear. One of the shots is so close that you can see the veins in her eyes, highlighting the extent to which her captors understand her as nothing more than flesh and blood to be devoured.

The gruesome tableau and family scene that Sally sees in *The Texas Chainsaw Massacre* alludes to Rockwell's *Freedom from Want* (1943), referencing that iconic image of an idealized heteronuclear family in order to underscore the sickness of Leatherface's clan. Instead of a table resplendent with fine china and a carefully prepared Thanksgiving meal, the table in *The Texas Chainsaw Massacre* appears dirty and scattered with bones and body parts. Rockwell's smiling faces of family members along the table and of the patriarch at its head are replaced in Hooper's film with the maniacal laughs and sneers of cannibals and the patriarch's corpselike body propped up at the end of the table. Leatherface has dressed in drag to play the role of Rockwell's matriarch, replacing his other masks with one adorned conspicuously with makeup. While Rockwell's painting shows the patriarch and matriarch of the family proudly displaying the turkey to be served, Hooper's film shows us the scene from the point of view of the "meat" herself.[23]

One of Rockwell's most famous paintings, *Freedom from Want* has been imitated and parodied in a range of contexts including *National Review*, *Advertising Age*, the animated Fox series *The Simpsons*, the ABC sitcom *Modern Family*, the PBS children's series *Sesame Street*, and a movie poster for Marvel's anti-superhero movie *Deadpool*. Many parodies poke fun at the racialized, classed, and gendered implications of the original, including the *Mad* magazine cartoon that supplants Rockwell's original figures with what Redmond calls "toxic" white women celebrities in various states of intoxication and undress.[24]

Another parody addresses the politics of gender and the objectification of women, by recalling the intertextual relationship between *Freedom from Want* and *The Texas Chainsaw Massacre*. As I discuss more fully in chap-

---

23. The affinities between Rockwell's image and this shot from *Texas Chainsaw Massacre* have been acknowledged by multiple fans and critics online. For instance, in a review posted on *Letterboxd*, Willow Catelyn describes the "composition at the table" as illustrating "perverse family values" and having "eviscerated" Norman Rockwell as a metonym for sanitized and sentimental figurations of the middle class. Likewise, the *Collection Connections* website, which specializes in the preservation of ephemeral media objects, includes a side-by-side comparison of the images in its digital archives. These readings of *Texas Chainsaw Massacre* reflect the description by *AV Club*'s Keith Phipps of the film as depicting a "bloody backlash from an American family closer to E.C. Comics than Norman Rockwell." Such readings resonate with film critic Robin Wood's sense that *Texas Chainsaw Massacre* is a kind of dark mirror for the Rockwellian vision of family life presented by the Hollywood musical *Meet Me in St. Louis* (Vincent Minnelli, 1944). See Wood, "American Family Comedy."

24. Redmond, "Sensing Celebrity."

ter 4, Kardashian appeared on a 2014 cover of *Paper* magazine in a series of images, created by Jean-Paul Goude, that were designed to be controversial. One image featuring Kardashian's bare buttocks became both the target of critique for its misogynoir and the subject of numerous misogynistic and racist parodies, in which Kardashian's buttocks were replaced with other objects (including parts of animal anatomy) or edited into other images, including *Freedom from Want*. In place of Rockwell's Thanksgiving turkey, the meme offers up Kardashian's backside on a platter. The joke of this image derives from the contrast between the presumed wholesomeness of Rockwell's image and the purported salaciousness of Kardashian's, wherein the Kardashian parody laments a supposed loss of innocence in which freedom from want has been transformed into unrestrained want. The meme makes Kardashian the literal butt of the joke and participates in the practice of blaming her for a supposed loss of cultural values metonymically associated with Rockwell. The image of Kardashian as Thanksgiving turkey also illustrates the normalization of misogyny and violence against women, signaling harms often inflicted on women's bodies, both literally and symbolically, in representations that Laura Mulvey might describe as sadistic and fetishistic.

It bears noting that Marilyn Burns, the actress who played Sally in *The Texas Chainsaw Massacre*, has indicated that the horrors of the film were not confined to its onscreen depictions, describing her on-set treatment as terrifying and violent. For instance, in the scene in which characters feed her blood to the family patriarch, an actor actually cut Burns and drew blood without her consent, and toward the end of filming the dinner scene, Burns became worried that men with whom she acted were going to harm her. Of course, violence toward women on film sets is not unique to *The Texas Chainsaw Massacre* or even to horror or exploitation production sites. As #MeToo and #TimesUp make clear, harassment and assault have long been a part of the film industry, which has often enabled powerful (white) men to exploit and abuse women with impunity. For example, actress Tippi Hedren, who starred in Hitchcock's *The Birds* (1963) and *Marnie* (1964), has spoken out about the director's abuses of her, inspiring the 2012 HBO film *The Girl* (Julian Jarrold). That same year, Anthony Hopkins starred as the eponymous lead in the biopic *Hitchcock* (Sacha Gervasi), which implies that the director also terrified Janet Leigh on the set of *Psycho*, threatening her with a real knife to elicit an authentic reaction from her.

Such gender violence is characterized by concomitant hypervisibility and invisibility; images of women experiencing violence, both fictional and factual, abound in US media culture, and yet (or, perhaps, therefore) incidents of gender violence are often overlooked or ignored as misogyny has been normalized.[25] In their conspicuous attention to women's eyes, *Psycho, The Texas Chainsaw Massacre, Silence of the Lambs,* and *A Single Man* register the extent to which women experience and understand (which is to say, *see*) their vulnerability to such violence and the extent to which the positioning of their bodies as the targets of an objectifying gaze can engender forms of violence against them. In *Psycho, The Texas Chainsaw Massacre,* and *Silence of the Lambs,* this violence is quite literal and graphic, whereas *A Single Man* addresses more subtle forms of misogyny. The film's emphasis on Charley's beauty routines signals her dependence on signifiers of feminine beauty as indices of her perceived self-worth. Offering very little development of Charley's character beyond depicting her makeup routines, substance-use habits, and the luxe mise-en-scène of her home and wardrobe, *A Single Man* depicts her as flattened by hegemonic gender and sexual norms into a series of surfaces. Charley has no sense of self beyond her image and other people's views of her, as if her life has no value outside its currency in a heteronormative economy, which leaves her isolated, lonely, and depressed.

Collectively, these films and their attention to women's reciprocal capacities to see and be seen illustrate that violence against women exists on a continuum, wherein normative expectations about women's beauty and objectification become participant in the cultural devaluation of women's subjectivities and bodies that authorizes material forms of violence against them. The close-ups of women's eyes make clear that they are neither oblivious to nor impassive about their subject positions in patriarchal cultures but are, instead, attuned to the norms imposed on them and agentic in relation to them. This textual assemblage demonstrates the ubiquity of misogyny and violence as through-lines in the lives of women, on- and offscreen—as connective tissues between their bodies, famous and not. It is that commonality that such hashtags as #MeToo and #YesAllWomen aim to capture. But these textual connections also illustrate how such vulnerabilities are unevenly distributed.

Let us return to the case of Jodie Foster, for example. Her choice not to come out until decades into her career is likely owed to the intersecting oppressions of misogyny and homophobia and to her recognition of her own vulnerability. At the same time, her choice as a wealthy, white cis woman in the public eye not to come out constituted an injury and insult to many of those who lacked her privilege and power, as demonstrated by Deb Baer's declaration of queer women's anger that Foster waited so long to come out.[26] Such silence arguably compounds already poor working conditions for queer

---

25. Manne, *Down Girl,* 5.
26. Baer, "Why I'm So Angry."

women, especially BIPOC queer women, in Hollywood, where they already lack "access to the necessary networks, capital or resources"[27] to pursue their own projects or "subvert the white male gaze."[28]

Conversely, consider the example of the 1994 Best Actor acceptance speech by Tom Hanks, a straight cis white man, who played a gay man with AIDS but refused to kiss his onscreen love interest for a film whose story was based on the lives of actual gay men who died of the disease. Without Hanks's star power and privilege, that story likely would not have been told in 1993; but, in taking that part, Hanks shored up his persona as a noble straight savior and was duly rewarded. Hanks's speech briefly acknowledges those who lack his privilege, including the many people who lost their lives to AIDS; he also describes his costar Washington as the only actor in the film to really put his career at risk but never names racism or white supremacy in Hollywood and does little, if anything, to challenge such injustice. Also during this speech, Hanks expresses gratitude toward the two gay men he knew in his youth, whose examples, he suggests, enabled him to play his role in *Philadelphia*. Never mind that one of those men—Hank's high school drama teacher—was not out to his local community at the time that the Hollywood star called him by name on the Oscars telecast. This accidental *outing* became the subject of the comedy *In & Out* (Frank Oz, 1997), which stars straight actors Kevin Kline and Tom Selleck, who had previously sued *National Enquirer* for claiming he was gay.

Hanks's expressions of gratitude reveal hegemonic structures, such as white masculinity and the Hollywood film industry, as networks dependent on and exploitative of the vulnerability, precarity, and suffering of others— even while claiming (or perhaps even intending) to be benevolent to those precaritized others, including women and BIPOC, queer, and/or disabled people. As Towns explains, whiteness and masculinity use the bodies of those they oppress as mediums—not unlike "the printing press, the television, or even the Web"—for the reproduction of their privilege and power.[29] Case in point, Hanks went on to win his next Best Actor Oscar playing a man with intellectual and physical disabilities.

The calls from LGBTQ activists for Foster to come out at a time of increased threat to queer people or for straight stars like Hanks not to treat queer or disabled parts as opportunities to "pad out their canon and their legacy"[30] resonate with Brittney Cooper's 2016 critique of white women for enabling

---

27. "Cross-Post."
28. Denton-Hurst, "Seen on Screen."
29. Towns, "Toward a Black Media Philosophy," 869.
30. King, "Not Only the Brave."

the election of Donald Trump as the forty-fifth US president. Cooper frames Trump's victory as a failure of accountability on the part of white women, who "did not come get their people." Cooper admonishes white women for not doing the work of calling out both white men and white women for their participation in structures of oppression and for failing to "make the leap toward solidarity" based on understanding of how "the project of white supremacy" affects both Black women and white women. Cooper writes, "White women and, specifically, white feminists have to reckon with their complicity and often full participation in this set of social narratives about Black sexuality that has been exceedingly dangerous to the well-being of Black lives."[31] The refusal to address such complicity is a failure of response-ability. As Butler argues, to recognize human interconnectedness and interdependency requires accepting humans' obligations to preserve not only the self but also the lives of others.[32]

As a hyperbolic example of interconnectedness, celebrity culture makes clear that networks are never drawn along equivalent lines of power. In fact, celebrity culture offers a particularly visible demonstration of the Foucauldian claim that all relations (social and textual) are power relations. To call attention to these linkages through metonymic criticism, however, is not merely a descriptive act that reveals how networks operate. It is also a normative one that positions attention to both interconnectivity and power as a precursor for an ethics of care, and it is a call for accountability from those in hegemonic positions not merely to acknowledge their privilege but also to marshal it as a resource.

---

31. Cooper, *Eloquent Rage*, 171, 180, 196.
32. Butler, *Force of Nonviolence*.

CHAPTER 4

Emotional Icons

Digital Culture, Networks of Affect, and Kim Kardashian

> "What is the operation by which a self relates itself to its own self, transparently? Selfie."
> —Kim Kierkegaardashian, @KIMKIERKEGAARD

> *Kim Kardashian was in* Deep in the Valley *with Denise Richards, who was in* Wild Things *with Kevin Bacon.*

During the 2016 Paris Fashion Week, five masked men disguised as paparazzi and police officers robbed Kim Kardashian at gunpoint. Binding and gagging Kardashian, the assailants fled with millions of dollars' worth of her possessions. Almost immediately, news outlets alerted audiences to the breaking story, speculating about Kardashian's emotional state and her next moves. Public figures and social media users remarked on Kardashian's plight, and while some expressed empathy, others blamed Kardashian for the assault and/or seized the opportunity to make jokes at her expense. For example, designer Karl Lagerfeld told reporters on a Paris red carpet, "You cannot display your wealth and then be surprised that some people want to share it with you." Late-night television host Jimmy Kimmel feigned disbelief that the robbers could find the one moment when Kardashian wasn't being followed by cameras. Following the attack, some retailers offered "bound and gagged" Kardashian Halloween costumes.

Twitter discourse was largely unkind, calling the robbery a publicity stunt, photoshopping images of Kardashian's bruised and lacerated body, recirculating the well-known meme of her "cry face," or asserting that she deserved to die.[1]

---

1. While multiple images of Kardashian crying have circulated online, the most iconic one originated in *Kortney and Kim Take New York*, a spin-off of the reality series *Keeping Up With the Kardashians*. This still image of Kardashian with her eyes partially closed and mouth agape in anguish has been memed and even turned into consumer objects. On celebrity memes, see Rojek, *Fame Attack*, 90–91.

Occasionally, tweets referenced other celebrities, including jokes that Taylor Swift engineered the attack or that Kardashian faked the robbery, not unlike Ryan Lochte during the 2016 Olympics in Brazil. Celebrity and social media personality Chrissy Teigen framed Kardashian's experience as illustrating the paradoxes of celebrity culture, declaring that famous people are expected to love their audiences "while also knowing [they would] make a meme of [their] dead bodies to get retweets." Other online respondents addressed the misogyny structuring many of the jokes about Kardashian, including Matilda Dixon-Smith's remarks that Kardashian's treatment illustrates the victim blaming and slut shaming experienced by women every day.[2]

After the attack, Kardashian stepped away from social media for a three-month hiatus before returning with a notable, but temporary, change in her Instagram posts. In place of selfies and glamorous photographs taken in couture fashion at red-carpet events, Kardashian shared seemingly candid pictures. Grainy and faded, as if aged or taken on Polaroid film, these images feature Kardashian and then spouse Kanye West with their children in a sparsely decorated home. The amateurish aesthetic of the images and their supposed scenes of everyday life correspond to public rhetoric in which Kardashian claimed to be enjoying a "slower life" in the wake of the attack and feeling grateful for lessons she learned from the event.[3] This stylistic change implies that the traumatic experience led Kardashian to re-evaluate her priorities, illustrating a redemption narrative of sorts. Eight days later, her posts resumed the sensibilities with which she had been associated, emphasizing luxury and excess.

The mediation of Kardashian's experience illustrates the centrality of melodrama to celebrity culture and its articulations with metonymy as a rhetorical form. This chapter argues that both melodrama and metonymy invite recognition of vulnerability, interdependence, and contingency as definitive of human signification and subjectivity. Taking up figurations of Kardashian as a metonym for the melodramatic affects of celebrity culture, this chapter critiques the gender and race politics of Kardashian's persona while also finding resources within her public image for challenging hegemonic discourses about selfhood in the US.

KEEPING UP WITH MELODRAMA

Born in Los Angeles, California, Kardashian gained fame through her relationship with socialite Paris Hilton; but it was the 2007 circulation of *Kim*

---

2. Dixon-Smith, "Reaction to Kim Kardashian's Robbery."
3. Grossman, "Why Kim Kardashian Is 'Grateful.'"

Kardashian Superstar, a sex tape made with musician and reality television personality Ray J, that led to her becoming a household name and to her family's reality television series, *Keeping Up With the Kardashians* (*KUWTK*). Prior to becoming famous herself, Kardashian grew up amid celebrity culture: her father, Robert Kardashian, was friends with O. J. Simpson and was involved with his 1995 trial, and her mother was married to Olympic athlete Caitlin Jenner. Kardashian's inherited association with celebrity and participation in the genre of reality television account for frequent descriptions of her as "famous for being famous," but Kardashian has also built an expansive commercial empire.[4]

Beyond her family's reality series and its spin-offs, Kardashian has produced other television series, owned a retail store, designed a clothing line for QVC, served as a spokesperson for multiple product lines, developed her own line of cosmetics, created a book, and licensed multiple digital applications, including the mobile game *Kim Kardashian: Hollywood*, the shopping app Screenshop, and her own line of emoji, Kimoji. Active on social media, including Snapchat, Twitter, and Instagram, Kardashian helped define the online marketing category of "influencer." As Sharon Marcus contends, "If you have bought milk or toilet paper in the past ten years, you have seen the Kardashians on the covers of magazines and are likely to recognize their faces, even if you cannot tell Kim from Khloe and have never heard of, let alone watched, the television shows that made them famous."[5] While many have critiqued Kardashian as emblematic of digital-era narcissism run amok, others have called her a pioneering artist akin to Warhol, Virginia Woolf, or the Brontës.[6] As Maureen Dauphne says, "Kardashian may very well be the greatest performance artist of our time. Or she's the worst example of our culture's snowballing narcissism and vanity."[7]

Kardashian's brand offers access to her and her family, including her mother, her siblings, her romantic partners, and her children. Kardashian has deployed both reality television and social media to share personal information about herself ranging from her medical history to her fitness and diet regimens to moments of familial and marital discord, and her near-constant

---

4. The packaging for the *Superstar* DVD relies on this rhetoric of fame by association, describing her as the "daughter of O. J. Simpson lawyer Robert Kardashian, the stepdaughter of Olympic Gold Medalist [Caitlin] Jenner, and the best friend of Paris Hilton." The blurb references the size of her partner's genitalia in relation to the theory of "six degrees," positioning Kardashian as "9½ [inches] from stardom."

5. Marcus, "Celebrity 2.0," 23.

6. Newell-Hanson, "Kim Kardashian West"; Saltz and Wallace-Wells, "How and Why"; Riviere, "Kardashian Sisters." For a more cynical discussion of her image culture that mocks the notion that she is an artist, see Jones, "Kim Kardashian's *Selfish*."

7. Muller, "Surprising High-Art Theory."

selfies encourage feelings of intimacy and immediacy for her audiences.[8] For example, a 2016 episode of *KUWTK* shows the Kardashian sisters undergoing a BRCA gene test, and later that year, Kardashian shared selfies of herself taking a pregnancy test on an airplane. This emphasis on the emotional and personal dimensions of Kardashian's life typifies celebrity culture's reliance on the sensibilities and affects of melodrama. As Barbara Walters reported, "The Kardashians are everywhere, their empire endlessly self-replicating with spin-off after spin-off, a strange mix of trashy sex, upscale excess . . . tabloid melodrama and suburban family life."[9]

An essential function of celebrity culture is the performance of emotional labor aimed at guiding public attitudes and feelings. As Christine Gledhill contends, "stars function as signs in a rhetorical system" that we might call melodramatic. The "conceptual link" Gledhill identifies "between melodrama and stardom" should be understood in the context of the histories and theories of melodrama.[10] Peter Brooks argues, "The desire to express *all* seems a fundamental characteristic of the melodramatic mode," which takes shape through expressions of the "deepest feelings" and an insistence on excess.[11] Elisabeth Anker similarly characterizes melodrama as depicting "dramatic events through moral polarities of good and evil, overwhelmed victims, heightened affects of pain and suffering, grand gestures, astonishing feats of heroism, and the redemption of virtue."[12]

Histories of melodrama identify the genre as originating in the theater of eighteenth-century France just before the revolution. Jean-Jacques Rousseau coined the term *melodrama*, or *mélodrame*, as a portmanteau from the Greek word for music (*melos*) and the French term for drama (*drame*) to differentiate his work *Pygmalion*, which alternates spoken words with music, from Italian opera, in which all the lines are sung. Borrowing from Greek mythology, Rousseau's melodrama tells the story of sculptor Pygmalion's love for his marble creation Galatea, who comes to life and assumes an identity of her own. Monique Rooney reads Rousseau's melodrama, which combines "various art forms or mediums (song, lyrical prose poem and dramatic action and gesture)," as a self-reflexive theorization of "transmediality," figuring Galatea as a metaphor for plasticity and transposition.[13]

---

8. Jerslev and Mortensen, "What Is the Self?"
9. McClain, *Keeping Up*, 1.
10. Gledhill, "Signs of Melodrama," 207. See also DeAngelis, *Gay Fandom*.
11. Brooks, *Melodramatic Imagination*, 4.
12. Anker, *Orgies of Feeling*, 2.
13. Rooney, *Living Screens*, 24.

Melodrama migrated to the United States in the nineteenth century in theatrical and literary forms before gravitating in the twentieth century toward the cinema. The performative stylistics of theatrical melodrama enabled the transition from stage to big screen, as silent films borrowed from theatrical melodrama's "repertory of gestures, facial expressions, bodily postures and movements" to convey meanings and emotions without the assistance of synchronized sound.[14] Even after the advent of talkies, cinematic melodrama demonstrated an affinity for heightened affects and hyperbole via music and mise-en-scène. Cinematic melodramas experienced popularity in the 1940s and 1950s, often being called "women's films" or "weepies" because of their associations with women characters and spectators. A prominent cinematic subgenre, maternal melodramas depict loss and sacrifice cathected in the mother–daughter relationship, replicating scenarios in which women give up aspects of themselves for the sake of their children. For example, Douglas Sirk's *Imitation of Life* (1954), which derives from Fannie Hurt's 1932 novel and its 1934 film adaptation by John Stahl, depicts two women's conflicts between their desires and those of their daughters: one woman, a wealthy, white Broadway star, struggles to maintain a career and love life without damaging her relationship with her daughter; the other, a Black woman who works as a housekeeper for the actress, relinquishes her ties to her daughter who wants to pass as white.

At the height of melodrama's cinematic glory, the advent of television suggested new potentialities for the genre. Lynne Joyrich argues, "In the late 1950s, television erupted in the American home and placed itself firmly within the realm of family, domesticity, and consumerism, the ground of the family melodrama." Focused on interpersonal relationships and domestic conflicts, melodrama was suited for the imagined intimacy of the small screen, giving shape to such genres as soap operas and reality television. As Joyrich explains, the move of melodrama to television was so pervasive that "it becomes difficult to locate as a separate TV genre."[15] Such transformations illustrate Gledhill's figuration of melodrama not as a discrete genre but as a contradictory mode that cuts across many genres, mediums, and contexts.

Celebrity culture illustrates another melodramatic site, as demonstrated by the fact that, in addition to *Imitation of Life*, many Hollywood melodramas are about celebrity, including *Sunset Boulevard* (Billy Wilder, 1950), *The Bad and the Beautiful* (Vincente Minnelli, 1952), *The Barefoot Contessa* (Joseph Mankiewicz, 1954), *An Affair to Remember* (Leo McCarey, 1957), and the four versions

---

14. Brooks, *Melodramatic Imagination*, x.
15. Joyrich, "All That Television Allows," 129, 131.

of *A Star Is Born*, which themselves remake *What Price Hollywood?* (George Cukor, 1932). Samantha Barbas notes that the US star system has encouraged audiences to seek emotional connections with famous people, often leading fans to attempt direct contact with or involvement in the lives and careers of stars.[16] Characterized by "exaggerated fluctuations," "discontinuit[ies] of emotional experience," and "dramatic moments of outbreak and collision before sudden reversals of fortune begin the movement again," celebrity culture demonstrates melodramatic form.[17]

Consider the dominant fictions of celebrity discourse: inspiring stories of aspiring stars who overcome adversity and sacrifice everything to pursue their dreams; salacious stories of scandal and disgrace and the attendant rituals of mortification aimed at redemption; and/or heart-wrenching stories of stars who suffer hardships and trauma, often in relation to the vulnerability that their visibility entails. Kardashian's experience in Paris conforms most closely to the conventions of this latter category, while her public persona has also taken shape through the intersection of narratives about aspiration and scandal, including the release of *Superstar*, which is rumored to have been leaked by her mother and manager, or "momager."

The affinities between melodrama and celebrity culture can be traced to their Rousseauian origins. The French term *célébrité*, notes Antoine Lilti, "has been in frequent use since the second half of the eighteenth century," peaking between 1760 and 1780.[18] It was during this time that Rousseau coined the term *melodrama* and created *Pygmalion*. Lilti notes that Rousseau was himself famous, experiencing "more celebrity than any writer before him" and often drawing crowds when in public. Fame was, accordingly, a subject of significance to Rousseau, and Lilti reads Rousseau's book *Rousseau, Judge of Jean-Jacques* as a meditation on celebrity in which Rousseau describes his own fame as subjecting him "to the gaze of others" and prohibiting "normal relations with them." Anticipating, or even prefiguring, much rhetoric of contemporary celebrity, Rousseau describes feeling vulnerable and "split" between his "personal identity" and his "social identity," as illustrated by his choice to write this book as a dialogue between fictionalized versions of himself.[19]

Rousseau's works also suggest anxiety that fame diminishes a subject's agency over their own image as they are exposed to the opinions and judg-

---

16. Barbas, *Movie Crazy*, 4.
17. Joyrich, "All That Television Allows," 131.
18. Lilti, "Writing of Paranoia," 55. See also Goodman, "Between Celebrity and Glory."
19. Lilti, "Writing of Paranoia," 68–70. Terry Eagleton further describes Rousseau as introducing traditionally feminine sensibilities into public discourse. See Eagleton, "What Would Rousseau Make?"

ments of others. To demonstrate, in *Pygmalion* an artist attempts to sculpt his creation according to his own desires before discovering that, once complete, his creation is no longer his to control. Originating with Ovid, this myth has been reimagined in myriad texts, including George Bernard Shaw's famous version from 1913, which inspired the Broadway musical *My Fair Lady* (1956) and George Cukor's 1964 Hollywood adaptation. In Shaw's iteration and its derivations, a phonetician falls in love with a woman of lower socioeconomic status, whose class standing he aims to improve by changing her manners of speech and public presentation.

Critics have also read *Six Degrees of Separation* as an iteration of Pygmalion mythology, as Paul "is taught refined manners and pronunciation in exchange for sexual favors by his white Pygmalion."[20] The Pygmalion story anticipates the norms of celebrity culture and its roots in the star system, wherein image-makers (such as filmmakers, studio executives, managers, and publicists) mold would-be stars into idealized types in search of public adoration. For example, tabloids have accused Will Smith of playing Pygmalion to his wife Jada Pinkett Smith, attempting to refine her style through etiquette lessons the couple calls "My Fair Jada."[21]

While the Pygmalion allusion applies to celebrity culture generally, it has been linked directly to Kardashian. For example, ABC's 2014 sitcom *Selfie* updated Shaw's narrative by alluding to Kardashian and the category of "influencer" with which she is associated. The sitcom focuses on a young woman pursuing social media fame and on the marketing expert who helps her craft her image. In addition to *Selfie*, allusions to *Pygmalion* have made multiple appearances in public discourse about Kardashian. For example, filmmaker John Bailey describes Kardashian as the contemporary Galatea to Andy Warhol's Pygmalion, having inherited the artist's capacity to pioneer new pop forms and his rather naked interest in cultivating fame. Bailey suggests that one might imagine the artist's "Jackie O and Marilyn silkscreens usurped by ones of the Armenian-American diva," had Warhol lived long enough to see Kardashian's rise to fame.[22]

Likewise, commentators argue that Kanye West demonstrated Pygmalion-like impulses toward Kardashian, having shaped her appearance and fashion choices.[23] Kardashian has affirmed this rhetoric, noting in *Interview* magazine, while dressed as Jackie Kennedy Onassis, "I usually go to Kanye for advice about my brand, my life, my image." Kardashian's app *Kim Kardashian: Hol-*

---

20. Bouchard, *Theater and Integrity*, 162.
21. Shipp, "Inside Will Smith's Pygmalion Obsession."
22. Bailey, "Kardashian Selfies."
23. See Jones, "Kim Kardashian Is Assed Out," and Caramanica, "Agony and the Ecstasy."

lywood extends this imagined creative control to ordinary people who play the game, allowing them to style and dress the star's avatar for her public events (using digital versions of her own line of beauty products).

In 2016 West enacted Pygmalion mythology literally, creating a sculptural replica of Kardashian's body for a music video and art exhibition at the Blum & Poe Gallery in Los Angeles.[24] Reversing the Pygmalion myth, *Famous* features a silicone double of Kardashian, West, and other famous figures, including Taylor Swift, Donald Trump, and Bill Cosby. The installation features these fabricated body doubles, which seem to breathe in rather lifelike fashion, in bed together, fully undressed; Kardashian lies on her stomach with her buttocks exposed.[25] The description for the installation reads, "*Famous* reduces a modern pantheon of celebrity figures to a group of vulnerable—nude, yet desexualized—sleeping partners, stripped cleanly of any artifice or pretense that invokes celebrity." While this caption positions celebrity and vulnerability as antithetical or even mutually exclusive, the value of melodramatic celebrity culture is paradoxically its capacity to call attention to vulnerability as a constitutive aspect of human subjectivity.

CELEBRITY SPREADS

Articulations of melodrama and celebrity abound in US culture. Noting that "melodrama is more than a film, literary, or cultural genre," Anker understands it as a "genre of national political discourse" that emphasizes vulnerability.[26] She identifies the genre as having "exploded" in popularity in the US after the 9/11 attacks in 2001, when rhetorics of trauma and victimization circulated prevalently in public discourse. The explosion of melodrama in political discourse should also be understood in relation to the prolifera-

---

24. West's multimedia installation also takes inspiration from Vincent Desiderio's mural *Sleep* (2008), which depicts over twenty bodies, asleep in one bed, and alludes to Leonardo da Vinci's *The Last Supper* (1495–98).

25. Kardashian has herself duplicated Kanye's sculptural approach; in 2018 she created a bottle for her perfume, KKW Body, as a reproduction of her body styled as a classical sculpture. The bottle features her torso but neither her head nor her legs, which Kardashian cites as an allusion to statues she has in her own home, and the packaging places the bottle on a pedestal, recalling the display practices of museums. Kardashian shot the advertising campaign in the studio of Vanessa Beecroft, a sculptor and performance artist who had also made works for Kardashian and West's wedding ceremony and home. Of the pieces for the wedding, which she calls "mimetic pieces" and which feature both cuts of marble and living models, Beecroft says, "I wanted to transform the women into marbles, or into something between women and marbles." See Pasori, "Artist Vanessa Beecroft."

26. Anker, *Orgies of Feeling*, 2.

tion of celebrity culture in the early 2000s. Although the fame industry had been in place for nearly a century, celebrity culture expanded during this period through reality television and the internet, and it continued to proliferate through the development of social media.[27] For example, a subgenre of celebrity-focused reality television series appeared in the two years following 9/11, including *I'm a Celebrity . . . Get Me Out of Here*, *The Osbournes*, *The Simple Life*, and *The Surreal Life*.[28] Such shows expanded the genre's focus from the tales of ordinary people seeking fame through television appearances to onscreen depictions of celebrities' purportedly real lives that promise audiences more intimate access to the rich and famous.

The expansion of celebrity culture, its association with reality television and social media, and their shared claims of authenticity have further blurred the supposed boundaries between entertainment and news. Attendant to this convergence of media modalities has also been the increased permeability of the boundaries between entertainment and politics, celebrities and politicians. S. Elizabeth Bird describes this transformation as a convergence between "dominant" and "tabloid" news media. While Bird notes that *National Enquirer*'s coverage of the Gary Hart scandal in 1987 and tabloid interest in the Simpson trial in 1995 indicate that the porousness of these boundaries is not new, she posits that the increasing omnipresence of celebrity gossip makes the tabloid no longer a *discrete* or stand-alone category; rather, the "personality-driven" stories that characterize contemporary coverage of both celebrities and politicians have "swamped all genres of mainstream news."[29] P. David Marshall suggests that "celebrity as a formation of contemporary individuality has migrated out of entertainment culture into a wider political culture" because of its capacity to construct and circulate personalities.[30]

Todd Gitlin frames this change as a "tabloidization" of the public sphere that risks the "trivialisation of public affairs" and "usurpation of public discourse by soap opera."[31] Graeme Turner notes that such suspicious takes on the proliferation of celebrity exist in tension with more generous renderings of this process as enabling a democratization of the public sphere through

---

27. The years between 1999 and 2001 were crucial in the development of reality television and its increased "discursive currency." See Holmes and Jermyn, "Introduction," 3.

28. Kardashian made some of her earliest appearances on television in episodes of *The Simple Life*, which followed socialites Paris Hilton and Nicole Ritchie in their attempts to hold down jobs and live as ordinary people. Prior to the development of her show *KUWTK*, Kardashian pitched a sequel to this show, titled *I'm a Rich Kid . . . Get Me Out of Here!* in which she would star.

29. Bird, "Converging into Irrelevance?," 193, 209.

30. Marshall, *Celebrity and Power*, xxxiii.

31. Gitlin, "Anti-political Populism of Cultural Studies," 35.

"democratainment," which offers so-called ordinary people greater access to the realms of both political discourse and celebrity.[32] Turner's position mirrors feminist critics' arguments that oft-maligned genres such as melodrama and soap opera (and their not-so-distant relative, the talk show) can operate as important counterpublic sites that call attention to subjects often considered too taboo or too private for consideration in the public sphere.[33]

While Anker notes that melodramas have demotic impulses and have historically focused on "the sufferings of ordinary people," rather than nobility or the elite, the melodramatic registers of celebrity culture often function to cast famous people as ordinary or relatable in their *just-like-us-ness*.[34] At the same time, celebrity discourse figures stars as leading lives that are as inaccessible and otherworldly as the celestial metaphor of stardom would suggest. To demonstrate, *KUWTK* focuses on both the everyday conflicts of family life and the wealthy family's extravagant lifestyles and shocking experiences, including Kardashian's robbery. This paradox between ordinariness and extraordinariness illustrates but one of the structuring tensions that defines celebrity as a melodramatic economy.

Additional structuring oppositions within celebrity culture further illustrate the articulation of melodrama and metonymy. To begin, celebrity depends on a structural tension between absence and presence. Although celebrities remain absent, at least physically, from most of their audiences' lives, existing primarily as abstractions, they also assume a great deal of metaphorical presence in their followers' lives. Gledhill notes that the presence of stars relates both to the presumed indexicality of photographic mediums—pictures of celebrities document the appearance of a person who was "really there"—and the surfeit of representations of them.[35] The figurative presence of celebrities is also embodied through connotations of excess in their onscreen performances and their offscreen personae, which coextensively imitate and instantiate the sensibilities of melodrama. The title of Kardashian's reality series illustrates such a tension, as the phrase "keeping up" suggests both the expectation of tracking and documenting the famous family's presence and an impulse toward conspicuous consumption and social climbing.

Much of celebrity culture's allure derives from the opposition between perceptions of stars' *having-been-there-ness* and the rarity of actual co-presence with them. This dynamic reveals a disconnect in celebrity culture between the industry's promise of authentic access to a celebrity and the open secret that

---

32. Turner, *Ordinary People*, 16.
33. See Kaplan, *Motherhood and Representation*; and Kuhn, "Women's Genres."
34. Anker, *Orgies of Feeling*, 69.
35. Gledhill, "Signs of Melodrama," 219.

the public sees only a manufactured, or sculpted, public image. The coterminous push and pull between absence/presence and authenticity/artifice signal the extent to which celebrity culture manifests the instability of signification and the metonymic conditions of all language. The presumption of a difference, or discrepancy, between who a celebrity "really is" and who that person appears to be might reinforce investments in fantasies of stable, core selfhood—as if just the right amount of "keeping up" with a star could reveal their true self. And yet, the constant deferral of this reality and the lingering evidence that the gap between true self and public image can never be closed illustrate the illusoriness of that investment in the first place, suggesting that, all attempts at keeping up aside, there is no there *there*. The complex circuits of fame reveal the unavoidable gap between a referent and its signifier(s), the real and the symbolic.

The larger-than-life *presence* of stars also owes to their capacity to signify beyond themselves—their singularity registering what Derrida might describe as their "metonymic force."[36] As such, the concept of star presence derives from an additional tension between intimacy and iconicity. As Gledhill contends, both melodrama and celebrity depend on "personalizations" that give audiences access to the particularities of individuals, including their emotional lives and embodied states; but melodrama and celebrity also operate through personification, "whereby actors—and fictional characters conceived as actors in their diegetic world—embody ethical forces."[37] Such personification operates through metonymy as stars, like the figures in melodramatic narratives, stand in for ideals or types, emblematically signifying concepts that exceed their individual identities. For example, the public image of Kardashian has associations with two sites of melodramatic enactments: reality television and social media. As perhaps melodramatic celebrity culture's quintessential metonym, Kardashian stands in for the accessibility and inaccessibility—ordinariness and extraordinariness—of stardom in the digital era. This metonymic register can be seen, for instance, in Lagerfeld's and Kimmel's responses to Kardashian's robbery, which make jokes about the star's trauma in relation to her mediated presence and hypervisibility.

The embodied character of stardom exists in tension with its associative qualities, as any image of a celebrity articulates with other sites, texts, and mediums that stitch together a concatenated phantasm, or *imago*. As Gledhill notes, "Star personae are produced through . . . repetition, differentiation, sedimentation and interchange," developing like genres, through assemblage

---

36. Derrida, "Deaths of Roland Barthes," 286.
37. Gledhill, "Signs of Melodrama," 211, 210.

and accumulation. As actors develop personae, they no longer play singular roles but incorporate those parts into an assemblage of their physical embodiment, perceived personality, and associated past roles.[38] The condensation of these various iterations takes shape through the operations of metonymy (the forging of associations) while also striving toward metaphorization (claims of an essential identity).

Metonymy is central to celebrity culture because melodrama is a mode that is deeply concerned with signification and its limits. The "metonymic slide" that characterizes theorizations of melodrama—which has been defined as not just a genre but also a "style, mode, sensibility, aesthetic, and rhetoric"—might be understood to derive from characteristics of melodrama itself and, in particular, melodrama's interest in plasticity and metamorphosis.[39] This slipperiness also signals melodrama's theorization of the inadequacies of signification, highlighting "the limitations of the conventions of language and representation" and their incapacity to capture the intensities of human experiences.[40] For example, the suffering and sacrifice, longing and loss, deferrals and disappointments that typify melodramas stand in for the lack that constitutes human subjectification in/by language, wherein the tragic failures of characters to fulfill their desires and dreams anxiously replay the failure of unicity that delimits signification.

Yet, while melodrama recognizes that "the signifier cannot cover the possibilities of the signified" and can never be adequate to the real, it attempts to "force meaning and identity from the inadequacies of language."[41] Rousseau's *Pygmalion* inaugurates such a sensibility, using music and gestures to supplement language in its depiction of a vivified statue who gains meaning and identity that exceed her intended symbolic capacity. Likewise, those formal and stylistic elements of cinematic melodrama that engender its excesses—bodily expressions, music, spectacle, and mise-en-scène—attempt to convey meanings that words cannot represent. Brooks notes that if all language is metonymic, melodrama's formal and stylistic devices strive toward the concatenating impulse of metaphor while demonstrating the operations of catachresis as they attempt to make up for the lack of any better words.[42] Thus, Brooks's contention that a defining characteristic of melodrama is the "desire to express *all*" should be understood more precisely to illustrate melodrama's

---

38. Gledhill, "Signs of Melodrama," 215.
39. Zazosa, "Melodrama," 237. See also Mercer and Shingler, *Melodrama*; and Rooney, *Living Screens*.
40. Gledhill, "Melodramatic Field," 33.
41. Gledhill, "Melodramatic Field," 33.
42. Brooks, *Melodramatic Imagination*, 72.

acknowledgment of the impossibility of expressing all and its attendant efforts to try *nonetheless*. The excess that is often described as a stylistic norm or deficit of melodrama performatively enacts this impossibility, restaging language's failure (a paranoid disposition) while also hoping for possibilities that exceed signification (a loving gesture of reparation).

This paradox of melodrama has ideological implications. For example, melodrama's recognition of the instability of signification suggests the corresponding realization that a category like *woman* is necessarily a catachrestic one that maintains illusions of stability through the metonymic associations that accrete to it. And yet, melodrama's insistence on the manifestations of affects through formal and stylistic excesses also acknowledges that, however fictional, a category like *womanhood* is felt as real and cannot be extricated from conditions of materiality and embodiment. Rousseau's *Pygmalion* and its adaptations address this problematic, depicting men who aim to recreate women in line with their own fantasies, only to find that these women as embodied subjects never match (and often exceed) these expectations. Perhaps this reading of melodrama helps account for its peculiar tendency toward cruelty to those who are presumed to be its primary consumers: women. Feminist critics have read melodrama's treatment of women as expressing the pain women experience within patriarchal society and allowing for the "articulation of unconscious female needs, desires, and frustrations."[43] Furthermore, melodrama stages a fraught confrontation with the paradoxes of signification and subjectification: although the signifiers with which we name and identify ourselves have no actual referents or stable meanings, humans often need, as Spivak might suggest, to identify and live strategically as if they do.

The example of celebrity as a melodramatic site becomes instructive in this context. Celebrity culture is invested in discourses of individualism and authenticity, promising audiences that they might get to know the "real" person behind the celebrity images they admire.[44] Richard Dyer demonstrates that claims to intimacy and accessibility have always been hallmarks of celebrity discourse, but the emergence of reality television and social media have amplified these impulses. Such discourses might be understood to reaffirm fantasies of whole, coherent, and essential subjectivity. At the same time, celebrity culture flaunts evidence of its artifice and contingency: actors dress up and play parts, celebrities often assume taxonomic and generic types ("America's Sweetheart," "The Girl Next Door," or "It Girl"), social media influencers display the practices (and even medical procedures) with which they craft their

---

43. Kaplan, "Melodrama/Subjectivity/Ideology," 12. See also Gledhill, "Melodramatic Imagination."
44. Nunn and Biressi, "'Trust Betrayed.'"

appearances. Celebrity is an industry built on the impossible promise of access to a *someone* who does not really exist, and the making of celebrity images restages the drama of catachresis that defines not just fame but human subjectivity. The value of celebrity as a case derives from its tenuous position with respect to cultural fantasies about the wholeness and coherence of subjectivity. While often tasked with reinforcing narratives about the subject's unity and sovereignty, celebrity culture also has the potential to undo, or rewrite, these narratives.

KIM KARDASHIAN: SUPERSTAR

Cultural anxieties about the status of such catachrestic categories as *womanhood, nationhood,* and *whiteness* cathect around Kardashian as a celebrity who is blamed for myriad social and cultural harms. Such critiques reveal how her persona exposes ruptures within celebrity culture and hegemonic discourses in US culture about what it means to be a subject. Kardashian's image culture emphasizes, rather than obfuscates, the performativity of subjecthood and the consequent instability of such allegedly instantiating categories as gender and race.

Media discourse about the "Kardashian brand of fame management is almost always framed universally in 'derogatory' terms."[45] Critics have described Kardashian's media stunts as distracting audiences from traditional values, interpersonal connections, and the kind of "Norman Rockwell day(s)" to which families are allegedly meant to aspire.[46] Other critics have framed Kardashian as threatening traditional norms of femininity, blaming her for damaging young girls' self-esteem and "ruining womanhood." For instance, Hadley Freeman accuses Kardashian and her family of destroying "wholesome" aesthetics of girlhood in favor of "terrifying sex glamazon" sensibilities that are predicated on artificiality, cosmetic enhancements, and overt sexualization. Dubbing the spread of this aesthetic as the "Kardashianizing" of femininity, Freeman worries whether young girls and women will ever feel able to "be themselves" again, which presumes that such innocence or authenticity has ever been possible (not to mention desirable) in the first place.[47]

There are also those who have painted Kardashian as complicit in the loss of truth and objectivity. For example, Ellis Cashmore writes, "Thanks to the Kardashians and you, readers, the first casualties of the digital age are rational-

---

45. Brady, "Keeping Away," 115. See also McClain, *Keeping Up,* 114.
46. Stanik, "Even If."
47. Freeman, "How the Kardashians."

ity, logic and common sense."[48] Such rhetoric figures Kardashian as a catalyst for the spread of infotainment and the misdirection of news coverage away from real stories and toward fake, or at least frivolous, ones. To demonstrate, a tweet by @Améliebaron asserts, "You bet Kardashian gets more public's attention than #Haiti & #Jamaica facing hurricane, #ColombiaVota and, needless to say, #Aleppo." An Occupy Wall Street protester's sign similarly casts Kardashian as a symptom of misaligned priorities within US political culture, asserting, "If you don't understand why we are here, but you can name all of the Kardashians, it is time to Turn off The TV and PAY ATTENTION!" Kardashian's fame has also been critiqued as distracting attention from activism against anti-Black racism, as illustrated by a tweet falsely attributed to Will Smith. Posted by a white man impersonating Smith, it reads, "WE live in America where a girl that threw flour on Kim Kardashian was arrested on site. But the man who KILLED Trayvon Martin is still free."[49] These accusations suggest that complex histories of injustice, inequity, and violence could be remedied if people would just stop keeping up with the Kardashians.

Some detractors have cited Kardashian as complicit in Donald Trump's election as the forty-fifth US president, which is itself figured as a sign of a loss of an idealized vision of democratic practice. For instance, Trump has been called the "Snapchat" or "reality show" candidate, as well as the "Kim Kardashian candidate."[50] A political cartoon by artist Jess Rotter from the (now defunct) online feminist newsletter *Lenny* positions Kardashian as part of a shocking circuit that gave life to Trump's monstrosity. Referencing Frankenstein iconography, the image depicts Trump strapped to a gurney with bolts of electricity surging through his body. Surrounding him and delivering this electric power are three cell phones: the first displays an image from Trump's reality television series *The Apprentice* and the phrase "You're fired," the second features illustrations of "like" and "hate" buttons in the style of the Facebook interface, and the third presents one of Kardashian's most famous mirror selfies, in which she wears a white swimsuit that leaves most of her buttocks uncovered. Rotter's image accompanies a *Lenny* article that critiques media culture for privileging "entertainment over education," names reality television as helping to "invent" Trump, and chastises citizens for not "paying

---

48. Cashmore, *Kardashian Kulture*, 11.

49. Although this tweet was falsely linked to Smith, many Black celebrities engage in antiracist activism on Twitter. See Duvall and Heckemeyer, "#BlackLivesMatter"; and Jackson et al., *#Hashtag Activism*.

50. Ingleton and York, "From Clooney to Kardashian," 365. See also Ouellette, "Trump Show."

attention."[51] The article warns, "When we put reality-television stars [like Kardashian] on the Time 100 list . . . we raised this kind of vote."[52] Such critiques liken Kardashian to the Snapchat filters with which she is associated, as if she obfuscates what is real by privileging surfaces over substance.[53]

Lynn Stuart Parramore also links Kardashian and Trump in a narrative of American decline, deploying the language of melodrama to cast America as "the love child of Kim Kardashian and Donald Trump." Positioning Kardashian as sharing Trump's "garish" taste and role as a cultural signifier of "excess," she describes the two public figures as perfecting reality television as a melodramatic genre that "thrives on high drama, outsized personalities and loud-mouthed conflicts" and censures them for having "acted as barometers for how far a person can go and how low a culture can sink."[54] This moral panic mirrors Tina Brown's assertion that Trump's brand is the "Kardashian Camelot, fueled by ostentatious displays of money, supermarket-tabloid celebrity, comprehensive fakery, indiscriminate access, and a preposterously (and prosperously) good-looking family." Such scapegoating of Kardashian buttresses nostalgic (and sexist and classist) fantasies about a pure democratic past, while covering over the histories of injustice and inequity that have long preceded (and further enabled) Trump's election.

I do not intend to assert that Kardashian's public image is or is not guilty of such harms, because the rhetoric of loss is, in these cases, predicated on

---

51. Grillo, "Time to Listen."

52. *Time*'s 2015 list included Kardashian among the year's most influential people, with an article written by celebrity chef and reality television star Martha Stewart naming Kardashian the "first lady of #fame."

53. In 2017, as part of a segment critiquing Trump as inauthentic, the television talk show *The View* photoshopped an oversized image of his face onto an image of Kardashian's body published on a controversial cover of *Paper*, in which a bottle of champagne spills onto her buttocks.

54. Parramore, "How America Became." The notion that Trump and Kardashian illustrate how "low" people might "sink" echoes through frequent characterizations of the 2016 presidential election as a "Milgram experiment." This comparison references the notorious obedience experiments conducted by social psychologist Stanley Milgram at Yale in the 1960s. For example, Chris Ladd describes the election as a "mass rerun of Stanley Milgram's experiments on obedience and morality, with all of us as test subjects." Beyond this metaphoric connection and an impulse to "shock" people, Trump and Kardashian might be said to have a genealogical connection to the social psychologist as well. Milgram's experiments, in which he compelled individuals to administer electric shocks to strangers, were inspired, at least in part, by Allen Funt's *Candid Camera*, one of the earliest examples of reality television and a predecessor to Trump's and Kardashian's televisual genre of choice. Having studied social psychology himself, Funt began his career making serious documentaries about the ethical limits of human behaviors, which would transform into the "what will people do" logic of *Candid Camera*. Milgram, who would go onto become a filmmaker himself, studied Funt's programming and conducted research about it. See McCarthy, "Stanley Milgram, Allen Funt, and Me," 26.

catachrestic fantasies that the notions of womanhood or nationhood can be understood as unified or monolithic forms. The claim that Kardashian has endangered particular cultural or political values presupposes a coherence and stability to these categories that never existed and reinforces investments in fantasies of unified and coherent signification and subjectivity. Just as the idealized fixation on celebrities as discrete and unique individuals demonstrates an impulse to maintain such figurations of selfhood, the scapegoating of (some) celebrities as threats to hegemonic cultural narratives and institutions reflects an anxious defense of the fantasy of unicity and a disavowal of signification's instability.

The value of this rhetoric about Kardashian lies in what it reveals about the logic of attribution characteristic of misogyny, which often fetishizes women and blames them for social problems, including their own victimization. The accusations that Kardashian is "radically changing" or even "destroying" America illustrates, Diane Negra and Su Holmes argue, "the extent to which contemporary female celebrities are placed to operate as lightning rods for a range of concerns."[55] Castigatory fixation on famous women demonstrates what Kate Manne describes as a larger tendency to treat all women as "representative targets" and "scapegoat[s] for a resented absence."[56] Manne describes this kind of targeting as a typical feature of misogyny, which feminist media scholarship has shown as taking virulent (and often racialized and/or classed) aim at countless women celebrities, from early Hollywood film star Clara Bow to the more contemporary celebrity Britney Spears.[57] Such targeting illustrates what Jacqueline Taylor calls the "burden of synecdoche," wherein one member of a minoritized or marginalized group must stand in as a representative of the whole, akin to the "burden of representation" theorized by Kobena Mercer.[58] As Ella Shohat and Robert Stam argue, "Representations thus become allegorical; within hegemonic discourse every subaltern performer/role is seen as synecdochically summing up a vast but putatively homogenous community."[59]

To note the misogyny at work in public discourse about Kardashian is not to excuse her image from its own enactments of the synecdochal logic of fetishism. As many Black and women of color feminists have noted, Kardashian's persona and commercial empire depend on layered appropriations of Black cultures. For example, in 2017 many commentators accused Kar-

---

55. Negra and Holmes, "Going Cheap?"
56. Manne, *Down Girl*, 58, 108. For examples of these critiques, see Callahan, "How a Decade"; and Obeidallah, "Are the Kardashians."
57. Studlar, "White Trash Celebrity"; Williamson, "Female Celebrities."
58. Taylor, "On Being," 70. See also Mercer, "Black Art."
59. Shohat and Stam, *Unthinking Eurocentrism*, 183.

dashian of engaging in multiple examples of blackface: a cover story for *Interview* magazine in which her skin seemed darkened, an advertisement for her beauty products for which her skin also appeared darkened, and a Halloween costume in which she dressed as Black R&B singer Aaliyah.[60] Kardashian and her sisters have also been critiqued for appropriating hairstyles with historical ties to Blackness, including cornrows, bantu knots, box braids, doobie wraps, and durags, and for glamorizing physical attributes, including full lips and large buttocks, which white culture has denigrated via their association with Black women and women of color.

Kardashian has access to white and/or light-skin privilege but also has the capacity to present as not white, leading many women of color critics to identify her as illustrating what Priscilla Peña Ovalle calls "racial mobility."[61] As Sesali B. argues, Kardashian has the ability to deploy cultural signifiers of Blackness to "legitimate" her "relevancy" at the same time that she can "disassociate" herself from Blackness when it suits her, illustrating white supremacy's concurrent fascination with Blackness and lack of "investment in the lived experiences or material conditions of Black people."[62] Kardashian's capacity to move between racial and ethnic categories also signals economic privilege, as she can modify herself through physical, chemical, and even surgical means.

Kardashian has acknowledged these critiques, incorporating them into public narratives about her identity. For example, she appeared on the short-lived CW reality show *H8R*, which stages meetings between celebrities and ordinary people who claim to dislike them. In a 2011 episode, Kardashian meets a Black woman named Deena, or "The Hater," who appears under the pretense that she is auditioning for a different reality show. The show's host, Mario Lopez, explains that Deena has no idea that Kardashian will see footage of her criticizing the celebrity. In a direct-address confessional, which Lopez calls a "rant," Deena explains that she does not like what Kardashian "stand[s] for," characterizing the star's physique as fake and calling Kardashian a "thief" who steals Black women's "asses" and men.

Kardashian appears in the episode with a caption that labels her "The Celebrity," explaining that she feels "nervous" to watch video footage of her critic—after which she demurs, "Gosh, I would never say that to someone." The following sequence, dubbed "The Ambush," involves a confrontation between The Hater and The Celebrity, in which Kardashian promises to show Deena who she "really is." Kardashian and Lopez ambush Deena during what

---

60. Critiques of Kardashian's participation in practices of blackface resurfaced in 2019, following a cover shoot for *Hollywood* magazine, which darkened her skin. See Dicker, "Kim Kardashian Accused"; and Virk and McGregor, "Blackfishing."

61. Ovalle, *Dance and the Hollywood Latina*, 7.

62. B., "Flirting with Blackness."

she thinks is a shoot for an instructional yoga video; but rather than confront Deena, Kardashian greets her with compliments and affection, promising to "give love." Lopez claims to fear Deena's "rage," feigning concern that she might attack his "dear friend." The women then spend time together, leading Deena to declare newfound respect for the celebrity she once hated.

H8R operates at melodramatic registers in multiple ways—using music, dramatic pauses, and paratextual devices to add affective intensity and structuring its narrative around tropes of "victimization and vilification."[63] Like Kardashian's larger image culture, this episode participates in what Linda Williams describes as a US variant of melodrama: the racial melodrama. Williams traces the development of racial melodrama through *Birth of a Nation* (D. W. Griffith, 1915), *The Jazz Singer* (Alan Crosland, 1927) *Gone with the Wind* (Victor Fleming, 1939) and the miniseries *Roots* (ABC, 1977) to the media spectacle surrounding the 1995 murder trial of O. J. Simpson, arguing that racial melodramas proffering narratives of Blackness and whiteness are "deeply embedded in the structure of American popular culture."[64] Melodrama, argues Daphne Brooks, must be understood in relation to the history of minstrelsy, from which melodrama borrowed "the production of a spectacular and 'suffering' black body" as an allegorical signifier.[65] At the center of racial melodramas are questions of "racial legibility," wherein narratives about conflict between races reproduce interarticulated sets of binaries, in which race is often imagined as only Black or white and in which a racialized subject is either a victim or a villain.[66]

The Kardashian episode of *H8R* offers a complex, if not contradictory, narrative about victimization. The episode emphasizes injuries done to Deena, who critiques Kardashian's harmful appropriation of Black culture. Furthermore, the subterfuge and ambuscade deployed to engineer the confrontation between Deena and Kardashian position Deena as vulnerable, if not exploited. Yet the reality series also marks its celebrity as victimized, diluting the force of what Brittney Cooper might call Deena's "eloquent rage" about the Kardashians' imperialist practices. For example, *H8R* calls Deena "jealous" of Kardashian's wealth, in contrast to its depiction of Kardashian as clement toward and wounded by her "hater." The episode further undercuts Deena's critique by concluding with a scene in which she apologizes for not keeping up with

---

63. Williams, *Playing the Race Card*, 5.
64. Williams, *Playing the Race Card*, 309. Kardashian's participation in racial melodrama might be understood, to a certain extent, as an inherited role, as her father was a public loyalist to Simpson during his trial, and at least some of the drama of the trial took place in Kardashian's home, as Simpson reportedly threatened suicide in her childhood bedroom in her father's presence.
65. Brooks, *Bodies in Dissent*, 30.
66. Williams, *Playing the Race Card*, 367.

the positive contributions the Kardashians have made to Africa and the "Black community," reaffirming the trope of the white savior.

H8R is complicit in the ongoing privileging of non-Black womanhood over and against the experiences of Black women, perpetuating narratives about white innocence and Black anger, revaluing the currency of "white-lady tears as a form of political capital," and reinforcing the logic of gaslighting.[67] One aspect of the show, however, suggests a moment of rupture within the normative logics of "black and white melodrama" and misogyny: the positioning of Lopez as the engineer of the conflict between "The Hater" and "The Celebrity." Intercutting shots of Kardashian's anxious walk to meet Deena with footage of Lopez watching video of Kardashian's confrontation with Deena on the monitor in his luxury SUV, *H8R* depicts Lopez as he leans toward the television screen and leers in anticipation of conflict between the women. As not only host but also executive producer, Lopez appears as a nefarious character in this melodrama: the sculptor of a plot aimed at humiliating women.[68] At the same time that this episode illustrates patriarchal investments in conflicts between Black and white women, it also demonstrates how often white women align themselves with patriarchal structures at the expense of Black women and women of color.[69]

A generous reading of this show might understand it as critiquing melodrama's and celebrity culture's tendency to scapegoat women, revealing how frequently mediated conflicts between women are staged for the enjoyment of spectators and the service of patriarchy. Reading this episode reparatively also reveals theorizations of the relationship between the melodramatic operations of celebrity culture and metonymic discourses about race and gender in the United States. As much as *H8R* seems to reify such categories as Celebrity/Hater, victim/villain, white/black, it betrays the instability of such taxonomic structures; as much as the series deploys the rhetoric of authenticity, it also lays bare its own artifice. The episode is, after all, built around deception and duplicity, making clear that Deena has participated in the show because she wants to pursue an acting career and/or fame herself. In fact, one shot of Dee-

---

67. Cooper, *Eloquent Rage*, 175.

68. The social engineering at work in this episode through the staging of encounters meant to test social norms also suggests a Milgramesque sensibility, experimenting with its subjects to see just what they might do. In fact, in her analysis of the series, Kimberly Springer likens the conventions of the show to those of *Candid Camera*. Springer, "Beyond the H8R."

69. Lopez's identity as Latinx matters in this instance. The casting of a man of color in this role may suggest efforts to mitigate against this effect; one could imagine, for instance, that the presence of a white man in this role would make the power imbalances and exploitative logics of the series even more apparent, but it also demonstrates what Vanessa Díaz describes as celebrity culture's long-standing practices of exploiting Latinx folks. See Díaz, *Manufacturing Celebrity*.

na's direct-address "rant" (accidentally?) reveals a script in her hands, which she consults before dropping it to the floor.

These complex attitudes toward the uncertainty of identity categories align with melodrama's interest in the indeterminacy and inadequacy of language, as demonstrated by the title of the show. Mimicking shorthand often used in text messages and internet slang, this title suggests H8R's attempt to reach younger, digitally savvy audiences; but the phonetic substitution of the number 8 for the letters *a-t-e* also registers the malleability and arbitrariness of signification.[70] As a visual pun, H8R alludes to the frequency with which women's bodies are positioned at the center of such melodramas. The phrase "figure 8" describes an idealized shape for women's bodies, which is characterized by ample breasts, a small waist, and large hips. Kardashian is an oft-cited exemplar of this body shape, even developing her own brand of waist-trainers, or compression garments, used to reduce the size of one's waist and to attain a "figure 8" body shape.[71] Operating as a synecdoche for Kardashian's larger image culture, which itself functions as an urtext for the operations of celebrity culture in the context of networked publicity, this episode of H8R makes clear that the interdependence that characterizes all subjectivity creates conditions of possibility not only for connection and shared vulnerability but also for exploitation and precaritization.

MAKING KIM KARDASHIAN KIM KARDASHIAN (AGAIN)

Rather than disavow the claim that she is "famous for being famous," Kardashian leans into this accusation, curating a public image that is conspicuously self-referential. I take this tautology seriously, reading Kardashian as an expert on celebrity whose image culture explicates what and how fame means.[72] Typified by self-reflexive attention to both synecdoche and mimesis as metonymic operations, Kardashian's iconography considers the relationship

---

70. This titular choice recalls the linguistic play that is common within internet lingo. For example, it resembles leetspeak (a contraction of the words "elite" and "speak"), which replaces letters with symbols or numbers that visually resemble them, such as substituting a numeral 3 for the letter *E*.

71. The visual metonymy between women's bodies and the numeral 8 has been so normalized that the marketing for International Women's Day, which has taken place on March 8 since 1914, has often used the number as a stand-in for women's bodies.

72. The notion that Kardashian's work operates as a site for cultural and/or political theorization has been inspiration for online parody. For example, an article for *W* teasingly imagines what might happen were Kardashian and her then spouse Kanye West to take "the academic world by storm," speculating that their curriculum might include such classes as "Famous: Celebrity Culture and Authorship of the Self." See Marine, "What If."

between signification and subjectivity through two primary examples: Kardashian's line of bespoke emoji and her impersonations of other celebrities.

First, in 2015 the Kimoji app became one of the original proprietary lines of emoji to feature images of a celebrity. Consumers who purchased the app could insert Kardashian-associated icons, or "stickers," into electronic messages, allowing them to forge an association with the Kardashian brand. On the day of the app's launch, so many consumers attempted to purchase Kimoji that the Apple App Store crashed; although Kardashian discontinued the app in 2018, Kimoji helped inaugurate the genre of the "celebremoji," with a number of public figures subsequently creating their own versions, including Amber Rose's MuvaMoji, Lady Gaga's GagaMoji, Justin Bieber's Justmoji, Stephan Curry's StephMoji, and Gabby Douglas's Gabbymoji. Trump's image has also been rendered in emoji form by such apps as Trumpoji, and the Trump campaign lobbied (unsuccessfully) to get Twitter to create a custom Hillary Clinton emoji as a supplement to or substitute for the hashtag "CrookedHillary." Customizable emoji also exist for nonfamous smartphone users who can such apps as Bitmoji to create their own personal avatars.

Emoji function through synecdoche and metonymy, deploying parts of the human body to stand in for a whole person and for the range of emotions with which those parts have become associated: elevated thumbs to indicate approval, upturned mouths to mean joy, heart shapes as signifiers of hearts-as-organs as signifiers of love. Within Kimoji, synecdochal and metonymic links become even more specific, referencing images, body parts, and products and practices with which Kardashian is associated. Kimoji icons include Kardashian's "cry face"; the mirror selfie of her in the white one-piece swimsuit; a depiction of her hand holding a phone to take a selfie; various products from Kardashian's cosmetics line; speech bubbles of such internet slang as "BAE," "FML," and "NSFW"; and a cream-covered peach emoji, which itself references the Unicode peach emoji.

The same year Kardashian released Kimoji, the *Oxford English Dictionary* named the "Face with Tears of Joy" emoji its "word" of the year, marking the first time a pictograph received this honor and acknowledging the increasingly important role of emoji and emoticons in human communication. Vyvyan Evans indicates that one function of emoji is to replace nonverbal cues that are significant within face-to-face interactions but absent from electronic communication; emoji have also begun to replace internet slang—substituting bodily expressions of emotions for linguistic abbreviations, such as using the "Face with Tears of Joy" emoji in place of the abbreviation "LOL."[73] Much like non-

---

73. Evans, *Emoji Code*, 25.

verbal cues that supplement spoken language and the audiovisual flourishes of melodrama, emoji register the incompleteness of language and the inability of written words to fully capture affects.

Emoji, Luke Stark and Kate Crawford argue, "create new avenues for digital feeling" by constructing a "new visual vernacular." They aim to capture affect as both an intelligible, or narrativizable, emotion and a source of capital. As Stark and Crawford explain, "These graphic forms are exemplary of the tension between affect as liberating human potential, and as a productive force that the market continually seeks to harness through the commoditization of emotional sociality."[74] For example, Facebook's 2016 decision to expand its "Like" button from a thumbs-up to a series of "Reactions" allows users to nuance their responses to a post and enables the site to more accurately track and commodify public feelings. These icons—a heart, a laughing face, a face with a gaping mouth, a crying face, and a grimacing red face—go by the respective names Love, Haha, Wow, Sad, and Angry. In 2020, in response to the COVID-19 pandemic, Facebook added Care, which depicts a smiling face hugging a heart.

The celebrifying of emoji reveals that, beyond the rather obvious fact that consumers expect celebrities to deploy new media technologies to brand themselves, there are conceptual links binding celebrity culture and the digital icons we call emoji and emoticons. Celebrities and emoji play homologous cultural roles as emotional icons, which Kimoji seems to embrace. Emoji bear traces of the melodramatic in multiple ways, displaying emotions and signaling the extent to which affects are, as Erin Rand argues, "vital forces and intensities that exceed linguistic capture."[75] Emoji reflect what Ben Anderson calls the "excess of affect," attempting to capture in visual form, not unlike pantomimic gestures, what words cannot express.[76]

Like melodrama, emoji operate at the juncture between absence and presence, making present affects and sensations that might have been absented by recourse to networked technologies: a cry that can't be heard, a smile that can't be seen, a hand that can't be felt. The emotional icons also rely on the productive tensions between iconicity and intimacy, embodiment and association, rendering emotion by referencing the human body via synecdoche and metonymy; and while emoji often act as literal signifiers of all kinds of bodily matter—hands, mouths, excrement—they also reference bodies at symbolic registers, as illustrated by the popularity of eggplants and peaches as eroticized signifiers. These two-dimensional images have also been transfigured back

---

74. Stark and Crawford, "Conservatism of Emoji," 1, 2.
75. Rand, "Bad Feelings," 161.
76. Anderson, "Modulating the Excess," 161.

into material objects and consumer goods, including the perfume bottle that Kardashian modeled after her peach Kimoji and launched on World Emoji Day in 2018.

Celebrities similarly act as emotional icons that drive affects and render them legible. P. David Marshall writes, "The celebrity works in the culture as a figure who wrests the various forms of affective power into rationalized configurations" under the auspices of "consumer capitalism."[77] Celebrities become sites for the attribution of affects and sites around which affects accrete and are made meaningful, offering resources to their audiences for managing the excesses of affect. As Sara Ahmed notes, affect depends on metonymy, or conditions of relatedness that involve contingency and proximity. Because affect itself exceeds signification, it must exist in relation to signs and objects with which it is associated: affect must be experienced in terms of something else. One can affect and be affected by only those things to which one comes into contact, with which one has an association—even if only virtually. Affective charges accrue to artifacts through their repetition and circulation, and over time these contingent connections may come to feel inherent or innate. Celebrities, not unlike emoji, often become these objects of attachment, or stickiness.

The claim that celebrities and emoji perform correlative cultural functions is literalized by an animated film about anthropomorphized emoji inhabiting a digital city inside one teen's smartphone: *The Emoji Movie* (Tony Leondis, 2017). The commercially successful but critically lambasted film depicts the social worlds of emoji moving through digital platforms, including Instagram and Twitter. Replaying the tale of Galatea, *Emoji Movie* tells the melodramatic story of Gene Meh, an emoji who finds that his feelings exceed those he is designed to signify. In this world, the most popular emoji gain access to VIP events and red-carpet treatments, while the less favored ones find themselves exiled to the basement-level "loser lounge." The film casts its emoji characters as celebrities and influencers whose visibility across various social media determines their cultural capital, and each emoji achieves (or fails to achieve) such visibility based on the persona they craft and image they cultivate.[78] This treatment of anthropomorphized emoji as celebrities makes visible its chiasmic counterparts: celebrities as emoji (literally) and emotional icons (figuratively).

---

77. Marshall, *Celebrity and Power*, 56.

78. The *Today* show literalized the link between emoji and celebrities, generating their own list of emoji and the actors who should play them because of metonymic attachments to their personae. For example, an online article by Chris Serico casts Will Smith as "smiling face with sunglasses," referencing *Men in Black* (Barry Sonnenfeld, 1997). See Serico, "Emoji Movie."

Similarly, Kimoji attends to the emotional labor assigned to celebrities as signifiers to which personal and public feelings attach and through which they move. The Kimoji stickers register the affective stickiness that typifies celebrity as well as what Ahmed describes as the interplay between movement and attachment. Affect is what moves us, but it is also "what connects us to this or that." As Ahmed writes, "What moves us, what makes us feel, is also that which holds us in place, or gives us a dwelling place."[79] Ongoing processes of circulation, or movement, become anchored by moments of stickiness, or attachment. Consider the coverage of Kardashian's hostage situation: this experience of actual capture also became a moment of virtual capture, or captivation—a site to which affects and attentions became temporarily attached. Many of those who encountered stories and images of Kardashian's ordeal felt moved to respond, putting mediated renderings of Kardashian's experience into further circulation. When audiences comment on, like, or share celebrity stories, images, or messages, they perform the operations of movement and attachment, further circulating and disseminating a digital artifact while also attaching themselves to it and its source. Such practices allow the fan to become associated with the celebrity in question and to become articulated with networks of other intimate strangers, generating both feelings of community and communities of feeling, which Marshall calls "micropublics" of association and Peter Turner dubs "interstellar communities."[80]

Second, Kardashian's image culture marks mimesis as central to the production of public renown. While behind-the-scenes access to famous people has become de rigueur in contemporary celebrity culture, Kardashian draws hyperbolic attention to her processes of image-making. Staples in her image culture include scenes of her being styled by a team of professionals, videos in which she or a stylist uses her face to offer makeup tutorials, and footage of her undergoing cosmetic medical procedures. Her social media accounts abound with photographs of her getting fitted in clothes for special events, as well as photographs of her being photographed. For instance, a 2014 *Vogue* cover story features a two-page Annie Leibowitz photograph of Kardashian taking a selfie in front of a mirror while Kanye West photographs her on an iPad. Captioned "Screen Time," the photo presents two versions of Kardashian: one captured by Leibowitz's camera and the other captured by West's, but the image also implies the absent presence of at least two other images: what Kardashian sees on the screen of her phone and her reflection in the mirror behind her.

---

79. Ahmed, "Skin of the Community," 100.
80. Marshall, "Persona Studies"; Turner, "Fast Marketing," 469.

This multiplication of Kardashian's image, between mirrors and cameras, in the process of self-portraiture recalls Rockwell's famous *Triple Self-Portrait* (1960), in which the capturing of one's image is depicted not as a solitary act but as a self-conscious collaboration with other image makers. Although Rockwell's painting was created decades before digital selfies were possible, the Norman Rockwell Museum (NRM) has anachronistically noted affinities between Rockwell's self-reflexive painting and the genre of the selfie with which Kardashian is associated. For instance, on their Instagram account in 2008, NRM posted a photograph of *Triple Self-Portrait* with the caption "The original selfie" and the hashtag #selfie. In 2014 the museum offered visitors an interactive exhibition, titled "Triple Selfie," that allowed participants to capture selfies in a replica of the studio from *Triple Self-Portrait* and streamed video footage of visitors to the exhibit via Facebook Watch.

Kardashian's selfies also became the subject of arthouse publisher Rizzoli New York's 2015 coffee-table book, *Selfish*, which conspicuously resembles the book of portraits from Marina Abramović's performance *The Artist Is Present*.[81] *Selfish* features previously circulated images and private ones, including nude photographs that had been leaked one year prior (presumably without Kardashian's consent) as part of "The Fappening."[82] This choice illustrates what Caitlin Lawson describes as "tensions between celebrities' desire to maintain private selves and the public's desire for an authentic, intimate glimpse of those private selves," which have been exacerbated by the "affordances of digital technology."[83] Not unlike *Triple Self-Portrait*, which shows Rockwell at work creating his rendition of himself, *Selfish* focuses on Kardashian creating her own image and "engaged in the work of celebrity."[84] Multiple "mirror selfies" show Kardashian working to photograph herself, and approximately twenty-five images depict Kardashian sitting at a makeup table, applying makeup, or having it applied for her by a stylist.[85] The book frequently references "Old Hollywood," describing the aesthetics associated with classic movie stars as one of Kardashian's preferred looks to imitate; the blurb for *Selfish* describes Kardashian as the "modern-day personification of Marilyn Monroe," leading one reviewer to claim that the book "may end up being just as much a part of pop-art history as when Andy Warhol painted soup cans."[86]

---

81. Abramović et al., *Marco Anelli*.

82. These leaked photographs, some of which were circulated as part of "The Fappening," appear in the middle of the book, and they are the most sexually explicit images in *Selfish*.

83. Lawson, "Pixels, Porn, and Private Selves," 608. See also Rojek, *Fame Attack*, 81.

84. Butkowski and Humphreys, "Gendered Art, Work, and Self-Representation," 167.

85. The second edition of the book, published in 2018, features eight additional such images, including one in which Kardashian was styled to resemble Marilyn Monroe.

86. Pesce, "'Selfish.'"

Kardashian has also made a habit of publicly imitating or masquerading as other celebrities. Beginning in 2013, fashion commentators began to suggest that Kardashian was becoming the "spitting image" of Abramović, borrowing several elements of the artist's signature sartorial style.[87] In 2014 Kardashian dressed as *Vogue* editor Anna Wintour for Halloween and appeared in an advertising campaign for an energy drink dressed as Audrey Hepburn. In 2017 Kardashian wore multiple costumes replicating famous white women celebrities—Cher, Madonna (doing her impersonation of Marilyn Monroe), and Pamela Anderson—as well as a number of famous Black women and women of color, including Aaliyah, Lil' Kim, and Selena Quintanilla.[88]

Also in 2017, Kardashian appeared in a cover story for *Interview* magazine dressed as Jacqueline Kennedy Onassis, a frequent subject of Warhol, the magazine's creator. The cover story, which contains photographs of Kardashian and her oldest daughter alongside an interview by Janet Mock, was one of Kardashian's media appearances that garnered critique for the apparent darkening of her skin. The photo spread includes a series of medium close-ups of Kardashian-as-Kennedy with a pillbox hat atop bouffant hair that are presented in a grid, imitating Warhol's *Nine Jackies* (1964). The article's tag line describes Kardashian as recalling "another mother whose every move captivated the American imagination: First Lady Jacqueline Kennedy Onassis."[89] The interview's discussion of Kardashian's famous, empire-building family further implies connections to the Camelot myth, which Kennedy Onassis introduced in a now-famous *Life* interview following JFK's death.[90]

Suggesting that Kardashian is imitated as much as she imitates, the 2018 season of Kanye West's fashion line Yeezy featured a social media campaign of paparazzi-style photographs of Paris Hilton and various "internet-famous" women of different racial and ethnic backgrounds impersonating Kardashian.

---

87. Wilkinson, "Kim Kardashian."

88. In 2015 Kardashian also appeared as Marilyn Monroe for the cover story of *Vogue* Brazil and was photographed while being styled as Elizabeth-Taylor-as-Cleopatra; in 2019 she recreated a sequence from the film *Legally Blonde* (Robert Luketic, 2001), imitating Reese Witherspoon's fictional character in the video, and she posed for the cover of *7Hollywood* magazine in a costume that was described as imitating Sophia Loren and/or Elizabeth Taylor.

89. The comparison of Kardashian to a First Lady recalls the controversial cover of *Cosmopolitan* in 2015 that describes the Kardashians as "America's First Family." The cover inspired a great deal of criticism, much of which suggested that the cover erased the Obamas. The cover appeared just two months after Kanye West announced during an acceptance speech at the MTV Video Music Awards that he intended to run for president in 2020.

90. Kennedy Onassis's references to Camelot derive less from the narratives of English literature and folklore than from the hit 1960 Broadway musical *Camelot*, written by Alan Lerner (a former classmate of JFK) and Frederick Loewe. At the time of *Camelot*'s production, Lerner and Loewe had already made names for themselves with their hit musical *My Fair Lady* (1956), which adapts George Bernard Shaw's version of *Pygmalion*.

These advertisements style the women to look exactly like Kardashian (as styled by West) and recreate mock paparazzi images of Kardashian running errands, which she circulated online prior to the release of the new line.[91] With captions such as "McDonald's run," "Smoothie run," and "FedEx run," these images of Kardashian and their imitations assert the everydayness of the star's style and behaviors. Other images for the campaign featured more high-art stylistics, including Kardashian look-alikes presented in Warhol-inspired grids. The contrast between these aspects of the campaign reflects the constitutive tension within celebrity culture between rhetorics of accessibility and inaccessibility, ordinariness and extraordinariness, likeness and difference.

Attention to imitation within Kardashian's iconography illustrates an appeal to potential consumers who might like to copy, and therefore forge an association with, the Kardashian brand. This mimetic practice, argues Marcus, is central to a paradox of celebrity culture, in which celebrities cement their unique status and fame by imitating and being imitated. Marcus notes, for example, that Madonna's allusions to Marilyn Monroe reinforce her Madonna-ness, just as Lady Gaga's imitations of Madonna's imitations of Monroe solidify her Gaga-ness.[92] The same paradox applies to Kardashian's production of the Kardashian brand, amplifying her Kardashian-ness by replicating the fame of others and adding a new register of meaning to the phrase "famous for being famous," which might be amended to say "famous for being someone else famous." The more on-brand Kardashian's image becomes, the more it signals its own performativity, acknowledging the extent to which citation, imitation, and even parody typify the production of public images and "ordinary" identities as well.

Kardashian's iconography also acknowledges that all subjectivity is constituted via metonymy. If fantasies of stable signification and masterful subjectivity imagine subjects as metaphors—as having an essential identity or self-sameness, as if we can become our "true selves"—then Kardashian underscores the extent to which subjectivity is always formed through association with and in relation to others. While impersonation may seem to illustrate the logic of metaphor—substituting one person for another because of shared likenesses—look-alikes always suggest repetitions with a difference, reminding us that likenesses are often more feigned than inherent. Calling as much attention to the absence of the referent as its presence, mimesis, argues Freder-

---

91. This advertising campaign references Kardashian's 2012 lawsuit against The Gap for an Old Navy commercial that featured reality television actor and model Melissa Molinaro, styled to resemble her. In 1984 Jacqueline Kennedy Onassis filed a similar impersonation lawsuit against fashion house Christian Dior for its use of a look-alike model, Barbara Reynolds.

92. Marcus, "Celebrity 2.0," 36.

ick Burwick, is more metonymic than metaphorical.[93] Furthermore, these acts also create contiguities between those imitating and those being imitated in yet another iteration of associative micropublics. And not unlike the *Pygmalion*-inspired *My Fair Lady*, these mimetic acts involve tactical performances aimed at elevating the performer's status and associations. Taken together, Kimoji and the mimesis within Kardashian's image culture suggest that we might consider Kardashian's iconography to be metatropological, revealing the extent to which all associations between signifiers and signifieds are arbitrary and must be forged.

PHOTO CHOPPING

One month after her hostage situation in Paris, Kardashian appeared on the cover of *Paper*, inaugurating the magazine's trademarked "Break the Internet" feature. Two different versions of the cover promised to generate enough traffic to shut down the internet, which proved largely true, as the magazine's website did crash under the weight of searches for the images. One cover shows Kardashian standing in profile on a stool in a black evening gown and holding a bottle of champagne that spews bubbles over her head and into a champagne glass resting on her protruding buttocks. Highly sexualized, this image evokes the "money shot" in pornographic films, including Kardashian's own sex tape. The other cover shows Kardashian mostly naked, her skin oiled and her backside facing the camera. Mimicking the ancient *Venus Callipyge* sculpture and illustrating the artistic device of anasyrma, Kardashian lowers her dress below her buttocks and looks over her shoulder with a smile.

Both photographs were taken by French photographer Jean-Paul Goude, a white cishet man whose work has been described as blurring the bounds between commerce and high art and critiqued as sexist, racist, and colonialist, given its tendency to depict Black women in sexualized, exoticized, or animalistic scenes. Goude's photograph of Kardashian with the champagne bottle remakes an image he took in the late 1970s. The original image, titled *Carolina Beaumont* (or, *The Champagne Incident*), features Toukie Smith, a Black model and actress from the United States.[94] Wearing nothing but gold hoop

---

93. Burwick, *Mimesis*, 8.

94. Born in Philadelphia, Toukie Smith was known primarily for her role in the NBC sitcom *227*. She is also the sister of fashion designer Willi Smith—who is not to be confused with Will Smith, who was also born in Philadelphia. A predecessor of *The Fresh Prince of Bel-Air*, the sitcom *227* focused on a mostly Black cast and was a star vehicle for Marla Gibbs, who had gained fame as Florence Johnston on *The Jeffersons*, another predecessor of *The Fresh Prince of Bel-Air*, which also focused on an affluent Black family. Gibbs reprised her role as Johnston in the series finale of *The Fresh Prince of Bel-Air* in 1996.

earrings with her hair pulled to a point high above her head, Smith performs the champagne trick replicated in the Kardashian photo. Describing images (and sculptures) he made of Smith, Goude fetishistically compares her buttocks to "*la croupe d'un cheval*" ("the rump of a horse").[95]

Black women critics, including Bethonie Butler and Blue Telusma, have noted that the original image of Smith and its Kardashian remake recall the colonialist racism of nineteenth-century caricatures of Saartje Baartman, a South African woman who was held captive and exhibited in European museums and freak shows under the name *Hottentot Venus*.[96] An image of Baartman appeared in a book picturing African bodies claiming that the illustrations present "each animal" in profile to better display their "physiognomy." The book's explicit comparisons between Baartman's body and such primates as orangutans and monkeys, argues T. Denean Sharpley-Whiting, perpetuates "associations of black femaleness with bestiality and primitivism."[97]

Goude's image of Smith appears in his 1981 book *Jungle Fever*, whose cover photo depicts Goude's partner at the time, Black model, actress, and musician Grace Jones. The image, *Do Not Feed the Animal*, features Jones naked, on her hands and knees, inside a cage, which sits on a stage in front of a gold curtain. Inside and scattered around the cage are raw meat and bloodied animal bones, and the hand of a white man extends a microphone toward her as she looks at the camera, her mouth opened as if she is growling.[98] *Jungle Fever* includes photographs and illustrations of Jones and other Black women, including Smith, that hyperbolize depictions of their lips and buttocks, as well as many colonialist and racist tropes including blackface, offensive epithets, and caricatures of Indigenous clothing and rituals.

Critiques of the *Paper* cover link Goude's and Kardashian's problematic histories of appropriating and exploiting Black culture. Erica Schwiegershausen reads Goude's images of Black women, which often feature manipulations and "distortions" to amplify supposed phenotypic signifiers of Blackness,

---

95. Goude, *Jungle Fever*, 41.
96. See Butler, "Yes, Those Kim Kardashian Photos"; and Telusma, "Kim Kardashian."
97. Sharpley-Whiting, *Black Venus*, 23, 24.
98. In 2009 model Amber Rose, then dating Kanye West prior to his marriage to Kardashian, imitated this pose in a photograph taken by white photographer Matt Doyle for *Complex* magazine, along with a number of other images of Grace Jones. In 2010 West used one of Doyle's images of Rose, which was cut from the *Complex* magazine spread, on his website. The original image, titled *[N——] Arabesque*, first appeared in Goude's *Jungle Fever* and then on the cover of Jones's 1989 album *Island Life* before making its way in mimetic form to West's site. Each image features its mostly nude subject holding an arabesque pose in one hand and a microphone in the other.

as promoting the "objectification and eroticization of black women."[99] This critique parallels Dorothy Musariri's argument that the twenty-first-century trend of white women attempting to pass as Black on social media both imitates the image-making practices of the Kardashians and illustrates the "long history of objectification and exploitation of black women."[100] At the same time, Telusma suggests that Kardashian may have been manipulated by Goude, becoming the "butt" of his joke rather than being "in" on it.[101] Such a rendering of Kardashian as oblivious to the controversial history of her *Paper* cover figures her as being sculpted in rather Pygmalion-like fashion by Goude.

Both *Paper* covers have also been the subject of racist and sexist parody and memeification. Many parodies replace the bottle of champagne from Kardashian's version of *Carolina Beaumont* with the body of Black men ejaculating into the champagne glass resting on her backside, making the evocation of the money shot quite explicit. The partially nude *Paper* cover has been subject to even more parody, with multiple images making animalistic references. Some parodies replace Kardashian's buttocks with the hind quarters of a horse, evoking Goude's description of Toukie Smith in relation to *"la croupe d'un cheval,"* or the buttocks of a baboon, making almost direct reference to bestial figurations of Baartman. As noted earlier, another animalistic meme casts Kardashian's buttocks as the Thanksgiving turkey in Norman Rockwell's *Freedom from Want*.[102] This parody synecdochally reduces Kardashian's personhood into parts, offering her compartmentalized body as an object for consumption and signifying how common it is for gender violence to be treated as a source of horror and humor, as illustrated by the many memes and Halloween costumes poking fun at Kardashian's actual kidnapping.

Kardashian's impersonation of Toukie Smith also makes clear the double bind often faced by Black women and women of color, wherein their bodies are objectified and imitated while also being erased. The synecdochization of Black women's bodies moves in both of the trope's directionalities: from whole to part and from part to whole. Such synecdoche involves the reduction of Black women's personhood to their sexualized and racialized parts. Deborah E. McDowell describes the buttocks, historically, as the "most synecdochical

---

99. Schwiegershausen, "So, Was That Kim Kardashian."
100. Musariri, "White Women."
101. Telusma, "Kim Kardashian."
102. This parody was not the only time Kardashian was linked to Rockwell and the iconography of holiday culture in the US. In 2018 Kardashian posted a photograph of Christmas-themed artwork created by her daughter, North West, who was five years old at the time. Poking fun at Kardashian's and then husband Kayne West's self-stylizations as artists and art collectors, *W* sardonically likened the child's work to such figures as Robert Rauschenberg and Andy Warhol and contrasted it with Rockwell's art. See Munzenrieder, "North West."

signature of the 'black female' form."[103] But synecdochization also positions individual women to stand in for larger social bodies and to bear the burden of representation. Kardashian-as-Smith demonstrates how non-Black women's participation in this appropriative and mimetic process yields paradoxical results in which Black women are rendered hypervisible and invisible at the same time. Like metonymy, this synecdoche becomes an act of both articulation and displacement, combination and supplantation.

The coextensivity of articulation and displacement in this synecdochal process is literalized in the process Goude used to create images like *Carolina Beaumont* and ones featuring Grace Jones. Dubbed "The French Correction," Goude's technique involves literally cutting and pasting different images into one composite. Goude explains, "The aim of French Correction was to play with changing the proportions of people's bodies, pre-Photoshop. Chopping up photos and rearranging them in a montage to elongate limbs or exaggerate the size of someone's head or some other aspect appealed to me."[104] *Jungle Fever* includes multiple images that were modified in this way, such as a photograph of Jones posed in an arabesque and an image of the "French Correction" in process, with the cuts and pieces of tape still visible.

In 2012 Le Musée des Arts Décoratifs in Paris held an exhibition of Goude's work, *Goudemalion: The Jean-Paul Goude Retrospective*, that featured approximately six hundred works of his creation. One review frames the exhibition as celebrating Goude's attempts at "glorifying and revealing the body, by exaggerating and subliming it. He redesigns the bodies of his models, photographing then transforming them."[105] The choice to title the exhibition *Goudemalion* references that fact that Goude has likened himself to Pygmalion, particularly in relationship to Jones as one of his favorite subjects for image "correction" and as his former lover.

Promotional materials for the retrospective describe Goude as "ahead of his time," framing "French Correction" as having anticipated the capabilities of digital media and software such as Photoshop. Despite the supposedly futuristic qualities of Goude's work, however, we may trace its genealogy through

---

103. McDowell, "Afterword," 306. See also Nash, "Black Anality"; and Hammons, "Black (W)holes."

104. Wessang, "Jean-Paul Goude." In *Jungle Fever*, Goude writes, "I first photographed her in different positions that I combined in a montage. I cut her legs and neck to lengthen them, and I turned her body to face like an Egyptian bas-relief." See Goude, *Jungle Fever*, 102–3. An issue of *Esquire* magazine from 1974, when Goude was art director, also includes an article explaining the "French Correction." The article includes an image of a Black woman model that had been modified and images of Goude himself, and it offers a "how to" guide for readers interested in trying the process themselves.

105. Houssin, "Jean-Paul Goude's First Paris Exhibition."

much older practices, including violence done to Baartman. Goude's remaking and remapping of Black women's bodies imitates colonialist practices of creating "racialized categories" to mark Africans as "fundamentally different from and inferior to white Europeans."[106] The "French Correction" of Smith's and Jones's bodies harks back to nineteenth-century France—where Baartman was held under duress—as a "society that routinely used scientific racism and Enlightenment rationale to justify the subjugation of blacks."[107] In much the same way that Goude's image of Kardashian remakes his earlier image of Smith, "French Correction" replays the logic of the *mission civilisatrice* at the heart of French colonialism.

Goude's stitching together of these images of Smith and Jones also replays figurations of Baartman as a new category of human: "*Homo sapiens monstrous*, a kind of Frankenstein's monster scarcely capable of emotion and intelligence."[108] This assertion inspired French naturalist and zoologist Georges Cuvier's 1815 decision to dissect Baartman's body; display her skeleton and sexual organs; and, in an inversion of the Pygmalion story, remake her body with a plaster cast.[109] The dissecting and Frankensteinian reassembling of images of Smith's and Jones's bodies had already been prefigured and authorized by the literal dismemberment and reconstruction of Baartman's body in a process that synecdochized the logics of colonialism.[110] Alexandra Sastre argues that fetishizations of Kardashian's body should be understood in relation to this history, writing, "In Kardashian's case, the fragmentation is not literal,

---

106. Conklin, *Mission to Civilize*, 9.
107. Tillet, "Black Girls in Paris."
108. Crais and Scully, *Sara Baartman*. 2.
109. Goude acknowledges that his work has been misinterpreted in relation to Pygmalion mythology. Referencing philosopher Edgar Morin, Goude explains, "He used to say: Goude is mistaken about himself, he is not a Pygmalion. If Pygmalion falls in love with a statue that comes to life, Goude falls in love with real women whom he tries to transform into statues. It's not the same thing at all." See Couturier, "Jean-Paul Goude."
110. Overlaps between Pygmalion and Frankenstein mythologies deserve further discussion. After its origination in Mary Shelley's novel *Frankenstein: Or, the Modern Prometheus*, the story of Frankenstein's monster took a rather melodramatic turn. As Emma Raub explains, the first adaptation of the novel for the stage was a melodrama written by Richard Brinsley Peake in 1823, which derived from the conventions established by Rousseau's *Pygmalion*. This theatrical version of the narrative introduces dramatic changes from the source novel—many of which have persisted in subsequent adaptations of it. Chief among these adaptations is Peake's choice to render the monster mute. Raub reads this muteness, which requires the monster to communicate through bodily expression and gesture, as indicative of melodrama, recurring in melodramatic performances and illustrating the fact that melodrama was "born of, and intimately tied to, language restriction." Raub situates melodrama as a genre attentive to both the limitations of language and the possibilities of signification beyond it. See Raub, "Frankenstein," 443, 437.

but as a representational pulling-apart it is more than metaphoric," rendering Kardashian's buttocks "a synecdoche for the authenticity of her entire self."[111]

These examples illustrate the tropological operations of race and gender: the synecdochization of particular bodies and body parts "metonymically groups people and marks difference by mapping meaning onto observable, phenotypic traits," creating catachrestic illusions of coherence, stability, and meaning within such groups and the subjects that purportedly constitute them.[112] If catachresis may be defined as a "figure without a referent," then the figuration of actual bodies creates the illusion of a preexisting referent.[113] The double synecdochization of Black women's bodies—from whole to part and part to whole—allows for the reduction of individual Black women to the status of objects and reifies notions of Blackness into signifiers that white culture can appropriate and deploy as paradoxical evidence of its own wholeness and universality. Much as celebrities imitate others to cement their identities, whiteness exploits Blackness to assert its wholeness. The *Paper* magazine cover and its entanglement with histories of objectification and violence toward Black women's bodies confirm that Kardashian's iconography warrants suspicious consideration and critique, as her image culture is responsible for considerable harm against Black women. This violence should be understood as symbolic, emotional, and material, and its implications should be taken seriously; but there also exists space for reading Kardashian's mimetic image culture otherwise in order to minimize, or even counteract, its harms.

PHOTOGRAPHIC GESTURES OF LIFE

A 2007 appearance in *Playboy* helped establish Kardashian as a popular cover model. In 2010 Kardashian appeared in the nude on the cover of *W* magazine's art issue, looking at the camera with tussled hair and parted lips in a pose reminiscent of the sensibilities of *Playboy* covers. Overlaid on the photograph of Kardashian's body, covering her breasts and genitals, is text by Barbara Kruger, with words printed in white type on red blocks in the artist's characteristic style: "It's all about me/ I mean you/ I mean me." A block of text next to Kardashian's body on the cover identifies the art issue as "starring" a number of public figures, including Kruger, Pee-wee Herman, Salvador Dali, and Jürgen Teller, who would later also photograph Kardashian. A parenthetical remark beneath this list of names claims, "Warhol would be proud."

---

111. Sastre, "Hottentot in the Age of Reality TV," 133.
112. Gilbert and Rossing, "Trumping Tropes," 95.
113. Bollobás, "Circumference & Co.," 274.

Affirming the logic of the "famous for being famous" tautology, the tagline for the Kardashian cover story reads, "Kim Kardashian can't sing, act, or dance, but she's found the role of a lifetime in the fine art of playing herself," and the interview promises "behind the scenes" access to the "queen of reality TV." Reading this tagline alongside Kruger's interview suggests that the text on the cover ("It's all about me/ I mean you/ I mean me") illustrates suspicion toward the star, implying an indictment of Kardashian's alleged narcissism and selfishness. Yet there is also ambivalence in the phrasing that suggests other more generous, interpretations of it—particularly when read alongside the final words from *Pygmalion*.

At the end of Rousseau's melodrama, an enlivened Galatea speaks to her creator. Touching herself, Galatea says, "Moi" ("Me"), to which Pygmalion responds in kind. She then touches herself again and reasserts, "C'est moi" ("This is me"), before touching a block of marble to declare, "Ce n'est plus moi" ("Now, that is not me"). Finally, Galatea touches her creator and says, "Ah! Encore moi" ("Ah! This is still me," or, translated otherwise, "This is me again"). Such words and their accompanying gestures encourage reading Rousseau's *Pygmalion* as an allegory for the production of the self as a "figure, or form."[114] Galatea's equivocal language asserts that she has agency and cannot be defined by her creator or the materials from which she was created, but her final words also indicate her realization that she does not exist independently from her creator. Rather, the self always exists in relation to others, and while both figures are distinct, they also remain interarticulated and interdependent. Galatea maintains a metonymic relationship with Pygmalion, who is "still" (or "again") part of her but never fully definitive of or equivalent to her, and her liminal position mirrors that of all subjects who are affected by signifying practices that precede them but who also have agency to affect them. That is, Galatea signifies Enikö Bollobás's reading of catachresis as "the trope of performativity par excellence."[115]

Rousseau is a forebearer of the confessional mode associated with Kardashian, as his book *Confessions* is considered one of the earliest examples of the tell-all autobiography. Although both St. Augustine and St. Teresa had written spiritual autobiographies, Rousseau inaugurated a genre more focused on personal experiences, including shameful or salacious details about his private life and his relationship with his own fame. Descriptions of Kardashian as fine-tuning the art of playing one's self parallel the opening lines of Rousseau's tell-all: "I have resolved on an enterprise which has no precedent and

---

114. Rooney, *Living Screens*, 13.
115. Bollobás, "Circumference & Co.," 274.

which, once complete, will have no imitator. My purpose is to display to my kind a portrait in every way true to nature, and the man I shall portray will be myself."[116] Rousseau's remarks illustrate what will become one of the constitutive paradoxes of celebrity: a claim to authenticity (the natural self) that is hinged on representationality (the portrait). These lines also signal that the construction of self is an enterprise dependent on the presence (even if only imagined) of an other to whom such a portrait will be offered, illustrating Laura Rascaroli's figuration of the self-portrait as a "contradictory genre, which merges the most intimate artistic gesture with the most public display of image management."[117]

Rousseau's work invites a different interpretation of Kardashian's *W* cover, not as an iteration of self-absorption or self-centeredness but as an illustration that the "me" always exists in relation to the "you." The equivocation of the lines, implicitly attributed to Kardashian, acknowledges the subject's interstitiality and interdependence, enacting an intersubjective figuration of selfhood as an unstable and ongoing process. This reading of the cover conflicts with much of the conventional wisdom about Kardashian; after all, her coffee-table book of photographic self-portraiture bears the title *Selfish*. Yet close reading of *Selfish* supports the argument that neither it nor the photographic genre of the selfie should be dismissed as merely symptomatic of narcissism and ego investment but should be acknowledged as a gesture of recognition, an admission of vulnerability, and an acceptance of intersubjectivity.

Writing about iconic photographs, Robert Hariman and John Louis Lucaites remind us that still images often refuse to sit still. Addressing AP photographer Joe Rosenthal's famous photograph of the flag-raising at Iwo Jima, for example, Hariman and Lucaites attend to its afterlives: its circulation, appropriation, adaptation, reenactment, and imitation across a range of mediums and sites, both purposeful and accidental. The reinterpretation and reuse of a photograph keep the original image and its afterimages in motion, signaling the "plasticity" and "ambiguous potentiality" of images.[118] The transmutations of an iconic image like Rosenthal's underwrite the concept of abundance that Hariman and Lucaites identify as central to photography. They write, "The habitus of photography becomes a place where images and the image world as a whole are continuously developing through use as they circulate beyond local boundaries, being taken up by others here and there, and then again somewhere else, and again and again."[119]

---

116. Rousseau, *Confessions*, 17.
117. Rascaroli, "Self-Portrait Film," 63.
118. Hariman and Lucaites, *No Caption Needed*, 44–45.
119. Hariman and Lucaites, *Public Image*, 236.

The *Paper* magazine photographs, which imitate and are imitated, illustrate this process rather melodramatically, but abundance is not simply a matter of circulation. The concept of abundance also refers to the polysemic character of images—their "radical plurality"—as well as to the plentitude of meanings that audiences might find in their encounters with images. Moreover, abundance does not solely characterize iconic images; it also characterizes the most banal, ordinary, and forgettable of images—as illustrated, Hariman and Lucaites note, by the scores of photographs uploaded to social media every hour and every minute of every day. In the context of networked digital media and the sharing economy, we find ourselves facing an "embarrassment of riches." Banal, or ephemeral, images have an abundant quality to them not only because of their omnipresence but also because of the close encounters they offer with everyday life and the condition of "something *like* intimacy" that they suggest.[120]

Hariman and Lucaites encourage us to respond to these images generously, writing, "Photography cannot be resolutely serious, however, as it remains ridiculously ubiquitous. It is everywhere, from the image on the cereal box to the lunchtime digital news scan to the selfie uploaded in the evening." Such "supersaturation," they argue, offers a "sign of cultural vitality" and a reminder that life always exceeds the boundaries, or borders, that seek to contain it.[121] The claim that ephemeral or forgettable images can engender experiences of abundance applies to even the form of image-making that is arguably the most banal: the selfie.

Jerry Saltz offers a history of the selfie both as descended from the transmedia genre of self-portraiture and as a distinct genre with its own conventions, tropes, and structuring logics. He notes genealogical points of articulation between contemporary selfies and pre-selfie images such as Parmigianino's *Self-Portrait in a Convex Mirror* (1523–24) or Van Gogh's 1889 *Self-Portrait*. These images are more akin to selfies than to other kinds of self-portraiture because they display the artist's attempts to render their own image. Parmigianino's painting reveals the subject's hand holding the mirror with which he sees his image; Van Gogh's depicts the artist holding the palette and brushes with which he will paint himself.[122] To this assemblage of image, we might add Rockwell's *Triple Self-Portrait*, as well as a host of early daguerreotypes and photographs in which photographers (including, famously, the Grand Duchess Anastasia Nikolaevna of Russia) rely on mirrors to capture themselves, making their photographic equipment visible in the image, or extend their

---

120. Hariman and Lucaites, *Public Image*, 15, 55, 237.
121. Hariman and Lucaites, *Public Image*, 24.
122. Saltz, "Art at Arm's Length."

arms to hold their cameras away from their bodies, their lenses turned back on themselves.[123]

As Saltz notes, "Selfies are nearly always taken from within an arm's length of the subject. For this reason, the cropping and composition of selfies are very different from those of all preceding self-portraiture. There is the near-constant visual presence of one of the photographer's arms, typically the one holding the camera."[124] As Paul Frosh contends, this arm is both "mediating"—it facilitates the photographic event—and "mediated"—it is depicted in the image and becomes a signifier of the "selfieness" of the image.[125] Even in those selfies in which the photographing arm is not mediated—having been cropped out of the frame—its presence is implied and leaves tell-tale traces in the image's composition, including camera angle, height, and distance.

What, if anything, is significant about the presence of these mediating and mediated markers—hands, arms, mirrors, tools—of the photographic event? Might not the visible arm and the awkward angle its extension creates be seen simply as deficits of the genre? Saltz suggests that these conventions help explain how the selfie engenders what Geoffrey Batchen describes as "the shift of the photograph [from] memorial function to a communication device."[126] These conventions of the selfie manifest and acknowledge its sociality or its status as what Frosh calls a "gestural image," in which the image not only depicts the mediated gesture with which the image is made but also performs a "gesture of inclusion," inviting the viewer "to look, be with, and act."[127] As Anne Jerslev and Mette Mortensen argue, the selfie performs an "act of becoming" that is aimed at an other.[128]

This gesture toward connectivity, Frosh argues, illustrates the extent to which figurations of selfies as purely narcissistic enterprises are reductive, missing much of what selfies reveal about the construction of selves and social relations in and through photography. The genre is multiply reflexive: displaying self-referentiality about its status "as an image" and demonstrating "personal reflexivity" by showing a "self, enacting itself." This paradox "reveals the very instability of the term 'self'" in ways that resonate with Rousseau's figuration of his confessional narrative as both a revelation of his authentic self and a representation, or portrait.[129] These elements of the selfie acknowledge

---

123. Gilbert, "World's Earliest Selfies."
124. Saltz, "Art at Arm's Length."
125. Frosh, "Gestural Image," 1611.
126. Saltz, "Art at Arm's Length."
127. Frosh, "Gestural Image," 1619.
128. Jerslev and Mortensen, "What Is the Self?"
129. Frosh, "Gestural Image," 1621.

the production of subjectivity as a performative process dependent on citation and imitation of others. Extending Frosh's argument, I understand selfies as making clear that subjects not only are the effects of citational, mimetic gestures but also exist only in metonymic relation to others.

Just as all textuality is, in Kristevan terms, intertextuality, all subjectivity is, in fact, intersubjectivity. While Frosh reads selfies as similar to phatic communication in their revelation that individuals need to exist in sociable conditions, I read selfies as reenacting the process through which subjects are formed always in relation to others. For this reason, it seems worth noting that the arm's length that is definitive of most selfies is the same distance at which infants are first able to discern faces such as those of the caregivers who hold them. Selfies make it clear that humans exist in relation to other subjects as well as to objects that affect and are affected by such prosthetic relations.

The gesture of the selfie is, thus, not merely an invitation; it is an expression of vulnerability and an assumption of risk, but this extension of the self suggests an inclination toward abundance, rather than scarcity, as a condition of life. This gesture assumes, or at least hopes, that there are more, rather than fewer, others who will respond to this invitation; it imagines that opportunities for connectivity are more plentiful than they are lacking. We might, then, understand the selfie as performing a disposition that is more reparative than paranoid and as operating more through accretion and association than through distancing and disidentification. Unlike Goude's "French Correction," which seeks an image of wholeness and seamlessness, selfies understand subjectivity as a network of interdigitated relations. Life is abundant because it always exceeds—or, overflows—the bounds of individuation, in much the same way that the body of the selfied subject typically exceeds the bounds of the frame.

That the selfie captures only part of the self (or group) reminds viewers that life depends on contiguity with others and, consequently, on contingency. Such conditions can signify scarcity, as in lack, absence, or loss; but these conditions also signify the possibility of life's abundance. Just as body parts synecdochize whole bodies, individuals signal larger collectives that exist through practices of association. In contrast to more traditional norms of portraiture, selfies do not reinforce fantasies of masterful, autonomous, or individuated subjects; rather, they understand the subject's relationality to wholeness, wherein wholeness is synonymous not with completeness or totality but with contingent connectivity. The incompleteness of the individual is a sign not of scarcity but of intersubjective abundance.[130]

---

130. Hariman and Lucaites, "Hands and Feet."

Let us return, then, to Kardashian's *Selfish*. At first glance, the title of this book suggests the kind of suspicious attitude toward its subject that typifies much of Rousseau's work on the harms of fame, and the book itself offers evidence of the greed, superficiality, and self-centeredness that trouble Rousseau. It might even be said to illustrate the worst form of amour propre: an obsession with the opinions of others and a performance of the self in relation to (or anticipation of) those imagined judgments. As James Delaney puts it, "If Rousseau was wary of *amour-propre*'s dangers in more populated areas like the Paris of his time, what would he think of forums like Facebook and Twitter?"[131] What would he think of Kardashian? These questions, however, are not the ones I am interested in asking, as I am not invested in Rousseau's paranoid disposition or in Pygmalion's inclination toward mastery. Instead, I am foregrounding notions of relationality and subjective interdependence as productive ways of imagining selfhood. ("This is me" and "This is still me.") Intersubjectivity always entails risk and vulnerability, exploitation and abuse. But intersubjectivity also means that all subjects have potential for connection with and responsibility to one another.

The selfies in Kardashian's photographic memoir—her visual *Confessions*—expose signs of openness and vulnerability; they reveal skin, as Sara Ahmed might describe it, as both a border and a point of contact, as both a defense and a site of susceptibility. Like those images of Kardashian being "made up" by a stylist, selfies indicate the performative dimensions of subjectivity and its relationality, showing the self to be not stable or unified but, all at once, catachrestic, metonymic, and synecdochal. Within the title itself, the suffix *-ish* means "of the nature of, approaching the quality of, somewhat." We see this meaning of *-ish* in its contemporary colloquial use to mean "sort of." In this sense, this title tells us that *Selfish* offers us something approaching the quality of Kardashian's self, but it also reminds us that subjectivity is always experienced and shared as something *like* a self. The selfie recalls the melodrama as a genre that wants to express all but, knowing that it cannot, gestures toward such expression nonetheless.

Critics of Kardashian may be right that her iconography and penchant for selfies made her more vulnerable to the specific attack in Paris, but this melodramatic example reminds us that all lives lived in public experience vulnerability. At the same time, the particularities of Kardashian's attack also serve as paradoxical reminders that some lives are made more vulnerable, or precarious, than others. The fact that Kardashian's image-making practices create conditions of possibility for both exploiting and exposing the vulnerabilities

---

131. DeLaney, "Rousseau."

of others mirrors the tensions that define selfies more broadly. As Sanaz Raji argues, the emancipatory capacities of selfies for "Black, PoC, disabled and other non-normative groups" must be understood in relation to their capacity to enable surveillance of and violence toward those same bodies.[132]

Critics and theorists of selfies must ask, as Adi Kuntsman encourages, "Who has the ability—and the safety—to star in a selfie?" While "selfie visibility" can signify privilege, its visibility may be, for many, "neither always available nor desirable."[133] The emancipatory affordances of selfies may also be co-opted. For example, Aria Dean describes Black women's and femmes' early adoption of selfie culture in the early 2000s as a form of resistance that was appropriated and displaced by white or white-presenting (cis and nondisabled) women whose images aligned more closely with the hegemonic beauty norms that guide image cultures in the US.[134]

I will conclude with attention to practices of image-makers using selfies, often at great peril, to resist oppressive structures while also questioning the constraints of the genre and the intersubjective relations it enables. Examples include the "interjected" selfies of Raju Rage, a transgender queer of color artist who took selfies at a European exhibition of LGBTQ art that excluded queers of color in order to interrupt the art's whitewashing with their literal and photographed presence, or the "selfless selfies" of the "Chupacabra Selfie Project" in which undocumented immigrants take selfies while obscuring their identities with Chupacabra masks in order to signify the ways that white supremacist rhetoric in the US has cast them as monsters.

Consider also the work of new media and performance artist Shawné Michaelain Holloway, whom Dean cites as resisting the kind of "basic-bitch politic of visibility" that adopts either a paranoid or a reparative lens for seeing the acts of seeing and being seen.[135] Self-describing as an artist who uses "rhetorics of technology and sexuality" to expose and challenge "structures of power," Holloway, who is Black, features scores of selfies, mirror selfies, and computer screen selfies on her Instagram account (@cleogirl2525) that emphasize malleable forms of self-presentation. Alternating between and/or commingling hyperfemme and butch stylistics, they demonstrate self-reflexivity about their mediation.

One post from 2019 depicts Holloway and a companion via a mirror selfie in a New York City bodega. The image reflected back at the two subjects originates in a surveillance screen in the store. Appearing at a canted angle, the

---

132. Raji, "'My Face,'" 153.
133. Kuntsman, "Introduction," 17.
134. Dean, "Closing the Loop."
135. Dean, "Closing the Loop."

selfie shows the two figures pressed against a wall of shelves in an overstuffed chip aisle; Holloway's gaze is directed at the surveillance screen on which the two bodies are captured, while the other photographed/photographing subject looks at the phone documenting the doubled image. This photograph of two subjects rendered visible on two screens between two rows of shelves makes visible the kind of "Du Boisian double consciousness that has characterized Black life for centuries" and that is becoming increasingly felt by "every single networked human being" in an age of near-constant image making.[136] Such an image manifests the vulnerability felt by all subjects while also highlighting the precarity of some—including those who may find the possibility of being subjected to or taken hostage by state violence to be as ordinary as the banal act of buying chips at a convenience store.

As a cultural formation, celebrity is both hyperbolic and hypertrophic, and Kardashian is one of the twenty-first century's most visible iterations of these qualities. The harms that her image culture has engendered against women of color, and Black women in particular, are both unique to her brand and illustrative of ongoing practices of misogynoir that have been normalized in white supremacist cultures for centuries. Kardashian's hypervisibility is grounds for both suspicious and generous responses, as it perpetuates her privileged position at the same time that it lays bare the often-injurious practices on which fame depends. While conditions of semiotic interdependence and intersubjectivity mean that powerful figures such as Kardashian can exploit those with less privilege through various forms of appropriation and mimesis, these same conditions allow others to resignify these images in ways that disrupt and destabilize their hegemony. It is precisely Kardashian's disposition toward metatropological sensibilities that enables the conditions of her image culture's own remaking.

---

136. Dean, "Closing the Loop."

EPILOGUE

> The portmanteau word is a monster, a word that is not a word, that is not authorized by any dictionary, that holds out the worrying prospect of books which, instead of comfortingly recycling the words we know, possess the freedom endlessly to invent new ones.
> —Derek Attridge

At the time of its release, *Six Degrees of Separation* (Fred Schepisi, 1993) was one node in a larger network of small-world films. These include *Short Cuts* (Robert Altman, 1993), *Fragments of a Chronology of Chance* (Michael Haneke, 1994), *Before the Rain* (Milcho Manchevski, 1994), *Exotica* (Atom Egoyan, 1994), and *Pulp Fiction* (Quentin Tarantino, 1994); they are characterized by an ensemble of characters with discrete storylines that intersect through various "contingent links," accidents, or associations. The "narration alternates among various lives so that no one character emerges as a protagonist," asking audiences to "trace out a web of personal relationships among the characters."[1]

These associational narratives again gained prominence during the late 1990s and early 2000s with a focus on the traumatic registers of networks, including tragedies or catastrophes, that often bring people into "unwanted" contact with each other. Examples include *Magnolia* (Paul Thomas Anderson, 1999), *Traffic* (Steven Soderbergh, 2000), *Amores Perros* (Alejandro Gonzalez Iñárritu, 2002), *21 Grams* (Alejandro Gonzalez Iñárritu, 2003), *Crash* (Paul Haggis, 2004), *Syriana* (Stephen Gaghan, 2005), and *Babel* (Alejandro Gonzalez Iñárritu). These films, Neil Narine contends, chart a "perhaps unconscious epistemological shift toward cognitively mapping social life in the global age

---

1. Bordwell, *Poetics of Cinema*, 190.

as a network."[2] Films with interlocking narratives also exist at the intersections of melodrama and romantic comedy, including *Love Actually* (Richard Curtis, 2003), *Happy Endings* (Don Roos, 2005), *Hereafter* (Clint Eastwood, 2010), *Valentine's Day* (Garry Marshall, 2010), and *New Year's Eve* (Garry Marshall, 2011). Critics and theorists have given these films multiple names: *network films, global network films, hyperlink films, multiplex films, multi-protagonist films*, and *database narratives*.[3]

Related to this body of films are anthology films, in which multiple discrete short films, sometimes with different directors, are presented together.[4] While such films often share unifying threads, their narratives do not typically intersect. Examples include *New York Stories* (Woody Allen, Francis Ford Coppola, and Martin Scorsese, 1989), *Four Rooms* (Allison Anders, Alexandre Rockwell, Robert Rodriguez, and Quentin Tarantino, 1995), *11'09"01 September 11* (Youssef Chahine, Amos Gitai, Shôhei Imamura, Alejandro G. Iñárritu, Claude LeLouch, Ken Loach, Samira Makmalbaf, Mira Nair, Idrissa Ouedrogo, Sean Penn, and Danis Tanovic, 2002), and *Coffee and Cigarettes* (Jim Jarmusch, 2003). This category of films also goes by multiple names: *anthology films, package films, omnibus films*, and *portmanteau films*.

As David Bordwell and others have noted, network films register the cultural, social, political, and aesthetic impacts of new communication technologies and digital forms of mediation. Network and anthology films also capitalize on the celebrity industry with ensemble casts featuring multiple stars. Those network films that focus on trauma also animate what Narine calls the "Hollywood humanitarian-star economy," or the neoliberal expectation that famous individuals perform "ethical stances" and idealized forms of global citizenship.[5] Both network and anthology films recognize relationality and interdependence as constitutive of human experience, demonstrating that subjects always exist in relation to others and framing vulnerability as threading together its ensemble of characters.

Mapping the Stars has focused on the metonymic registers of celebrity culture, but I conclude with attention to another rhetorical device integral to the networked logics and aesthetics of celebrity: the portmanteau. Not simply a category of films, the portmanteau is a morphological form of pun combining the sounds and meanings of words into one. Although often described as a discrete figurative device distinguishable from metonymy, the portmanteau

---

2. Narine, "Global Trauma," 213.
3. Quart, "Networked"; Simons, "Complex Narratives."
4. These categories of films are sometimes considered interchangeable and described variously. See Spicer, "Author as Author"; and Barber, "Fragmentation Games."
5. Narine, "Global Trauma," 211.

extends and even amplifies metonymic logic by suggesting that all signifiers exist through relations of contiguity or association. What remains implied in metonymy—the interdependence and interrelation of signifiers—becomes explicit in portmanteaus, which "flagrantly" announce the instability of signification. Derek Attridge argues, "The portmanteau shatters any illusion that the systems of difference in language are fixed or sharply drawn, reminding us that signifiers are perpetually dissolving into one another." In this way, the portmanteau suggests both the instability of all words and the consequent "freedom endlessly to invent new ones."[6]

The word *celebrity*, contends Tim Edwards, has itself become a "portmanteau term" used to explain, if not contain, the "shifting terrain" of publicness, sociality, and fame in Western cultures.[7] And, literally, portmanteaus abound within rhetoric about stars, as illustrated by many words that have made appearances throughout this book: *melodrama, momager, celebutante, emoticon, celebremoji, Kimoji*. Neologisms frequently recur in discourse about media and popular culture because the rapid changes and hybridizations in these arenas often necessitate new vocabularies, but the device also occupies a prominent place in the lexicon of celebrity culture within the journalistic trend of naming famous couples with portmanteaus, as in *Bennifer* (Ben Affleck and Jennifer Lopez), *Brangelina* (Brad Pitt and Angelina Jolie), *J-Rod* (Jennifer Lopez and Alex Rodriguez), and *Kimye* (Kim Kardashian and Kanye West). This trend has also engendered parodies, such as the Twitter account for Kim Kierkegaardashian, which mashes up phrases evocative of Kim Kardashian's sensibilities with philosophical musings suggestive of Kierkegaard's existentialism, such as "Matte makeup reminds a person of what he truly is—nothing" or "Eyebrows on fleek. This is as close as I can come to approaching the absolute."

The presence of portmanteaus within celebrity discourse should be understood as more than mere coincidence. As Ruben Borg explains, portmanteaus rely on properties of metonymy and the related functions of synecdoche. Like metonyms, portmanteaus operate as substitutions hinged on associational contiguity between terms at linguistic, phonological, and sometimes conceptual levels; portmanteaus also illustrate synecdochic operations wherein linguistic parts stand in for wholes.[8] The term *portmanteau* derives from the French words meaning to carry (*porter*) and cloak (*manteau*), and its earliest usage denoted a large trunk or suitcase that opens in two parts. As a figurative device, portmanteaus signify two words that have been blended to combine

---

6. Attridge, *Peculiar Language*, 196.
7. Edwards, "Medusa's Stare," 155.
8. Borg, "Neologizing in Finnegan's Wake," 150.

their sounds and meanings, as in *smog* (smoke and fog), *motel* (motor and hotel), or *brunch* (breakfast and lunch). Literary and rhetorical scholars attribute the first figurative use of the term *portmanteau* to Lewis Carroll's *Through the Looking Glass* (1871), in which Humpty Dumpty explicates neologisms in the poem "Jabberwocky," such as *slithy* ("lithe and slimy") and *mimsy* ("flimsy and miserable"), which feature "two meanings packed up into one word."[9] The portmanteau assumed its prominent role in rhetoric about stardom in the US during Hollywood's earliest decades, with an early example referring to the shared residence of celebrity couple Mary Pickford and Douglas Fairbanks. Named *Pickfair*, their Beverly Hills estate became a gathering space for some of the most notable figures of the twentieth century, including *Pygmalion* playwright George Bernard Shaw, Charlie Chaplin, Greta Garbo, gossip columnist Louella Parsons, and President Calvin Coolidge. The first portmanteau applied directly to a celebrity couple was *Gilbo*, appearing in a 1928 fan letter to *Picture-Play* magazine about Greta Garbo's relationship with John Gilbert.[10]

Portmanteaus became increasingly important to celebrity culture as the gossip industry developed, chiefly because of Walter Winchell. Beginning his career at William Randolph Hearst's *New York Daily Mirror* in 1929, Winchell penned the first syndicated gossip column, "On-Broadway," and went on to have one of the highest-rated radio shows at the time.[11] Covering high-profile celebrity scandals, Winchell influenced Ed Sullivan and Louella Parsons, helping to create the gossip industry as we know it today. As Neil Gabler writes, Winchell "helped inaugurate a new mass culture of celebrity," which was "fixated on personalities, promulgated by the media, predicated on publicity, dedicated to the ephemeral and grounded on the principle that notoriety confers power."[12] Deploying network logic, Gabler continues, "If one surveys this culture of Monica Lewinsky and O. J. Simpson and constant gossip and salaciousness, and one tries to trace the roots, you find yourself at Walter Winchell." John Blades describes Winchell's influence in even more paranoid terms: "Winchell is the virus responsible for the present epidemic of celebrity chatter and prattle."[13] Winchell might also be seen to have anticipated,

---

9. Carroll, *Through the Looking Glass*, 101. In 1974 Norman Rockwell's son Thomas Rockwell and daughter-in-law Gail Rockwell published an illustrated children's book, *The Portmanteau Book*, which includes a number of poems written in nonsensical language in homage to Carroll.

10. Williams, "'Gilbo-Garbage,'" 24.

11. In 2002 *Six Degrees of Separation* playwright John Guare helped adapt the film *Sweet Smell of Success* (Alexander Mackendrick, 1957), which was based on Winchell, into a Broadway musical.

12. Gabler, *Winchell*, xiii.

13. Blades, "Godfather of Gossip."

if not animated, the demands for nonstop news within the information age. John Katz posits, "The real roots of the exploding computer culture aren't only in MIT labs or hacker bedrooms, but equally in the far-reaching visions of Frankenstein-like innovators Winchell and Hearst."[14]

Winchell's column was classic melodrama, reporting "who was romancing whom, who was cavorting with gangsters, who was ill or dying, who was suffering financial difficulties, which spouses were having affairs, which couples were about to divorce, etc." While "what made him a national phenomenon was gossip," Winchell's "vivid prose helped transform the style of journalism and made him a popular curiosity."[15] He expanded US American vernacular with numerous portmanteaus, such as *infanticipate* (the anticipation of a new child), *keptives* (women in relationships with married men, who were both "kept," or taken care of, and "captive," or held hostage by the relationship), *frenemies* (referring in 1935 to Russia as both "friends" and "enemies" of the United States), and *celebutantes* (describing famous socialites, or debutantes). Such forms of "slanguage" and the journalistic style they inspired have since been called *Winchellisms*.

The celebrity portmanteau gained new prominence in the early 2000s, as Winchell-style celebrity gossip intensified and demands for intimate access to celebrities increased. As noted in chapter 4, the rise of reality television programming and the internet amplified the celebrity gossip industry. For example, *People* magazine lost its stronghold on the celebrity human-interest market with the arrival of a number of competing magazines and websites. After the rebranding of *Us* magazine from an industry-oriented monthly to a celebrity-focused weekly, other tabloids appeared, including *In Touch*, in 2002, and *Life & Style*, in 2004. Celebrity gossip websites and blogs, such as *TMZ* and *Perez Hilton*, appeared in 2005, making it clear that "celebrity gossip was reaching an all-time zenith," as tabloids sought the status that Winchell had pioneered. Print and online publications fought to distinguish their coverage, and one tactic to "draw and maintain readership" was the coinage of celebrity-couple names. Although there was no consensus about what to call this category of names, dubbed "uni-names, bundled names, combined names, name meshing, name blends or celebrity couple portmanteaus," their success, notes Vanessa Díaz, "sparked a race between celebrity magazines to come up with the next catchy portmanteau."[16]

There are numerous ways to account for the presence of the portmanteau within rhetoric about celebrities and celebrity couples. There is an economic

---

14. Katz, "Winchell."
15. Gabler, *Winchell*, xii.
16. Díaz, "'Brad & Angelina,'" 278, 275.

logic to the tactic that helps brand, by association, the entity that coins the phrase while also cashing in on the cultural capital of the individuals with a combination that is greater than the sum of its parts. As Maria Pramaggiore argues, celebrity-couple portmanteaus deploy a "synergistic and multiplicative logic," in which the capital of the paired individuals outstrips "the value associated with the two stars as individuals."[17] The logic of the celebrity-couple portmanteau reduplicates the logics of consolidation and conglomeration that have become hegemonic in the global entertainment market since the Reagan era.[18]

Celebrity nicknames also appeal to audience expectations about the supposed *just-like-us-ness* of stars, implying intimacy between celebrities and their fans.[19] For example, both Fox News and the *New York Times* have described celebrity nicknames as affording audiences a sense of agency over and access to celebrities' lives.[20] Even when coined by media outlets, such sobriquets enable audiences to forge metonymic connections with stars and to link themselves to larger networked publics. The names themselves also take on metonymic functions, communicating ideas about the celebrity couple and their cultural significance. For instance, Díaz describes an article on *People.com* in which one half of a celebrity couple references another famous couple by their portmanteau to distinguish their respective public personae, demurring that his and his wife's wedding anniversary was not going to be "all *Brangelina*." Implying that his celebration would be much more in line with what ordinary couples might experience, this celebrity uses *Brangelina* metonymically to signify "extravagant travelling, spontaneity or something 'sexy.'"[21]

Pramaggiore suspiciously reads celebrity-couple portmanteaus as illustrating the hegemony of heterosexuality in Hollywood, noting that despite the increasing presence of same-sex couples in US media culture, no LGBTQ couples have (as of yet) earned a "conjoined name." The prominence of celebrity-couple portmanteaus can also be read suspiciously as signifying the compulsory logic of coupledom in US culture. Yet Pramaggiore also suggests, more generously, that celebrity portmanteaus do enable new relational structures and models of kinship. She emphasizes that these nicknames typically use celebrities' first names, rather than surnames, which she interprets as an emphasis on "romance rather than reproduction" and a form of relationality that is not necessarily tied to "traditional marriage."[22]

---

17. Pramaggiore, "Filial Coupling," 78.
18. Petri, "Just Say No."
19. Díaz, "'Brad & Angelina,'" 282.
20. "Blame Bennifer"; Cave, "What's in a Nickname?"
21. Díaz, "'Brad & Angelina,'" 285.
22. Pramaggiore, "Filial Coupling," 79.

I also read the celebrity-couple portmanteau generously, interpreting the recurrence of the portmanteau within rhetoric about stars as signaling intersubjectivity and relationality. Combining two names into one, portmanteaus demonstrate the unfixity and contingency that define both signification and subjectivity. In portmanteaus, Borg argues, "synecdochic containment of the whole within the part" suggests a "sense of organic completeness, of structural unity" at the same time that the portmanteau betrays a "tendency to exceed its own structure, to unmake itself with every performance." Borg continues: "As a synecdochic fragment" suggests "its own totality," it also reveals the limitations, if not impossibility, of "successful communication."[23] This reading of the synecdochic elements of the portmanteau mirrors Jeffrey Adams's contention that "all texts are produced in the complex dialectic involving simultaneous affirmation and negation of other texts." Portmanteaus acknowledge that "words, images, and sounds are all penetrated by other words, images, and sounds" and are therefore always "polyphonic and heterogeneous, never univocal or semantically self-contained."[24] To Adams's assemblage of "words, images, and sounds," I would add *subjects,* which are consequently never fully univocal or uniform, self-contained or self-same.

Amplifying metonymic impulses, portmanteaus signal humans' fraught relationship with interconnectedness, manifesting the instability and vulnerability of subjecthood itself. Portmanteaus remind us of the affective and symbolic networks of interdependence that constitute both signification and subjectification. And like melodrama, the portmanteau carries with it a sense of anxiety or loss that might prompt paranoia and/or call for a reparative response insofar as it lays bare the impossibility of wholeness or completion. Paul Saint-Amour defines the portmanteau as a "relic of melancholia, or mourning for the self." He writes, "This mourning orbits around two realizations of loss: first, that the self is dislocated, and must pack for exile; second, that the self is neither containable nor continent."[25] It matters that the metaphorical understanding of the portmanteau is first articulated by Humpty Dumpty—who, upon falling, cannot be put back together again. Humpty Dumpty's articulation of the portmanteau, argues Saint-Amour, illustrates a "wishful coinage" derived from an "embodied yearning"—which is to say, a reparative response—at the same time that it also reveals a paranoid fear of becoming monstrous in the wake of falling apart and being reassembled.

There is something rather Frankensteinian about the portmanteau, which Attridge calls a "monster word" (or, Creation) that stitches together two words

---

23. Borg, "Neologizing," 150, 151.
24. Adams, "Sublimation," 699.
25. Saint-Amour, "Over-Assemblage," 52.

such that the seams between them remain both absent and present—the words' individual histories, sounds, and meanings conjoined, however imperfectly.[26] In fact, a literal portmanteau plays a significant role in Mary Shelley's novel *Frankenstein*, and although Shelley's novel predates Carroll's coinage of the portmanteau metaphor by a little more than fifty years, *Frankenstein* demonstrates an interest in the relationship between signification and subjectivity. Abandoned by his creator Victor Frankenstein, the monster finds a leather portmanteau filled with several works of literature, including John Milton's *Paradise Lost,* a volume of Plutarch's *Lives of the Noble Greeks and Romans,* and Johann Wolfgang von Goethe's *The Sorrows of Young Werther,* which introduce him to the conditions of being human. Upon reading these works, the monster describes feeling both "ecstasy" and the "lowest dejection," as he experiences identifications *and* disidentifications with the characters he encounters and his feelings of connectedness to them reinforce his lack of connection to others in his everyday life.[27] This portmanteau of books concurrently demonstrates to the monster his agency and vulnerability—his capacity to create and to be destroyed.

Frankenstein posits the dangers of impossible fantasies of wholeness and mastery, with the monster standing in for the paranoid anxieties that subjects might feel about their own uncertain, uneven, and unstable constitutions in and beyond signification. The monster is not a monster at all but a reminder of the fragility, imperfection, and compositeness that define all bodies and subjects; monstrousness itself is a projection resulting from cultural disavowal of such aspects of human existence. We might therefore read *Frankenstein* as an allegory about the networked form of bodies and subjectivities and the perils of inattention to such interdigitations.

That Shelley's novel is centrally concerned with the sensibilities and politics of networks can be seen, argues Andrew Burkett, in its many adaptations for "immersive electronic environments, hypertext online resources, and digital humanities initiatives." Shaped by such new nineteenth-century technologies as electricity, the mechanical printing press, locomotion, and photography, *Frankenstein* is "deeply concerned with the nature and function of 'information' and especially with media(tion)." Like *Six Degrees of Separation,* Shelley's *Frankenstein* demonstrates attention not only to new forms of communication technologies but also to the dogsled as a medium for transmitting people and, consequently, information. It is a dogsled on which Captain

---

26. Attridge, *Peculiar Language,* 196. The term *Frankenword* is a kind of portmanteau used in popular media discourse, which combines *Franken* with other words, such as *Frankenfood* or *Frankenstorm.* See Doll, "Rise of Frankenwords"; and Bodle, "Frankenwords."

27. Shelley, *Frankenstein,*177.

Walton first sees the creature traveling in the Artic, and it is a dogsled that transmits Frankenstein and his remarkable story to Walton, who transmits these stories to the book's imagined readers. Burkett thus reads the novel as a hypertextual, or "pre-cybernetic," narrative.[28] *Frankenstein* also links itself to a network of other texts, including those in the monster's portmanteau, and it is itself composed by epistolary form and multivocal narration, asking audiences, not unlike network films, to trace lines of connection between its characters.

Within the nested narratives composing *Frankenstein* is attention to fame and its potentially harmful implications, which helps explain the various "cameos" of the monster and his creator throughout this book.[29] Set in the late eighteenth century, when the discourse of celebrity was first emerging, the novel opens with letters written by Captain Walton, a failed writer who has journeyed to the North Pole in search of fame. His story recalls that of Victor Frankenstein, whose scientific endeavors are motivated by a desire to make a name for himself, which ultimately results in his making a name for his creature. Even the creature himself illustrates the potentially traumatic character of fame insofar as he is crafted by a Pygmalion-like creator, or image-maker, making his image largely beyond his control.

Shelley's interest in celebrity is owed perhaps to being the child of two well-known authors and being in the company of Lord Byron, a poet famous (or infamous) for his interest in his own fame, when she wrote the first draft of her novel. And it was upon seeing a staged melodrama based on her novel that Shelley realized that she was a celebrity, remarking, "But lo and behold! I found myself famous."[30] As David Marshall demonstrates, Shelley's novel also seems influenced by Jean-Jacques Rousseau, including not only *Pygmalion*'s story of a man who gives life to a creature he cannot control but also Rousseau's autobiographical works. Marshall notes, for example, that in his anxious accounts of his fame and his consequent inability to control his image, Rousseau describes himself in *Rousseau: Judge of Jean-Jacques* as being perceived as

---

28. Burkett, "Mediating Monstrosity," 580, 581, 591.
29. The cameos resonate with those made by Trump and Warhol, each of whom has his own articulations with the literary figure. For example, many political commentaries have framed Trump as the GOP's Frankenstein, a monster of their own creation who has become powerful enough to destroy them. See, for example, Heer, "Like Dr. Frankenstein." In the case of Warhol, Paul Morrissey's film *Andy Warhol's Frankenstein* alludes to the artist's personal trauma after a gunshot wound "gave Warhol's torso a network of Frankenstein scars." See Stevens, "Day Andy Warhol Was Shot Dead." Warhol also had affinities with Humpty Dumpty, who was one of the featured figures in Warhol's famed and fragile collection of cookie jars. See Wetmore, "Warhol's Cookie Jar."
30. Raub, "Frankenstein," 437.

a "monster" by the public.[31] We might also note that Shelley's novel takes shape as a series of "concentric" autobiographies: that of "Walton, then Frankenstein, then the monster, then Frankenstein and Walton again."[32] This network of interlocking autobiographical narratives hinges on a cluster of figures defined by either the quest for fame and/or the experience of having a public image thrust upon them. When packaged together, these stories consider the extent to which all identities remain subject to interpretation and, consequently, misinterpretation. Like the "parallel lives" of the noble Greek and Roman men the monster learns of in Plutarch's volumes, these figures operate as nodal points around which Shelley's consideration of ambition and fame articulate.

It is through tales of lives both parallel and intersecting that Shelley's novel addresses how characters take shape in relation to one another. Steven Vine argues, "The self in Frankenstein emerges on the basis of figure: the self acquires face and form only by way of figures which reside beyond it." Through its complex form of networked stories that open onto one another like a series of portmanteaus, the novel "unfolds this logic of the self's figural emergence in a relentless staging of selfhood as the repetition of *other* faces and figures."[33] Mirroring the interlocking relationships between Walton, Frankenstein, and the monster, the novel signals interarticulations of different registers of intersubjectification wherein subjects take effect in relation to other figures: the embodied, literary, and/or public figures that shape their lives and the figures of speech that come to define, or name, them. The monster's experiences of violence and ostracism manifest the extent to which cultural norms and social hierarchies participate in and help shape this process as well.

Frankenstein suggests a rather paranoid vision of subjectivity's fragile assemblage, and this vision of the monster resonates with anxieties within *Six Degrees of Separation*. Paul's tragedy takes shape as he assembles a persona for himself, stitching together bits and pieces of other people's stories; but whereas Frankenstein's monster finds his creator's name imposed on him erroneously in his intertextual afterlives, Paul consciously adopts the names of his "fathers" (Sidney Poitier and Flan Kittredge) to feign association with them. Also like *Frankenstein*, *Six Degrees of Separation* frames Paul's tragedy as belonging not entirely to him but also to those who desire to craft and/or exploit his image, as illustrated by its structure as a series of unfolding stories offered by different narrators. The figures of Frankenstein's monster and Paul, thus, might be understood to replay anxiously and hyperbolically the unstable, uneven, and often unpredictable process by which all subjects come into being with and

---

31. Marshall, *Surprising Effects of Sympathy*, 182, 191.
32. Vine, "'Frankenstein,'" 249.
33. Vine, "Frankenstein," 247.

through others. In these characters, we might also see evidence of precarity; while all subjects are defined by the vulnerability that inheres in the process of intersubjectification, some are positioned to be more vulnerable than others.

This theory of networked subjectivity imagines the subject as constelled in relation to a range of animate and inanimate actants. These relations necessarily entail vulnerabilities, but they also engender agency, or what Butler describes as the coextensivity of vulnerability and agency. It is this quality of concatenation that renders the portmanteau valuable for considering relations among subjects (and objects) and between subjectivity and signification. By concluding with attention to portmanteaus, I aim to make a further case for the value of rhetorical theory as a lens for seeing and understanding the figural relations that constitute, constrain, and enable subjects. And through the prominence of the portmanteau within celebrity culture, we might glimpse yearnings—both suspicious and hopeful—to acknowledge the extent to which all subjects remain tethered to and defined, at least in part, by their relations with others. With all its many faults, the culture of celebrity offers resources for imagining and creating conditions of possibility for new, hopeful, and more compassionate modes of being with others.

BIBLIOGRAPHY

Abramović, Marina, Klaus Biesenbach, Chrissie Iles, and Marco Anelli. *Marco Anelli: Portraits in the Presence of Marina Abramović.* Bologna, Italy: Damiani, 2012.

Abramovitch, Seth. "'After Earth' as Scientology Propaganda: What Critics Are Saying." *Hollywood Reporter,* May 31, 2013. https://www.hollywoodreporter.com/news/earth-as-scientology-propaganda-what-559943.

———. "'New Yorker' Cover Artist Kadir Nelson on Police Killings: 'These Young Men Are Real People.'" *Hollywood Reporter,* July 7, 2016. https://www.hollywoodreporter.com/lifestyle/lifestyle-news/new-yorker-cover-artist-kadir-909232/.

Adams, Henry. *Eakins Revealed: The Secret Life of an American Artist.* Oxford: Oxford University Press, 2005.

Adams, Jeffrey. "Sublimation, Intersubjectivity, and Artistic Identity." *Psychoanalytic Review* 93, no. 5 (October 2006): 687–711.

Adorno, Theodor W., and Anson G. Rabinbach. "Culture Industry Reconsidered." *New German Critique* 6 (1975): 12–19.

Agyeman-Fisher, Abena. "Is Will and Jaden Smith's 'After Earth' Being Sabotaged by Racists?" *NewsOne,* June 4, 2013. https://newsone.com/2530136/after-earth-movie-review-racism/.

Ahmed, Sara. "The Skin of the Community: Affect and Boundary Formation." In *Revolt, Affect, Collectivity: The Unstable Boundaries of Kristeva's Polis,* edited by Tina Chanter and Ewa Płonowska Ziarek, 95–112. Albany: State University of New York Press, 2012.

Alberoni, Francesco. "The Powerless Elite: Theory and Sociological Research on the Phenomenon of the Stars." In *Sociology of Mass Communications,* edited by Denis McQuail, 75–98. Harmondsworth: Penguin, 1972.

Alzamora, Geane Carvalho. "A Semiotic Approach to Transmedia Storytelling." In *The Routledge Companion to Transmedia Studies,* edited by Matthew Freeman and Renira Rampazzo Gambarato, 438–46. London and New York: Routledge, 2019.

Anderson, Ben. "Modulating the Excess of Affect: Morale in a State of 'Total War.'" In *The Affect Theory Reader*, edited by Melissa Gregg, Greggory J. Seigworth, and Sara Ahmed, 161–85. Durham, NC: Duke University Press, 2010.

Anderson, Melissa. "Closet Case." *Art Forum*, December 7, 2009. https://www.artforum.com/film/melissa-anderson-on-a-single-man-24339?utm_source=pocket_mylist.

Anderson, Reynaldo, and Charles E. Jones. "Introduction: The Rise of Astro-Blackness." In *Afrofuturism 2.0: The Rise of Astro-Blackness*, edited by Reynaldo Anderson and Charles E. Jones, vii–xvii. Lanham, MD: Lexington Books, 2016.

Anker, Elisabeth. *Orgies of Feeling: Melodrama and the Politics of Freedom*. Durham, NC: Duke University Press, 2014.

Annesley, James. "Being Spike Jonze: Intertextuality and Convergence in Film, Music Video, and Advertising." *New Cinemas: Journal of Contemporary Film* 11, no. 1 (2013): 23–37.

Arcy, Jacquelyn. "The Digital Money Shot: Twitter Wars, *The Real Housewives*, and Transmedia Storytelling." *Celebrity Studies* 9, no. 4 (2018): 487–502.

Aretxaga, Begoña. "Madness and the Politically Real: Reflections on Violence in Postcolonial Spain." In *Postcolonial Disorders*, edited by Mary-Jo DelVecchio Good, Sandra Teresa Hyde, Sarah Pinto, and Byron J. Good, 43–61. Berkeley: University of California Press, 2008.

Arntfield, Mike. "Hegemonic Shorthand: Technology and Metonymy in Modern Policing." *Communication Review* 11 (2008): 76–97.

Artavia, David. "*Sordid Lives* Actor Alleges Mogul Benny Medina Tried to Rape Him." *Advocate*, November 10, 2017. https://www.advocate.com/crime/2017/11/10/sordid-lives-actor-alleges-mogul-benny-medina-tried-rape-him.

Åsberg, Cecilia. "Feminist Posthumanities in the Anthropocene: Forays into the Postnatural." *Journal of Posthuman Studies* 1, no. 2 (2017): 185–204.

Atkinson, Nathalie. "Parting Is Such Stylish Sorrow." *National Post*, December 9, 2009. https://www.pressreader.com/canada/national-post-latest-edition/20091214/282213711926496.

Attridge, Derek. *Peculiar Language: Literature as Difference from the Renaissance to James Joyce*. London and New York: Routledge, 1988.

Aurthur, Kate. "Jodie Foster's Coming Out Speech at the Golden Globes." *Buzzfeed*, January 13, 2013. http://www.buzzfeed.com/kateaurthur/jodie-fosters-coming-out-speech-at-the-golden-glo.

Austin, Thomas. "Star Systems." In *Contemporary Hollywood Stardom*, edited by Thomas Austin and Martin Barker, 25–29. New York: Oxford University Press, 2003.

B., Sesali. "Flirting with Blackness." *Feministing*, July 17, 2015. https://feministing.com/2015/07/17/flirting-with-blackness/.

Backstrom, Lars Paolo Boldi, Marco Rosa, Johan Ugander, and Sebastiano Vigna. "Four Degrees of Separation." In *WebSci '12: Proceedings of the Fourth Annual ACM Web Science Conference*, 23–42. New York: Association for Computing Machinery. https://doi.org/10.1145/2380718.2380723.

Baer, Deb. "Why I'm So Angry About Jodie Foster's Coming Out Speech." *HuffPost*, January 14, 2013. https://www.huffpost.com/entry/why-im-so-angry-about-jodie-foster-coming-out-b_2471770.

Bailey, John. "Kardashian Selfies, Warhol Superstars and 'Famehood.'" *American Cinematographer*, June 21, 2015. https://ascmag.com/blog/johns-bailiwick/kardashian-selfies-warhol-superstars-and-famehood.

Baldwin, Keith. "The 5 Worst Movies of the Decade All Starred Will Smith." *Popdust*, December 18, 2019. https://www.popdust.com/worst-movies-of-the-decade-2641640527.html.

Banet-Weiser, Sarah. *Authentic™: The Politics of Ambivalence in a Brand Culture.* New York: New York University Press, 2012.

Barabási, Albert-László. *Linked: How Everything Is Connected to Everything Else and What It Means for Business.* New York: Basic Books, 2014.

Barad, Karen. *Meeting the Universe Halfway: Quantum Physics and the Entanglement of Matter and Meaning.* Durham, NC: Duke University Press, 2007.

———. "Posthumanist Performativity: Toward an Understanding of How Matter Comes to Matter." *Signs* 28, no. 3 (2003): 801–31.

Barbas, Samantha. *Movie Crazy: Stars, Fans, and the Cult of Celebrity.* New York: Palgrave, 2001.

Barber, Nicholas. "Fragmentation Games: The Return of the Portmanteau Film." *The Guardian,* March 17, 2015. https://www.theguardian.com/film/2015/mar/17/portmanteau-films-wild-tales-pulp-fiction-short-cuts.

Barker, Martin. "Introduction." In *Contemporary Hollywood Stardom,* edited by Thomas Austin and Martin Barker, 1–24. New York: Oxford University Press, 2003.

Barthes, Roland. *Image, Music, Text.* Translated by Stephen Heath. New York: Hill and Wang, 1977.

———. *Mythologies.* Translated by Annette Lavers. New York: Noonday Press, 1972.

Basil, Michael D. "Identification as a Mediator of Celebrity Influence." *Journal of Broadcast and Electronic Media* 40, no. 4 (1996): 478–95.

Bataille, Georges. *Literature and Evil.* Translated by Alastair Hamilton. New York: Penguin Books, 2012.

Bell, Christopher E. *American Idolatry: Celebrity, Commodity, and Reality Television.* Jefferson, NC: McFarland & Company, 2010.

Bennett, James. "Historicising Celebrity Studies." *Celebrity Studies* 1, no. 3 (2010): 358–59.

Berlant, Lauren. "Slow Death (Sovereignty, Obesity, Lateral Agency)." *Critical Inquiry* 33, no. 4 (2007): 754–80.

Berridge, Robert. "Escape from Celebrity: How Rockwell Reconnected with the Common Man." *Saturday Evening Post* 283, no. 6 (November–December 2011), 80.

Bertetti, Paolo. "Toward a Typology of Transmedia Characters." *International Journal of Communication* 8 (2014): 2344–61.

Bird, S. Elizabeth. "Converging into Irrelevance?: Supermarket Tabloids in the Post-9/11 World." In *Journalism After September 11,* edited by Barbie Zelizer and Stuart Allan, 191–211. London and New York: Routledge, 2002.

Blades, John. "Godfather of Gossip." *Chicago Tribune,* June 18, 1990. https://www.chicagotribune.com/news/ct-xpm-1990-06-18-9002190689-story.html.

"Blame Bennifer: Celeb Uni-Names Multiply." *Fox News,* January 13, 2005. https://www.foxnews.com/story/blame-bennifer-celeb-uni-names-multiply.

Bliss, Michael, and Christina Banks. *What Goes Around Comes Around: The Films of Jonathan Demme.* Carbondale: Southern Illinois University Press, 1996.

Bodle, Andy. "Frankenwords: They're Alive! But for How Long?" *The Guardian,* February 5, 2016. https://www.theguardian.com/media/mind-your-language/2016/feb/05/frankenwords-portmanteau-blend-words.

Bollobás, Enikő. "Circumference & Co.: Catachresis as the Trope of Performativity in Emily Dickinson's Poetry." *Hungarian Journal of English and American Studies* 18, nos. 1–2 (Spring-Fall 2012): 271–92.

Booker, Bobbi. "Award-Winning Illustrator Kadir Nelson to Discuss His 'Search for Truth.'" *Philadelphia Tribune,* January 7, 2018. https://www.phillytrib.com/lifestyle/award-winning-illustrator-kadir-nelson-to-discuss-his-search-for-truth/article_cbd0219a-4735-51f1-a503-cfff03220954.html.

Boone, Joseph, and Nancy J. Vickers. "Introduction: Celebrity Rites." *PMLA* 126, no. 4 (2011): 905–15.

Boorstin, Daniel. *The Image: Or What Happened to the American Dream.* London: Weidenfeld & Nicholson, 1962.

Bordwell, David. *Poetics of Cinema.* New York and London: Routledge, 2008.

Borg, Ruben. "Neologizing in *Finnegans Wake*: Beyond a Typology of the Wakean Portmanteau." *Poetics Today* 28, no. 1 (Spring 2007): 143–64.

Boston, Nicholas. "The Underlying Lesbophobia of Will Smith's Slap." *Gay City News,* April 4, 2022. https://gaycitynews.com/the-underlying-lesbophobia-of-will-smiths-slap/.

Bouchard, Larry D. *Theater and Integrity: Emptying Selves in Drama, Ethics, and Religion.* Evanston, IL: Northwestern University Press, 2011.

Boucher, Brian. "Did Obama Troll Donald Trump with a Norman Rockwell Painting in Oval Office Meeting?" *Artnet News,* November 22, 2016. https://news.artnet.com/art-world/obama-troll-donald-trump-norman-rockwell-757778.

Brady, Anita. "Keeping Away from the Kardashians: Celebrity Worth and the Re-Masculinising of Caitlin Jenner." *Celebrity Studies* 1, no. 1 (2016): 115–18.

Braidotti, Rosi. *Metamorphoses: Towards a Materialist Theory of Becoming.* Cambridge: Polity Press, 2002.

Brier, Jennifer, and Matthew Wizinsky. "Worlds of Signification: Power and Subjectivity in Global AIDS Posters." In *Up Against the Wall: Art, Activism, and the AIDS Poster,* edited by Donald Albrecht and Jessica Lacher-Feldman, 9–24. Rochester, NY: RIT Press, 2021.

Brooks, Daphne. *Bodies in Dissent: Spectacular Performances of Race and Freedom, 1850–1910.* Durham, NC: Duke University Press, 2006.

Brooks, Peter. *The Melodramatic Imagination: Balzac, Henry James, Melodrama, and the Mode of Excess.* New Haven, CT: Yale University Press, 1976.

Burke, Kenneth. *A Rhetoric of Motives.* Berkeley: University of California Press, 1969.

Burkeman, Oliver. "Will and Jaden Smith Give the Most Bizarre Interview in Hollywood History." *The Guardian,* May 30, 2013. https://www.theguardian.com/commentisfree/2013/may/30/will-smith-new-york-magazine-interview.

Burkett, Andrew. "Mediating Monstrosity: Media, Information, and Mary Shelley's 'Frankenstein.'" *Studies in Romanticism* 51, no. 4 (Winter 2012): 579–605.

Burman, John. "Forbes' Star Currency." *Forbes,* February 10, 2009. https://www.forbes.com/2009/02/10/star-currency-hollywood-star-currency-09-business-0210_star_currency_lander.html#3ef5c4d855c2.

———. "Hollywood's Most Valuable Actors." *Forbes,* February 10, 2009. https://www.forbes.com/2009/02/10/forbes-star-currency-business-media-star-currency-09_0210_star_currency.html#34dc8b20361b.

Burwick, Frederick. *Mimesis and Its Romantic Reflections.* University Park: Pennsylvania University Press, 2001.

Bush, Vannevar. "As We May Think." *Atlantic Monthly,* July 1945, 101–8.

Butkowski, Chelsea, and Lee Humphreys. "Gendered Art, Work, and Self-Representation: A Comparative Analysis of Camera-Photographic and Painted Self-Portraits." In *The Routledge Companion to Mobile Media Art,* edited by Larissa Hjorth, Adriana de Souza e Silva, and Klare Lanson, 164–73. London: Routledge, 2020.

Butler, Bethonie. "Yes, Those Kim Kardashian Photos Are About Race." *Washington Post,* November 21, 2014. https://www.washingtonpost.com/blogs/she-the-people/wp/2014/11/21/yes-those-kim-kardashian-photos-are-about-race/.

Butler, Jeremy G. *Television: Critical Methods and Applications.* London and New York: Routledge, 2011.

Butler, Judith. *Bodies That Matter: On the Discursive Limits of Sex.* London: Routledge, 1993.

———. *The Force of Nonviolence: An Ethico-Political Bind.* London: Verso, 2021. Kindle.

———. *Frames of War: When Is Life Grievable?* London: Verso, 2010.

———. *Gender Trouble: Feminism and the Subversion of Identity.* London: Routledge, 1990.

———. "Imitation and Gender Insubordination." In *Inside/Out: Lesbian Theories, Gay Theories,* edited by Diana Fuss, 13–31. New York: Routledge, 1991.

———. "Performativity, Precarity, and Sexual Politics." *AIBR: Revista de Antropología Iberoamericana* 4, no. 3 (2009): i–xiii.

———. *Precarious Life: The Powers of Mourning and Violence.* London: Verso, 2006.

———. *The Psychic Life of Power: Theories of Subjection.* Redwood City, CA: Stanford University Press, 1997.

———. "Rethinking Vulnerability and Resistance." In *Vulnerability in Resistance,* edited by Judith Butler, Zeynep Gambetti, and Leticia Sabsay, 12–27. Durham, NC: Duke University Press, 2016.

Callahan, Maureen. "How a Decade of the Kardashians Radically Changed America." *New York Post,* September 23, 2017. https://nypost.com/2017/09/23/how-a-decade-of-the-kardashians-radically-changed-america/amp/.

Canby, Vincent. "Methods of Madness in 'Silence of the Lambs.'" *New York Times,* February 14, 1991, 70.

Caramanica, Jon. "The Agony and the Ecstasy of Kanye West." *New York Times,* April 20, 2015. https://www.nytimes.com/2015/04/10/t-magazine/kanye-west-adidas-yeezy-fashion-interview.html.

———. "This 'Imagine' Cover Is No Heaven." *New York Times,* March 20, 2020. https://www.nytimes.com/2020/03/20/arts/music/coronavirus-gal-gadot-imagine.html.

Carlson, Marvin. "Invisible Presences—Performance Intertextuality." *Theatre Research International* 19, no. 2 (1994): 111–17.

Carroll, Lewis. *Through the Looking Glass and What Alice Found There.* Chicago: Henneberry Company, 1917.

Carter, Christopher. *Metafilm: Materialist Rhetoric and Reflexive Cinema.* Columbus: The Ohio State University Press, 2018.

Cashmore, Ellis. *Kardashian Kulture: How Celebrities Changed Life in the 21st Century.* Bingley, UK: Emerald Publishing, 2019.

Castells, Manuel. *The Rise of the Network Society.* Hoboken, NJ: Wiley-Blackwell, 2009.

Cave, Damien. "What's in a Nickname? A Melding of Minds." *New York Times,* December 25, 2005, C3.

Chambers, Veronica. "On-Color Remarks." *Premiere,* January 1994, 32.

———. "Willing." *Premiere,* January 1994, 74–77.

Chang, Richard. "Artists Are Poster Boys, but Movie Ads Sizzle." *Times of India,* March 4, 2001, 12.

Chouliaraki, Lillie. "The Theatricality of Humanitarianism: A Critique of Celebrity Advocacy." *Communication and Critical/Cultural Studies* 9, no. 1 (2012): 1–21.

Christakis, Nicholas, and James Fowler. *Connected: The Surprising Power of Our Social Networks and How They Shape Our Lives.* New York: Little, Brown, and Company, 2009.

Chun, Wendy Hui Kyong. *Control and Freedom: Power and Paranoia in the Age of Fiber Optics.* Cambridge, MA: MIT Press, 2006.

———. "The Enduring Ephemeral, or the Future Is a Memory." *Critical Inquiry* 35 (Autumn 2008): 148–71.

Clinton, Paul. "Bloody 'Hannibal' Lacks Bite of 'Lambs.'" *CNN*, February 8, 2001. https://web.archive.org/web/20070225002414/http://archives.cnn.com/2001/SHOWBIZ/Movies/02/08/hannibal.review/index.html.

Cloud, Dana. "'To Veil the Threat of Terror': Afghan Women and the <Clash of Civilizations> in the Imagery of the U.S. War on Terrorism." *Quarterly Journal of Speech* 90, no. 3 (2004): 285–306.

Clover, Carol. *Men, Women, and Chain Saws: Gender in the Modern Horror Film.* Princeton, NJ: Princeton University Press, 1992.

Coates, Ta-Nehisi. "*After Earth*: What Was Will Smith Thinking?" *The Atlantic*, June 3, 2013. https://www.theatlantic.com/entertainment/archive/2013/06/-i-after-earth-i-what-was-will-smith-thinking/276466/.

———. *Between the World and Me.* New York: Random House, 2015.

Coggan, Devan. "*Bright* Is a Fantasy Buddy-Cop Movie That Fails Both Genres." *Entertainment Weekly*, December 21, 2017. https://ew.com/movies/2017/12/21/bright-review/.

Conklin, Alice L. *A Mission to Civilize: The Republican Idea of Empire in France and West Africa, 1895–1930.* Palo Alto, CA: Stanford University Press, 1997.

Connell, Catherine. "Contesting Racialized Discourses of Homophobia." *Sociological Forum* 31, no. 3 (2016): 599–618.

Cooper, Brittney. *Eloquent Rage: A Black Feminist Discovers Her Superpower.* New York: St. Martin's Press.

Corber, Robert J. "Joan Crawford's Padded Shoulders: Female Masculinity in *Mildred Pierce*." *Camera Obscura* 21, no. 2 (2006): 1–31.

Cosgrove, Ben. "The Photo That Changed the Face of AIDS." *Life*, n.d. https://www.life.com/history/behind-the-picture-the-photo-that-changed-the-face-of-aids/.

Couturier, Elisabeth. "Jean-Paul Goude remonte les temps." *Paris Match*, November 14, 2011. https://www.parismatch.com/Culture/Art/Jean-Paul-Goude-remonte-le-temps-156789.

Crais, Clifton, and Pamela Scully. *Sara Baartman and the Hottentot Venus: A Ghost Story and a Biography.* Princeton, NJ: Princeton University Press, 2009.

Crimp, Douglas. "Right On, Girlfriend!" *Social Text* no. 33 (1992): 2–18.

Crisler, B. R. "Footnotes on Pictures and People." *New York Times*, August 9, 1936, X3.

"Cross-Post: 20 Years of Black Lesbian Cinema Before Pariah." *Women and Hollywood*, January 3, 2012. https://womenandhollywood.com/cross-post-20-years-of-black-lesbian-cinema-before-pariah-9d156e6da608/.

Currid-Halkett, Elizabeth. *Starstruck: The Business of Celebrity.* New York: Faber and Faber, 2010.

Cvetkovich, Ann. *Depression: A Public Feeling.* Durham, NC: Duke University Press, 2012.

Danto, Arthur C. "Age of Innocence." *The Nation*, December 20, 2001. https://www.thenation.com/article/archive/age-innocence-0/.

Dargis, Mahnola. "A Love That Speaks Its Name." *New York Times*, December 10, 2009. https://www.nytimes.com/2009/12/11/movies/11singleman.html.

Davidson, Casey. "Philly, the Sequel? What Hollywood Will Now Do with AIDS." *POZ*, April 1, 1994, 18.

Davis, Ben. "Mi Gosh and By-heck: Deborah Solomon's Life of Norman Rockwell, Whose Art Looked Back to an America That Never Was." *Slate*, November 6, 2013. https://slate.com/culture/2013/11/norman-rockwell-biography-deborah-solomons-american-mirror-reviewed.html.

de la Bellacasa, Maria Puig. "Matters of Care in Technoscience: Assembling Neglected Things." *Social Studies of Science* 41, no. 1 (2011): 85–106.

Dean, Aria. "Closing the Loop." *New Inquiry*, March 1, 2016. https://thenewinquiry.com/closing-the-loop/.

DeAngelis, Michael. *Gay Fandom and Crossover Stardom: James Dean, Mel Gibson, and Keanu Reeves*. Durham, NC: Duke University Press, 2001.

———. "Queer Memories and Universal Emotions: A Single Man (2009)." In *Feminism at the Movies: Understanding Gender in Contemporary Popular Cinema*, edited by Hilary Radner and Rebecca Stringer, 25–35. New York: Routledge, 2011.

DeCordova, Richard. *Picture Personalities: The Emergence of the Star System in America*. Champaign: University of Illinois Press, 2001.

DeCurtis, Anthony. "Jonathan Demme on 'Philadelphia.'" *Rolling Stone* 678 (March 24, 1994): 60–65.

Deino, Daryl. "Will Smith and the History of Gay Rumors: Why Are People So Obsessed?" *The Inquisitor*, January 23, 2016. https://www.inquisitr.com/2731619/will-smith-and-the-history-of-gay-rumors-why-are-people-still-obsessed/.

Del Costello, Mark. "Movie Posters Being Coveted by a Collector Near You." *Chicago Tribune*, August 11, 1979, B13.

Delaney, James. "Rousseau, Self-Love, and an Increasingly Connected World." *OUPblog*, June 28, 2017. https://blog.oup.com/2017/06/rousseau-self-love/.

Denroche, Charles. *Metonymy and Language: A New Theory of Linguistic Processing*. New York: Routledge, 2015.

Denton-Hurst, Tembe. "Seen on Screen: Hollywood Needs to Recognize a World Where Black Girls Kiss." *Them*, February 7, 2020. https://www.them.us/story/hollywood-needs-to-recognize-a-world-where-black-girls-kiss.

"Denzel Washington: I Don't Think There's a System." *The Talks*, September 5, 2012. https://the-talks.com/interview/denzel-washington/.

Derrida, Jacques. "The Deaths of Roland Barthes." In *Philosophy and Non-Philosophy Since Merleau-Ponty*, edited by Hugh J. Silverman, 259–96. Evanston, IL: Northwestern University Press, 1988.

Díaz, Vanessa. "'Brad & Angelina.'" In *First Comes Love: Power Couples, Celebrity Kinships and Cultural Politics*, edited by Shelley Cobb and Neil Ewen, 275–94. New York: Bloomsbury, 2015.

———. *Manufacturing Celebrity: Latino Paparazzi and Women Reporters in Hollywood*. Durham, NC: Duke University Press, 2020.

Dicker, Ron. "Kim Kardashian Accused of 'Blackface' for Magazine Photo Shoot." *HuffPost*, December 20, 2019. https://www.huffpost.com/entry/kim-kardashian-blackface-magazine_n_5dfce39be4b0843d35faece9.

Dickinson, Greg. "Joe's Rhetoric: Finding Authenticity at Starbucks." *Rhetoric Society Quarterly* 32, no. 4 (2002): 5–27.

Dirvin, René, and Ralf Pörings, eds. *Metaphor and Metonymy in Comparison and Contrast*. Berlin: De Gruyter, 2009.

Dixon-Smith, Matilda. "The Reaction to Kim Kardashian's Robbery Reveals Some of Our Most Insidious Problems with Women." *Junkee*, October 4, 2016. https://junkee.com/reaction-kim-kardashians-robbery-reveals-insidious-problems-women/86541.

"Does Hollywood Create?" *Vogue* 81, no. 3 (February 1, 1913): 59+.

Doll, Jen. "The Rise of the Frankenwords." *The Atlantic*, November 1, 2012. https://www.theatlantic.com/culture/archive/2012/11/frankenstein-word-monster/321860/.

Donaldson, Lucy Fife. "Access and Excess in *The Texas Chainsaw Massacre*." *Movie: A Journal of Film Criticism*, no. 1 (2010). https://centaur.reading.ac.uk/36209/1/the_texas_chain_saw_massacre.pdf.

Doty, Alexander. *Flaming Classics: Queering the Film Canon*. London: Routledge, 2000.

Dovey, John. *Freakshow: First Person Media and Factual Television*. London: Pluto, 2000.

"Draws Boys and Not Girls." *Boston Daily Globe*, August 5, 1923, 70.

Dubrofsky, Rachel. "Authentic Trump: Yearning for Civility." *Television & New Media* 17, no. 7 (2016): 663–66.

Duffy, Brooke Erin, and Jefferson Pooley. "Idols of Promotion: The Triumph of Self-Branding in an Age of Precarity." *Journal of Communication* 69, no. 1 (2019): 26–48.

Duvall, Spring-Serenity, and Nicole Heckemeyer. "#BlackLivesMatter: Black Celebrity Hashtag Activism and the Discursive Formation of a Social Movement." *Celebrity Studies* 9, no. 3 (2018): 391–408.

Dyer, Richard. *Heavenly Bodies: Film Stars and Society*. London: BFI, 1986.

———. *Stars*. London: British Film Institute, 1998.

———. *White*. London: Routledge, 1997.

Eagleton, Terry. "What Would Rousseau Make of Our Selfish Age?" *The Guardian*, June 27, 2012. https://www.theguardian.com/commentisfree/2012/jun/27/rousseau-our-selfish-age-philosopher.

Edelstein, David. "Will and Jaden Take the Shyamalan Out of This Shyamalan Movie." *Vulture*, May 31, 2013. http://www.vulture.com/2013/05/movie-review-after-earth-will-jaden-smith.html.

Edwards, Tim. "Medusa's Stare: Celebrity, Subjectivity, and Gender." *Celebrity Studies* 4, no. 2 (2013): 155–68.

Ehrenreich, Barbara. *Bright-Sided: How Positive Thinking Is Undermining America*. New York: Henry Holt and Company, 2009.

Ehrlich, David. "'Bright' Review: Netflix's First Blockbuster Is the Worst Movie of 2017." *IndieWire*, December 20, 2017. https://www.indiewire.com/2017/12/bright-review-netflix-will-smith-max-landis-david-ayer-worst-movie-2017-1201909960/.

Ellis, John. "How to Be in Public: The Case of an Early Television Show." *Celebrity Studies* 6, no. 3 (2015): 355–69.

———. *Visible Fictions: Cinema, Television, Video*. London and New York: Routledge, 1982.

Evans, Vyvyan. *The Emoji Code: The Linguistics Behind Smiley Faces and Scaredy Cats*. New York: Picador, 2017.

Farred, Grant. "Achilles, Celebrity, Recluse." *PMLA* 126, no. 4 (2011): 1102–9.

Fawaz, Ramzi. *The New Mutants: Superheroes and the Radical Imagination of American Comics*. New York: New York University Press, 2016.

Felski, Rita. *The Limits of Critique*. Chicago: University of Chicago Press, 2015.

Fiske, John. "The Cultural Economy of Fandom." In *The Adoring Audience: Fan Culture and Popular Media*, edited by Lisa A. Lewis, 30–49. London and New York: Routledge, 1992.

———. *Television Culture*. London and New York: Routledge, 1987.

Ferriss, Suzanne. *Chick Flicks: Fashioning Femininity in the Makeover Flick*. London: Routledge, 2007.

Flanagan, Caitlin. "Feeling Special." *New York Times*, September 27, 2015, A13.

Fleming, Michael. "Kirkwood, Rockwell Paint Banner." *Variety*, December 18, 2001. https://variety.com/2001/film/news/kirkwood-rockwell-paint-banner-1117857547/.

Fleury, Rick. "The Most Powerful Icon of the '90s." *Brandweek* 33, no. 45 (November 30, 1992): 14.

Folsom, Ed. *Walt Whitman's Native Representations*. Cambridge: Cambridge University Press, 1994.

Foster, Helen. *Networked Process: Dissolving Boundaries of Process and Post-Process*. West Lafayette, IN: Parlor Press, 2007. Kindle.

Fowler, William M. *The Baron of Beacon Hill: A Biography of John Hancock*. Boston: Houghton Mifflin, 1980.

Frascina, Francis. "Advertisements for Itself: *The New York Times*, Norman Rockwell, and the New Patriotism." In *The Selling of 9/11: How a National Tragedy Became a Commodity*, edited by Dana Heller, 75–96. New York: Palgrave Macmillan, 2005.

Freeman, Hadley. "How the Kardashians Sold Their Terrifying Sex Glamazon Look to the World." *The Guardian*, June 13, 2018. https://www.theguardian.com/fashion/2018/jun/13/how-the-kardashians-sold-their-terrifying-sex-glamazon-look-to-the-world.

Frosh, Paul. "The Gestural Image: The Selfie, Photography Theory, and Kinesthetic Sociability." *International Journal of Communication* 9 (2015): 1607–28.

Fuller, Kathryn H. *At the Picture Show: Small Town Audiences and the Creation of Movie Fan Culture*. Charlottesville: University of Virginia, 1996.

Gabbard, Krin. *Black Magic: White Hollywood and African American Culture*. New Brunswick, NJ: Rutgers University Press, 2004.

Gabler, Neil. "We All Enabled Donald Trump: Our Deeply Unserious Media and Reality-TV Culture Made This Horror Inevitable." *Salon*, March 14, 2016. https://www.salon.com/2016/03/14/we_all_enabled_donald_trump_our_deeply_unserious_media_and_reality_tv_culture_made_this_horror_inevitable/.

———. *Winchell: Gossip, Power and the Culture of Celebrity*. New York: Vintage Books, 1995.

Gallagher, Victoria, and Kenneth Zagacki. "Visibility and Rhetoric: The Power of Visual Images in Norman Rockwell's Depictions of Civil Rights." *Quarterly Journal of Speech* 91, no. 2 (2005): 175–200.

Gamson, Joshua. *Claims to Fame: Celebrity in Contemporary America*. Berkeley: University of California Press, 1994.

Gates, Racquel. *Double Negative: The Black Image and Popular Culture*. Durham, NC: Duke University Press, 2018.

Gilbert, Christopher J., and Jonathan P. Rossing. "Trumping Tropes with Joke(r)s: *The Daily Show* 'Plays the Race Card.'" *Western Journal of Communication* 77, no. 1 (2013): 92–111.

Gilbert, Sarah. "The World's Earliest Selfies—In Pictures." *The Guardian*, July 21, 2014. https://www.theguardian.com/artanddesign/gallery/2014/jul/21/worlds-earliest-selfies-in-pictures-buzz-aldrin.

Gillan, Jennifer. "'No One Knows You're Black!': Six Degrees of Separation and the Buddy Formula." *Cinema Journal* 40, no. 3 (Spring 2001): 47–68.

Gitelman, Lisa. *Always Already New: Media, History, and the Data of Culture.* Boston: MIT Press, 2006.

Gitlin, Todd. "The Anti-political Populism of Cultural Studies." In *Cultural Studies in Question,* edited by Marjorie Ferguson and Peter Golding, 25–38. London: SAGE, 1997.

Gittell, Noah. "*Dallas Buyers Club*: An AIDS Drama the Tea Party Can Enjoy." *The Atlantic,* November 18, 2013. https://www.theatlantic.com/entertainment/archive/2013/11/-em-dallas-buyers-club-em-an-aids-drama-the-tea-party-can-enjoy/281421/.

Gladwell, Malcolm. *The Tipping Point: How Little Things Can Make a Big Difference.* New York: Little, Brown, 2006.

Gledhill, Christine. "The Melodramatic Field: An Investigation." In *Home Is Where the Heart Is: Studies in Melodrama and the Woman's Film,* edited by Christine Gledhill, 5–42. London: BFI Publishing, 1987.

———. "Signs of Melodrama." In *Stardom: Industry of Desire,* edited by Christine Gledhill, 207–29. New York and London: Routledge, 1991.

Gmiterková, Šárka. "Transmedia Celebrity: The Kardashian Kosmos—Between Family Brand and Individual Storylines." In *The Routledge Companion to Transmedia Studies,* edited by Matthew Freeman and Renira Rampazzo Gambarato, 116–23. London and New York: Routledge, 2019.

Goodman, Jessica. "Between Celebrity and Glory? Textual After-Image in Late Eighteenth Century France." *Celebrity Studies* 6, no. 4 (2016): 545–50.

Goude, Jean-Paul. *Jungle Fever.* New York: Xavier Moreau, 1981.

Graham, Renee. "In Casting Film Couples, Race Is Still a Black and White Issue." *Boston Globe,* March 8, 2005, C1.

Grainge, Paul. "Introduction." In *Ephemeral Media: Transitory Screen Culture from Television to YouTube,* edited by Paul Grainge, 1–22. London: Palgrave Macmillan, 2011.

Granovetter, Mark S. "The Strength of Weak Ties." *American Journal of Sociology* 78, no. 6 (May 1973): 1360–80.

Gray, Jonathan. *Show Sold Separately: Promos, Spoilers, and Other Media Paratexts.* New York: New York University Press, 2010.

Green, Jesse. "Flirting with Suicide." *New York Times,* September 5, 1996, SM39.

———. "The Philadelphia Experiment." *Premiere,* January 1994, 54–61.

———. *The Velveteen Father: An Unexpected Journey to Parenthood.* New York: Villard Books, 1999.

———. "The Year of the Ribbon." *New York Times,* May 3, 1992, V7.

Greenwood, Carl. "'Absolutely Not True': Will Smith's Ex-Wife Slams 'Secret Gay' Claims." *Mirror,* January 23, 2016. https://www.mirror.co.uk/3am/celebrity-news/absolutely-not-true-smiths-ex-7230618.

Greven, David. "The Death-Mother in *Psycho*: Hitchcock, Femininity, and Queer Desire." *Studies in Gender and Sexuality* 15, no. 3 (July 2014): 167–81.

Griggs, Brandon. "Kevin Bacon on 'Six Degrees Game': 'I was Horrified.'" *CNN,* March 12, 2014. https://www.cnn.com/2014/03/08/tech/web/kevin-bacon-six-degrees-sxsw/index.html.

Grillo. "Time to Listen." *Lenny Letter,* March 30, 2018. https://www.lennyletter.com/story/time-to-listen.

Grindstaff, Laura, and Susan Murray. "Reality Celebrity: Branded Affect and the Emotion Economy." *Public Culture* 27, no. 1 (2015): 109–35.

Grossberg, Lawrence. *We Gotta Get Out of This Place*. London: Routledge, 1992.

Grossman, Jonathan. *Charles Dickens's Networks: Public Transport and the Novel*. Oxford: Oxford University Press, 2012.

Grossman, Lena. "Why Kim Kardashian Is 'Grateful' for Frightening Robbery in Paris." *E! News*, October 21, 2018. https://www.eonline.com/news/979123/why-kim-kardashian-is-grateful-for-frightening-robbery-in-paris.

Guare, John. "My Dinner with Donald, and Other Happenings." *New York Times*, January 15, 1998. Available at https://www.nytimes.com/1998/01/25/archives/my-dinner-with-donald-and-other-happenings.html.

Guinn, Jeff, and Douglas Perry. *The Sixteenth Minute: Life in the Aftermath of Fame*. New York: Tarcher, 2005.

Gulla, Emily. "Kanye West Called Out Will Smith and Jada in New Kim Kardashian Interview." *Cosmopolitan*, January 25, 2022. https://www.cosmopolitan.com/uk/entertainment/a38881507/kanye-west-called-out-will-smith-jada-kim-kardashian-interview/.

Guthrie, Ricardo. "The *Real* Ghosts in the Machine: Afrofuturism and the Racial Space in *I, Robot* and *DETROPIA*." In *Afrofuturism 2.0: The Rise of Astro Blackness*, edited by Reynaldo Anderson and Charles E. Jones, 45–60. Lanham, MD: Lexington Books, 2016.

Hackett, Pat. *The Andy Warhol Diaries*. Edited by Pat Hackett. New York: Warner Books, 1991.

Halberstam, Jack. *In a Queer Time and Place: Transgender Bodies, Subcultural Lives*. New York: New York University Press, 2005.

———. "Mackdaddy, Superfly, Rapper: Gender, Race, and Masculinity in the Drag King Scene." *Social Text* 52–53 (Autumn-Winter 1997): 104–31.

Hall, Stuart. "Encoding/Decoding." In *Media and Cultural Studies: Keywords*, edited by Meenakshi Gigi Durham and Douglas M. Kellner, 166–76. Malden, MA: Blackwell Publishing, 2001.

———. "On Postmodernism and Articulation: An Interview with Stuart Hall." In *Stuart Hall*, edited by D. Morley and D-K. Chen, 131–50. London: Routledge, 1996.

———. "The Work of Representation." In *Representation: Cultural Representations and Signifying Practices*, edited by Stuart Hall, 13–74. London: SAGE, 1997.

Halpern, Richard. *Norman Rockwell: The Underside of Innocence*. Chicago: University of Chicago Press, 2006.

Hammons, Evelynn. "Black (W)holes and the Geometry of Black Female Sexuality." *differences* 6, nos. 2–3 (Summer–Fall 1994): 126–45.

Haralovich, Mary Beth. "Advertising Heterosexuality." *Screen* 23, no. 2 (July–August 1992): 50–60.

Haraway, Donna. "Awash in Urine: DES and Premarin® in Multispecies Response-ability." *WSQ: Women's Studies Quarterly* 40, nos. 1–2 (August 2016): 301–16.

———. *When Species Meet*. Minneapolis: University of Minnesota Press, 2008.

Harding, Cortney. "It's a Wonderful Afterlife." *Billboard: The International Newsweekly of Music, Video and Home Entertainment* 122, no. 25 (June 26, 2010): 16–18.

Hariman, Robert, and John Louis Lucaites. "Hands and Feet: Photojournalism, the Fragmented Body Politic and Collective Memory." In *Journalism and Memory*, edited by Barbie Zelizer and Keren Tenenboim-Weinblatt, 131–47. London: Palgrave Macmillan, 2014.

———. *No Caption Needed: Iconic Photographs, Public Culture, and Liberal Democracy*. Chicago: University of Chicago Press, 2007.

———. *The Public Image: Photography and Civic Spectatorship*. Chicago: University of Chicago Press, 2018.

Harris, Daniel. *The Rise and Fall of Gay Culture*. New York: Hyperion, 1997.

Hassenger, Jesse. "Gemini Man Is a Cinematic Throwback, but It May Be the Future of Blockbusters, Too." *The Verge,* October 16, 2019. https://www.theverge.com/2019/10/16/20915178/gemini-man-will-smith-ang-lee-blockbuster-future-digital-de-aging-wild-west-matrix.

Hearn, Alison. "'Meat, Mask, Burden': Probing the Contours of the Branded 'Self.'" *Journal of Consumer Culture* 8, no. 2 (2008): 197–217.

Heer, Jeet. "Like Dr. Frankenstein, Republicans Now Face the Monster They Created." *The Nation,* November 13, 2019. https://www.thenation.com/article/archive/fuentes-alt-right-republican-trump/.

Hemmeter, Thomas. "Hitchcock's Melodramatic Silence." *Journal of Film and Video* 48, no. 1 (1996): 32–40.

Hershkovits, David. "How Kim Kardashian Broke the Internet with Her Butt." *The Guardian,* December 17, 2014. https://www.theguardian.com/lifeandstyle/2014/dec/17/kim-kardashian-butt-break-the-internet-paper-magazine.

Herzog, Charlotte, and Jane Gaines. "'Puffed Sleeves Before Tea-Time': Joan Crawford, Adrian, and Women Audiences." *Wide Angle* 6, no. 4 (1985): 24–33.

Hitchon, Jacqueline, and Jerzy Jura. "Allegorically Speaking: Intertextuality of the Postmodern Culture and Its Impact on Print and Television Advertising." *Communication Studies* 48, no. 2 (1997): 142–58.

Hoffman, Claire. "Will Smith and His Fresh Prince." *New York,* June 3–10, 2013, 50–56.

Holifield, Ryan. "Defining Environmental Justice and Environmental Racism." *Urban Geography* 22, no. 1 (2001): 78–90.

Hollenbaugh, Lindsay. "Rockwell Goes Digital." *The Berkshire Eagle,* January 6, 2011. https://www.berkshireeagle.com/stories/rockwell-goes-digital,450091.

Holmes, Su, and Deborah Jermyn. "Introduction." In *Understanding Reality Television,* edited by Su Holmes and Deborah Jermyn, 1–32. London and New York: Routledge, 2004.

"Homage to Rockwell." *Esquire,* April 1971, 84–85.

Hou, Mingyi. "Social Media Celebrity and the Institutionalization of YouTube." *Convergence: The International Journal of Research into New Media Technologies* 25, no. 3 (2019): 534–53.

Houssin, Lauren. "Jean-Paul Goude's First Paris Exhibition." *Elle,* November 11, 2011. https://www.elle.com/culture/art-design/news/a7747/jean-paul-goudes-first-paris-exhibition-32463/.

Howard, Sheena. *Encyclopedia of Black Comics.* London: Fulcrum, 2017.

Howard, Sheena C., and Ronald L. Jackson III. *Black Comics: Politics of Race and Representation.* London: Bloomsbury, 2013.

Hu, Tung-Hui. *A Prehistory of the Cloud.* Cambridge, MA: MIT Press, 2015.

Hughes, Robert. "The Rembrandt of Punkin Creek: Death Comes to a Reticent Monument of America." *TIME Magazine* 112, no. 21 (November 20, 1978): 110.

Hughes, Sarah Anne. "Will Smith Recycles Joke about Playing President Obama." *Washington Post,* May 22, 2012. https://www.washingtonpost.com/blogs/celebritology/post/will-smith-recycles-joke-about-playing-president-obama/2012/05/22/gIQAT55WiU_blog.html.

Hughey, Matthew. *The White Savior Film: Content, Critics, and Consumption.* Philadelphia: Temple University Press, 2014.

Huliaras, Asteris, and Nikolaos Tzifakis. "Personal Connections, Unexpected Journeys: U2 and Angelina Jolie in Bosnia." *Celebrity Studies* 6, no. 4 (2015): 443–56.

Hummler, Richard. "Cats." *Variety,* October 13, 1982. https://variety.com/1982/legit/reviews/cats-1200425296/.

Ingleton, Pamela, and Lorraine York. "From Clooney to Kardashian: Reluctant Celebrity and Social Media." *Celebrity Studies* 10, no. 3 (2019): 364–79.

Inglis, Fred. *A Short History of Celebrity*. Princeton, NJ: Princeton University Press, 2010.

Irwin, William. "Against Intertextuality." *Philosophy and Literature* 28, no. 2 (October 2004): 227–42.

Jackson, Sarah J. *Black Celebrity, Racial Politics, and the Press: Framing Dissent*. London: Routledge, 2014.

Jackson, Sarah J., Moya Bailey, and Brooke Foucault Welles. *#Hashtag Activism: Networks of Race and Gender Justice*. Cambridge, MA: MIT Press, 2020.

Jagoda, Patrick. *Network Aesthetics*. Chicago: University of Chicago Press, 2016.

Jakobson, Roman. "The Metaphoric and Metonymic Poles." In *Metaphor and Metonymy in Comparison and Contrast*, edited by René Dirvin and Ralf Pörings, 41–48. Berlin: De Gruyter, 2009.

Jenkins, Henry. *Convergence Culture: Where Old and New Media Collide*. New York: New York University Press, 2006.

———. *Textual Poachers: Television Fans and Participatory Culture*. London and New York: Routledge, 1992.

Jensen, Charles. "Megan Volpert: Six Degrees of Andy Warhol." *Lambda Literary*, February 21, 2012. https://lambdaliterary.org/2012/02/megan-volpert-six-degrees-of-andy-warhol/.

Jerslev, Anne, and Mette Mortensen. "What Is the Self in the Celebrity Selfie? Celebrification, Phatic Communication and Performativity." *Celebrity Studies* 7, no. 2 (2016): 249–63.

Johnson, E. Patrick. "The Specter of the Black Fag: Parody, Blackness, and Hetero/Homosexual B(r)others." *Journal of Homosexuality* 45, nos. 2–4 (2003): 217–34.

Johnson, Paul Elliott. "The Art of Masculine Victimhood: Donald Trump's Demagoguery." *Women's Studies in Communication* 40, no. 3 (2017): 229–50.

Jones, Jonathan. "Kim Kardashian's *Selfish*: A Nail in the Coffin for Artistic Photography?" *The Guardian*, May 5, 2015. https://www.theguardian.com/lifeandstyle/shortcuts/2015/may/05/kim-kardashian-selfish-book-photography-selfies.

———. "Norman Rockwell's Statue of Liberty Can Point Trump Towards Decency." *The Guardian*, November 23, 2016. https://www.theguardian.com/artanddesign/jonathanjonesblog/2016/nov/23/norman-rockwell-statue-of-liberty-can-point-trump-towards-decency.

Jones, Luvvie Ajayi. "Kim Kardashian Is Assed Out for Attention and She Should Stop." *Awesomely Luvvie*, October 15, 2012. https://awesomelyluvvie.com/2012/10/kim-kardashian-is-assed-out-for-attention.html.

Jones, Robert. *The End of White Christian America*. New York: Simon & Schuster, 2016.

Joyrich, Lynne. "All That Television Allows: TV Melodrama, Postmodernism and Consumer Culture." *Camera Obscura* 6, no. 1 (1988): 128–53.

Kakoudaki, Despina. "Spectacles of History: Race Relations, Melodrama, and the Science Fiction/Disaster Film." *Camera Obscura* 50, no. 17 (2002): 109–53.

Kaplan, E. Ann. "Melodrama/Subjectivity/Ideology: Western Melodrama Theories and Their Relevance to Recent Chinese Cinema." In *Melodrama and Asian Cinema*, edited by Wimal Dissanayake, 9–28. Cambridge: Cambridge University Press, 1993.

———. *Motherhood and Representation: The Mother in Popular Culture and Melodrama*. London and New York: Routledge, 1992.

Kapoor, Ilan. *Celebrity Humanitarianism: The Ideology of Global Charity*. London and New York: Routledge, 2012.

Karinthy, Frigyes. "Chain-Links." In *Everything Is Different*, 21–26. Budapest: Atheneum Irodalmi és Nyomdai RT, 1929.

Kasindorf, Jeanie. "Six Degrees of Impersonation: The Scammer Who Inspired John Guare's Hit Play Is Still At It." *The New Yorker*, March 25, 1991, 40–46.

Katz, John. "Winchell: An Unlikely Liberator of the Information Era." *Wired*, February 1, 1995. https://www.wired.com/1995/02/winchell-an-unlikely-liberator-of-the-information-era/.

Keillor, Garrison. "Norman Rockwell, the Storyteller." *New York Times*, December 19, 2013. https://www.nytimes.com/2013/12/22/books/review/american-mirror-the-life-and-art-of-norman-rockwell-by-deborah-solomon.html.

Kerr, Mark, and Kristin O'Rourke. "Sedgwick Sense and Sensibility: An Interview with Eve Kosofsky Sedgwick." January 19, 1995. http://nideffer.net/proj/Tvc/interviews/20.Tvc.v9.intrvws.Sedg.html.

Khamis, Susie, Lawrence Ang, and Raymond Welling. "Self-Branding, 'Micro-Celebrity' and the Rise of Social Media Influencers." *Celebrity Studies* 8, no. 2 (2017): 191–208.

King, Barry. "Embodying an Elastic Self: The Parametrics of Contemporary Stardom." In *Contemporary Hollywood Stardom*, edited by Thomas Austin and Martin Barker, 45–61. New York: Oxford University Press, 2003.

King, Claire Sisco. *Washed in Blood: Male Sacrifice, Trauma, and the Cinema*. New Brunswick, NJ: Rutgers University Press, 2011.

King, Emily. *A Century of Movie Posters: From Silent to Art House*. Hauppauge, NY: B.E.S. Publishing, 2003.

King, Geoff. *New Hollywood Cinema: An Introduction*. New York: Columbia University Press, 2002.

———. "Stardom in the Willenium." In *Contemporary Hollywood Stardom*, edited by Thomas Austin and Martin Barker, 62–73. New York: Oxford University Press, 2003.

King, J. L. *On the Down Low: A Journey into the Lives of "Straight" Black Men Who Sleep with Men*. New York: Broadway Books, 2004.

King, Jack. "Not Only the Brave: Why Straight Actors Playing Gay Are No Longer Automatically Acclaimed." *The Guardian*, June 18, 2021. https://www.theguardian.com/film/2021/jun/18/how-straight-actors-playing-gay-went-from-brave-to-blacking-up.

Kitch, Carolyn. *The Girl on the Magazine Cover: The Origins of Visual Stereotypes in American Mass Media*. Chapel Hill: University of North Carolina Press, 2001.

Klinger, Barbara. *Beyond the Multiplex: Cinema, New Technologies, and the Home*. Berkeley: University of California Press, 2006.

Koojiman, Jaap. "The True Voice of Whitney Houston: Commodification, Authenticity, and African American Superstardom." *Celebrity Studies* 5, no. 3 (2014): 305–20.

Kosenko, Kami, Andrew Binder, and Ryan Hurley. "Celebrity Influence and Identification: A Test of the Angelina Effect." *Journal of Health Communication* 21, no. 3 (2016): 318–26.

Kramer, Larry. "Why I Hated 'Philadelphia.'" *Los Angeles Times*, January 9, 1994, 29.

Kristeva, Julia. *Desire in Language: A Semiotic Approach to Literature and Art*. Edited by Leon Roudiez. Translated by Thomas Gora and Alice Jardine. New York: Columbia University Press, 1980.

Kroll, Justin. "Nicholas Stoller to Rewrite 'Uptown Saturday Night' for Warners." *Variety*, November 25, 2013. https://variety.com/2013/film/news/nicholas-stoller-uptown-saturday-night-warners-1200883904/.

Kuchta, David. *The Three-Piece Suit and Modern Masculinity: England, 1550–1850*. Berkeley: University of California Press, 2002.

Kuhn, Annet. "Women's Genres: Melodrama, Soap Opera, and Theory." *Screen* 25, no. 1 (1984): 18–28.

Kuntsman, Adi. "Introduction: Whose Selfie Citizenship?" In *Selfie Citizenship*, edited by Adi Kuntsman, 13–20. Manchester: Palgrave Macmillan, 2017.

Kurzman, Charles Chelise Anderson, Clinton Key, Youn Ok Lee, Mairead Moloney, Alexis Silver, and Maria W. Van Ryn. "Celebrity Status." *Sociological Theory* 24, no. 4 (December 2007): 347–67.

Laclau, Ernesto. *The Rhetorical Foundations of Society*. London: Verso, 2014.

Laclau, Ernesto, and Chantal Mouffe. *Hegemony and Socialist Strategy: Towards a Radical Democratic Politics*. Translated by Winston Moore and Paul Cammack. London: Verso, 1995.

Lanham, Richard. *A Handlist of Rhetorical Terms*. Berkeley: University of California Press, 1991.

Latour, Bruno. *Reassembling the Social*. Oxford: Oxford University Press, 2005.

LaValle, Victor. *Victor LaValle's Destroyer*. New York: Simon & Schuster, 2017.

———. "Introduction." In *The Best of Richard Matheson*, edited by Victor LaValle, vii–xviii. New York: Penguin Classics, 2017.

Law, John. "Networks, Relations, Cyborgs: On the Social Study of Technology." In *Visualizing the Invisible: Towards an Urban Space*, edited by Stephen Read and Camilo Pinilla, 84–97. Spacelab 1. Amsterdam: Techne Press, 2006.

LaWare, Margaret R. "Encountering Visions of Aztlán: Arguments for Ethnic Pride, Community Activism, and Cultural Revitalization in Chicano Murals." *Argumentation and Advocacy* 34, no. 3 (1998): 140–53.

Lawson, Caitlin. "Pixels, Porn, and Private Selves: Intimacy and Authenticity in the Celebrity Nude Photo Hack." *Celebrity Studies* 6, no. 4 (2015): 607–9.

Lebo, Harlan. *Citizen Kane: A Filmmaker's Journey*. New York: Thomas Dunne Books, 2016.

Ledbetter, James. "The Unbearable Whiteness of Publishing, Pt. 1." *Village Voice*, July 25, 1995. https://www.villagevoice.com/2020/06/10/the-unbearable-whiteness-of-publishing-pt-1/.

Lee, Ashley. "'Bel-Air' Began as a $25,000 Short. It Might Be the Future of the TV Reboot." *Los Angeles Times*, February 9, 2002. https://www.latimes.com/entertainment-arts/tv/story/2022-02-09/bel-air-peacock-fresh-prince-will-smith-morgan-cooper-jabari-banks.

Lee, Chris. "Inside Hidden Hills, Shangri-La to the Kanye Set." *Vanity Fair*, November 21, 2017. https://www.vanityfair.com/style/2017/11/inside-hidden-hills.

"Lee Daniels Wants to Make a Gay Action Hero Movie." *Out*, October 9, 2013. https://www.out.com/entertainment/popnography/2013/10/09/lee-daniels-wants-make-gay-action-hero-movie-alex-pettyfer.

Leiter, Andrew B. *In the Shadow of the Black Beast: African American Masculinity in the Harlem and Southern Renaissances*. Baton Rouge: Louisiana State University Press, 2010.

Levine, Carolyn. *Forms: Whole, Rhythm, Hierarchy, Network*. Princeton, NJ: Princeton University Press, 2015.

Lilti, Antoine. "The Writing of Paranoia: Jean-Jacques Rousseau and the Paradoxes of Celebrity." *Representations* 103, no. 1 (2008): 53–83.

Love, Heather. "Truth and Consequences: On Paranoid Reading and Reparative Reading." *Criticism* 52, no. 2 (2010): 235–41.

Lowenthal, Leo. "Biographies in Popular Magazines." In *Radio Research*, edited by P. F. Lazarsfeld and F. Stanton, 507–48. New York: Duell, Sloan, and Pearce, 1944.

Lubin, David M. *Shooting Kennedy*. Berkeley: University of California Press, 2003.

Lucaites, John Louis, and Celeste Michelle Condit. "Reconstructing <Equality>: Culturetypal and Counter-Cultural Rhetorics in the Martyred Black Vision." *Communication Monographs* 57 (March 1990): 5–24.

Lundberg, Christian. *Lacan in Public: Psychoanalysis and the Science of Rhetoric*. Tuscaloosa: University of Alabama Press, 2012.

Lynch, Annette. *Dress, Gender, and Cultural Change: Asian American and African American Rites of Passage*. Oxford: Oxford University Press, 1999.

Madocs, Rita. "The Saturday People." *McCall's* 94, no. 1 (October 1966): 116+.

Magill, David. "Celebrity Culture and Racial Masculinities: The Case of Will Smith." In *Pimps, Wimps, Studs, Thugs and Gentlemen: Essays on Media Images of Masculinity*, edited by Elwood Watson, 126–40. Jefferson, NC: McFarland & Company, 2008.

Magnus, Kathy Dow. "The Unaccountable Subject: Judith Butler and the Social Conditions of Intersubjective Agency." *Hypatia* 21, no. 2 (Spring 2006): 81–103.

Manne, Kate. *Down Girl: The Logic of Misogyny*. Oxford: Oxford University Press, 2018.

Marcus, Sharon. "Celebrity 2.0: The Case of Marina Abramović." *Public Culture* 27, no. 1 (2015): 21–52.

Marine, Brooke. "What If Kim Kardashian and Kanye West Were the Next Great Academic Power Duo?" *W*, September 10, 2018. https://www.wmagazine.com/story/kanye-west-art-professor-college-syllabus/.

Marshall, Barbara, and Momin Rahman. "Celebrity, Ageing and the Construction of 'Third Age' Identities." *International Journal of Cultural Studies* 18, no. 6 (2015): 577–93.

Marshall, David. *The Surprising Effects of Sympathy: Marivaux, Diderot, Rousseau, and Mary Shelley*. Chicago: University of Chicago Press, 1988.

Marshall, P. David. *Celebrity and Power: Fame in Contemporary Culture*. Minneapolis: University of Minnesota Press, 2014.

———. "New Media New Self: The Changing Power of Celebrity." In *The Celebrity Culture Reader*, edited by P. David Marshall, 634–44. New York and London: Routledge, 2006.

———. "Persona Studies: Mapping the Proliferation of the Public Self." *Journalism* 15, no. 2 (2014): 153–70.

———. "The Promotion and Presentation of the Self: Celebrity as Marker of Presentational Media." *Celebrity Studies* 1, no. 1 (2010): 35–48.

Marshall, P. David, Christopher Moore, and Kim Barbour. *Persona Studies: An Introduction*. Hoboken, NJ: Wiley-Blackwell, 2019.

McAlpine, Kat J. "It's a Small World After All: 'Six Degrees of Peggy Bacon.'" *Smithsonian Magazine*, July 6, 2012. https://www.smithsonianmag.com/smithsonian-institution/its-a-small-world-after-all-six-degrees-of-peggy-bacon-806322/.

McCarthy, Anna. "'Stanley Milgram, Allen Funt, and Me': Postwar Social Science and the 'First Wave' of Reality TV." In *Reality TV: Remaking Television Culture*, edited by Susan Murray and Laurie Ouellette, 23–43. New York: New York University Press, 2009.

McClain, Amanda Scheiner. *Keeping Up the Kardashian Brand: Celebrity, Materialism, and Sexuality*. Lanham, MD: Lexington Books, 2014.

McCune, Jeffrey Q., Jr. *Sexual Discretion: Black Masculinity and the Politics of Passing*. Chicago: University of Chicago Press, 2014.

McDowell, Deborah E. "Afterword: Recovery Missions: Imaging the Body Ideals." In *Recovering the Black Female Body*, edited by Michael Bennett and Vanessa D. Dickerson, 296–318. New Brunswick, NJ: Rutgers University Press, 2000.

McLeod, Kembrew. "Authenticity within Hip-Hop and Other Cultures Threatened with Assimilation." *Journal of Communication* 49, no. 4 (1999): 134–50.

Mecklenburg, Virginia. *Telling Stories: Norman Rockwell from the Collections of George Lucas and Steven Spielberg.* New York: Harry N. Abrams, 2010.

Mendelson, Andrew. "Slice-of-Life Moments as Visual 'Truth.'" *Journalism History* 29, no. 4 (2004): 166–78.

Mennel, Barbara. *Queer Cinema: Schoolgirls, Vampires, and Gay Cowboys.* London: Wallflower, 2012.

Mercer, John. "Introduction: Sex and the Celebrity." *Celebrity Studies* 4, no. 1 (2013): 1–3.

Mercer, John, and Martin Shingler. *Melodrama: Genre, Style, Sensibility.* London: Wallflower, 2004.

Mercer, Kobena. "Black Art and the Burden of Representation." *Third Text* 4, no. 10 (1990): 61–78.

Meinhof, Ulrike, and Jonathan Smith, eds. *Intertextuality and the Media: From Genre to Everyday Life.* Manchester and New York: Manchester University Press, 2000.

Miller, Monica. *Slaves to Fashion: Black Dandyism and the Styling of Black Diasporic Identity.* Durham, NC: Duke University Press, 2009.

Milstein, Sarah. "Using E-Mail to Count Connections." *New York Times,* Dec. 20, 2001. https://www.nytimes.com/2001/12/20/technology/using-e-mail-to-count-connections.html.

Modleski, Tania. *Feminism without Women: Culture and Criticism in a "Postfeminist" Age.* London and New York: Routledge, 1991.

Moffatt, Laurie Norton. "The Norman Rockwell Museum Acquires the *Art Critic.*" *The Portfolio* 16, no. 1 (Spring 1999): 12–13.

Mole, Tom. "Hypertrophic Celebrity." *M/C Journal* 7, no. 5 (2004). https://doi.org/10.5204/mcj.2424.

Monaco, James. *Celebrity.* New York: Delta, 1978.

Montgomery, Alexander. "Centrality in Transnational Governance: How Networks of International Institutions Shape Power Processes." In *The New Power Politics: Networks and Transnational Security Governance,* edited by Deborah Avant and Oliver Westerwinter, 19–40. Oxford: Oxford University Press, 2016.

Montgomery, Elizabeth Miles. *Norman Rockwell.* New York: Smithmark, 1989.

Morganstern, Joe. "Muddle-'Earth': Is 'After Earth' the Worst Movie Ever Made?" *Wall Street Journal,* May 30, 2013. https://www.wsj.com/articles/SB10001424127887324412604578515000854294308.

Morley, David. *The Nationwide Audience: Structure and Decoding.* London: BFI, 1980.

Moylan, Brian. "The 6 Degrees of the O.J. Simpson Trial." *Vulture,* January 25, 2016. https://www.vulture.com/2016/01/oj-simpson-trial-six-degrees.html.

Muller, Daphne. "The Surprising High-Art Theory Behind Kim Kardashian's 'Selfish.'" *Salon,* May 8, 2015. https://www.salon.com/2015/05/08/the_surprising_high_art_theory_behind_kim_kardashians_selfish/.

Muñoz, José Esteban. *Cruising Utopia: The Then and There of Queer Futurity.* New York: New York University Press, 2009.

Munzenrieder, Kyle. "North West, 5, Makes Powerful Debut in the Conceptual Art Space." *W,* December 20, 2018. https://www.wmagazine.com/story/north-west-art-elf.

Murphy, Mekado. "Hand-Drawn Homage to Classic Films." *New York Times,* October 9, 2011, AR8.

Murray, Susan. *Hitch Your Antenna to the Stars: Early Television and Broadcast Stardom.* London and New York: Routledge, 2005.

Musariri, Dorothy. "White Women Are Posing as Black on Instagram. Are the Kardashians to Blame?" *New Statesman,* November 12, 2018. https://www.newstatesman.com/science-tech/social-media/2018/11/white-women-are-posing-black-instagram-are-kardashians-blame.

"Museum Shares Decade-Long Digitization Project with Worldwide Audience." *Norman Rockwell Museum,* January 3, 2011. https://www.nrm.org/2011/01/norman-rockwell-museum-announces-online-debut-of-projectnorman/.

Nama, Adilifu. *Black Space: Imagining Race in Science Fiction Film.* Austin: University of Texas Press, 2008.

———. *Superblack: American Pop Culture and Black Superheroes.* Austin: University of Texas Press, 2011.

Narine, Neil. "Global Trauma and the Cinematic Network Society." *Critical Studies in Media Communication* 27, no. 3 (2010): 209–34.

Nash, Jennifer C. "Black Anality." *GLQ: A Journal of Lesbian and Gay Studies* 20, no. 4 (2014): 439–60.

Negra, Diane, and Su Holmes. "Going Cheap? Female Celebrity in Reality, Tabloid, and Scandal Genres." *Genders,* December 2008. https://www.colorado.edu/gendersarchive1998-2013/2008/12/01/introduction-special-issue-going-cheap-female-celebrity-reality-tabloid-and-scandal.

———, eds. *In the Limelight and Under the Microscope: Forms and Functions of Female Celebrity.* London: Continuum, 2011.

Newell-Hanson, Alice. "Is Kim Kardashian West the Andy Warhol of Our Time?" *i-D,* May 20, 2015. https://i-d.vice.com/en_us/article/wj5z7x/is-kim-kardashian-west-the-andy-warhol-of-our-time.

Newman, Mark, Albert-László Barabási, and Duncan Watts. *The Structure and Dynamics of Networks.* Princeton, NJ: Princeton University Press, 2006.

Noble, Safiya Umoja. *Algorithms of Oppression: How Search Engines Reinforce Racism.* New York: New York University Press, 2018.

"Norman Rockwell Biography." *Saturday Evening Post.* https://www.saturdayeveningpost.com/norman-rockwell-biography/.

Norman Rockwell: Pictures for the American People: A Family Guide. Stockbridge: Norman Rockwell Museum, 1999.

Nunn, Heather, and Anita Biressi. "'A Trust Betrayed': Celebrity and the Work of Emotion." *Celebrity Studies* 1, no. 1 (2010): 49–64.

Obeidallah, Dean. "Are the Kardashians Destroying America?" *CNN,* November 8, 2011. https://www.cnn.com/2011/11/08/opinion/obeidallah-kardashian/index.html?no-st=1530297063.

Obell, Sylvia. "Can You Guess How Many Reality Shows Can Be Tied Back to the O.J. Simpson Trial?" *Buzzfeed,* April 5, 2016. https://www.buzzfeed.com/sylviaobell/the-house-that-oj-built.

O'Gorman, Ned. "Aristotle's Phantasia in the Rhetoric: Lexis, Appearance, and the Epideictic Function of Discourse." *Philosophy and Rhetoric* 38, no. 1 (2005): 16–40.

Oh, David. "K-Pop Fans React: Hybridity and the White Celebrity-Fan on YouTube." *International Journal in Communication* 11 (2017): 2270–87.

Olson, Lester. "Portraits in Praise of a People: A Rhetorical Analysis of Norman Rockwell's Icons in Franklin D. Roosevelt's 'Four Freedoms' Campaign." *Quarterly Journal of Speech* 69 (1983): 15–24.

Orr, Mary. *Intertextuality: Debates and Contexts.* Cambridge: Polity, 2003.

Orth, Maureen. *The Importance of Being Famous: Behind the Scenes of the Celebrity-Industrial-Complex.* New York: Henry Holt, 2004.

Ott, Brian, and Cameron Walter. "Intertextuality: Interpretive Practice and Textual Strategy." *Critical Studies in Media Communication* 17, no. 4 (2000): 429–46.

Ouellette, Laurie. "The Trump Show." *Television & New Media* 17, no. 7 (2016): 1–4.

Ouellette, Laurie, and James Hay. *Better Living through Reality TV: Television and Post-Welfare Citizenship.* New York: Wiley-Blackwell, 2008.

Ouellette, Laurie, and Susan Murray. "Introduction." In *Reality TV: Remaking Television Culture,* edited by Laurie Ouellette and Susan Murray, 1–22. New York: New York University Press, 2009.

Ovalle, Priscilla Peña. *Dance and the Hollywood Latina: Race, Sex, and Stardom.* New Brunswick, NJ: Rutgers University Press, 2011.

Palmer, Lorrie. "Black Man/White Machine: Will Smith Crosses Over." *Velvet Light Trap* 67 (Spring 2011): 28–40.

Papacharissi, Zizi. *A Networked Self: Identity, Community, and Culture on Social Network Sites.* New York and London: Routledge, 2011.

"Paparazzi on the Prowl." *Time,* April 14, 1961, 81.

Parramore, Lynn Stuart. "How America Became the Love Child of Kim Kardashian and Donald Trump." *Reuters,* February 25, 2016. https://www.reuters.com/article/parramore-trump/column-how-america-became-the-love-child-of-kim-kardashian-and-donald-trump-idUSL2N1641IZ.

Pasori, Cedar. "Artist Vanessa Beecroft Has Decorated Kim Kardashian and Kanye West's Wedding with 20 Sculptures." *Complex,* May 24, 2014. https://www.complex.com/style/2014/05/vanessa-beecroft-sculptures-at-kim-kardashian-and-kanye-west-wedding.

Pearl, Sharrona, and Dana Polan. "Bodies of Digital Celebrity." *Public Culture* 27, no. 1 (2015): 185–92.

Perez, Gilberto. *The Eloquent Screen: A Rhetoric of Film.* Minneapolis: University of Minnesota Press, 2019.

Perman, Cindy. "What's Your 'Bacon Number?' Just Ask Google." *CNBC,* September 13, 2012. https://www.cnbc.com/id/49020195.

Pesce, Nicole Lyn. "'Selfish,' Kim Kardashian's Book of 300 Selfies, Is Bound for a Coffee Table Near You." *New York Daily News,* April 15, 2015. https://www.nydailynews.com/entertainment/theater-arts/selfish-kim-kardashian-selfie-book-bound-thrill-fans-article-1.2185387.

Petri, Alexandra. "Just Say No to Portmanteaus." *Washington Post,* June 21, 2012. https://www.washingtonpost.com/blogs/compost/post/just-say-no-to-portmanteaus/2012/06/21/gJQAQfqetV_blog.html.

Peyser, Marc. "Tyranny of the Red Ribbon" *Newsweek,* June 27, 1993. https://www.newsweek.com/tyranny-red-ribbon-193796.

Phillips, Kendall. "Rhetorical Maneuvers: Subjectivity, Power, and Resistance." *Philosophy & Rhetoric* 39, no. 4 (2006): 310–32.

Plunkett, Stephanie. "Gallery Guide." In *American Chronicles: The Art of Norman Rockwell.* Stockbridge, MA: Norman Rockwell Museum, 2013.

Ponce de Leon, Charles L. *Human-Interest Journalism and the Emergence of Celebrity in America, 1890–1940.* Chapel Hill: University of North Carolina Press, 2003.

Pramaggiore, Maria. "Filial Coupling, the Incest Narrative and the O'Neals." In *First Comes Love: Power Couples, Celebrity Kinships and Cultural Politics*, edited by Shelley Cobb and Neil Ewen, 78–95. New York: Bloomsbury, 2015.

Pristin, Terry. "'Philadelphia' Screenplay Suit to Reach Court." *New York Times*, March 11, 1996, 47+.

Pullen, Christopher. "Heroic Gay Characters in Popular Film: Tragic Determination, and the Every Day." *Continuum: Journal of Media & Cultural Studies* 25, no. 3 (June 2011): 397–413.

Quart, Alissa. "Networked: Dysfunctional Families, Reproductive Acts, and Multitasking Minds Make for Happy Endings." *Film Comment*, July–August 2005, 48–51.

Radway, Janice. *Reading Romance: Women, Patriarchy, and Popular Literature*. Chapel Hill: University of North Carolina Press, 1984.

Rahman, Momin. "Is Straight the New Queer? David Beckham and the Dialectics of Celebrity." *M/C Journal* 7, no. 5 (2004). http://journal.media-culture.org.au/0411/15-rahman.php.

Raji, Sanaz. "'My Face Is Not for Public Consumption': Selfies, Surveillance and the Politics of Being Unseen." In *Selfie Citizenship*, edited by Adi Kuntsman, 149–60. Manchester, UK: Palgrave Macmillan, 2017.

Rand, Erin J. "Bad Feelings in Public: Rhetoric, Affect, and Emotion." *Rhetoric and Public Affairs* 18, no. 1 (Spring 2015): 161–76.

——. "An Inflammatory Fag and a Queer Form: Larry Kramer, Polemics, and Rhetorical Agency." *Quarterly Journal of Speech* 94, no. 3 (2008): 279–319.

Raphael, Laura. "Barack Obama Had a Hilarious Response to the Idea of Will Smith Playing Him." *Esquire*, October 8, 2017. https://www.esquire.com/uk/culture/tv/news/a16586/barack-obama-had-a-hilarious-response-to-will-smith-playing-him/.

Rascaroli, Laura. "The Self-Portrait Film: Michelangelo's Last Gaze." In *The Cinema of Me: The Self and Subjectivity in First Person Documentary*, edited by Alisa Lebow, 57–78. New York: Wallflower Press, 2012.

Raub, Emma. "Frankenstein and the Mute Figure of Melodrama." *Modern Drama* 55, no. 4 (Winter 2012): 437–58.

Ravid, Gilad, and Elizabeth Currid-Halkett. "The Social Structure of Celebrity: An Empirical Analysis of an Elite Population." *Celebrity Studies* 4, no. 2 (2013): 182–201.

Ray, Robert. *How Film Theory Got Lost and Other Mysteries in Cultural Studies*. Bloomington: Indiana University Press, 2001.

"The Red Ribbon Project." *Visual AIDS*. https://visualaids.org/projects/the-red-ribbon-project.

Redmond, Sean. "Sensing Celebrity." In *A Companion to Celebrity*, edited by P. David Marshall and Sean Redmond, 385–400. Hoboken, NJ: Wiley-Blackwell, 2015.

Remes, Tom. "Six Degrees of Rogers Hornsby." *New York Times*, August 17, 1997, 275.

Renggli, Gabriel. "Building Metonymic Meaning with Joyce, Deleuze, and Guattari." *Joyce Studies Annual* (2018): 122–46.

Rich, Frank. "'Six Degrees' Reopens, Larger but Still Intimate." *New York Times*, November 9, 1990, C5.

Richards, Cindy Koenig. "Inventing Sacagawea: Public Women and the Transformative Potential of Epideictic Rhetoric." *Western Journal of Communication* 73, no. 1 (2009): 1–22.

Rife, Katie. "Will Smith's Netflix Blockbuster *Bright* Is Stunning in Its Audacity—And Its Stupidity." *AV Club*, December 22, 2017. https://www.avclub.com/bright-is-stunning-in-its-audacity-and-its-stupidity-1821529051.

Riffaterre, Michael. "Intertextuality vs. Hypertextuality." *New Literary History* 25, no. 4 (1994): 779–88.

Riviere, Sam. "The Kardashian Sisters Are the True Heirs to the Brontës." *Telegraph*, May 5, 2015. https://www.telegraph.co.uk/culture/books/11584309/Kim-Kardashian-is-a-feminist-artist-for-our-time.html.

Robinson, Sally. *Marked Men: White Masculinity in Crisis*. New York: Columbia University Press, 2000.

Rockwell, Abigail. "Who Moved the Norman Rockwell in the Oval Office?" *Huffington Post*, November 11, 2016. https://www.huffpost.com/entry/who-moved-the-norman-rockwell-painting-in-the-oval_b_58333e46e4b08c963e344310.

"Rockwell Cover Joins Fight on AIDS." *New York Times*, December 18, 1987, 54.

"Rockwell May Decide to Remain." *Los Angeles Times*, February 11, 1930, A1.

Rockwell, Norman. *My Adventures as an Illustrator*. New York: Harry N. Abrams, 1995.

Roeper, Richard. "Put an Orc in It: Will Smith's Cop Fantasy 'Bright' a Netflix Disaster." *Chicago Sun Times*, December 26, 2017. https://chicago.suntimes.com/2017/12/26/18349192/put-an-orc-in-it-will-smith-s-cop-fantasy-bright-a-netflix-disaster.

———. "Six Degrees of Monica Lewinsky." *Entertainment Weekly*, February 13, 1998. https://ew.com/article/1998/02/13/six-degrees-monica-lewinksy/.

Rogin, Michael. *Blackface, White Noise: Jewish Immigrants in the Hollywood Melting Pot*. Berkeley: University of California Press, 1996.

Rojek, Chris. *Fame Attack: The Inflation of Celebrity and Its Consequences*. New York: Bloomsbury Publishing, 2012.

———. "Sports Celebrity and the Civilizing Process." *Cultures, Commerce, Media, Politics* 9, no. 4 (2006): 674–90.

Romney, Jonathan. "A Single Man, Tom Ford." *Independent*, February 14, 2010. https://www.independent.co.uk/arts-entertainment/films/reviews/a-single-man-tom-ford-100-mins-12a-1898713.html.

Rooney, Monique. *Living Screens: Melodrama and Plasticity in Contemporary Film and Television*. London and New York: Rowman & Littlefield International, 2015.

Rose, Steve. "Make Will Smith Great Again." *The Guardian*, December 22, 2016. https://www.theguardian.com/film/2016/dec/22/make-will-smith-great-again-collateral-beauty.

Rottenberg, Josh. "Denzel Washington Reflects on His Past." *Entertainment Weekly*, January 8, 2010. https://ew.com/article/2010/01/08/denzel-washington-reflects-his-past/.

Rousseau, Jean-Jacques. *Confessions*. New York: Penguin Classics, 1953.

Saint-Amour, Paul. "Over-Assemblage: Ulysses and the Boîte-en-Valise from Above." In *Cultural Studies of James Joyce*, edited by R. Brandon Kershner, 21–58. Amsterdam: Rodopi, 2003.

Saltz, Jerry. "Art at Arm's Length: A History of the Selfie." *Vulture*, January 26, 2014. https://www.vulture.com/2014/01/history-of-the-selfie.html.

———. "Has Money Ruined Art?" *New York Magazine*, October 5, 2007. http://nymag.com/arts/art/season2007/38981/.

———. "Middle Americana." In *Seeing Out Loud: Village Voice Art Columns Fall 1998-Winter 2003*, edited by Jerry Saltz, 116–18. Great Barrington, MA: The Figures, 2003.

Saltz, Jerry, and David Wallace-Wells. "How and Why We Started Taking Kim Kardashian Seriously (and What She Teaches Us about the State of Criticism)." *Vulture*, May 20, 2015. https://www.vulture.com/2015/05/saltz-how-kim-kardashian-became-important.html?mid=fb-share-vulture.

Sanderson, Katharine. "Six Degrees of Messaging." *Nature,* March 13, 2008. https://doi.org/10.1038/news.2008.670.

Sastre, Alexandra. "Hottentot in the Age of Reality TV: Sexuality, Race, and Kim Kardashian's Visible Body." *Celebrity Studies* 5, nos. 1–2 (2014): 123–37.

Scherstuhl, Alan. "After Earth: Smith Family Robinson." *Village Voice,* May 29, 2013. https://www.villagevoice.com/2013/05/29/after-earth-smith-family-robinson/.

Schueller, Malini Johar. "Decolonizing Global Theories Today." *Interventions* 11, no. 2 (2009): 235–54.

Schuessler, Jennifer. "Six Degrees Forevermore." *New York Times,* April 23, 2017, AR1.

Schwiegershausen, Erica. "So, Was That Kim Kardashian Cover Photoshopped?" *The Cut,* November 13, 2014. https://www.thecut.com/2014/11/was-that-kim-kardashian-cover-photoshopped.html.

Scott, A. O. "An I.R.S. Do-Gooder and Other Strangeness." *New York Times,* December 18, 2008. https://www.nytimes.com/2008/12/19/movies/19seve.html.

Sedgwick, Eve Kosofsky. *Touching Feeling: Affect, Pedagogy, Performativity.* Durham, NC: Duke University Press, 2003.

Serico, Chris. "Emoji Movie: 12 Characters We Want to See, and Which Stars Should Play Them." *Today,* July 22, 2015. https://www.today.com/popculture/emoji-movie-12-characters-we-want-see-which-stars-should-t33906.

Sexton, Jared. "The Social Life of Social Death: On Afro-Pessimism and Black Optimism." *InTensions,* 5 (2011). https://doi.org/10.25071/1913-5874/37359.

Shah, Beejoli. "Sporting Chance: How CTE Takes the Biggest Toll on Athletes of Color." *Bitch Media,* February 8, 2018. https://www.bitchmedia.org/article/nfl-cte-athletes-color.

Sharpley-Whiting, Tracy Denean. *Black Venus: Sexualized Savages, Primal Fears, and Primitive Narratives in French.* Durham, NC: Duke University Press, 1999.

Shelley, Mary Wollstonecraft. *Frankenstein: Or, the Modern Prometheus.* London: George Routledge and Sons, 1891.

Shepard, Joan. "Movie Posters Become Stars." *Chicago Tribune,* May 29, 1984, D_B4.

Shingler, Martin. "Star Studies in Mid-Life Crisis." *Celebrity Studies* 10, no. 4 (2019): 445–52.

Shipp, Patricia. "Inside Will Smith's Pygmalion Obsession." *National Enquirer,* May 16, 2013. https://www.nationalenquirer.com/celebrity/inside-will-smiths-pygmalion-obsession/.

Shohat, Ella, and Robert Stam. *Unthinking Eurocentrism: Multiculturalism and the Media.* London and New York: Routledge, 1994.

Simons, Jan. "Complex Narratives." *New Review of Film and Television Studies* 6, no. 2 (2008): 111–26.

Smee, Sebastian. "Nostalgia, Norman Rockwell, and . . . Donald Trump?" *Boston Globe,* June 30, 2016, N1.

Smith, Will. *Will.* New York: Penguin Press, 2021.

Snorton, C. Riley. *Nobody Is Supposed to Know: Black Sexuality on the Down Low.* Minneapolis: University of Minnesota Press, 2014.

Sobande, Francesca. "The Celebrity Whitewashing of Black Lives Matter and Social Injustices." *Celebrity Studies* 13, no. 1 (2022): 130–35.

Span, Paula. "Colored with Controversy." *Washington Post,* February 13, 1992. https://www.washingtonpost.com/archive/lifestyle/1992/02/13/colored-with-controversy/a362eee9-385b-421c-9943-e2dcd8f33fdc/.

Spicer, Andrew. "The Author as Author: Restoring the Screenwriter to British Film History." In *The New Film History: Sources, Methods, Approaches*, edited by James Chapman, Mark Glancy, and Sue Harper, 89–103. New York: Palgrave Macmillan, 2007.

Springer, Kimberly. "Beyond the H8R: Theorizing the Anti-Fan." *The Phoenix Papers* 1, no. 2 (2013). https://fansconference.org/dRuZ33A/wp-content/uploads/2013/07/Beyond-the-H8R-Theorizing-the-Anti-Fan-by-Kimberly-Springer.pdf.

Staiger, Janet. *Perverse Spectators: The Practices of Film Reception*. New York: New York University Press, 2000.

Stanik, Mary. "Even If It Isn't a Perfect Norman Rockwell Day, Let's Keep Thanksgiving a Real Holiday." *MinnPost*, November 14, 2014. https://www.minnpost.com/community-voices/2014/11/even-if-it-isnt-perfect-norman-rockwell-day-lets-keep-thanksgiving-real-hol/.

Stark, Luke, and Kate Crawford. "The Conservatism of Emoji: Work, Affect, and Communication." *Social Media + Society* 1, no. 2 (July–December 2015): 1–11.

Sternberg, Ernest. "Phantasmagoric Labor: The New Economies of Self-Presentation." *Futures* 30, no. 1 (January 1998): 3–21.

Sternheimer, Karen. *Celebrity Culture and the American Dream: Stardom and Social Mobility*. New York and London: Routledge, 2015.

Stevens, Christopher. "The Day Andy Warhol Was Shot Dead but Came Back to Life." *Daily Mail*, February 27, 2020. https://www.dailymail.co.uk/tvshowbiz/article-8048585/The-Day-Andy-Warhol-shot-dead-came-life.html.

Stewart, James B. "Norman Rockwell's Art, Sniffed at by Critics, Is Becoming Prized." *New York Times*, May 24, 2014, B1+.

Stitch. "The Will Smith & Chris Rock Slap Situation Is Not About You." *Teen Vogue*, March 28, 2022. https://www.teenvogue.com/story/will-smith-chris-rock-slap-situation-is-not-about-you.

Stuart, Tessa. "Sorry Kevin Bacon, Dennis Hopper Is Actually the Center of the Hollywood Universe." *Buzzfeed*, April 26, 2013. https://www.buzzfeed.com/tessastuart/sorry-kevin-bacon-dennis-hopper-is-actually-the-center-of-th.

Stubblefield, Thomas. "Disassembling the Cinema: The Poster, the Film, and In-Between." *Thresholds*, 34 (2007): 84–88.

Studlar, Gaylyn. "White Trash Celebrity in the Age of Eugenics: Desecrating Clara Bow." *Celebrity Studies* 11, no. 1 (2020): 60–74.

Sturley, Theresa. "New Again: Will Smith." *Interview*, March 26, 2013. https://www.interviewmagazine.com/film/new-again-will-smith. Originally published in October 1990.

Taubin, Amy. "Playing It Straight: R.E.M. Meets a Post-Rodney King World in Independence Day." *Sight and Sound* 6, no. 8 (1996): 6–8.

———. "Review: A Single Man." *Film Comment*, November–December 2009. https://www.filmcomment.com/article/review-a-single-man-tom-ford/.

Taylor, Derrick Bryson. "Alexis Arquette Drops Will Smith Gay Sex Bombshell." *Page Six*, January 20, 2016. https://pagesix.com/2016/01/20/alexis-arquette-claims-will-and-jada-pinkett-smith-are-gay/.

Taylor, Jacqueline. "On Being an Exemplary Lesbian: My Life as a Role Model." *Text and Performance Quarterly* 20, no. 1 (2000): 58–73.

Telusma, Blue. "Kim Kardashian Doesn't Realize She's the Butt of an Old Racial Joke." *The Grio*, November 21, 2014. https://thegrio.com/2014/11/12/kim-kardashian-butt/.

Teotonio, Isabel. "Google Adds Six Degrees of Separation to Search Engine." *The Star*, 13 September 2012. https://www.thestar.com/entertainment/2012/09/13/google_adds_six_degrees_of_kevin_bacon_to_search_engine.html.

Thomas, Sarah. "Celebrity in the 'Twitterverse': History, Authenticity and the Multiplicity of Stardom." *Celebrity Studies* 5, no. 3 (2014): 242–55.

Tillet, Salamishah. "Black Girls in Paris: Sally Hemings, Sarah Baartman, and French Racial Dystopia." *Callaloo* 32, no. 3 (Summer 2009): 935–36.

Toh, Justine. "The White Fireman and the American Heartland in the Memory of 9/11." *Critical Race and Whiteness Studies* 10, no. 2 (2014): 1–18.

Tollefson, Michael. "You're Not You When You're in a Snickers' Ad: Celebrity, Intertextuality, and Masculinity." *Qualitative Research Reports in Communication* 20, no. 1 (2019): 35–41.

Towns, Armond. "Toward a Black Media Philosophy." *Cultural Studies* 34, no. 1 (2020): 851–73.

———. "'What Do We Wanna Be?' Black Radical Imagination and the Ends of the World." *Communication and Critical/Cultural Studies* 17, no. 1 (2020): 75–80.

Treichler, Paula. "AIDS, Homophobia, and Biomedical Discourse: An Epidemic of Signification." *October* 43 (Winter 1987): 31–70.

Turner, Fred, and Christine Larson. "Network Celebrity: Entrepreneurship and the New Public Intellectuals." *Public Culture* 27, no. 1 (2015): 53–84.

Turner, Graeme. *Ordinary People and the Media*. London: SAGE, 2010.

Turner, Graeme. *Understanding Celebrity*. London: SAGE, 2004.

Turner, Peter. "Fast Marketing, Furious Interactions: An Interstellar Community on Instagram." *Celebrity Studies* 10, no. 4 (2019): 469–78.

van Dijk, Jan. *The Network Society*. London: SAGE, 1999.

Vera, Hernán, and Andrew M. Gordon. *Screen Saviors: Hollywood Fictions of Whiteness*. Lanham, MD: Rowman & Littlefield, 2003.

Vigdor, Neil. "Boy Scouts Will Sell Nearly 60 Norman Rockwell Works to Pay Sex-Abuse Claims." *New York Times*, March 2, 2021. https://www.nytimes.com/2021/03/02/us/boy-scouts-bankruptcy-norman-rockwell.html.

Vine, Steven. "Filthy Types: 'Frankenstein,' Figuration, Femininity." *Critical Survey* 8, no. 3 (1996): 246–58.

Virk, Kameron, and Nesta McGregor. "Blackfishing: The Women Accused of Pretending to Be Black." *BBC News*, December 5, 2018. https://www.bbc.com/news/newsbeat-46427180.

Vogel, Carol. "Three Rockwell Classics Bring Nearly 57.8 Million." *New York Times*, December 4, 2013, C1.

Volpert, Megan. *Sonics in Warholia*. Little Rock, AR: Sibling Rivalry Press, 2011.

Walker, Alexander. *Stardom: The Hollywood Phenomenon*. Middlesex: Penguin Books, 1974.

Wallach, Alan. "Norman Rockwell and the Representation of Social Conflict." In *Seeing High and Low: Representing Social Conflict in American Visual Culture*, edited by Patricia Johnson, 280–90. Berkeley: University of California Press, 2006.

———. "Norman Rockwell at the Guggenheim." In *Art and Its Publics: Museum Studies in the Millennium*, edited by Andrew McClellan, 97–116. Malden, MA: Blackwell, 2003.

Washington, Myra S. *Blasian Invasion: Racial Mixing in the Celebrity Industrial Complex*. Jackson: University of Mississippi Press, 2017.

Watts, Duncan. *Six Degrees: The Science of a Connected Age*. New York: Norton, 2004.

———. *Small Worlds: The Dynamics of Networks Between Order and Randomness.* Princeton, NJ: Princeton University Press, 1999.

Weinstein, Steve. "NBC Takes a Second Look at 'And the Band Played On.'" *Los Angeles Times,* March 28, 1994. https://www.latimes.com/archives/la-xpm-1994-03-28-ca-39481-story.html.

Wellman, Barry. "Little Boxes, Glocalization and Networked Individualism." In *Digital Cities II: Computational and Sociological Approaches,* edited by Makoto Tanabe, Peter Van Den Besselaar, and Toru Ishida, 10–25. Berlin and New York: Springer, 2002.

Wells, Jane. "Six Degrees of Simpson." *CNBC,* June 11, 2014. https://www.cnbc.com/2014/06/10/six-degrees-of-oj-simpson.html.

Wesolowski, Adrian D. "Beyond Celebrity History: Towards the Consolidation of Fame Studies." *Celebrity Studies* 11, no. 2 (2020): 189–204.

Wessang, Adeline. "Jean-Paul Goude Is Still Ahead of His Time." *Vice,* April 1, 2012. https://www.vice.com/en_us/article/avnk3j/jean-paul-goude-is-still-ahead-of-his-time.

West, Isaac. "Queer Generosities." *Western Journal of Communication* 77, no. 5 (2013): 538–41.

Wetmore, Brandon. "Warhol's Cookie Jar Collection." *PAPER,* November 21, 2018. https://www.papermag.com/calvin-klein-andy-warhol-cookie-jar-2621107484.html.

Whatling, Clare. *Screen Dreams: Fantasising Lesbians in Film.* Manchester: Manchester University Press, 1997.

Whedbee, Karen. "Perspective by Incongruity in Norman Thomas's 'Some Wrong Roads Lead to Peace.'" *Western Journal of Communication* 65, no. 1 (2001): 45–64.

Wicke, Jennifer. "Epilogue: Celebrity's Face Book." *PMLA* 126, no. 4 (2011): 1131–39.

Wickham, Phil. "Scrapbooks, Soap Dishes and Screen Dreams: Ephemera, Everyday Life, and Cinema History." *New Review of Film and Television Studies* 8, no. 3 (2010): 315–30.

Wiegman, Robyn. "Interchanges: Heteronormativity and the Desire for Gender." *Feminist Theory* 7, no. 1 (2006): 89–103.

———. "The Times We're In: Queer Feminist Criticism and the Reparative Turn." *Feminist Theory* 15, no. 1 (2014): 4–25.

Wiegman, Robyn, and Elizabeth Wilson. "Introduction: Antinormativity's Queer Conventions." *differences* 26, no. 1 (2015): 1–25.

Wilderson, Frank B., III. "Grammar and Ghosts: The Performative Limits of African Freedom." *Theatre Survey* 50, no. 1 (May 2009): 119–25.

Wilkinson, Isabel. "Kim Kardashian Is Now the Spitting Image of Marina Abramović." *Daily Beast,* March 14, 2013. https://www.thedailybeast.com/kim-kardashian-is-now-the-spitting-image-of-marina-abramovic-photos.

"Will & Jada's Divorce Secret: The Man Who Came Between Them." *Star,* March 19, 2012, 36+.

Williams, Christian. "Clement Greenberg: This, He Likes." *Washington Post,* May 24, 1980. https://www.washingtonpost.com/archive/lifestyle/1980/05/24/clement-greenberg-this-he-likes/96630bd6-c5ef-4389-86d8-afa4513b18c5/.

Williams, Linda. *Playing the Race Card: Melodramas of Black and White from Uncle Tom to O.J. Simpson.* Princeton, NJ: Princeton University Press, 2001.

Williams, Michael. "'Gilbo-Garbage' or 'The Champion Lovemakers of Two Nations': Uncoupling Greta Garbo and John Gilbert." In *First Comes Love: Power Couples, Celebrity Kinships and Cultural Politics,* edited by Shelley Cobb and Neil Ewen, 13–28. New York: Bloomsbury, 2015.

Williamson, Milly. "Female Celebrities and the Media: The Gendered Denigration of the 'Ordinary' Celebrity." *Celebrity Studies* 1, no. 1 (2010): 118–20.

Wilson, Mark. "Lecter's Bloody Second Course Has a Hollow Centre." *Independent,* February 6, 2001. https://web.archive.org/web/20090204142404/http://www.independent.co.uk/arts-entertainment/films/reviews/lecters-bloody-second-course-has-a-hollow-centre-690474.html.

Witchel, Alex. "Impersonator Wants to Portray Still Others, This Time, Onstage." *New York Times,* July 31, 1990: C13.

Wood, Andrew F., and Tyrone L. Adams. "Embracing the Machine: Quilt and Quilting as Community-Building Architecture." In *Cyberghetto or Cybertopia? Race, Class, and Gender on the Internet,* edited by Bosah Ebo, 219–34. Westport, CT: Praeger, 1998.

Wood, Robin. "The American Family Comedy: From *Meet Me in St. Louis* to *The Texas Chainsaw Massacre.*" *Wide Angle* 3, no. 2 (1979): 5–11.

Wright, Kai. "The Great Down-Low Debate." *Village Voice,* June 5, 2001. https://www.villagevoice.com/2001/06/05/the-great-down-low-debate/.

Write, Julie Lobalzo. *Crossover Stardom: Popular Male Music Stars in American Cinema.* New York: Bloomsbury, 2017.

Yancy, George. *Black Bodies, White Gazes: The Continuing Significance of Race.* Lanham, MD: Rowman & Littlefield, 2008.

Young, Elizabeth. *Black Frankenstein: The Making of an American Metaphor.* New York: New York University Press, 2008.

Young, Vershawn A. "Compulsory Homosexuality and Black Masculine Performance." *Poroi* 7, no. 2 (2011). https://doi.org/10.13008/2151-2957.1095.

Zachary, G. Pascal. "The Godfather." *Wired,* November 1, 1997. https://www.wired.com/1997/11/es-bush/.

Zazosa, Agustin. "Melodrama and the Modes of the World." *Discourse* 32, no. 2 (Spring 2010): 236–55.

INDEX

Abramović, Marina, 8, 16, 184–85

Academy Awards, 79n56, 105n25, 111. *See also* Oscars

Academy of Motion Picture Arts and Sciences, 116–17

actor-network theory, 55

affect: and celebrities, 182; and criticism, 55; and cultural discourses, 44; and emoji, 181; and identification, 9, 35, 91; and intertextuality, 51, 56; and Kardashian, 177, 183; and Kimoji, 183; and melodrama, 49, 151n15, 160, 162–63, 171; and metonymy, 182; and networks, 103; and paranoia, 104; and portmanteaus, 207; and Rockwell, 80, 88, 89; and *Single Man,* 151n16; and Smith, 138, 141, 143; and subjectivity, 33, 40, 50, 207

Afrofuturism, 138, 142–44

Afropessimism, 138, 143–44

After Earth (Shyamalan), 37, 110, 112, 136–45

AIDS, 2, 20, 97–107, 98n4, 100n11, 102n17, 148–50, 152n18, 157. *See also* HIV

AIDS Memorial Quilt, 98

American Dream, 8–9, 38, 43, 65, 112–13, 112n16, 117–19, 124, 128

Andy Warhol Museum, 129n60. *See also* Warhol, Andy

antinormativity, 60, 75–76, 81, 84, 90. *See also* queer feminist criticism

authenticity: as celebrity brand, 2, 5–6, 8, 17, 31, 110, 167–69, 184; and individualism, 13, 41, 47, 171; and Kardashian, 172, 178, 184, 192; and Rockwell, 59, 71–72; and selfhood, 17, 46, 194–96

Baartman, Saartje, 188–89, 191

Bacon, Kevin: and Balto, 28n24; and *Balto* (Wells), 28n24; and Francis Bacon, 52; and *Premiere* magazine, 22n2; and whiteness, 30, 30n36; game, 21–22, 31–32, 50, 100. *See also* six degrees of separation

Baker, Akai, 144–46

Baker, Dr. Josephine, 144–46

Baker, Josephine, 146

Balto, 28, 28n24, 103

Balto (Wells), 28n24

Banderas, Antonio, 101, 101n16

Barthes, Roland, 18, 31, 35, 74

Bechdel, Allison, 92

Bel-Air (Cooper), 146–47

239

Berg, Peter, 124. See also *Hancock* (Berg)
Black Frankenstein, 132, 134–35, 144
Black Lives Matter, 140
Black Panther, 128–29, 129n60
Black Panther (Coogler), 107, 129n60
Boy Scouts of America, 61, 61n8
Boyer, Charles, 69n27, 79n56
Break the Internet, 16, 187
Bridges, Ruby, 92, 92n73, 95n79
Brown, Michael, 140
Burke, Kenneth, 9, 35
Bush, Vannevar, 25n12
Butler, Judith, 18, 41, 43, 44–48, 78, 80, 84, 158, 211

Capra, Frank, 65, 69n27
Captain America, 93, 93n75, 129–30
Carroll, Lewis, 204. See also *Through the Looking Glass* (Carroll)
Cats, 25, 24n7, 24n8, 125n52
celebrity culture: and AIDS, 99, 106–7; and American Dream, 38, 113; and authenticity, 8, 13, 41, 46, 168, 171, 194; and banality, 13; and brand culture, 49; and emoji, 181; and *Frankenstein*, 208–9; and gossip, 8, 11, 17, 30, 55, 167, 204–5; and hegemony, 5, 18–19, 172, 106; and identification, 168; and identity, 4–5, 8, 35–36, 46, 50; and ideology, 37–38, 50; and individualism, 13, 40–41, 50, 107, 171; and intertextuality, 35, 51; and Kardashian, 160–62, 166, 169, 172, 178–79, 179n72, 183, 186; and *Mad* magazine, 92n74; and melodrama, 19, 160, 162–64, 166, 167–72, 178; and metonymic criticism, 9, 40, 107; and metonymy, 3, 4, 19, 20, 31–32, 35, 51, 107, 168–70, 178, 202; and mimesis, 186; and misogyny, 178; and networks, 13–14, 18, 23, 24–25, 27–29, 35, 51, 158, 183; and portmanteaus, 20, 202–7, 211; and power, 106, 158; and *Pygmalion*, 165–66; and race, 107, 178, 178n69; and reality television, 167, 169; and Red Ribbon Project, 99; and rhetoric, 3, 8–9, 31–32; and Rockwell, 62, 64–65, 67, 72, 75, 83, 89; and Rousseau, 164; and Shelley, 209; and Smith, 109, 112, 127, 131, 139, 147; and social media, 167, 169; and subjectivity, 10, 12, 24, 40, 49, 50–51, 107, 158, 169, 172; and trauma, 49; and Trump, 1–2; and vulnerability, 49; and Warhol, 186

celebrity-industrial-complex, 38, 106, 107, 131
Chambers, Veronica, 101–2, 104, 104n24, 105, 112n16
Chaplin, Charlie, 32, 67, 116, 204
Chupacabra Selfie Project, 199
cinema: and Black Frankenstein, 132; and celebrity, 3, 8; and ephemera, 12; and melodrama, 163, 170; and metonymy, 31n40; and movie posters, 114–15; and pleasure, 52; and Rockwell, 60, 64–65, 71; and Smith, 6n13, 7, 108, 118; and tragic gay narratives, 148, 152n18
Coates, Ta-Nehisi, 8, 129n60, 137, 141, 144–46
comic books, 71, 93, 93n75, 127–29, 129n60, 144n101
Coogler, Ryan, 107, 129n60. See also *Black Panther* (Coogler)
Cooper, Brittney, 48, 135, 157–58, 177
Cooper, Gary, 66, 116
Cooper, Morgan, 146–47
counterhegemony, 13, 18, 41, 120, 136
Crawford, Joan, 8, 23, 66, 77–79, 77n48, 79n56, 152
Cukor, George, 164, 165. See also *My Fair Lady* (Cukor)

Demme, Jonathan, 99, 101n14, 102, 148–49
Disney, 23, 64, 79n56, 150
Disney, Walt, 65, 65n22, 69n27, 71
dogsled, 28, 208–9
down low, 4, 17, 109
Dyer, Richard, 12, 35, 37, 43, 49–50, 171

Eakins, Thomas, 87
emoji, 19, 161, 180–82, 182n78, 203
Emoji Movie (Leondis), 182
ephemerality, 10–14, 16, 29, 154, 195, 204
exceptionalism, 23, 112–13
extratextuality, 20, 30, 37, 43, 69, 79, 82, 101, 109, 116, 134, 153, 153n19

Facebook, 15, 27, 30, 110, 112–13, 173, 181, 198
Facts of Life (Rockwell), 97
Falcon, The, 93n75, 128–30
fame: and AIDS, 106; and American Dream, 37, 43; and Bacon, 22; and Balto, 103;

INDEX • 241

and digital media, 11–12; and ephemerality, 10–12; and *Frankenstein,* 209–10; and hegemony, 18; and intertextuality, 29; and Kardashian, 5, 16–17, 23, 29, 160, 161n4, 164–65, 167, 169, 172–73, 174n52, 178–79, 186, 198, 200; in *Mad* magazine, 92n74; and networks, 23–24, 40; and Rockwell, 4, 19, 60, 67–68, 70–72, 79, 85, 96, 97; and Rousseau, 193, 198, 209; and politics of recognition, 46; and portmanteaus, 203; and self-reflexivity, 5, 6; and subjectivity, 2, 3, 5, 13, 50; in *Six Degrees of Separation,* 25, 28; and Smith, 19, 29, 109, 112, 120, 126–28, 139, 139n84, 143, 147; and taste, 4; and Toukie Smith, 187n94; and trauma, 49. *See also* celebrity culture

fan magazines, 28–29, 67, 115

fandom: and American Dream, 37; and criticism, 50–51; and identification, 35, 40; and intertextuality, 9, 52; and Kardashian, 16; and melodrama, 164; and networks, 29, 41, 183; and portmanteaus, 204, 206; and Rockwell, 14, 17, 59–60, 65, 67–68, 154n23; and Smith, 121, 146; and social media, 27

fantasy: and American Dream, 112; and Blackness, 135; and class, 4; of dependency, 44; and *Frankenstein,* 208; and individualism, 36, 107; and Kardashian, 174–75; and masculinity, 132; and post-raciality, 100, 113, 117, 119, 142; and *Pygmalion,* 171; and race, 4, 113, 118, 130; of relatedness, 35; and Rockwell, 67; of sameness, 34, 35; and selfhood, 5, 17, 47, 49, 55, 169; and signification, 175, 186; and Smith, 109, 127; and subjectivity, 9, 18, 20, 32–33, 36, 43, 50, 52, 54, 171–72, 175, 197; and whiteness, 135

Fappening, The, 17, 184, 184n82

Fish, Mr., 93, 93n75

Folsom, Ed, 39

For Freedoms (Tomas and Gottesman), 93

Ford, Tom, 148. *See also Single Man* (Ford)

Foster, Jodie, 149, 156

Four Freedoms (Rockwell), 73, 93, 95

Frankenstein, 127, 132–35, 143n99, 144, 146, 173, 191, 191n110, 205, 208–10. *See also Frankenstein* (Shelley); *Frankenstein* (Whale)

Frankenstein (Shelley), 19, 132–34, 146, 191n110, 208–10

Frankenstein (Whale), 117, 126, 132–35

Freedom from Fear (Rockwell), 73, 91, 92, 93, 112

Freedom from Want (Rockwell), 73, 92, 92n74, 93, 154–55, 189

French Correction, 190, 190n104, 191, 197

Fresh Prince of Bel-Air, The, 1, 4–6, 15, 37, 37n64, 43, 109, 121, 146, 187n94

Galatea. *See Pygmalion* (Rousseau)

Garbo, Greta, 31, 117, 204

Garner, Eric, 92, 140

Gay, Roxane, 129n60

Gere, Richard, 99, 150n9

Girl at Mirror (Rockwell), 66, 67, 75, 76, 79–80, 79n56, 82, 85

Girl Reading the Post (Rockwell), 65, 65n22, 67, 85

Girl with Black Eye (Rockwell), 75, 82, 84, 86

Going Out (Rockwell), 76–77, 79–80, 152

gossip, 8, 11, 16–17, 25, 26n15, 30, 55, 63, 92n73, 167, 204–5

Gossips, The (Rockwell), 24, 24n8, 92

Gottesman, Eric, 93

Goude, Jean-Paul, 69n28, 155, 187–91, 188n98, 190n104, 191n109, 197

Goudemalion, 190

graphic novels, 19, 142n93, 144, 145n103

Green, Jesse, 99, 102, 102n17

Guare, John, 1–2, 21, 24n7, 25, 26n15, 112n16, 149, 204n11

Guggenheim Museum, 7, 61n9

H8R, 176–79, 178nn68–69

Hampton, David, 21, 23, 24n7, 25, 26n15, 37n64, 101, 105, 149

Hancock. *See Hancock* (Berg)

Hancock (Berg), 6, 124–35, 146, 147

Hanks, Tom, 99–102, 101n16, 148, 157

Hannibal (Scott), 153

Hearst, William Randolph, 25–26, 26n15, 204–5

hegemony: and American Dream, 8, 9; and audiences, 29, 105; and authenticity, 47; and beauty norms, 83, 156, 199; and celebrity, 18, 106; and femininity, 153, 156;

and film studies, 52; and hermeneutics of suspicion, 57; and heterosexuality, 73, 125; and Hollywood, 105, 157, 158; and identity, 5, 10; and individualism, 8, 9, 23, 33, 44, 47; and Kardashian, 160, 172, 175, 200; and masculinity, 125, 157; and metonymy, 18, 33, 39; and middle-classness, 73, 90; and networks, 26; and Rockwell, 19, 60, 66, 92; and selfhood, 13; and subjectivity, 5, 10, 18, 23, 43, 107; and whiteness, 33, 73, 90, 119, 124, 125, 157

Hepburn, Audrey, 31, 185

heteronormativity, 19, 80, 85, 88, 92, 108–9, 156

Hilton, Paris, 23, 92n74, 160, 161n4, 167n28, 185

Hinckley, John, Jr., 2, 23n5

hitch, 38, 118, 119, 120, 121, 123

Hitch. See *Hitch* (Tennant)

Hitch (Tennant), 6, 118–20, 119n41

Hitchcock, Alfred, 23, 51, 150, 151, 151nn15–16, 152, 155

HIV, 105–6, 149. See also AIDS

Holloway, Shawné Michaelain, 199–200

Hollywood: and activism, 98, 105, 106; and AIDS, 98, 105; and Bacon, 22, 30; and Baker, 146; and *Black Panther*, 129n60; and Crawford, 78–79, 79n56; and Demme, 101n14; and Hanks, 157; and Hearst, 26, 26n15; and heteronormativity, 206; and homophobia, 156–57; and Kardashian, 161, 176n60, 184; and *Mad* magazine, 92n74; and makeover cinema, 6n13; and melodrama, 163–65; and metonymy, 31; and Metro-Goldwyn-Mayer, 26; and misogyny, 175; and moral panic, 3–4; and movie posters, 114, 133; and network films, 202; and *Premiere* magazine, 22; and racism, 103–5, 134, 143, 157; and Rockwell, 62–68, 63n15, 68n26, 72, 89, 129n60, 154n23; and Smith, 7, 7n16, 111, 123, 124–28, 142, 147; and star system, 27

Hooper, Tobe, 51, 153–54. See also *Texas Chainsaw Massacre* (Hooper)

Hopper, Hedda, 63

Hopkins, Anthony, 153, 155

Hudson, Rock, 99, 153n19

Humpty Dumpty, 204, 207, 209n29. See also *Through the Looking Glass* (Carroll)

hypertextuality, 30, 36, 209

iconography, 98, 100n11, 128, 132, 139, 173, 179, 186–87, 189n102, 192, 198

identification: and affect, 9, 13, 38, 91; and antinormativity, 75, 85; and Burke, 35; and *Frankenstein*, 208; and metonymy, 34, 35; and gender, 60, 75, 77–78, 80–81, 86; and recognition, 46; and Rockwell, 72, 83; and sexuality, 60, 86

individualism: and American Dream, 8, 9, 43; and authenticity, 13, 41, 171; and exceptionalism, 23; and subjectivity, 18, 33, 36, 44, 47, 50, 54, 107

influencers, 16, 161, 165, 171, 182

Instagram, 15, 16, 27, 28, 106n30, 160, 161, 182, 184, 199

internormativity, 9, 19, 90

intersectionality, 9, 90–91

interstellar communities, 27, 183

intersubjectivity: as becoming, 45; and *Frankenstein*, 210–11; and interdependence, 8–9, 18, 24, 44, 47, 54, 194, 198, 200; and internormativity, 19; and intertextuality, 40, 42, 44, 86, 197; and networks, 20; and portmanteaus, 207; and selfies, 199. See also subjectivity

Interview magazine, 110, 165, 176, 185

Jackson, Michael, 49, 69n27, 137

Jackson, Sarah J., 42, 107, 108, 131

Jenner, Caitlin, 161, 161n4

John, Elton, 20, 99, 152n18

Jones, Grace, 188, 188n98, 190

Kardashian, Kim: and Abramović, 185; and American Dream, 43; and anti-Blackness, 175–78, 188–92; and appropriations of Blackness, 175, 177; and authenticity, 5; and Baartman, 188, 191; and blackface, 176, 176n60, 188; and Break the Internet, 16, 187; and celebrity, 5, 19, 162, 164–66; and Cher, 6, 185; and cry face meme, 159, 183; and emoji, 19, 180–83; and ephemera, 11, 14, 16, 29; and Fappening, 17, 184; gossip, 16; and Goude, 155, 187–92; in *H8R*, 176–79; as Hepburn, 185; and Hidden Hills, 3–4; and Hilton, 23, 160, 185; and identification, 35; as influencer, 16,

161, 165; and Instagram, 160; and intertextuality, 43; in *Interview* magazine, 185; and Jenner, 161; in *Keeping Up With the Kardashians (KUWTK)*, 161; and Kennedy Onassis, 6, 185; and Kevin Bacon game, 22; and Kimoji, 180–81, 183; as Madonna, 6, 186; on magazine covers, 161; and melodrama, 19, 166–72; in memes, 16, 155, 159; and metacelebrity, 6, 8, 179–87, 179n72; and metonymic criticism, 8, 41; and Milgram, 174n54; and mimesis, 179, 184–85, 190, 200; and misogyny, 160, 175; as Monroe, 184, 184n85, 185n88, 186; in *Paper* magazine, 20, 155, 187–92; at Paris Fashion Week, 159–60; and parody, 189, 189n102; and portmanteaus, 203; and post-truth, 16, 172–73; and Pygmalion, 19, 165–66, 189; and *Pygmalion*, 19, 165; and racial melodrama, 177, 177n64; and reality television, 7, 161, 167n28, 168, 173; and Rockwell, 155, 172, 184, 189n102; and Rousseau, 19, 165, 193–94; and *Selfie*, 165; and selfies, 6, 162, 198–99; in *Selfish*, 19, 184, 194, 198; and Simpson, 161, 177n64; and six degrees of separation, 23; and Smith, 110, 173; and Snapchat, 161, 173; and social media, 7, 160, 161, 168, 183; and subjectivity, 18, 43, 172, 175, 186, 194; in *Superstar*, 161, 161n4; and synecdoche, 175, 179; as Toukie Smith, 6, 187; and transmediation, 29; and trauma, 49; and *Triple Self-Portrait* (Rockwell), 184; and Trump, 2, 4, 22, 173–74, 174nn53–54; and Twitter, 161; and virality, 16; in *Vogue* magazine, 183–84; in *W* magazine, 192–94; and Warhol, 185, 186, 192; and West, 3, 160, 165–66; and white privilege, 176

Karinthy, Frigyes, 21, 25, 25n12, 26

Keeping Up With the Kardashians, 159n1, 161

Kennedy, Jacqueline Onassis, 6, 40, 66, 165, 185, 185n90, 186n91

Kennedy, John F., 40, 66

Kierkegaardashian, Kim, 203

Kim Kardashian Superstar, 161, 161n4, 164

Kimoji, 161, 180–83, 187, 203

Kittredge, Flan. See *Six Degrees of Separation* (Guare); *Six Degrees of Separation* (Schepisi)

Kittredge, Ouisa. See *Six Degrees of Separation* (Guare); *Six Degrees of Separation* (Schepisi)

Kosofsky-Sedgwick, Eve, 50–51, 53–55, 89
Kramer, Larry, 100n11, 101n14, 149, 150

LaValle, Victor, 20, 144, 144n102, 145n103, 146
Legend of Bagger Vance (Redford), 118, 122, 127n55
Leondis, Tony, 182. See also *Emoji Movie* (Leondis)
Lewinsky, Monica, 22, 204
Little Girl Observing Lovers on a Train (Rockwell), 80–81
Lubin, David, 40
Lucas, George, 62, 65, 70n30

Mad magazine, 92, 92n74, 154
Madocs, Rita, 68, 68n26
Madonna, 6, 99, 185, 186
magazine covers, 10, 14, 16, 19–20, 85–86, 100, 110, 122, 138, 192
makeover cinema, 6, 6n13, 126
Marriage Counselor (Rockwell), 83–84, 86
Martin, Trayvon, 140, 173
mastery, 44, 47, 52–53, 55–56, 135, 198, 208
melodrama: and celebrity culture, 19, 49, 160, 162–64, 166, 168–69, 171; in cinema, 151, 151n15, 153n19, 163, 170; and emoji, 181; and *Frankenstein*, 191n110; and gender, 171, 178; in H8R, 177–79; and Kardashian, 160, 162, 174, 198; and metonymy, 4, 160, 168, 170–71, 179; and network films, 202; and portmanteaus, 203, 207; and reality television, 163, 167, 169, 171, 174; and Rousseau, 19, 162, 164, 193; and selfies, 198; and Shelley, 209; and Smith, 117–18; and soap opera, 163, 168; and Trump, 174; and Winchell, 205. See also racial melodrama

meme, 10, 16, 22, 155, 159–60, 159n1, 189
Men in Black (Sonnenfeld), 6, 182n78
Men in Black 3 (Sonnenfeld), 109, 118
metacelebrity, 5–6, 19, 85, 112, 127, 179
metaphor, 30–31, 33–35, 38–39, 46–47, 113, 140–41, 168, 170, 186–87, 192, 207–8
metatrope, 19, 187, 200
metonymic criticism, 3, 8–9, 18–19, 24, 39–42, 50, 54, 107, 113, 158. See also metonymy
metonymic processing, 32

metonymy: and affect, 182; and AIDS, 97–98; and American Dream, 113; and celebrity, 4, 30, 31, 35–36, 38, 41, 52, 169–70, 202, 206; and Crawford, 78; and down low, 4; and emoji, 180, 182n78; and femininity, 74–75, 84, 179, 192; and Frankenstein, 134; and hegemony, 18–19, 23, 39; and Hollywood, 31; and ideology, 33, 85, 107; and intertextuality, 32–33, 36–37; and John Hancock, 130; and Kardashian, 20, 155, 179, 186; and Kevin Bacon game, 22; and media, 31; and melodrama, 160, 168, 170–71, 178; and metaphor, 34, 35, 38–39, 46, 170; and mimesis, 179, 186–87, 197; and movie posters, 114; and networks, 23, 42, 52; and portmanteaus, 202–3, 207; and postraciality, 113; and power, 34, 40; and *Premiere* magazine, 22, 100, 100n11; and *Pygmalion*, 193; and race, 33–34, 102–3, 112n16, 127, 192; and Rockwell, 68, 69n27, 71, 75, 79, 83, 85, 88, 91, 154n23, 155; and selfies, 197; and signification, 32, 39, 41–43, 54, 169; in *Six Degrees of Separation* (Guare), 24; in *Six Degrees of Separation* (Schepisi), 22; and Smith, 19, 22, 37, 102, 111, 112n16, 113, 119–23, 128, 131–33, 138n84, 142; and subjectivity, 33, 39–40, 41–42, 45–47, 198; and synecdoche, 33, 179, 180–81, 190, 192, 198; theories, 3, 31; and Trump, 1; in *Victor LaValle's Destroyer*, 146; and visuality, 74; and Washington, 102

#MeToo, 155–56

micropublics, 183, 187

Milgram, Stanley, 21, 27, 174n54, 178n68

mimesis: and gender, 77–78, 80–81, 86; and Goude, 188n98; and Kardashian, 166n25, 179, 183, 186–87, 190, 192, 200; and metonymy, 186–87; and selfhood, 6, 43, 107; and selfies, 197; and *Six Degrees of Separation*, 103

misogynoir, 155, 200

misogyny, 109, 155–56, 160, 175, 178

Monroe, Marilyn, 8, 66, 184, 184n85, 185, 185n88, 186

Moore, Julianne, 106, 151–53, 153n19

movie posters, 3, 10, 19, 64, 19, 113, 114–17, 117n36, 118, 154

Muccino, Gabriele, 43, 110, 111, 122. See also *Pursuit of Happyness* (Muccino) and *Seven Pounds* (Muccino)

Murder in Mississippi (Rockwell), 74

Museum of Modern Art, 99n9, 116

My Fair Lady (Cukor), 6n13, 165, 187
My Fair Lady (Shaw), 165, 187

Nama, Adilifu, 123, 126, 128, 131–32
Nelson, Kadir, 112

network: aesthetics, 42; and Black Frankenstein, 132; and celebrity, 3, 5, 9, 18, 20, 23–25, 28–29, 41, 43, 106n30, 158, 179, 183; as form, 8, 42, 54, 56; in *Frankenstein* (Shelley), 208–10; and Hollywood, 157; and intertextuality, 9, 23, 24, 40, 42, 53, 56, 210; and Kevin Bacon game, 30; and media, 13, 15, 18, 26, 27–28, 104, 181, 195; and metonymy, 18, 20, 23, 34–35, 41, 51–52, 107, 158, 206; in *Philadelphia*, 104; and portmanteaus, 202, 207; and power, 42, 53, 107, 157–58; and *Premiere* magazine, 100, 103; and race, 6n13, 19; and Rockwell, 65–66; in *Six Degrees of Separation*, 23, 24, 104; and Smith, 19, 113, 119, 123; social, 15, 24, 26n15, 27–28, 41, 106n30; studies, 26–27, 32–33, 55; theory, 23n5, 24, 25, 55; trauma, 201

network films, 202, 209

networked individualism, 44–45. *See also* networked subjectivity

networked subjectivity, 18, 40, 42, 44–48, 50, 51, 197, 200, 211. *See also* intersubjectivity; networked individualism; subjectivity

New Kids in the Neighborhood (Rockwell), 74

New York Times, 15, 25, 38, 58, 91, 102n17, 104n22, 106n30

No Swimming (Rockwell, 1921), 86–87
No Swimming (Rockwell, 1929), 86, 88
No Swimming (Rockwell, 1956), 86–87

Norman Rockwell Museum (NRM), 14, 61–65, 61n10, 63n16, 70n30, 72–73, 73n34, 87, 95n79, 116, 129n60, 184

Norman Rockwell's Shuffleton's Barbershop (Jean), 70–71, 92n74

Obama, Barack, 94–95, 117, 139n84, 185n89

Oscars, 99, 105, 105n25, 109, 148, 150, 157. *See also* Academy Awards

Paper magazine, 16, 20, 155, 174n53, 187–89, 192, 195

paranoia: and AIDS, 104, 149; as hermeneutics of suspicion, 76; and networks, 55, 103–4; as queer reading practice, 53–55,

76, 103–4, 144; as sensibility, 15, 17–18, 197–99, 204, 207–8, 210
parody, 14, 20, 79n56, 93, 106, 154–55, 179n72, 186, 189, 189n102
Parsons, Louella, 26n15, 204
Paul. See *Six Degrees of Separation* (Guare); *Six Degrees of Separation* (Schepisi)
perspective by incongruity, 9
Peterson, Maurice "Pops," 92–93
Philadelphia, 109–10, 146, 187n94
Philadelphia (Demme), 99–106, 101n16, 148–50, 157
Pickford, Mary, 66, 204
Poitier, Sidney, 8, 21, 24–25, 37n64, 103, 105, 105n25, 107, 123, 134, 210
portmanteau, 17n51, 20, 162, 202–9, 211
Portmanteau Book, The (Thomas Rockwell), 204n9
portmanteau films, 202
postraciality, 100, 113, 117–19, 124, 142
precarity, 9–10, 15, 19, 47–49, 104, 109, 113, 135, 143
Premiere magazine, 20, 22, 22n2, 100–104, 100n11, 112, 121
Problem We All Live With, The (Rockwell), 74, 92, 95, 95n79
Psycho (Hitchcock), 51, 150–52, 151n15, 155–56
Pursuit of Happyness (Muccino), 43, 110–11, 122
Pygmalion (Rousseau), 19, 162, 164–65, 170–71, 185n90, 191n110, 193, 198, 209
Pygmalion (Shaw), 165, 185n90
Pygmalion, 6, 126, 132, 162, 165–66, 180–91, 191nn109–10, 193, 204, 209

queer feminist criticism, 19, 53, 59–61, 84, 90

racial melodrama, 177–78, 177n64
Rage, Raju, 199
Raige, Cypher, 137, 139–45
Raige, Kitai, 137, 139–41, 143–45
Reagan, Ronald, 2, 66, 106
reality television: and celebrity culture, 2, 7, 27, 29, 167, 167n27, 171, 205; and Kardashian, 5, 7, 16, 161, 169, 173–74, 174n52, 174n54, 186n91; and melodrama, 163, 169; and Trump, 173–74

Red Ribbon Project, 98–99, 106
Redford, Robert, 118. See also *Legend of Bagger Vance* (Redford)
reparation: and Kardashian, 178; and melodrama, 171; and paranoia, 54–55, 76, 104, 144, 199; and portmanteaus, 207; as queer feminist criticism, 53–55, 60; and reparative practices, 54, 60; and Rockwell, 83, 90; and selfies, 197; and signification, 17; and Smith, 113, 144; and trauma, 54
Rich, Frank, 21, 138n84
Rock, Chris, 105, 109, 110, 125, 135n80
Rockwell, Abigail, 94
Rockwell, Norman: and 9/11, 38, 91–92; and AIDS, 20; and American Dream, 43; and *American Mirror* (Solomon), 58; and Bacon, 28n24; and Balto, 28n24; and Bechdel, 92; and Boy Scouts of America, 61, 61n8; and celebrity, 8, 19, 29, 59–60, 62–63, 66–72; and Chaplin, 67; and cinema, 60, 63n16, 64, 70–71; and civil rights paintings, 74; and Cooper, 66; and Crawford, 66; and digital media, 14, 72–73; and Disney, 65, 65n22; as ephemera, 7, 11, 14; and epideictic, 73–74; and *Freedom from Fear* (Rockwell), 73; and *Freedom from Want* (Rockwell), 73, 92; and gender normativity, 75–86; and *Girl at Mirror* (Rockwell), 79–81, 79n56; and *Girl Reading Post* (Rockwell), 85–86; and *Girl with Black Eye* (Rockwell), 82–83, 84, 86; and *Going Out* (Rockwell), 79; and gossip, 16–17; and *Gossips* (Rockwell), 24, 24n8, 92; and Goude, 69n28; at Guggenheim, 61; and heteronormativity, 19; and Hidden Hills, 3–4; and Hollywood, 63–67, 63n15; and homosexuality, 17; and internormativity, 90–91; and Kevin Bacon game, 28n24; and *Little Girl Observing Lovers on a Train* (Rockwell), 81; and Lucas, 64–65, 70n30; and magazine covers, 74; and *Marriage Counselor* (Rockwell), 83–85, 86; and mass mediation, 14; and metacelebrity, 5–6; and movie posters, 64; and *Murder in Mississippi* (Rockwell), 25; in *New York Times*, 38; and "No Swimming" paintings, 87–89; at Norman Rockwell Museum, 61–66; and *Norman Rockwell's Shuffleton Barbershop* (Jean), 70, 71; and Obama, 94–95; and parody, 92–93, 93n75; and *The Problem We All Live With* (Rockwell), 74, 95n79; and queer feminist

criticism, 19, 59–60, 76, 90; and Saltz, 7, 14, 59n3; and *Saturday People*, 67–68; and self-portraiture, 5, 6; and sexuality, 59, 87–91; and *Shuffleton's Barbershop* (Rockwell), 70–72, 70n30; and six degrees of separation, 23; and Spielberg, 64–65; and *Statue of Liberty* (Rockwell), 94–95; and Struzan, 64; and subjectivity, 18, 43, 49; and *Triple Self-Portrait*, 68–70, 69n27, 69n28; and Trump, 94–95, 94n77; and virality, 16; and vulnerability, 49, 88, 96; and Warhol, 65; at White House, 94–95, 95n78

Rockwell, Thomas, 64, 204n9

Rose, Amber, 180, 188n98

Rose, Steve, 124–25

Ross, Alex, 93n75, 129n60

Rousseau, Jean-Jacques: and celebrity, 8, 19, 164, 194, 198, 209; and confessionals, 193–94, 196; and femininity, 164n19; and Kardashian, 194, 198; and melodrama, 19, 162, 193; and *Pygmalion*, 19, 162, 170–71, 193, 209

Saltz, Jerry, 7, 8, 14, 59n3, 195–96

Saturday Evening Post, 14, 61, 63, 63n15, 67, 75, 85, 94, 97

Saturday People, 67–68

Schepisi, Fred, 4, 24–25, 26n15, 100, 108, 120, 120n44, 121, 201. See also *Six Degrees of Separation* (Schepisi)

Scott, Ridley, 153. See also *Hannibal* (Scott)

self-brand, 2, 5

selfie: as gesture, 196–97; history, 195–96; and Kardashian, 6, 7, 19, 160, 162, 173, 180, 183, 184, 194; and metonymy, 197; as photographic abundance, 195; and power, 199–200; and race, 199; and Rockwell, 184; and subjectivity, 197–98; and vulnerability, 197–98

Selfie, 165

Selfish (Kardashian), 19, 184, 184n82, 194–98

self-portraits, 5–6, 69–70, 184, 194–96

Seven Pounds (Muccino), 7n19, 111, 117, 122, 124, 135–36

Shaw, George Bernard, 165, 185n90, 204. See also *Pygmalion* (Shaw)

Shelley, Mary, 8, 19, 132–34, 145, 145n103, 191n110, 208–10. See also *Frankenstein* (Shelley)

Shuffleton's Barbershop (Rockwell), 70–71, 70n30, 112

Shyamalan, M. Night, 17n51, 37, 110, 136. See also *After Earth* (Shyamalan)

signification: and affect, 182; in Afrofuturism, 142; and AIDS, 104; and celebrity, 13, 170; and *Frankenstein*, 208; and interdependence, 18, 40, 47, 160; and intertextuality, 32; and Kardashian, 186; and melodrama, 160, 170–71, 191n110; and metonymy, 32, 39, 41, 43, 160, 169–70; and paranoia, 57, 171; and portmanteaus, 203, 207; and reparation, 171; subjectivity, 3, 16–17, 19, 33, 39–41, 43, 47, 160, 171, 175, 180, 186, 211

Silence of the Lambs (Demme), 148–50, 151n15, 153, 156

Simpson, O. J., 5, 8, 22, 95n79, 131, 161, 161n4, 167, 177, 177n64, 204

Single Man, A (Ford), 148, 150–52, 151n16, 156

Six Degrees of Kevin Bacon, 21–22, 30. See also six degrees of separation

Six Degrees of Peggy Bacon, 22. See also six degrees of separation

six degrees of separation: and Bush, 25; and celebrity, 22–24, 23n5; and Kardashian, 23, 161n4; and Karinthy, 21, 25; as meme, 21, 22; and Netflix, 27; and Rockwell, 23; theory, 53; and Warhol, 40. See also *Six Degrees of Separation* (Guare); *Six Degrees of Separation* (Schepisi)

Six Degrees of Separation (Guare): and AIDS, 100–101; and *Catcher in the Rye*, 23n5; and *Cats*, 125n52; and celebrity, 24, 28; and Hampton, 149; and *Frankenstein*, 208, 210; and *Fresh Prince*, 37n64; and network anxiety, 103; and *Pygmalion*, 165; and race, 112n16; and small-worldness, 21, 28; and Smith, 112n16; and technology, 28, 208; and Trump, 1–2; and Warhol, 25; and Winchell, 204n11

Six Degrees of Separation (Schepisi): and AIDS, 100–101, 104; and Bacon, 28n24; and Balto, 28n24, 103; and *Balto* (Wells), 28n24; and celebrity, 24, 28; and Chambers, 101–2; and Hampton, 26n15; and homophobia, 101–2, 108; and *Fresh Prince*, 4, 15, 37n64, 111; and Kevin Bacon game, 100; and Metro-Goldwyn-Mayer, 26n15; and movie posters, 118, 120–21; and network anxiety, 103–4; and *Philadelphia* (Demme), 100–101, 103; and

Premiere magazine, 22, 100, 104; and race, 101, 104, 108, 120–21; and Smith, 15, 21–22, 101–2, 108, 111, 118, 120–21; and technology, 28; and Warhol, 25; and Washington, 101–2, 108

small-worldness, 15, 21, 24n8, 25, 27–28, 40, 50, 65, 104, 201

Smith, Jada Pinkett, 3, 105, 110

Smith, Jaden, 3–4, 112, 136–39, 142

Smith, Toukie, 6, 187, 187n94, 189

Smith, Will: and Afrofuturism, 142–43, 143n99; and Afropessimism, 142–43, 143n99; in *After Earth*, 37, 112, 136–45; and AIDS, 101; and American Dream, 43, 112–13, 117, 124; and authenticity, 5, 15, 110; and Bacon, 28n24; and Balto, 28n24; and *Bel-Air*, 146–47; and Black fame, 19, 123, 127–28, 131, 137, 147; and Black Frankenstein, 132–36; and Black masculinity, 124–25, 131, 139, 142; and charisma, 141–42; and Coates, 19, 136–37, 141, 144–45, 146; and comic books, 128–29; and critical disdain, 7, 7n19; and digital media, 15; and down low, 4, 17, 109; and emoji, 182; and ephemera, 11, 14; and Facebook, 112; and *Frankenstein*, 132–36; in *Fresh Prince*, 4, 15, 32, 37, 102, 110n8, 121, 146–47, 187n94; in *Gemini Man*, 147; and gossip, 16; and Guare, 112n16; in *Hancock*, 125–36, 125n52; and hegemony, 18, 41, 105, 125; and heteronormativity, 108; and Hidden Hills, 3–4; in *Hitch*, 118–19, 120; and Hollywood, 7, 7n16, 104–5, 111, 123, 127–28, 147; and homophobia, 17, 101–2, 109, 128; and homosexuality, 17, 110n8; in *Interview* magazine, 110; and Jada Pinkett Smith, 3, 105, 110, 111, 135n80, 165; and Jaden Smith, 3, 4, 112, 136–40, 142; and *Just the Two of Us*, 112; and Kardashian, 110, 173; and Kevin Bacon game, 28n24; in *Legend of Bagger Vance*, 118, 127n55; and makeover cinema, 6, 6n13; and melodrama, 117–18; in *Men in Black*, 123; in *Men in Black 3*, 119–20; and metacelebrity, 5–6, 19; and metonymic criticism, 8; and metonymy, 32, 111; and movie posters, 114, 117, 119–21, 127, 138; and Nelson, 112; and network anxiety, 15, 104; in *New York* magazine, 101n15, 111n14, 138–39, 138n84; and Obama, 117; and Oscars, 105, 105n25, 109; and parody, 15, 117; and Poitier, 103, 105n25; and postraciality, 112–13, 117, 124; in *Premiere* magazine, 20, 100–103, 112; as Pygmalion, 165; and racial melodrama, 118; and racism, 19, 104–5, 109, 118, 136, 139; and Rock, 105; as Sad Will, 124–25; and Scientology, 37; and self-branding, 5; in *Seven Pounds*, 117, 146; and Simpson, 131; in *Six Degrees of Separation*, 4, 15, 21–22, 100–104, 108, 110, 120–22, 123, 146–47; and slap, 105, 109; and subjectivity, 18, 41; and suit, 122–24; and superheroes, 128–29; and synecdoche, 139; and Toukie Smith, 187n94; and transmediation, 29; and *Victor LaValle's Destroyer*, 144, 144n102; and Washington, 101–5, 105n25, 123; and whiteness, 111, 118, 122–23; and zones of contradiction, 108–9, 119, 133

Snapchat, 16, 161, 173–74

social media: and authenticity, 2, 171; and celebrity, 3, 27–29, 114, 167, 171; in *Emoji Movie*, 182; as ephemera, 10–11; and Kardashian, 5, 7, 16, 159, 160–61, 169, 183, 189; and Kevin Bacon game, 22; and photography, 195; and self-branding, 2; in *Selfie*, 165; and small-worldness, 27; and Smith, 15, 19, 122; and West, 185; and Yeezy, 185

Solomon, Deborah, 17, 58, 61n9, 69n27, 91, 95

Sonnenfeld, Barry, 118, 182n78. See also *Men in Black* (Sonnenfeld); *Men in Black 3* (Sonnenfeld)

Spielberg, Steven, 62, 64–65, 94, 100n11

Spears, Britney, 49, 92n74, 175

Staiger, Janet, 51–52, 104, 149–50

star system, 26–27, 29, 38–39, 63, 106, 115, 164–65

stardom: and Gary Cooper, 116; and Kardashian, 161n4, 169; and melodrama, 162, 168; and Poitier, 107; and portmanteaus, 204; and Rockwell, 59, 60, 62, 67, 96; and *Six Degrees of Separation*, 28; and Smith, 29, 147; and subjectivity, 5, 13, 23, 44, 46, 50; and trauma, 49; and vulnerability, 49

Starling, Clarice, 150, 153

Statue of Liberty (Rockwell), 94–95, 95n78

Sternberg, Amanda, 136

Struzan, Drew, 64, 116–17

subjectivity: in *After Earth*, 143; and American Dream, 9; and celebrity, 3, 5, 8, 13, 40, 166, 171–72, 207; in *Frankenstein*, 208; and hegemony, 10, 23, 41; and identity, 8, 10; and individualism, 5, 23, 36, 41, 44, 51; and interdependence, 9, 18, 47, 175; and intersubjectivity, 3, 8–9, 18, 42, 47, 197;

and Kardashian, 160, 180, 186, 198; and Kimoji, 180; and mastery, 9, 18, 32–33, 54, 186; and melodrama, 160, 166; and metonymic criticism, 9, 39–41; and metonymy, 20, 32–34, 39, 41–42, 160, 186; and mimesis, 180, 186, 197; and networks, 13, 18, 40, 42, 44–45, 197, 211; and performativity, 43, 197–98; and *Philadelphia*, 104; and portmanteaus, 207, 211; and *Premiere* magazine, 104; and selfies, 197; and signification, 3, 20, 39, 175, 180, 186, 207, 208, 211; and *Six Degrees of Separation*, 104; and trauma, 54; and unicity, 32–33, 36, 43, 54, 171–72, 175; and vulnerability, 179; and Western, 51. *See also* intersubjectivity; networked subjectivity

superheroes, 93, 93n75, 124, 125–27, 128–29, 129n60, 130–31, 154

synecdoche, 33, 46, 139, 175, 179–80, 181, 189–90, 192, 203

Tennant, Andy, 118. See also *Hitch* (Tennant)

Texas Chainsaw Massacre (Hooper), 51, 150–51, 151n15, 153–54, 154n23, 155–56

Theron, Charlize, 22, 126, 127n55

Thomas, Hank Willis, 93

Through the Looking Glass (Carroll), 204, 204n9

Towns, Armond, 17, 33, 109, 113, 120, 157

transmediation, 29, 36, 52–53, 162, 195

trauma: and AIDS, 100; and celebrity, 49; and *Destroyer*, 145; historical, 38, 82, 91; and Kardashian, 160, 164, 166, 169; and network films, 201–2; and Rockwell, 68, 82, 91; and Smith, 100, 124, 126, 134, 137, 143, 146; and subjectivity, 54

Triple Self-Portrait (Rockwell), 68–69, 69n27, 69n28, 93, 184, 195

Trump, Donald: and celebrity culture, 1–2, 4–5, 8; and emoji, 180; and Frankenstein, 209n29; and Kardashian, 16, 158, 166, 173–74, 174n53, 174n54; and Kevin Bacon game, 22; and Rockwell, 93–95, 93n75, 95n77; and Smith, 124; and white supremacy, 158

Twitter, 27, 159, 161, 173n49, 180, 182, 198, 203

Two Old Men and Dog (Rockwell, 1953), 86, 89

Two Old Men and Dog (Rockwell, 1956), 86, 87

Van Sant, Gus, 148, 152, 152n18, 153

Victor LaValle's Destroyer (LaValle), 19, 144–46, 144n102

virality, 13–14, 16, 17n51, 92n73, 103, 106n30

vulnerability: and agency, 47, 211; and Black masculinity, 133, 135; and Black women, 48, 135; and celebrity, 49, 113, 164, 166; in criticism, 56; and Hollywood, 157; to homophobia, 156; and interdependence, 9–10, 18, 40, 47, 179, 202; and intersubjectivity, 9–10, 18, 40, 47, 166, 194, 198, 211; and Kardashian, 198; linguistic, 47; and melodrama, 160, 166; and metonymy, 160, 207; to misogyny, 156; and portmanteaus, 207–8; and precarity, 10, 19, 48, 157, 179, 200, 211; to racism, 48, 92, 104–5, 113, 133, 135–36; and Rockwell, 59, 66, 69, 92; in selfies, 197; to sexism, 48; and signification, 47; and Smith, 105, 140–41, 143–44, 146; and white femininity, 133, 135; and white masculinity, 157

W magazine, 192–93

Warhol, Andy: and celebrity, 5, 8, 11, 11n30, 12; and David Hampton, 25; and Frankenstein, 209n29; and Kardashian, 16, 161, 165, 185–86, 189n102, 192; and Kevin Bacon game, 22; and Rockwell, 65–66, 93n75, 129n60; and six degrees of separation, 40

Washington, Denzel, 99–106, 101n14, 105n25, 107, 123, 157

Wells, Simon. See *Balto* (Wells)

West, Kanye, 3, 110, 160, 165, 166n25, 179n72, 183, 185, 185n89, 188n98, 203

White House, 94–95, 95nn78–79

Williams, Richard, 92–93, 92n74

Winchell, Walter, 204–5, 204n11

#YesAllWomen, 156

Young, Elizabeth, 132–34

www.ingramcontent.com/pod-product-compliance
Lightning Source LLC
Chambersburg PA
CBHW030134240426
43672CB00005B/122